Holiday Coastal Spain

Katharine Wood-de Winne was born in Edinburgh in
1960 of Belgian and English parents. She was educated
there, reading Communications, then English Language
and Literature at Edinburgh University. Following a
period as a freelance public relations consultant she
entered the world of travel journalism. An eighteen-
month spell touring Europe and North Africa resulted
in the book *Europe by Train* (published by Fontana)
which is one of the UK's top-selling guidebooks. As
well as working on this series of Holiday Guides, she is
currently involved in several projects encompassing
every aspect of the travel industry – from backpacking
students to round-the-world first-class tours. In the
course of her work she travels extensively, and has so
far clocked up forty-six countries, including Spain,
which she knows well. She is married and lives in Perth,
Scotland with her husband, who works with her on
various guides, and young sons, Andrew and Euan.

George McDonald was born in Dumfries, Galloway, in
1955 and was educated at Fettes College and Edinburgh
University. Following a spell on the family farm he
toured Europe and North Africa to help research the
guidebook *Europe by Train*. He continues to travel for
a living, having spent a considerable part of the last year
in Spain, researching for the various guidebooks he is
involved in with Katie Wood, and is rarely in one place
for more than three weeks at a time. He spent a
considerable part of last year in Spain, where he was
researching for this guide. Home, when he's there, is
Guernsey in the Channel Islands.

Holiday
COASTAL
SPAIN

Compiled and Edited by
Katie Wood

Research Co-ordinator:
George McDonald

FONTANA/Collins

First published in 1989 by Fontana Paperbacks
8 Grafton Street, London W1X 3LA

Maps drawn by Rhona Cunningham

Set in Linotron Plantin

Printed and bound in Great Britain
by William Collins Sons & Co. Ltd, Glasgow

For Euan

Contents

ACKNOWLEDGEMENTS

Thanks are owed to our UK researchers – *Devin Scobie* for Costas del Sol, Almería, Brava and Blanca, and the Balearic Islands; *Gary Duncan* for the Canary Islands, Costas Dorada, del Azahar, Calide and de la Luz, and *Ishbel Matheson* for the Introduction and Gibraltar and Formentera.

We should also like to thank the Spanish Tourist Board in London for their support throughout the project.

On the home front, a personal thanks is owed to my mother who 'kept the home fires burning', new baby and all, and allowed me snatched moments of childless peace to get this book written, and, of course, a thank you to my wonderful husband without whose practical help and support this would not have been published.

WHAT THIS GUIDE IS ABOUT

For too long now there has been a gulf in the guidebook market. On the one hand there are 'heavies' – books which, though good in their way, assume the holiday-maker wants a stone-by-stone description of all the ancient remains in the country of their choice, and what's more, assume that their readership is middle-aged, middle-class and predominantly American with a lot of cash to splash about. At the other end of the scale are the back-packing, student-orientated, 'rough it on $15 a day' guides which assume the traveller wants to cover the maximum amount of ground possible and spend the absolute minimum doing so (even if this does mean surviving on one bowl of vegetable rice a day and no baths for two weeks).

But in the middle of these poles lies the vast majority of tourists: normal, fun-loving people who go on holiday to unwind from a year's toil, and who, though not able to throw cash about indiscriminately, are willing to spend enough to enjoy themselves. Predominantly, these people fall into the under-forty age group – the 'young ones' keen to see the countries they visit and have a good time in their own way. This guide is written for this sort of person.

It does not wade into pages of history – it just gives you the basics to enable you to make sense of the monuments and places you'll see while on holiday. It does not pretend to be a specialist guide for one group of people (watersports enthusiasts, nature lovers, archaeologists, etc.), but it does point you in the direction of where to pursue these types of hobbies once you are in the country. If any one 'hobby' is highlighted more than most it is that of 'sun-worshipping' and where best to do it, as time after time surf, sea 'n' sand still come top of most people's priorities for a good holiday.

Spain remains one of the most popular holiday destinations in Europe. Over two hundred tour companies offer packages to mainland Spain, the Balearic and Canary Islands. This guide will look at the options open to would-be travellers and at the pros and cons of all the different packages offered by tour operators. Independent travellers are remembered too, and we look in great detail at the crucial decision of whether to opt for a package or an independent holiday. All the relevant up-to-the-minute info is in Part One – Before You Go.

Our recommendations for restaurants, nightlife, hotels, etc. start at the lower end of the market, since we believe the art of using money when on holiday lies in saving it without sacrificing the holiday spirit.

We hope this guide will help you to have a rewarding time in Spain, a country whose diversity and range of attractions never fail to amaze visitors. We have concentrated on the 'Costa Spain' because it is here that the heart of the Spanish tourist industry lies. If you feel we've missed anything out, let us know. This is a different type of guide: informal and chatty, not academic and definitive. We are not setting ourselves up as *the* authority on Spain. We know a lot and have travelled there extensively, but our knowledge is more on where the best places for different types of holidays are, than on Spanish history. If any of our recommendations fails to come up to the mark, or if you find a super undiscovered beach which you are willing to share, or a new lively taverna, write and tell us about it. After all, we all want the same in the end – the memory of at least two glorious, fun-filled weeks to sustain us through the long, dark, winter nights.

Part One

BEFORE YOU GO

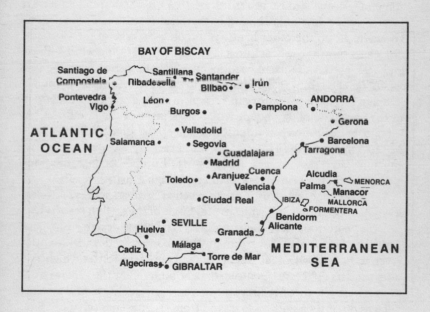

BAY OF BISCAY

Santiago de
Compostela Santillana Santander
Ribadesella Bilbao Irún

Pontevedra Léon ANDORRA
Vigo Burgos Pamplona

ATLANTIC
OCEAN Salamanca Valladolid Gerona

Segovia Barcelona
Guadalajara Tarragona
Madrid

Cuenca Alcudia
Toledo Aranjuez Palma MENORCA
Valencia Manacor
Ciudad Real IBIZA MALLORCA
FORMENTERA

Huelva SEVILLE Benidorm
Granada Alicante

Cadiz Málaga MEDITERRANEAN
Algeciras GIBRALTAR Torre de Mar SEA

What to Expect

Spain constantly defies expectations. If you thought the Spanish coastline was simply a rash of ugly concrete boxes, exhibiting the worst effects of mass tourism, then you will be surprised to find that some of Europe's most beautiful art treasures and architecture are located only a few miles inland at the historic centres of Seville and Granada. If, on the other hand, you took a package to the Costa del Sol, expecting (as the brochures say) a land of sparkling white villages and dark-eyed Andalusian beauties, the first glimpse of Torremolinos would be enough to make you want to take the next flight home.

Spain was the first country in Europe to really experience the effects of the package-holiday boom which took place in the late fifties. As foreign holidays were suddenly no longer the domain of the well-heeled, Spain with its long golden beaches, days of cloud-free sunshine and easy access from North Europe seemed the ideal alternative to the prospect of cold and rain in a British resort.

Since the first waves of tourism reached Spanish shores, development has been rapid and widespread. Some of the earliest resorts have become notorious for their ugliness and bad design, but later additions have been more thoughtfully constructed with attention given to how they look as well as to the kind of amenities which they offer tourists. The latest complexes to be built follow the general trend in the rest of the Mediterranean for high-quality self-contained villages often set a mile or so inland from the most densely populated tourist areas. These usually provide an abundance of sporting and leisure activities – the idea being, of course, that you can spend the entire duration of your two-week break quite happily in your holiday village.

In recent days, despite heavy promotion of newer, more exotic destinations such as Turkey or North Africa, Spain constantly perplexes its critics by continuing to attract more holiday-makers each year than any other Mediterranean country. The truth is that coastal Spain is everything that anyone has said about it – and it flaunts it. Yes, it is ridiculously commercialized in some places – 'English' pubs do line the streets of Torremolinos, and yes, restaurant menus in Benidorm do boast fish 'n' chips and bacon 'n' eggs – but there is great fun to be had. Coastal resorts at the height of the season buzz with life virtually twenty-four hours a day, and for a 'sun, sand and sea' break at prices you can afford, there simply is no better place to go than Spain.

The Spanish resorts on the mainland are also the ideal location for those who enjoy a few days' sightseeing in the middle of their beach holiday. The spectacular Alhambra in Granada, or colourful Barcelona, or that curious British enclave, the Rock of Gibraltar, are some of the best sights in Europe and are easily accessible from the coastal towns. If it is a quieter, 'get-away-from-it-all' holiday you're in search of, turn away from the mainland and head for one of the lesser-known Canary or Balearic Islands, where mass tourism is less known.

The Spanish coastline is usually split up into eight tourist sections. From north to south these are the Costa Brava, running forty miles north-east of Barcelona; the Costa Dorada, south from Barcelona to Tarragona; the Costa del Azahar from Vinaroz, sweeping around the Gulf of Valencia; the Costa Blanca, past Benidorm to Cartagena; the Costa Cálida, tucked in between the Costa Blanca and the Costa de Almería; then the Costa del Sol which encompasses the famous resorts of Málaga, Marbella and Torremolinos. On the western-facing Atlantic, sandwiched between Tarifa and Portugal is the Costa de la Luz. Of these areas, it is undoubtedly the Costa de la Luz which is the least developed in terms of tourist facilities. This is partly due to its location as the Atlantic Ocean tends to cool down more quickly than the Mediterranean. Nevertheless if you're looking for a quiet resort on the Spanish mainland, the Costa de la Luz offers fine beaches in traditional settings far from the madding crowds.

Off the Spanish coastline lie the equally famous holiday destinations of Majorca, or Mallorca as it is known in Spanish, Ibiza and, to a lesser extent, Menorca and Formentera. These islands make up the Balearics and have long proved to be popular among package holiday-makers. Majorca is the best known of the group and it welcomes hundreds of thousands of tourists to its golden shores every year. It is not difficult to see the secret of the island's success. Well-developed facilities, numerous fine beaches and some wonderful, unspoilt scenery prove irresistible to those in search of a relaxing two weeks in the sun. Ibiza, the other big crowd-puller in the Balearic Islands, has a totally different character. It tends to attract the younger set and a real spirit of *laissez faire* prevails. Anything goes in Ibiza and no-one cares – a great place to have an outrageously good time.

Also under Spanish dominion are the Canary Islands lying off the coast of North Africa. Volcanic in origin, there are seven islands in the archipelago – Tenerife, La Palma, Gomera and Hierro in the west, Gran Canaria, Fuerteventura and Lanzarote in the east. Tenerife and Gran Canaria have been established as firm favourites among British holiday-makers for some years now, and first-time visitors can look forward to sophisticated, modern resorts with plenty to offer the tourist in the way of sightseeing excursions and sporting activities. Lanzarote tends to be a quieter holiday destination but for the nature-lover, this is potentially the most fascinating island in the group with its dramatic landscapes of rock-strewn deserts and dormant volcanic cones. All the islands have extremely warm winters and consequently have become popular as winter holiday destinations among holiday-makers from colder climes.

Not surprisingly the Spanish package holiday scene is well developed, with over 200 tour-operators offering packages to the mainland, the Canaries and the Balearics. These companies range from the 'big boys' such as Thomson's or Thomas Cook, to small specialist organizations, who offer holidays 'with a difference' – which include anything from specially arranged golf-holidays to spending two weeks touring historic Spanish houses. More will be said about these options later on in the book, but whatever you end up choosing, you can rest assured that by travelling with a tour company, you are opting for the most cost-effective and hassle-free way of arranging a holiday to Costa Spain. Many hotels are block-booked by tour operators and the prospect of finding decent accommodation in a popular resort if you are travelling independently without pre-booking is pretty grim. That said, if you're not too fussy about what kind of place you end up staying in, the outlook for independent travellers is not too bad. Internal communications (road, rail and air) are of a reasonable standard (even if the trains and buses never run to time) and the cost of living in Spain can be reasonably cheap – if you're not lured by the gloss and glamour of places like Marbella or La Manga.

The Climate

COASTAL WEATHER

Lapped by the temperate waters of the Mediterranean, the south-east coast of Spain and the Balearic Islands are warm virtually the whole year round. In December, temperatures average 56°F/13°C at coastal resorts, while in the summer months, things are hotting up to around the 78°F/25°C mark and can soar as high as 90°F/32°C during the peak months of July and August.

Average daily temperatures, based on Málaga (Costa del Sol):

	JAN	FEB	MAR	APR	MAY	JUNE
°F	56	56	59	63	67	74
°C	13	13	15	17	19	23

	JULY	AUG	SEPT	OCT	NOV	DEC
°F	76	77	75	68	61	56
°C	25	25	24	19	16	13

INLAND WEATHER

Without the moderating influence of the sea, the inland areas of southern Spain experience the greatest extremes of temperature: stiflingly hot in summer but cool and rainy in the winter months.

Average daily temperatures, based on Seville:

	JAN	FEB	MAR	APR	MAY	JUNE
°F	51	54	59	63	68	77
°C	11	12	15	17	19	25

	JULY	AUG	SEPT	OCT	NOV	DEC
°F	82	83	78	69	59	53
°C	28	28	25	20	15	12

In the Canary Islands, there is an appreciable climate gradient running from east to west. Overall, the islands lying to the west tend to enjoy higher summer temperatures of around 77°F/25°C compared to 71°F/24°C in the eastern Canaries. However, all the islands are distinguished for their remarkably warm and sunny winters, which have contributed to the Canaries' popularity as a winter-holiday destination. Even in the coldest months of December and January, temperatures still average 68°F/19°C.

When To Go

All over Spain, July and August are the warmest and driest months, so if you are only interested in a beach holiday with some lively nightlife in the evening, this is the best time to pack your bags and head for the sun. On the other hand, these months are also the tourist industry's busiest season, so if you go at this time of the year, any sizeable resort will be jam-packed with holiday-makers, and you will have to pay peak season prices for the use of amenities such as hire of sporting equipment, etc. If this is not your idea of getting away from it all, then late spring or early summer is a good time to visit Spain. The weather is still warm enough to cultivate a tan, and the countryside is at its best at this time of the year. Only a mile or so inland from the coastal strip, wild flowers and tree blossoms brighten up the countryside with their colourful display.

A holiday in September or October is also a possibility for those who want to escape the crowds and you have the added bonus of paying off-season prices. By this time, however, the busiest tourist areas are worn out by the hectic summer season, and you may find the service in restaurants and hotels not up to the standard you expect. It is worth bearing this in mind if you are deciding when to go to Spain as it is the small things, such as the attention and courtesy of hotel staff, which can make an important contribution to the enjoyment of your holiday.

WINTER HOLIDAYS

Winter holidays in Spain or the Canary Islands have long been popular among people wanting a short break from the cold dreary climes of northern Europe. The advantages of holidaying during the winter months are pretty obvious: while friends and neighbours are shivering in Britain, you can bask in the Spanish sunshine and swim in the warm Mediterranean Sea.

On the financial side of things, holidaying out of season can also work out almost half the price of the same package taken in July or August and in an attempt to attract customers, tour operators will sometimes throw in extra perks, such as free car-hire or bigger discounts for children. It also works out cheaper to stay longer (sometimes the price difference between staying one week or two is minimal), and for those who wish to avoid winter weather altogether, some tour operators do special packages which entail a one- or two-month stay. This last option is particularly popular among older, retired people as such packages are likely to work out cheaper than spending the winter in Britain and paying for heating bills – and there is also the added bonus of being able to see the sun every day! One point to remember is that prices for winter breaks become more expensive again over the festive period (from 4 – 24 December), so if you're working on a tight budget, arrange your holiday to avoid these times.

Holidaying out of season does have its drawbacks too. You may find that some of the tourist facilities are closed down, not to speak of a dearth of activity on the social scene. The range of resorts and accommodation offered by tour operators is also cut substantially, so the choice of locations may be rather more limited if you choose to holiday during the winter months.

Where To Go For What

People often spend weeks deliberating which country to choose for their holiday destination, then leave the final choice of where they stay within the country to either a photo and brief, optimistic write-up in a travel brochure, or to the discretion and persuasive talk of a travel agent (many of whom haven't actually visited the country). This lottery results, not surprisingly, in people having a disappointing holiday simply because they got the facts wrong on this crucial decision. If anything, the decision about which part of the country you base yourself is more important than the choice of country itself for there is good and bad in every country – Britain, for example, offers the tourist a superb holiday destination, but if the visitor were to opt for two weeks in Sheffield when he really wanted a 'get away from it all' type of break, he would be sadly disappointed. Don't think that the Spanish equivalents of Sheffield aren't on offer. They are, but unless you're careful you will not know if you've landed them until you've paid your hundreds of pounds and arrived at the resort.

In order to match your needs to the most suitable resorts we have divided holiday-makers into certain stereotypes. Doubtless most of you fall into several of the categories, but the idea is to find which resorts crop up under the headings which interest you, and match your needs accordingly.

The following symbols representing the various interests appear throughout this book as an easy guide to the places likely to be of interest to you:

The Sun Worshipper

The Sightseer

The Socialite

Sporting Holidays

The Nature Lover

The Recluse

Family Holidays

The Naturist

 The Sun Worshipper: *Surf, Sea and Sand*

For a 'surf, sea and sand' holiday which won't knock a huge hole in your annual budget, there simply is no better holiday destination than Spain. Practically the whole Mediterranean coastline from Rosas to Cádiz is one long sandy strip. Not that this is as monotonous as it sounds, for each part of the coast has a distinctive character all its own. The Costa Brava in the north-east has a rugged shoreline, interspersed by sandy coves and backed by pine forests. The Costa Dorada and Costa del Azahar, by contrast, are much flatter and have long swathes of fine, golden sand. The Costa Blanca, as the name suggests, is distinguished by beaches of stunning white sand, while the Costa del Sol (surprisingly, considering its popularity among holiday-makers) has coarser sand which is greyish in colour. The Atlantic-facing Costa de la Luz has fine long beaches, but tends to feel the effect of strong sea winds, making things rather uncomfortable for would-be sun worshippers.

The Balearic Islands, too, differ substantially from each other. Majorca has many fine sandy stretches threading in and out of the coastline. The most popular beaches among holiday-makers are those which are in the greatest proximity to the large resorts, but if you take advantage of the extensive road network on the island, there are numerous sandy coves to be discovered on the north or east coasts. Less popular among holiday-makers, the smaller island of Menorca certainly has no shortage of fine beaches, but does tend to feel the effects of a brisk north wind. As a holiday destination, the island promotes itself as a quiet, get-away-from-it-all location and consequently, you may find the choice of off-beach entertainment limited with little in the way of the international buzz which is part of the allure of Majorca and Ibiza.

Ibiza itself has lots of secluded little beaches tucked away in its rocky coastline and a crystal-clear sea, ideal for swimming or wind-surfing. The island has a reputation as the most outrageous of the Balearics, which means anything goes . . . and, in some cases, everything comes off, as nudist sunbathing is common. Formentera, Ibiza's neighbour, seems dull in comparison. Tourist development has been limited and there is a lack of accommodation which tends to prevent huge crowds flocking onto the island. However, it does have some beautiful white beaches which are relatively quiet compared to Ibiza's, and as the island is only an hour's ferry ride away, it is suitable as a day-tripping destination if you want to get away from the hustle and bustle of its bigger sister.

In the Canary Islands, Gran Canaria has some wonderful rolling sand-dunes where the beach bum can flop and cultivate his tan. By contrast, Tenerife suffers from a lack of natural golden sand. There are strips – but nothing like as impressive as the beaches to be found on Gran Canaria. To compensate for this, hotels have installed huge swimming pools and certainly, no-one seems to complain about the lack of sand. On Lanzarote, the east coast is the place for the sun worshipper to concentrate. Choose one of the smaller resorts and the wide fringes of golden sand are only a couple of steps from the front door of your hotel.

Overall, then, there is no shortage of variety when it comes to choosing your location and resort. There are splendid beaches located right in the heart of the largest resorts of Benidorm and Torremolinos, but for those who prefer not to be one of the crowd toasting like rows of sardines on the beach, there is always a more secluded spot to be found only a short walk or bus ride away.

Practically any resort in Spain will supply you with the sand and sun to cultivate that rich, bronzed look, but here are a few suggestions for the most spectacular, notorious or beautiful holiday destinations that Spain has to offer.

BENIDORM (**Costa Blanca**) Criticized alternately for its blatant commercialism and its ugly built-up sea-front, despite all the scorn that is poured upon it, Benidorm still remains one of the most popular resorts in the Mediterranean. The secret of the resort's continuing success is that it attracts all sorts. Both young and old fill the huge hotels and apartment blocks every year, and the place really does have a buzz of its own. The beach is a major crowd-puller. The four-mile stretch of sand which sweeps the bay is one of Benidorm's most magnificent attractions.

PUERTO BANUS (**Costa del Sol**) Situated five miles west of the centre of Marbella, Puerto Banus has all the trappings one would expect from this most fashionable of Spanish resorts. Luxury yachts crowd into the bay and the jet set are in evidence – not really the place to spend a two-week holiday, as prices are shockingly expensive for both accommodation and food. However, it does boast a seventeen-mile stretch of sand, and it's worth taking a day trip here just to laze on the beach and see how the other half live.

PLAYA SANTA CRISTINA (**Costa Brava**) Just a few miles south of Lloret de Mar, one of the Costa Brava's largest resorts, Playa Santa Cristina nestles between outcrops of rock on one side and pine forests on the other. An attractive spot for sunbathing, it also has crystal-clear blue waters to take a dip in and sun-loungers to toast on.

MASPALOMAS, GRAN CANARIA (**Canary Islands**) This seven-mile stretch of beach, located in the south of the island, is backed by miles of rolling sand-dunes. The perfect place for those wishing to cultivate a sun tan, there are also many watersports on offer to occupy the more energetic members of your group.

FORMENTOR (**Majorca**) If you can stand the hairpin bends and sheer drops as the road edges its way to the most northerly tip of the Island, you are more than rewarded with stunning views of high cliffs, scented pine forests and sunny little coves. Formentor itself is a good get-away-from-it-all destination, with just enough development so you don't have to rough it in a local pension, but not so built up as to detract from the air of peace and tranquility. As for sunbathing, you have the choice of a number of sandy coves, one of the prettiest of which is **Puerto Pollenso** set against a backdrop of blue mountains.

PLAYA CABELLET (**Ibiza**) This is the official nudist beach on the island, so don't head here unless you are prepared to join in the fun. Over the other side of the dunes is the beach of **La Salinas**. Nudists are in evidence here too, but there are also modestly dressed family groups, including grannies, grandpas and kids who don't bat an eyelid at the full-frontals lying on the beach beside them.

The Sightseer: *Sights, Historical Monuments and Archaeological Remains*

The real bonus for visitors to Spain is that some of the best sights the country has to offer are within easy day-tripping distance from the major resorts on the coast. It is quite possible to enjoy all the benefits of a cheap 'sun, sea and surf' package based in the Costa del Sol as well as sampling some of the country's rich cultural and historical background by hopping on a train to Seville or Granada. Even if you are reluctant to move away from the coastal strip, there is plenty to see and do, if you choose the right resort, in old cities such as Valencia or Barcelona which have some quite superb art treasures and architecture.

On the islands, the attractions are natural rather than man-made. Lanzarote is strikingly different from anything else in Spain. The landscape is more lunar than terrestrial, with its extinct volcanic cones and grey sandy deserts. On Majorca, despite a fringe of development around the shoreline, the interior of the island remains largely unspoilt and contains some of the most beautiful scenery in Spain. For more spectacular sight-seeing, boat trips take holiday-makers to the extraordinary sea-caves which are a special feature of the coastline. On Menorca, there are the mysterious and impressive remains of an ancient civilization dotted around the island. The purpose of the *tayalots*, conical-shaped rock structures, and the *taulas*, tables made of rock slabs, have baffled professionals for decades. Whatever their original use, a trip up to the most isolated and windswept of these silent monuments is an eerie and awe-inspiring experience.

For those who do not just want to make short sightseeing trips, but to really soak up the history and atmosphere of this colourful and complex country, a stay in the Spanish paradors is worth considering. These state-owned luxury accommodations are usually situated in places of historical or scenic interest throughout the country. The parador buildings are often converted monasteries or castles and those which have been built specially for the purpose have been designed to harmonize with the architecture typical of the area. Similarly, the food which is served for guests' consumption has a special emphasis on the culinary specialities of the region. (For more detailed information, turn to the section on parador holidays on page 89.)

Here are some of the main sights which can be the highlight of any sightseeing tour.

BARCELONA There's more to this city than bullfighting and football. A lively, shopping centre, it also contains some first-rate museums and art-gallerics, which will delight even the most reluctant of sightseers. Spain's most famous twentieth century artist, Picasso, has a whole building dedicated to his work (the **Picasso Museum**), while some of the most exciting modern architecture in the world can be found in Antonio Gaudi's weird and wonderful **Church of the Holy Family**. For those who want a flavour of all Barcelona's colourful diversity, take a walk down the **Ramblas**, Barcelona's equivalent of Les Champs Elysées. This is an endless circus of street-sellers, locals, artists and sightseers.

MONTSERRAT If you're staying on the Costa Brava, and want a day steeped in magic and legend, take a trip to the mountain and monastery of Montserrat. This is said to be where the legendary **Holy Grail** was found, and is actually the home of the famous **Black Virgin** statue, supposedly transported to Spain by St Peter.

SEVILLE Flamboyant and colourful, Seville is the essence of the Spanish spirit. Delicate lace ladies' fans, ripening oranges, Carmen, bullfights et al. are all part and parcel of the historic and romantic appeal of the city. The cathedral is well worth a visit. A huge monument to workmanship and the dedication of sixteenth-century craftsmen, the building is the biggest Gothic construction in the world. One word of warning: don't be tempted into pinching one of the luscious-looking oranges hanging on the trees. Seville oranges are extremely sour, used for marmalade, not for quenching thirst.

GRANADA The chief reason for a day trip to Granada is to see the **Alhambra**, one of the most fabulous buildings in Spain. Built by the Muslims in the thirteenth-century, the Alhambra is the best-preserved example of Moorish architecture in existence – you just have to look in awe at the amazing ceilings and intricate Moorish carvings. Outside, are the beautiful gardens of the Generalife and cool oases of fountains and gushing water.

VALENCIA Palm trees and a distinctive old colonial atmosphere make this an attractive city to visit – and easy access to good beaches nearby means this is an excellent holiday destination if you want to combine a beach holiday with a few days' serious sightseeing. The **museum** attached to the cathedral claims to house the mythical Holy Grail, said to be used by Christ at the Last Supper, and the **Fine Arts Museum** contains one of the most comprehensive collections of Spanish Art in the country.

GIBRALTAR This little piece of England stands in striking and somewhat bizarre contrast to Spain. While Spain feasts, celebrates and basks in lazy somnolence, only a couple of miles off the coast English bobbies keep the peace, sterling is the official currency and British pubs line the streets. The Rock is well worth a visit if you're staying in one of the major resorts in the Costa del Sol and souvenir-shopping is cheaper here, so take plenty of extra cash with you. When on the island, a visit to the apes is a 'must'; a cable-car will take you to the top of the Rock, where you can see the only wild apes in Europe and take in some marvellous views of the island.

MAJORCA The train journey from Palma to the East Coast must rate as one of the most scenic rail routes in all Spain. During the one-hour trip the train winds its way at a leisurely pace through the beautiful and luscious interior, ending up at the pretty seaside resort of **PUERTO SÓLLER** in time for lunch.

LANZAROTE Excursions can be taken to the cone of the extinct volcano, **La Corona**. You can walk along **Los Verdes**, a huge three-and-a-half-mile-long tunnel which was once a channel for burning hot lava. Close by La Corona is the extraordinary spectacle of

Jameo del Agua. An underground lake fed by subterranean sea channels, it now resounds with the latest chart hits from the trendy nightclub which has been installed in this most unlikely of settings.

Obviously the sights listed above only scrape the surface of what there is to see from the Spanish resorts. For more details turn to the individual sections of the book.

The Socialite: *People-watching, Nightlife etc.*

Many popular holiday destinations in the Mediterranean attract crowds of holiday makers each year, by virtue of their 'sun, sand and sea' image. More often than not, however, it is only after the sun has set on your first day in foreign climes, that you discover the social scene is woefully inadequate. A few tavernas and the local disco with seventies music is likely to be your lot – if you're lucky. But, if this is the case in other parts of the Mediterranean, it's not true of Spain. The Spanish have been cashing in on the tourist boom for twenty years now, and they're shrewd enough to realize that the average holiday-maker doesn't take a package to the sun to learn about local habits. They want a good time, to meet new people and take home loads of holiday snaps full of smiling, bronzed faces.

This means that if you choose your resort carefully, you'll never be at a loss for something to do in the evening. During July and August, Spanish resorts are a social whirl. The options range from exuberant Spanish fiestas and carnivals, to bopping the night away in one of the nightspots in town. Prices vary, but in general, those who enjoy a hectic social life won't have their style cramped by having to pay crippling prices for drinks and nightclubs. The obvious exception to this is Marbella – the glamour of mixing with the young, gilded rich here soon wanes off when you see the bill for a round of drinks.

The colourful fiestas which liven up Spain's social scene are numerous throughout the year, and there is no charge for going along to spectate. Sometimes these events may simply be lively processions through the centre of town or they may be bigger affairs with fireworks, feasting, music and dancing. The larger festivals which are particularly worth noting are **Holy Week**, held during April in Málaga, when huge processions carry jewelled statues of the Holy Virgin through the streets; the **Horse Fair** (Jerez de la Frontera, near Cádiz) has riding displays, singing, dancing and bullfights. In Alicante during the month of June, the festival celebrating the **Bonfires of San Juan** culminates in the burning of bonfires in addition to parades, fireworks, religious pageants and bullfights. In September, the **Grape Harvest Festival** held in Jerez de la Frontera near Cádiz celebrates the first glass of wine of the season with flamenco displays, bullfights and a colourful cavalcade. For fuller details contact local tourist offices or the Spanish Tourist Board at 57-58 St James's Street, London SW1A 1LD. Tel: (01) 499 0901.

Bullfighting is not just a social event in Spain, but also a way of life. The fervour it arouses in its country of origin is equivalent to the emotion the World Cup raises in this country. Foreigners may find it difficult to relish the spectacle of six bulls being killed just as much as the Spaniards seem to, but many people go along out of curiosity. Definitely not an option for animal-lovers, though. The bullfighting season starts in March and ends in October, and bullfights are always held in the afternoon. There are around 300 bullrings throughout the country, and in the South most of the major towns have a ring. Despite the popularity of the event, an outing to a bullfight can be quite expensive – the cheapest seats sell at around £4 – £5. Tickets can be purchased for the afternoon's fights at the ticket-office connected to the ring, or at travel agents in town. During the summer months, it's better to buy tickets in advance of the fight or you are likely to be turned away at the gate.

Another unavoidable event in the Spanish social scene is the **flamenco**. Originating from the popular tradition of folk music, this gypsy lament has evolved into the well-known spectacle of swirling dresses, snapping castanets and clicking feet. Flamenco shows frequently charge high entrance prices, and it has to be said that some of these are second-rate, specifically laid on for unsuspecting tourists. Andalucía, encompassing the Costa del Sol, is the homeland of the flamenco, so it is here that you are most likely to get the authentic version of the dance, performed in all its colour and virtuosity.

For prime nightlife spots the areas that the Socialite should concentrate on are the Costa del Sol, the Costa Blanca and the Costa Brava on the Spanish mainland, Majorca and Ibiza on the Balearics and Gran Canaria and Tenerife on the Canaries. On the Costa del Sol, it is the big resorts of MÁLAGA, MARBELLA and TORREMOLINOS which have the most to offer in the way of bars, restaurants and nightclubs. BENIDORM on the Costa Brava has become a by-word among package holiday-makers, as *the* place in Spain where a good time can be had by all the family. Far from being just a 'sun, sea and sand' location, Benidorm has something to please everyone, from the old-time dancing and hotel cabaret for grannies and grandpas, to flashy nightclubs and beach barbeques for the younger crowd. Further north, LLORET DE MAR is a good choice for the socialite. All kinds of night-time entertainment are available, with discos and bars open well into the next morning . . . and if you want to capitalize on the allure of your nice new tan, there is an elegant promenade to strut down and eye up the local talent.

On Majorca, the capital PALMA is the place to base yourself. The best nightclubs and discos in town are to be found in the **Plaza Gomila**. No complaints about second-rate clubs and seventies-style discos here – the glitzy, modern establishments will rival, and probably outshine, what your home town has to offer. Ibiza is also a safe bet for some lively socializing. Night-time is *the* time to see the island as the place is transformed from dusk onwards into a heady cocktail of music, dancing and romance. Ibiza town itself is the largest resort on the island, and it has more than enough to keep even the most tireless socialite occupied for two weeks. On the Canaries, stick to the resorts **Puerto de la Cruz** or **Playa de las Americas** in Tenerife, **Playa del Ingles** on Gran Canaria, and **Puerto del Carmen** on Lanzarote. These are the biggest and busiest holiday destinations in the Canaries archipelago, and have the most to offer in terms of lively bars, quality restaurants and sophisticated nightclubs.

RECORDING YOUR HOLIDAY

Video cameras are taking over as the new form of home movies. The trend is set and each year an increasing number of people discover the delights of taking their holiday on film to be played back on their telly and watched from the comfort of their armchair in the dark winter months. Though a video rig-out is still an expensive business, it's the sort of equipment which once you've had, you feel you can never do without. Photos, slides and cine films just aren't the same after a full colour and sound film, and on holiday where the sky and sea are so blue, and the colours so much more vibrant, a video camera really comes into its own.

Those on the market now are well adapted to travelling: light and easy to handle. If you feel £1200 is a bit too much to splash out, consider hiring. That way you can have the fun of taking a film of your holiday for not much more than the equivalent you'd spend on conventional films, processing, etc. Hiring is widely available in all areas of the UK and is becoming, like the video camera itself, very much a thing of the future.

The Sportsperson: *The Great Outdoors*

Spain is well-equipped to cope with sporty types, whether they be complete beginners or muscle-rippling experts. A wide range of sports is on offer and in general, sporting facilities are well maintained and of a reasonable standard. Among the sports available at major resorts are golf, tennis, squash, archery and rifle shooting, horse-riding and a full range of water sports: sailing, water-skiing, pedalos, scuba diving, wind-surfing, sea-fishing, and, of course, swimming.

Overall, equipment-hire for popular activities, such as wind-surfing or horse-riding, is reasonably priced and in the major resorts, tuition is often available for those wanting to try out a new sport. Many hotels provide something in the way of sporting amenities for their guests. Table tennis, a tennis court, or a swimming pool are usually available to those who want to spend an afternoon in their hotel. If you're staying in a more up-market establishment, you can look forward to having the use of a private gymnasium and sauna. Villa and apartment complexes often have a swimming pool located in the vicinity. However, a hefty fee is sometimes charged for the use of these communal pools, so you'd do better to swim in the sea, which is warm, safe – and free!

Practically every tourist resort, from the smallest to the largest, has something sporty to offer holiday-makers. Wind-surfing, water-skiing, sailing and fishing-boat hire, usually run by enterprising locals, are available even in the quietest holiday. Nearer the bigger resorts, the range of options increases (as does the price) and there are some first-class golf courses, tennis complexes and horse-riding centres. The mild climate means that it is possible to indulge in outdoor activities for most of the year. The only exception to this is the Atlantic-facing Costa de la Luz, which tends to be cool and windswept during the winter months.

For some sports, Spain offers outstanding facilities, and **golf** is the foremost of these. The Costa del Sol boasts the largest number of golf courses to be found anywhere in Spain. Resorts for the golf-conscious to consider are MARBELLA, MIJAS and ESTEPONA, all of which have easy access to a number of courses. Further along, on the Costa Cálida, is situated **La Manga Club**. This prestigious and world-famous club is the sporty equivalent of Marbella, which means money, as well as sporting inclinations, is an important consideration in this holiday destination. But if you are really keen, not to say wealthy, or looking for a golfing holiday of a lifetime then this resort is a good bet. La Manga is not just restricted to golfers. It contains the most comprehensive selection of sports and leisure facilities in Spain – tennis, cricket, bowls and horse-riding can all be pursued here. In the Balearics, Majorca offers a number of fine golf courses which are located in the west of the island, and the resorts of **Palma Nova** and **Magaluf** provide easy access to courses as well as all the usual 'sun, sand and sea' entertainment for non-golfers. There are many golf tournaments running throughout the year. Some are for professionals only, but there are plenty for the amateur enthusiast to try his or her luck in. The Costa del Sol is the focus for most of the competitions and galas, and amateur tournaments are held at **Hotel Mijas**, during the months of November and March.

Tennis players are also well catered for in Spain. Apart from La Manga, **Ben Vista**, situated 7 miles outside Marbella, is a specially built complex which offers both sports and accommodation facilities. There are thirteen all-weather courts, as well as a golf course, gymnasium and swimming pools on site.

If you are a real golf or tennis enthusiast, it may be worthwhile taking a package with a tour operator who specializes in your

particular sport. These companies arrange deals especially suited to
your needs, and offer special rates on things like court hire or green fee
rates. If you are planning to play golf or tennis often, it is worth
checking on these companies – it could well work out cheaper
travelling with a specialist company than taking a straightforward
package through one of the large tour operators. For more information, see 'Who Specializes in What' on page 83.

There are many opportunities for **sea fishing** in Spain. Fishing
from rocks as well as offshore is likely to yield results. Mullet and bass
can be caught along the coastline, and if you have a boat the range
increases to include whiting, sardines and eels. The seas around the
Balearic and Canary Islands are particularly well stocked, although
the southern Atlantic is also popular among amateur fishers. For the
more adventurous, shark-fishing from MARBELLA makes a change
from the smaller fry. Dinghies with outboard motors can usually be
hired right along the coastline – wherever there are marina facilities,
there are usually a few boats for hire. The best way to procure a safe
dinghy, whose motor isn't going to give out in mid-ocean, is to head
for the local travel-agent's office. These usually rent out a couple of
boats at reasonable prices. Unless you know a lot about boats, steer
clear of what the local entrepreneurs have to offer. Their prices may
be cheaper, but the boats do not appear to be subject to any rigid
safety standards.

For those who enjoy the open-air life, the national parks of
SERRABIA DE RONDA and CORTES DE LA FRONTERA in Andalucía
provide plenty of challenging routes for hikers and rock-climbers.
Although not quite as spectacular as the Sierra Nevada in the
north-east, these parks are situated close to the major sea-side resorts
around Marbella and Cádiz and can be reached easily by car or local
bus. It comes as a culture shock to discover that, only a few miles
inland from all the built-up coastal strip, herds of wild goats, roe deer
and ibex run wild. There are numerous mountain peaks to be
conquered, ranging between 1,000 metres in the East and 1,919
metres in the West. On the higher peaks, refuge huts are available to
accommodate walkers staying overnight.

Back at the coast, the best facilities for **water-sports** tend to be
concentrated on the Costa del Sol, the Costa Blanca and Costa Brava
on the mainland, and the larger resorts on Majorca, Ibiza and the

Canary Islands. It goes without saying that places like Marbella, Benidorm and Lloret de Mar have masses to offer the water-sport enthusiast. For quieter waters though, it is worth considering the lesser-known resorts such as ROQUETAS DE MAR on the Costa Almería, or CALELLA DE PALAFRUGELL on the Costa Dorada. ESTARTIT, also on the Costa Dorada, is particularly good for beginners as it has a water-sports centre which offers instruction (in English) for watery activities such as scuba-diving and wind-surfing. On Majorca, the two biggest resorts PALMA NOVA and MAGALUF have some more unusual water-based activities to offer, including parasailing and trips in a glass-bottomed boat. In Ibiza, the crystal-clear waters tempt pleasure-lovers and enthusiasts alike and are ideal for all sports from snorkelling to water-skiing. The resorts of ES CANA and PUERTO SAN MIGUEL have fine beaches, a range of water-sports and good fishing to occupy holiday-makers. On Tenerife, the busy resort of PLAYA DE LAS AMERICAS has a water-park, where 'thrills, spills and splashes' for kids of all ages can be enjoyed. For the more serious-minded, there are some excellent water-sports facilities at the nearby **Los Cristianos**. On Gran Canaria, wind-surfing is particularly good beside the holiday-village of BAHIA FELIZ, and equipment and tuition are available for hire. Otherwise the large resorts of PLAYA DEL INGLES and SAN AGUSTIN have plenty to occupy those who have sporting and non-sporting interests.

For further details concerning the sporting scene in Spain or for more information about the range of sports listed above, contact the Spanish National Tourist Board at their address in London, 57-58 St James's Street, London, SW1A 1LD. Tel: (01) 499 0901.

Spa Holidays

Spain is well endowed with 'healing', mineral waters and many people travel to Spanish spas each year either in search of a cure, or simply a relaxing, healthy holiday. Most spa towns have sporting facilities, parks, cinemas, etc. to entertain the influx of visitors, and if you choose your spa carefully, there is no reason why your 'cure' cannot be combined with a spot of sightseeing in nearby towns or cities.

In the south of Spain, there are spas at FUENTE AMARGA on the Costa de la Luz, TOLOX, ALHAMA DE GRANADA, LANJARON, SAN NICHOLAS on the Costa del Sol and Costa Almería, FORTUNA on the Costa Almería, MONLLEO and GOLOFRE on the Costa Azahar, BROQUETAS, FORNS and PRATS near Barcelona. These are only a selection of the spas available to visitors. For a comprehensive list apply to the Spanish Tourist Office, 57-58 St James's Street, London SW1A 1LD Tel: (01) 499 0901.

The Nature-Lover

Majorca and the Canary Islands are the areas where the nature-lovers should concentrate their attentions. Although holiday resorts are prolific on the shores of the islands, there has been little tourist development away from the coast. The advantages of this are obvious – you can take a cheap package to one of the coastal resorts and make tours inland to explore the lovely natural landscapes of the islands.

Majorca has a bewildering variety of landscapes and scenery. Fruit orchards, orange groves, olive terraces and fragrant pine forests are just a few delights awaiting those who venture out of their resort for a day. The Tramontana mountain range, running along the centre of the island, is dotted with some lovely peacful havens while the Formentor peninsula in the north of the island provides some spectacular views of the rocky coastline. At the other end of the island, close to the port of Alcudia is **La Albufera**, an area of swampy lands which has lagoons, reed beds and water birds. Of special interest to ornithologists, those who are keen to visit this unique landscape must apply to the offices located in the Playa Esperanza Urban Development for authorization. Some of the most amazing natural phenomena on Majorca are actually located under this island, in the form of vast subterranean caves. The **Drach** caves are the most famous – and it is not difficult to see why. Boat trips through the caves reveal clusters of stalactites and stalagmites hanging in incredibly intricate formations from the darkened walls. The journey culminates in the amphitheatre

– a huge underground cavity where a concert takes place each day from one of the small ships which floats on the lake.

The Canary Islands are volcanic in origin, and their landscapes are characterized by grey carbonized deserts and numerous, dormant volcano cones. GRAN CANARIA has been called a 'miniature continent' because of the sheer diversity of its terrain. Abrupt cliffs and rugged ravines alternate with fertile valleys which grow banana plantations, almond trees, vineyards and tomato fields. The island affords endless days of walking and discovery, but perhaps one of the most accessible places to head for is ARUCAS. Located a mile or so inland, amid banana plantations, the town is set picturesquely against the backdrop of an extinct volcano. TENERIFE's landscape is distinguished by its unusual black beaches and the spectacular crater, **Caxadas del Teide**, which measures twelve miles in diameter. Further north stands the impressive **Pico del Teide**. At 12,270 feet above sea-level it is the highest peak in Spain, and during the winter months becomes white with snow.

LANZAROTE is famous for its awe-inspiring vistas of volcanic desolation and desertion. Camel trains take a lonely path over stoney deserts to the gulf of Montaña de Fuego where there is the unforgettable sight of 300 volcanic cones rising up all round the horizon. At La Geria, the island's lava interior, hostile nature has been harnessed by resourceful islanders and the ground is a series of tiny craters which are cultivated to grow a wine-yielding vine.

The smaller islands of GOMERA and LA PALMA also deserve a mention. Remote from the hustle and bustle of their sister islands, they are rich in geographical interest and don't have herds of loud tourists charging around spoiling the peace and quiet. Green, terraced hills and abundant fruit orchards are part of the geography of these islands, with huge volcanic cones and black beaches adding some drama to the landscapes.

On the mainland, the countryside around the coastal strips cannot claim to rival the richness and diversity of the islands – but a few miles inland from the coastal resorts can be found hilly uplands which are teeming with wild game like deer, partridge, ibex and fox. Depending on how energetic you are, there are a number of hill walks (or car drives) to be taken which afford fine views of the coastline and neighbouring mountain ranges.

PRIVATE.
Keep Out

The Recluse

A 'get-away-from-it-all' holiday destination is not the image which most people have of Spain. Nevertheless, pockets of peace and quiet remain – if you make the effort to find them. The Atlantic-facing Costa de la Luz has managed to escape the effects of mass tourism and there is no shortage of little villages and resorts which are havens of peace and quiet. TARIFA is a charming village with an authentic Moorish ambience and lovely stretches of undiscovered beaches. CONIL rates as slightly more touristy, but if you can avoid peak season, you are guaranteed hours of undisturbed pleasure on the fine beaches lapped by a warm Atlantic.

Apart from the Costa de la Luz, options for the recluse become more limited. Resorts on the Costa Cálida and Costa Almería tend to be quieter, family destinations, but even these have the standard sprinkling of touristy nightclubs and bar-restaurants full of loud, jolly holiday-maker types. Better to leave the mainland behind altogether and head for one of the lesser-visited islands.

In the Balearics, the main ones to consider in this respect are Formentera and Menorca. There are plenty of remote little nooks on the island where you can bury yourself in relative peace and quiet. If you have a tent, you can strike out in any direction from the island's capital Mahón – and take pot-luck where you end up. If you're relying on less basic forms of accommodation, take a bus and head north to CALA MESQUIDA and FONELLS, or to CALA SANTA GALDANA on the other side of the island. All of these have some tourist development – but not sufficient to spoil the sleepy, small town atmosphere. Formentera has some stunning white beaches which still remain relatively quiet – even during peak season. Shortage of accommodation is a problem which prevents many people staying on the island, but again, if you're camping, there are many idyllic spots to pitch your tent – and no-one to move you on. PUGOLS is the main package-tour holiday destination on the island, and as such, it is a moderately developed resort with the usual array of hotels, restaurants and bars. A better option for those seeking seclusion, is CALA SAHONA on the east of the island. It boasts a largish, family-run hotel built right beside a long stretch of pine-fringed beach.

On the Canaries, the islands of **La Palma** and **Gomera** have so far managed to escape the eagle eye of the large tour operators and those who stray here are likely to have the pick of the lovely pools and beaches which are dotted around the coastline. For quiet locations, try the village of PUERTO DE NAOS (notable for its beach of black sand) or the slightly more touristy BREÑA BAJA on La Palma. On Gomera, SAN SEBASTIAN, the capital, is a small bustling town which should provide for your accommodation needs – or for an even further-flung destination, try the picturesque fishing village of PLAYA SANTIAGO.

Holidaying out of season is another option which the recluse should consider seriously. Then, smaller resorts along the Costa Cálida and Costa Almería are at their quietest, and the temperatures are still hot enough to have a few days' sunbathing. If you enjoy sightseeing, but can't stand herds of holiday-makers, then October through to March is also a good time to soak up the historic and cultural pleasures of places like Barcelona or Valencia. Broadly speaking, if you are not too fussy about the weather, and peace and quiet are your main priorities, then the winter months represent your best opportunity to come to Spain and avoid the crowds.

 Family Holidays

Many families, especially with young children, will want to avoid the biggest resorts of Torremolinos and Benidorm. Petty crime rates are high in these areas and some parts of town can be seedy – definitely not the place to turn young teenagers loose in. However, there is no shortage of alternatives to choose from – almost all the towns along the shoreline have a good variety of activities to keep young people occupied while the seas are safe and warm for swimming.

Some of the best resorts on the mainland to consider are SALOU on the Costa Dorada with its funfair, excellent beach and sporting amenities and CALELLA DE PALAFRUGELL on the Costa Brava with its gently shelving beaches which are particularly suitable for younger bathers. For a quieter holiday destination, ROQUETAS DE MAR on the Costa de Almería offers a wide range of water-sports and easy access to the pretty Andalusian villages in the mountains while on the Costa de la Luz, CONIL is a good choice if you're looking for a relaxing, unsophisticated family holiday.

Choosing your hotel can often be as important as choosing your resort when it comes to having a holiday that can be enjoyed by all the family. If you have younger offspring, take note of what the brochures say about children's facilities. Most hotels have a playpool and cots (although you may have to pay a bit extra for these) and some establishments provide early suppers and highchairs if requested. Babysitting services are often available in larger hotels, although it is always wise to check with your tour operator first. Generally, the bigger tour operators tend to pitch themselves at the family-holiday market, so will have most to offer in the way of these types of facilities. If in doubt, go for holidays which say they are specifically recommended for families – that way you have a come-back if the resort is not up to scratch from the children's facilities' point of view. As for the 'one child free' option, if you read the small print, you'll soon realize that such places are limited and allocated on a first-come, first-served basis – so early booking is essential if you want to take advantage of these offers. However, watch out for this seemingly attractive proposition. There may be a good reason why tour operators have to offer this extra concession to fill up a hotel during peak-season, or else you'll find the savings made on one child's place will be eaten up by other 'hidden' expenses. Also, if you're the type who thinks your children are fine, but other people's en masse are not, avoid these hotels as they are invariably reminiscent of summer camps in peak season.

Away from the coast, Majorca, Ibiza and the Canary Islands of Tenerife and Gran Canaria are your best bets for family-holiday destinations. On Majorca, resorts which are particularly good are CALAS DE MALLORCA, a small development with a more personable atmosphere than some of the larger resorts, CALA MOREYA with its no-through-traffic restrictions and PUERTO POLLENSA, a small, picturesque resort which has a plethora of water-based activities as well as easy access to a number of quiet coves along the coast.

On Ibiza, the resort of PLAYA D'EN ROSSA is an ideal location for a family holiday. A relatively new resort, it boasts some excellent amenities for children: a huge aquatic park, a funfair and a sports centre are only a few of the attractions on offer. Otherwise, the nearby town of TALAMANCA is a popular choice for family groups. The beaches remain relatively uncrowded, even during the summer months, and the resort is well placed for leisurely sightseeing trips, with Ibiza Town, the island's capital, only a short bus trip away.

On Tenerife, PLAYA DE LAS AMERICAS is a bright, big modern resort, with a water-slide park, play areas and activity pools to entertain kids. For families with older children, PLAYA PARAISO, with its relaxed surroundings and good variety of sporting facilities, is worth considering. On Gran Canaria, PUERTO RICO is an attractive resort with safe bathing and a playground for younger members of the family, while the major resort of PLAYA DEL INGLÉS has something to offer everyone from camel rides to mile upon mile of golden, sandy beach.

 The Naturist

For the serious naturist, there are several special beaches and centres throughout coastal Spain and the islands, and their number is increasing each year. International Naturists Federation (INF) cards are not always necessary, but most operators try to encourage membership while balancing the number of singles. For more information apply to The General Secretary, The Central Council for British Naturism, Assurance House, 35-41 Hazelwood Road, Northampton NN1 1LL or The Spanish Tourist Office, 57-58 St James's Street, London SW1A 1LD, Tel. (01) 499 0901, which keeps a list of all nudist beaches in Spain. Specialist tour operators include Peng Travel, 86 Station Road, Gidea Park, Essex, Tel. (04024) 71832 for COSTA NATURA on the COSTA DEL SOL, about sixty miles from MALAGA, and Eden Holidays, 92 The Avenue, Sunbury on Thames, Middlesex TW16 5EX, Tel. (0932) 784041 for COSTA NATURA, VERA PLAYA, LANZAROTE and GRAN CANARIA.

Practicalities

RED TAPE

Visitors holding British (or British Visitor's), Canadian or American passports are allowed to stay in the country for three months without a visa. If you are planning to stay longer, apply for a special visa before you leave. Nationals of Australia, New Zealand and South Africa require a visa to enter the country, and these may be obtained from Spanish consulates in the country concerned.

Embassy and Consulate Addresses

Visas may be obtained from the Spanish Consulate General, 20 Draycott Place, London SW3 (Tel: (01) 581 5921).

The Spanish embassy in the USA can be found at 2,700 15th Street, 20009 Washington DC. In addition, there are consulate offices in major cities throughout the country.

In Canada, the embassy is located at 350 Sparks Street, Suite 802, Ottawa, KIR-758. Consulates can be found in Vancouver, Edmonton Alta, Halifax, Quebec and St John's in Newfoundland.

HEALTH FORMALITIES

No vaccinations are required for visitors from the United Kingdom, North America or Continental Europe.

CUSTOMS

Although there is no limit to the amount of foreign currency or the amount of pesetas which may be taken into Spain, visitors may not take out over 500,000 pesetas in the equivalent foreign currency or 100,000 pesetas in Spanish notes.

Tourists (over seventeen years of age) may import the following duty-free goods: 2 litres of table wine; 1 litre of brandy or liqueurs (over 22%) or 2 litres (up to 22%); 200 cigarettes or 250 grams tobacco or 50 cigars; 1/4 litre toilet water; 50 grams perfume; gifts up to 5,000 pesetas.

Personal effects such as clothes, luggage, small stocks of your favourite tea or coffee are not questioned providing they are not carried in obviously excessive amounts. The same goes for more expensive items which you might conceivably be carrying – such as a portable typewriter or cameras – although it may be worthwhile taking your receipts with you, so there's no chance of being charged duty on these items.

MONEY

The monetary unit of Spain is the peseta. Notes and coins are issued in the following denominations:

Coins: 1, 2, 5, 10, 25, 50, 100 pesetas

Notes: 100, 200, 500, 1,000, 2,000 pesetas

For customs regulations governing money, see the section on 'Customs' above.

How to Take Your Money

The exchange rate for the Spanish peseta stays reasonably constant at about 200 pesetas to the pound so there is no particular advantage taking peseta traveller's cheques in preference to sterling or American dollar traveller's cheques as both are widely accepted throughout the country. However, it is a good idea to take some Spanish currency with you. This is readily available from larger travel agents or banks and will tide you over the first few hours in Spain when you are still finding out the location of banks and exchanges.

Traveller's cheques in your own currency can be exchanged in hotels, banks, tourist offices and some restaurants. The commission fee charged by banks for changing money is low, so it makes sense to use these instead of hotels and restaurants. Always go for a well-known bank or credit card company, i.e. American Express, Thomas Cook or Bank of England, otherwise you could have difficulties in some small resorts or rural towns. Remember also, that you may be required to produce your passport as proof of identity before you can cash your cheques.

The major *credit cards* (Visa, Diner's Club, American Express, etc.) are accepted in most tourist resorts, and this is a safe and convenient way to carry your cash. It is not a method to be relied upon as your sole source of money, however, and a stock of traveller's cheques should be taken to cover items which can't be paid for by credit card.

Personal cheques Eurocheque Card and Eurocheques (available from your bank) are becoming increasingly popular among holiday-makers. These need to be ordered a few days in advance, but once you have them you can use them to sign cheques abroad just as you would at home. While this form of money is widely acceptable in the busy resorts on the coast, the situation is different in the more rural areas of the interior – so if you are planning to travel extensively take a credit card or traveller's cheques as a back-up.

Where to Exchange

Traveller's cheques, foreign currency and personal cheques can all be exchanged at banks, travel agencies, exchange bureaux and at some hotels and restaurants. Banks and travel agencies will invariably offer the best rates of exchange, and the daily rate is usually on clear display in the window. Exchange bureaux located in railway stations and airports generally offer less favourable rates, and changing money at hotels and restaurants should be avoided if possible, as commission fees are high and rates of exchange low. At the end of your holiday, try to get rid of most of your pesetas before returning to this country; you will always lose out by exchanging from Spanish to British currency.

To summarize, then, all these methods have their advantages and disadvantages. Like most holiday-makers, you will probably weigh up the odds and decide that only a combination of the alternatives gives the security and flexibility you require: some ready cash in pesetas and then a choice of traveller's cheques, a credit card or Eurocheques. Overall, traveller's cheques in your own currency are the best to carry the bulk of your money if you are planning to travel extensively, although Eurocheques or a credit card are equally acceptable in the main tourist centres. If you have a credit card, it's a good idea to take it with you as a back-up to traveller's cheques. One final point to remember – take some of your own currency with you! It's amazing how many people manage to successfully negotiate the foreign currency maze abroad and completely forget to take some ready cash with them in preparation for buses, taxis, etc. on their return to this country.

BANKING

Opening hours are 9am – 2pm, Monday to Friday, and 9am – 1pm, Saturday. During the summer, banks at airports and some of the main tourist centres extend their opening times.

INSURANCE

It really is foolhardy to cut back on holiday insurance, yet each year thousands of people make this false economy and live to regret it. Increasingly if you're taking a package holiday you'll have no say in the matter and insurance will be added on to your final bill whether you like it or not. While this is at least makes sure you get some sort of cover, remember you are not obliged to take this policy.

Note, then, that you are under no obligation to accept the insurance policy offered by your travel agent. In some instances these are not as detailed as policies bought from large reputable companies and all too often the package policies mean long delays in the settlement of claims as they're snowed under at the peak of the tourist season. On the plus side, however, the rep at your resort will have been trained in how to handle claims and this will take some of the strain off you. Tour companies also represent a formidable force in the insurance market and their buying power means that they can usually offer a cheaper insurance policy than could be bought on your own. The secret is to read the small print of the insurance policies carefully. Don't assume that because it has the backing of a 'big name' insurance company that it is necessarily the right policy for you.

If you consider the inclusive package as inadequate for your needs, the best advice is to go to an insurance broker, tell him what you're taking (remember photographic equipment, etc.), what you envisage doing, e.g. if you plan spending a lot of time doing water-sports, and how long you'll be away. This is a particularly good idea if you're planning on taking some new, expensive equipment with you (many package policies put a limit of around £200 per item on your valuables) or if your chances of requiring medical treatment are higher than average. Also check out the liability clause for delays if it's important that you get home by the date stipulated.

For most people, then, the basic insurance policy offered by tour companies will be sufficient. But for those who are looking elsewhere, Lloyds of London are particularly good and will provide travel insurance for people who normally find it difficult, e.g. disabled people and pregnant ladies. Independent travellers are especially advised to arrange a good insurance policy for themselves as if anything goes wrong, they have no one (such as ABTA or a travel agent) to argue their case for them.

In terms of medical insurance, most comprehensive travel insurance policies incorporate some kind of coverage for medical costs incurred abroad. The amount which will be reimbursed varies from company to company, but many of the major tour operators offer to cover costs up to £500,000. Reciprocal health agreements exist between Spain and Britain and, on production of the proper documents (see 'Health' section below), British citizens are entitled to emergency medical treatment free of charge. However, for more serious illnesses, a good insurance policy is essential. If you already have a medical insurance policy in this country, it is worth finding out if this covers you for travel abroad.

North American travellers and those from further afield are strongly advised to procure good travel insurance cover before leaving home.

HEALTH

If you are travelling to Spain from Britain or North America, you are not required to obtain any medical vaccinations (*see* 'Health Formalities', page 30), although it is a good idea, as with all the Mediterranean countries, to have a typhoid/polio booster before you go.

The standards of hygiene in most tourist resorts are reasonable and you should have no cause for complaint. If you are travelling independently to some of the smaller Balearic or Canary Islands, you may find the local customs a little hard to live with, so be sure to pack your own loo-roll, soap and a first-aid kit. A good health insurance policy is also essential. Officially, tap-water is safe to drink – but you'd be advised not to risk stomach upsets and drink mineral or distilled water.

In general, the standard of medicine practised is acceptable, and in larger towns and hospitals there should be no problem finding a doctor who speaks English. If it is something minor that is bothering you, try a *farmacia* first. Spanish pharmacists are well trained and should be able to guide you around the array of unfamiliar drugs until you get what you want.

Medical attention is not free in Spain and *it costs* – even for the quickest visit to the doctor. Theoretically, British people are entitled to free emergency medical treatment on production of an E111 certificate (available from your local DHSS offices). However, in practice, the local doctor may not be too impressed and an E111 is no substitute for a good medical insurance policy, which will cover the costs of a more serious or prolonged illness.

Medical insurance is often integrated into a basic insurance policy offered by tour operators or insurance companies, but if you want to take out a separate medical insurance policy, then check out the AA, RAC and Lloyds, who all offer good deals. The cheapest medical insurance Britons can get, and probably one of the best, is given by Europe Assistance Ltd, 252 High Street, Croydon, Surrey, CRO 1NF. For a small premium (average £15 per person travelling by car) you get a twenty-four-hour advice telephone link with the UK and a guarantee of on-the-spot cash for emergency services. This insurance also covers the expenses that can arise from a car accident (hiring another car, flying out spare parts, etc.).

PRE-PLANNING AND FREE INFO

The more you know about a country before going, the more you'll get out of your holiday once you're there. For the latest, up-to-date information write to the Spanish Tourist Office, 57-58 St James's Street, London SW1A 1LD (Tel: (01) 499 0901). They have stacks of leaflets and brochures which they will send out, free of charge, if you write to them asking for general tourist literature. If you have any specific interests which you want to pursue when you are on holiday (such as golfing or fishing) ask them their advice on where best to go and to send you any leaflets that they might have. Remember to ask for a map and accommodation listings if you are touring independently. These are also free and save you buying maps and guide-books at the other end.

When you're choosing your resort, another extremely useful source of information (again, free and impartial) comes from the travel agent Hogg Robinson. They produce resort reports, which go into detail on what to expect, and give an unbiased report on all the hotels used by the tour operators. These files can be consulted free of charge in any of their agencies.

Thomas Cook also produce resort reports and these can be taken away by the public. Much smaller, and with no detail on specific hotels, these do, however, contain condensed information on the main resorts, sightseeing, best buy etc. and they give a good idea of how expensive drinks and meals will be once you get there. Lunn Poly do a similar kind of thing; their *Guide to Good Hotels* is compiled on the basis of customers' actual experiences, and hotels are featured according to their recommendations and comments.

Another source of free information on Spain is your local library. Reams have been written about Spain, covering just about every imaginable interest, from Moorish influences to Spanish folktales. The country has also inspired many British writers to put pen to paper, both in the form of fictional literature and travel accounts. Some of the best of these are: *Spain* by Jan Morris, an evocative and descriptive introduction to the country; Laurie Lee's work *As I Walked Out One Summer's Day* and Hemingway's novels *Death in the Afternoon* and *For Whom the Bell Tolls*, both of which give you a flavour of Spain's drama and colour.

As far as bought sources go, there are a few other guide-books worth considering: Collins' *Welcome to Spain* is a fairly detailed book which is worth considering if you have a specialist interest or if you're planning to do the country in depth; Fodor's *Spain* (Hodder and Stoughton) is pretty standard stuff, well researched, comprehensive and informative, but a bit too middle-aged and middle-class to be of much practical use for young(ish) package-tour holiday-makers. The

Rough Guide to Spain (Routledge and Kegan Paul) is another publication worth considering. Although it is really geared towards student back-packing types, don't be put off as the guide is well compiled and especially good for the independent traveller, with detailed accounts of the more far-flung places in Spain.

And, of course, you are already reading the guide best suited to all your travel needs!

BUDGETING

Spain is a good country for the cost-conscious to visit. True, prices are marked up in most tourist resorts, but even so, the cost of eating out or day-tripping is considerably cheaper than can be found in Britain. As far as getting there is concerned, lower air fares and increased competition among tour operators means that there will undoubtably be a deal which suits your requirements as well as your pocket.

Major tour companies aim to keep prices down and to be competitive so if you choose carefully, a cheap package holiday need not be at the expense of quality accommodation or service. If you are working with limited resources it is worth considering companies such as Martin Rooks or Tjaereborg – these specialize in offering budget holidays to those who want two weeks in the sun but can't afford to spend a fortune. Another possibility to 'break away on a budget' is to holiday in the off-season months rather than the July/August period. Out-of-season breaks can often be at least a third cheaper than the same package taken in mid-summer. Similarly, late bookings advertised in travel agents' windows are a good way to keep costs down. At least 80% of late bookings on offer are to Spanish destinations, so if you're flexible and willing to take pot luck, pack a bag and head for the sun . . .

There are various accommodation choices open to the holiday-maker in Spain which can range from expensive luxury hotels to the humble family-run pension. Most people will opt for hotel accommodation, either bed and breakfast or half/full board. Although full board is the cheapest option, your palate may become a bit jaded once you have eaten your way through the chef's repertoire twice. Don't be too wary of taking half board. As long as you're not expecting to sample exotic delicacies in restaurants, the food in Spain is hearty, filling and relatively cheap. A basic three-course meal is likely to set you back around £4.50, and a bottle of cheap wine is around £1.50.

Imported food is more expensive, and this includes tea. A nice cuppa can cost up to three times as much as you would pay in Britain – so take your own teabags and ask for hot water. If you're travelling with Junior and are fussy about what your baby eats, take your own supply of baby food, as again, it can be quite pricey to buy. If you're in self-catering, go to the local markets and choose from a vast array of fruits, vegetables and fish. Supermarkets with a high proportion of canned and packaged food tend to be more expensive, but usually they have refrigerated cheese and meat counters which you may prefer, for the hygiene aspect, to the open-air stalls in markets.

As for nightlife, if you are a disco fan without much money, you have to pick and choose your nightspots carefully. Some of the glitzy, new discos can be very expensive while others are on a par with their British equivalents. Beware of nightclubs that offer the first round of drinks free with the entrance fee. When you do eventually make it up to the bar, four drinks are likely to set you back a cool £10. Cheaper entertainment altogether is found at a local fiesta or listening to folk music in a local bar. Popular leisure activities such as wind-surfing or pedalos are not beyond the limits of most people's budgets although, obviously, you will have to pay more if you want to practise your golf game on one of the coast's top-class golf clubs.

Although an all-inclusive package holiday is the cheapest way to spend two weeks in the sun, if you are keen to go it alone you won't find yourself paying the price for it. It is possible to get yourself a pension for £5 a night, but for those who don't fancy roughing it, a single room in a cheap hotel, including breakfast, might cost you somewhere in the region of £7–£8 a night.

Undoubtedly the biggest expense involved in going it alone will be moving around the country. A week's car hire of a Fiat Uno or Renault 5 hatchback is likely to set you back £85 – £90 basic rate. On top of that you will have to pay VAT (currently running at 12%) plus a collision damage waiver insurance if you are hiring through one of the big rental firms. It usually works out cheaper to book a car in advance with your tour operator than to hire through one of the international car-hire firms based in Spain.

A far better way to travel, without forking out vast sums of money, is to use the local bus or train services. Fares on these are low and for train travel, there are several discount tickets available. It is possible to buy a Chequetren which costs around £9 and can be shared between six people. If you are travelling in a group of ten or over, you can get discounts of up to 50% – the same applies to old age pensioners and children under fourteen years of age.

Further discounts on museum entrances are available to students in possession of a valid International Student Identity Card.

Finally, when working out your budget, remember that it's easier to take too much money with you than to have money transferred to your account or sent on. A credit card is the ideal stand-by for emergencies, but an extra £100 or so in your current Eurocheque account or in traveller's cheques does not go amiss. If you do not use all your sterling traveller's cheques in Spain, you can cash them in at face value on return to this country. No commission will be charged if you are exchanging them in a bank or building society where you have an account. When abroad, change money in small amounts, enough to do you for a couple of days. There are two advantages in this: firstly it is safer as chances of loss through theft are reduced; secondly, you will be able to keep track of precisely how much money is being spent and budget accordingly. Having small quantities of currency also cuts down the chances of having to change back large quantities of pesetas into sterling (at a frequently disadvantageous rate) before you leave the country.

Getting Yourself Organized

WHAT TO TAKE WITH YOU

Package-tour holiday-makers should take the minimum of luggage. Think back to previous years when you returned home with half the clothes unused and remember you'll need to allow a bit of extra room in your luggage for any items you buy over there or for your duty free. Try to travel with hand luggage. If you're going for a two-week 'sun, sand and sea' holiday there is no reason why you shouldn't be able to pack everything you need into a small lightweight bag which can be carried as hand-luggage. Think of the advantages of not having to wait in the baggage collection queues wondering if what you checked in will actually reappear. A word of caution though. It really will have to be a very neat bag, as there's not much room on charter aircraft and the staff are very reluctant to let you take large bags on board.

As for the actual clothes themselves, light casual garments plus a showerproof raincoat and a sweater should be all you require. If you're going on a winter holiday, it's a good idea to pack an extra jumper as temperatures can cool down quite rapidly after nightfall. Dress is not usually formal in hotels, so there is no need to pack a suit or evening dress, unless you are staying in a five-star Grand Hotel.

If you're travelling independently, aside from taking the absolute minimum of lightweight kit, you might consider taking a few extra items such as a travelling alarm clock (for early starts) and an empty water-bottle to fill up with drinking water when you get the chance. For those camping or hostelling, it's advisable to take a money-belt to keep your valuables in and a padlock for youth hostels. A good first-aid kit is a must for independent travellers heading off to remote parts, and a phrase book would not go amiss either.

Although the best advice that can be offered to any holiday-maker is to travel light, taking only the essentials, there are a few items which definitely merit packing:

(1) Take all photographic equipment that you are likely to need. Camera film, such as Kodak or Agfa, is *always* more expensive to buy in a big tourist resort, compared with the prices at your local chemist at home. If you do have to buy an extra roll of film, check the expiry date to ensure that it is not out of date. This is especially important in Mediterranean countries where the heat can distort photographic colours over a period of time.

(2) Take any English-language books or magazines you're likely to want for beach reading. Spanish newsagents often carry a stock of second-hand British and American books, but these tend to be Mills & Boon types or seedy horror stories that other people have discarded. Whatever is on offer is generally overpriced – on average, it will set you back about £5 for a grimy paperback.

(3) If you are travelling with a young child and prefer certain brands of baby food, it's a good idea to take your own supply with you. British brands are available in supermarkets but, again, are much more expensive than at home.

(4) Toiletries and medicines should also be brought with you (and this includes suntan preparations, which are more expensive in the resorts than back at home). There are few countries which offer cheaper toiletries than Britain, and even if you do find some, the quality could well be questionable. Any prescribed medicines should definitely be brought from home as often the equivalent drug will not be available abroad.

(5) Loo-paper and soap are essential to any traveller – whether you're on a package or going independently. Although most hotels and larger resorts are well acquainted with North European habits, once you strike out to the smaller towns and islands, you can't be sure they will be so enlightened.

(6) If you're planning on visiting any of the churches in the country, it is regarded as a mark of respect that women should cover up bare arms and legs before entering. Take a light shawl to throw across your shoulders and pack a shirt in your day-bag before going on sightseeing tours.

THE HOLIDAY INDUSTRY

Tourism is big business these days, and, realizing the vast potential market which exists, more manufacturers each year are entering the business of catering for the holiday industry, designing and marketing products specifically for the traveller. Photographic goods, electrical gadgets, luggage, clothing, toiletries . . . the list goes on, all produced with the annual two weeks in the sun in mind. Look through a good, objective magazine such as *Which* to spot the best buys (local libraries often have back copies).

Some travel products are excellent; some do not merit the expense involved and some are just plain awful. As full-time travellers we have the opportunity to try out many products in this category, and here we bring you a list of some of our personal recommendations which we found useful and worth investing in.

Travelling with Babies and Young Children

The addition of babies and children to the travelling duo *does* make a difference, there's no point denying this, but with a bit of careful pre-planning and the purchase of a few items, taking your youngsters on holiday abroad can be a relatively easy experience, and there is certainly no need for the commonly held belief that foreign travel has to stop with the arrival of tiny feet.

Today there is a whole range of well-designed products on the market for the holidaying parent. The recent introduction of these goods has revolutionized family travelling, and with the ever-increasing awareness on the tour operators' part that families make up a sizeable part of their market, the situation is improving each year.

Your children will invariably be the best introduction to the locals you can have. Babies particularly are a passport to conversation, for even without being able to speak the language your brood will be adopted by the local mamas and grandmas, and you'll find pleasant little surprises – your ice creams will be that bit bigger, your service that bit friendlier.

Babies under six months generally make excellent holiday-makers. They are not yet mobile, tend to be up late anyway, and will not be too upset about being out of their normal environment. Before they are weaned, feeding is a lot simpler, and you don't need to transport a plethora of favourite toys with you yet. Three months is a particularly good age, as, if you're lucky, they're just about sleeping through the whole night; are still easily fed; still take daytime naps; and are at the stage when the bustle and activity in places like airports will keep them entertained and quiet. Under three months it is still perfectly possible to go on holiday, but obviously they are that bit younger and more prone to infection, etc.

Between six months and a year, as every parent will tell you, it gets a bit hard. A crawling baby is not the best passenger, but having said that, if you're sensible about your flight timings and the transfer times from airport to hotel, it can still work. Feeding is more of a problem, but this can be overcome by taking instant dried baby foods and supplies of milk and juice granules. Products such as Milupa Herbal Drink Granules, Milupa or Boots dried baby food and SMA Ready to Feed UHT Baby Milks, which come in cartons, are ideal. The latter was new on the market in 1988 and makes travelling with bottle-fed babies far easier as there is no need to find sterile water etc. All these products are available in High Street chemists throughout the UK. At this stage, if your child is difficult, you may find it easier to go for a self-catering holiday based in a villa away from other people.

Toddlers and young children need constant amusement, so choose your resort carefully. Regular bedtimes are important, too, so somewhere with a reliable babysitting service should be on your list of priorities unless you want it to be a real home from home.

Our family researchers have tested all the products they could find on the market for travelling babies and children, and recommend the following items. In every case the cost was more than justified by the added convenience and peace of mind.

For Babies

A lightweight pushchair from home is an essential piece of equipment for all children under two and a half. If the one you have is heavy or cumbersome try to borrow a lighter one, or, if you're planning on doing a lot of travelling, or are buying one for the first time with travelling in mind, the best thing to do is look at the MacLaren range. They have several lightweight buggies which are easily steered, quick to fold into an umbrella shape, and have available all the weatherproof attachments you need, and a useful playtray which helps at feeding times. For a very young baby the lie-back multi-position *Dreamer* is a good alternative.

In some holiday destinations it is possible to hire prams, but in our experience this is not a good idea as foreign makes tend to be less well designed and sometimes do not meet with British Safety Standards. And it does not solve the problem of how to transport your baby from home to your holiday destination.

Do not check in your pushchair with your other luggage at the airport. Instead tell the airline that you require it until the last minute and hand it to the baggage handlers on the tarmac as they load the plane. This way you have your hands free for duty-free shopping, etc. (An alternative would be to take a papoose.)

The business of cots on holiday can present unforeseen problems if you are not aware in advance of the cost involved or you are going to a small hotel or villa where a cot cannot be supplied. Most tour operators will endeavour to get a cot for you if you stipulate this on your booking form but costs vary dramatically (anything from £5 to £25 per week), so check first. Again, check with your operator that the cot you are hiring meets British Safety Standards.

The alternative to hiring is to take your own travel cot with you. For a very young baby a Moses basket is best, but after six months a full-size travel cot is necessary. Mothercare have two very good designs: one small and light, the other sturdier, and suited to the older child. Either of these could easily be taken as luggage on a plane. They weigh 15.4lb and 24.2lb, and retail around £40 and £60 respectively (mattresses are included in the price), but obviously their usefulness is not restricted to foreign holidays alone, and if you are being charged a comparable sum merely for the hire of a cot in your hotel the purchase of a travel cot would make a lot of sense. An alternative for an older child is the Boots Bed Barrier which allows any conventional bed to be used, and stops the child from rolling out.

Other pieces of equipment to bring from home are portable seats to make meal times easier. Two very well-designed, low-priced and highly portable models are the Babydiner and the Tota Portable High Chair. Both clip on to most conventional tables (the Babydiner will not fit on tables with any substantial structure below the worktop such as farmhouse-style tables) and are invaluable for feeding babies in restaurants and places where highchairs are not available. The Tota product is more expensive, but is more sturdy and fits on to more styles of tables. It is heavier, takes a child up to five stone, and is likely to last longer.

Another useful product suited to toddlers and young children is the Tamsit Baby Chair Harness – a cloth harness which fits over a chair and restrains the child while eating. This folds into the size of a scarf and can be used in any location: a café, restaurant, etc. These products are available from leading baby stores or through the John Lewis Partnership.

One item found to be useful in coping with 'little emergencies' was the Bubble Potty, produced by Babydiner. This plastic blow-up potty with disposable liners fits in a corner of a suitcase and is very useful for virtually potty-trained youngsters, as one thing's for sure – if they're going to 'forget' you can be sure it'll be at the airport, in the heat of the moment! For around £3 this little piece of additional luggage could save a lot of problems.

Feeding Babies on Holiday

Young babies still on a milk diet are far easier to travel with than older ones. Obviously breast-feeding is the perfect answer in that no equipment is necessary, and it doesn't matter where you are (nursing babies are a common sight in all major holiday destinations).

Bottle-feeding is possible abroad with a bit of pre-planning and the purchase of a few essential items: sterilizing tablets are easier than liquid, and to immerse the bottles and teats try an old ice-cream carton, rather than taking a big sterilizing unit. Unless you can be certain that a constant supply of sterile water will be available at your hotel/villa (and that means it must have boiled for at least ten minutes to kill off the bacteria) you should take one of the following from home: either a 'mini boiler' – a heating element which is immersed in the water to be heated (for which you can easily ask for a cup from the hotel) – or a jug kettle.

The former is obviously far smaller and more convenient. Pifco makes an ideal model which has a universal voltage. Traveller International also makes two alternatives: Hot Rod, an immersion heater which can boil water in two minutes, and Travel Jug, which acts as a mini jug kettle making cuppas for Mum and Dad as well as boiling water efficiently for Junior's feed. If you're on a driving holiday they also produce a car jug 'Pit Stop' which you plug into the cigarette lighter. This way you can brew up in a lay-by and feed the baby en route. One final alternative is to buy bottled mineral water, but the problem there is heating up the milk once made if your baby will not take it cold.

You would be best advised to take your normal formula from home as a foreign-bought one could easily upset your baby's digestive system for a few days.

Weaning babies require more equipment. Although weaning foods are available in all the major holiday destinations, again you would be better to bring products from home which your baby is used to and you know he will eat. The 'instant' dried varieties are lightest and more convenient to carry. Also available now are granules to make up drinks for babies, which are far better for them than syrupy juices and, again, far easier to carry. Lightweight plastic feeding equipment (such as the Boots Red Range) is a good idea to bring from home. A bowl, beaker, and spoon are the absolute basics.

If you'll be away for a long time, or are self-catering, the Moulinex Baby Chef will earn its space in the suitcase as it allows you to purée your own food. Its screw-lid jars can be used for taking food on outings.

Changing, Washing, Emergencies . . .

Disposable nappies are available now in almost every major holiday resort, but the quality and sizing systems vary enormously. Again, it's really better to bring your own from home. They don't weigh much, so it won't affect your baggage allowance; it's just the bulk involved. Disregard any thought of terry nappies and daily washings early on. Even in self-catering it isn't a good idea. Washing machines are not generally provided, and after all, it is your holiday too!

As regards washing baby clothes, take a little container of soap flakes from home. Invariably you cannot find a small enough packet of soap powder in the shops, and if you resort to using the local soap you will often find that it leaves colour and scum on the fabrics. A small plastic bottle filled with soft rinse wouldn't go amiss either to counteract the hard water, if you have any space left.

To clean baby at change times Baby Wipes of some sort are a good idea. Baby Lotion Wipes were the ones our researchers found best. They do the job of both soap and water and are easy to carry and convenient. At bath times a bath additive which doubles as a shampoo will save duplicating. Don't count on baby baths being available, even in high grade hotels. You'll have to make do with the wash-hand basin for tiny babies, or the big bath for older ones.

Apart from a range of baby toiletries, paediatric medicines are definitely best brought from home. British pharmaceutical products are better than any you're likely to get abroad, and cheaper too. Don't leave home with a baby or child without a first-aid kit which includes gripe water, Paracetamol, pain-relief syrup, and nappy-rash cream.

Remember the effect the sun has on babies. If your child seems especially grumpy, tired and miserable it may just be that you have had him in the direct sun for too long. Be very careful about the length of exposure a young baby gets. Put on a protective sun block/screen at all times, and give plenty of drinks to counteract dehydration. (This is when the drink granules come in handy, rather than giving milk which is not as thirst quenching, and is a food as well.)

Children on Holiday

Keeping young children amused on a journey and while on holiday can be a problem. If yours are the restless type bear this in mind when choosing your resort and choose a hotel where special children's facilities are laid on, and which has something like 'Recommended for Families' in the write-up. Check beforehand exactly what is meant by this, as it can mean anything from 'a full range of games, toys and a professional child-minding service', to 'a small dirty paddling pool is available', depending on the tour operator.

Try buying a new toy which is only brought out on the journey to keep the children preoccupied, and also pack a couple of old favourites from home so they have a familiar face for night-times. There are a whole range of well-designed toys on the market today. The Early Learning Centre and Boots are two of the best stores stocking toys ideal for travelling: both lightweight and durable. Firm favourites for travelling are: pop-up storybooks; novelty rattles and similar toys for babies; small Lego toys; and a double-sided playboard which can occupy two children at a time. Other favourites seem to be the Turn 'n' Learn Key Sorter: Lift-out Shape Puzzles; Toddler's Puzzle Sets; and Fisher Price's Activity Centre (for car travel). Giant Snap Lock Beads are also good. Obviously each child has their own special favourite, but these all worked a treat on all the travelling toddlers we tried them with, and as they're available from Early Learning, they're easy to locate.

Don't be too ambitious about the amount of nightlife you will be able to get in the first few days. Young children are often upset enough being in a strange place without having 'funny-looking' (in their eyes) babysitters thrust upon them right away as well. It's best to give it a few nights until they're used to their surroundings before leaving them in care.

With older children the hardest thing is to keep them from getting bored. If your brood are of this nature, consider a two-centre holiday, or an activity or touring type. Before leaving, try to instil into them a little background knowledge of the country you are travelling to. Once interested in their destination, they will make their own discoveries and amuse themselves to a far greater extent when they are there.

Toiletries

On the toiletries side, Boots have two first-aid kits which are exceptionally well packed, nicely presented and good value. The Trip Kit contains a survival kit for those attempting an adventurous holiday such as skiing, mountaineering, etc.; it has the equipment to cope with sprains, pains and general nasties. The Holiday Kit is for your average two-weeks-in-the-sun holiday-maker; it provides you with the basics for the sort of things you're likely to be stricken with. Each costs only £7 – you'd be hard pressed putting a first-aid kit of your own together for this price.

At holiday time you will also find ranges of travel toiletries available in chemists: small plastic bottles containing just enough for a couple of weeks. Despite their slightly inflated prices these products are a good idea and save you carrying surplus or dangerous glass bottles.

Electrical Goods

Turning to electrical goods: if you're on the point of buying a shaver, hairdryer, iron, electric toothbrush, alarm clock, etc., just bear in mind that for very little extra cost one can buy an appliance which will operate abroad, on a different voltage, and can therefore be used on holiday. Granted, an international adaptor (Traveller International does one for around £5) will allow you to use any appliance anywhere in the world, but if you're buying a new electrical appliance, it is a good idea to consider the following:

Shavers – The Braun System 1-2-3 Universal is a good choice. This rechargeable shaver can be used anywhere and performs extremely well. Once recharged it will last for about a week's use. The Braun Battery 2001 is another ideal travelling shaver. Being battery-operated it too can be used anywhere and as battery shavers go this is one of the best available. The Philips Battery Ladyshaver is another good model and the Boots Rechargeable 1500 is another option.

Battery and rechargeable shavers are a decided asset when travelling, and are well worth the few extra pounds for the convenience. Carmen produce a couple of good travel products for ladies: the Bikini Line and the Smoothie Too. Complete with travel bags, these shavers are aimed specifically at the holiday-maker, and are well designed and efficient. Panasonic's Wet and Dry Shavers give you the best of both worlds and their ES862 is recommended.

Black & Decker, a name previously associated with the other end of the electrical market, has now launched a range of travel products under the collective name of Stowaway. Included in the range are travel irons (dry or steam. The steam model is particularly recommended); two travel hairdryers – the 1000 with a folding handle, and the 1500 in a travel bag, and the capacity to dry even the longest hair in record time after a day at the beach; curling tongs, and a battery-operated ladyshaver.

Travel irons entered the market only a few years ago and in that time about a dozen manufacturers have started to produce them. At first they may strike you as an unnecessary luxury, but once you've had one you'll wonder how you ever managed without. The ability to press the creases from your clothes as they emerge from the suitcases looking as if you've slept in them, and to launder and wear again what you bring, is a great asset, and considering travel irons sell around the £12 mark they are a good long-term investment. Worth considering are: Traveller International's Smoothie steam iron, the Pifco, the Prestige, the Black & Decker travel irons, and the Braun travel-iron attachment to the Compact 1200 hairdryer. This latest model (collectively known as the Travelcombi PGI 1200) is an ingenious device which actually clips on to the model of Braun hairdryer and gives you an efficient dry or steam (separate spray provided) iron.

Travel hairdryers – The basic difference between an ordinary hairdryer and a travel model is the dual voltage of the latter, enabling it to be used abroad without fear of it exploding, fusing or taking an age to heat up. A continental plug adaptor must, of course, be used with all British 13 amp appliances, but these are widely available. Travel adaptors can be bought everywhere from supermarkets to the airport duty free. Traveller International is a reliable make; Travel Accessories' products also work fine, and they are that bit more competitively priced. Travel hairdryers are also smaller and neater to pack, and as there is no real price difference involved, and the level of efficiency is just as high, it does make sense to choose one if you're planning on doing any globetrotting at all.

There are numerous models available. Out of the extensive range on offer we have singled out the following: the Boots 1200 Travel represents very good value; the Braun Silencio 1200 Travelair, with its folding handle and quiet performance; the Philips Voyager 1200 is an excellent folding dryer; the Carmen Romany is neat and powerful. The Black & Decker range proved very popular: the 1000 Foldaway is the most compact dryer on the market, and the 1500 Fastdry one of the most powerful; lastly the Braun Compact 1200 has the added advantage of doubling up as a power source for the travel iron attachment (see above). Hair stylers and tongs have also been given the travel treatment of late. The breakthrough in this field has got to be the Braun Independent Styler GC 2. Using butane gas for power, this styler allows complete freedom of use and is small, compact and extremely efficient into the bargain. It is ideally suited to the traveller, the only – extremely important – point to note being that it is strictly illegal to take refills of butane gas on to an aircraft for reasons of combustion. This means that you can pack a styler containing a gas unit in your luggage and it must be checked in and travel in the hold. You must not take a refill. As a full styler gives you about a week's average use, or two weeks' sparing use, this should suffice for an average holiday anyway.

Alternative hair stylers for travelling are: the Carmen Heatwave, which has dual voltage and retractable bristles, and the Black & Decker Stowaway Styler, again with retractable bristles and universal voltage. Carmen have also introduced travel heated rollers, though there are mixed reports on them.

Other useful appliances for the holiday-maker include the new Braun voice control AB 312 vsl travel alarm, and the Traveller International equivalent World Alarm, which is even smaller.

Travel toothbrushes are also a good investment. The Braun Travel d3t is a very good system and comes complete with travel case.

For those who, like me, suffer from mosquitoes making life miserable on holiday, you could try a new product I certainly feel has helped. It's called Spira-No-Bite, and is distributed through Travel Accessories, 10 Shelley Drive, Lutterworth, Leics. It's available either as an electrical device with tablets, or fuelled by meths for situations where no electricity exists (i.e. camping). Traveller International do a similar product called Buzz Off.

Another product of interest to those whose mental arithmetic isn't up to much is Travel Accessories' X-Changer – a tiny calculator which you programme with the current rate of exchange, then all you have to do is feed in the price in the foreign currency, and, hey presto, you know how much that beer's costing you. You may have seen these in Scotcade's catalogue – they cost around £6, but for a regular holiday-maker they can soon pay their way.

A couple of interesting little travel gadgets are made by Allcord Ltd, Ilford Road, Newcastle-upon-Tyne, and are available by post. One is a knife-and-spoon set which would double up for feeding children or camping; the second is a miniature camera tripod. This is of good design, weighs only 90 grams and folds in 5in x 1in. Another new product to make life easier for the traveller is 'washaway' detergent tablets. For around £1 you get twelve foil-wrapped tablets of detergent which are light and easy to carry and work well. Most major chemists, including Boots, sell them.

One final thing well worth considering if you're the type who would kill for a good cuppa after a week of dishwater, is a Travel Jug (*see* 'Feeding Babies' section).

The Luggage Revolution

For most travellers packing a suitcase for a holiday is a chore – rushed and often frustrating. It needn't be, however, if you follow a few simple guidelines, and choose your cases carefully in the first place. In recent years there has been something of a revolution in luggage design. Pull-out handles and cases on wheels are just two of the innovations which have taken much of the strain out of travelling; cabin cases, which fit neatly under the seat in an aircraft, are another. The advantage of these is that you miss out the chore of having to check in your luggage and wondering if you'll see it again at the other end of the journey. In Britain there are numerous luggage manufac-turers offering a whole range of goods, from the craftsman-made bags to plastic cases, which after only a couple of trips will be falling to bits. Buying cheap luggage is a false economy which many people make. Luggage is one area where you definitely get what you pay for. When it comes to deciding between hard shell and soft-top luggage, bear in mind that hard-shell cases (such as the Delsey Club) stand up better to the rigours of baggage handling than cheaper soft tops, but if you don't fill them you will find the contents rattling around the case.

More can actually be crammed into a soft-top case, particularly if, like the Antler cases, they have a wide gusset. The top range soft tops are made out of incredibly strong stuff (Antler use up to 1000 denier nylon), so they will withstand any normal batterings.

Three reliable manufacturers are Delsey, Samsonite and Antler. They produce a wide range of cases, from luxury executive models to basic yet sturdy cases aimed at the annual holiday-maker. The Delsey Club and Helium; Antler's Stag, Airlight and Shires, and Samsonite's Scope and Rhapsody fall into the latter category. The more expensive ranges, such as Antler's Harrier and Signature, Samsonite's Silhouette and Delsey's Airstyle Deluxe, stand up better to more frequent travel, and if you travel a lot or want to make a good investment for the future then consider these ranges. Cheaper cases (especially those bought from magazine offers, e.g. three cases for £50) are unfit to travel after only a month or so's continual use.

When the new Heathrow Terminal 4 was having its luggage equipment tested the cases to come out best were the Antler Harrier (top of the range due to its double aluminium frame), with the Signature coming not far behind – a good result for a range which concentrates so heavily on style.

When packing for a trip make a list of what you want to take. Gather all the things together, then halve it. This is a perfectly serious statement as we all take far too much with us, year after year. List what you're left with so you can check it off when packing for the return journey. Try to choose clothes that mix and match so you get maximum use from them, and remember that most of the time you will be wearing very little. Modern-day fabrics mean you don't have to interleave clothes with tissue paper, as you did in the past, but it is still advisable to roll whatever you can to ensure the minimum of creasing. To get rid of residual creasing either invest in a travel iron (see page 49), hang the clothes in a steamy bathroom, or invest in a Rowenta Steam Brush, which steams and presses clothes in one. Always pack shoes at the bottom of the case, against the hinge. This will prevent them moving up and squashing clothes. Don't pack large bottles of make-up, perfume or suntan oil; you won't use it all up – buy small bottles or transfer toiletries into lightweight pots or plastic bottles and pack them all into a safe waterproof bag.

Use the bottom half of the case for jumpers, lingerie, shirts, trousers and accessories and fold everything – except trousers – lengthways, and then roll up. Pack dresses and suits in the top half of the case, and fold them as flatly as possible. These few guidelines will ensure you get as much as possible out of the space available.

For carrying photographic equipment, it's a good idea to take a proper photographic equipment bag. These ensure that delicate items such as lenses are properly buffered against knocks, and they're handy for keeping all the camera equipment together for when you're out and about, taking photographs. One of the best, in terms of value and quality, is the Cullmann brand, available from Boots. Photographic equipment is nearly always cheaper in the UK than buying abroad; a couple of exceptions to this rule are West Germany and Holland. Where possible, buy own-brand goods, such as Boots, which are equally good in terms of quality and represent considerable savings.

Part Two
HOW TO GO

Package v. Independent

If money is your only consideration, then without doubt, the package-tour holiday-maker comes off best in Spain. Not that travelling independently in Spain is likely to be extortionately expensive, but tour operators, who are dealing with literally hundreds of thousands of customers, can afford to offer accommodation, car hire, etc. to customers at lower prices than could be obtained if you were freelancing.

Some tour operators recognize that people want freedom to travel about and see something of the country that they're holidaying in. With this in mind, there are the special fly/drive deals on offer from a few of the larger tour operators. If you take advantage of this option, you can go wherever you want in the country, without having the additional problems of organizing flights or hiring cars before you go. Otherwise, car hire is often available at very competitive rates through major companies and worth considering if you want to spend a few days out and about exploring the countryside.

However, the most popular option which tour operators offer to independent travellers is their chartered flights (see 'Independent Travel, By Air' on page 97). This is one of the cheapest and quickest ways to get to Spain, and once you're there, it's entirely up to you to make your own travel and accommodation arrangements. The only drawback is that a return fare on a chartered flight is usually only valid for a one- to two-week period, so is not wholly suitable for those who are planning to stay in Spain for a couple of months.

In terms of accommodation, Spain is well equipped to cope with the huge influx of holiday-makers into its coastal resorts, and even at peak season you should be able to find a room in a small *pensione* somewhere. If it is a family group which is travelling, you could have more problems, and prior booking for hotels is strongly advised. If you're put off taking a package holiday because of the unbearable crowds of other holiday-makers in your hotel, then consider the 'small hotels/*pensiones*' option which some larger tour operators offer (see page 88).

How to get around the country once you're there is another problem facing independent travellers. The options are discussed later in this chapter, but overall, internal communication in Spain is reasonable, with extensive air, bus and road networks to serve holiday-makers.

It is entirely up to the individual's preferences and interests whether you travel independently in Spain or take a package holiday. If you don't mind sitting back and letting all the arrangements be made for you, then a package is the ideal option. On the other hand, if you don't want to be one of the crowd, travelling independently in Spain has few of the hassles to be found in some other Mediterranean countries.

Package Holidays

TOUR OPERATORS IN BRITAIN OFFERING PACKAGES TO SPAIN

There are over 200 British tour operators who offer holidays to Spain. Some of these are specialists, others offer only one or two Spanish destinations as part of their overall package programme.

Resort	*Tour Operator*
MAINLAND SPAIN	
Aguadulce, Almería	Intasun, Horizon, Airtours, Carousel, Thomson Holidays.
Aiguablava	Hotels in Spain.
Alicante, Costa Blanca	Falcon, Iberotravel, Mundi Color, Wings Ltd., Airtours, Carousel, Lancaster.

Algeciras, Costa del Sol	Cadogan Travel, Intasun, Mundi Color, Thomson.
Almería, Costa Almería	Carousel, Intasun, Mundi Color, Saga, Global, Iberotravel, Airtours, Thomson Holidays.
Ampuria Brava	Lancaster.
Avila, Inland Spain	Mundi Color, Hotels in Spain.
Antequera	Hotels in Spain.
Arcos de la Frontera	Hotels in Spain.
Barcelona, Costa Dorada	Global, Iberotravel, Mundi Color, Sovereign, Saga, Marsans, Airtours, Carousel, Hotels in Spain, Falcon.
Bayona, Galicia	Mundi Color.
Benalmadena, Costa del Sol	Allegro, Bath Travel, Cadogan Travel, Carousel, Thomas Cook, Enterprise, Flair, Global, Horizon, Intasun, Lancaster, Martin Rooks, Panorama, Portland, Falcon, Sunstart, Wings Ltd., Airtours, Hotels in Spain.
Benidorm, Costa Blanca	Arrowsmith, Cosmos, Enterprise, Flair, Global, Falcon, Horizon, Intasun, Lancaster, Martin Rooks, Mundi Color, Portland, Saga, Sunstart, Thomson Holidays, Hotels in Spain, Wings, Airtours, Tjaereborg, Sunflight.
Benicasim, Costa del Azahar	Saga.
Blanes, Costa Brava	Cosmos, Global, Horizon, Intasun, Lancaster, Panorama, Sunstart, Falcon Holidays, Airtours, Carousel, Sunflight, Thomson Holidays.

Cádiz	Iberotravel, Hotels in Spain.
Calella de la Costa, Costa Dorada	Cosmos, Enterprise, Flair, Global, Horizon, Intasun, Lancaster, Martin Rooks, Panorama, Portland, Sunstart, Thomson Holidays, Twentys Holidays.
Calella de Palafrugell, Costa Brava	Thomson Holidays, Sunflight.
Calonge	Lancaster.
Calpe, Costa Blanca	Thomson Holidays, Wings Ltd., Global, Saga.
Cambados, Galicia	Mundi Color.
Cambrils, Costa Dorada	Thomson Holidays, Intasun, Horizon.
Cardona, Pyrenees	Mundi Color, Hotels in Spain.
Carmona	Hotels in Spain.
Cordoba, Inland Andalucía	Global, Mundi Color, Saga, Iberotravel. Hotels in Spain.
Denia, Costa Blanca	Enterprise, Martin Rooks, Global, Portland, Flair, Airtours, Carousel, Sunflight, Horizon.
Estartit, Costa Brava	Cosmos, Martin Rooks, Panorama, Sunfare, Thomson Holidays, Wings Ltd., Lancaster, Falcon.
Estepona, Costa del Sol	Cadogan Travel, Cosmos, Carousel, Enterprise, Intasun, Tailor Made Holidays, Wings Ltd., HCI, Hourmont Tours, Hotels in Spain.
Fuengirola, Costa del Sol	Allegro, Arrowsmith, Cosmos, Enterprise, Global, Horizon, Intasun, Lancaster, Mundi Color, Portland, Saga, Sunstart, Tailor Made Holidays, Thomas Cook, Thomson Holidays, Tjaereborg, Wings Ltd., Flair, Hotels in Spain, Falcon.

Gandia, Costa Blanca	Falcon.
Gerona	Iberotravel, Wings Ltd.
Granada, Inland Andalucía	Global, Mundi Color, Saga, Iberotravel, Hotels in Spain.
Gredos, Inland Spain	Mundi Color.
Jaen, Inland Spain	Mundi Color, Hotels in Spain.
Javea, Costa Blanca	Mundi Color, Paloma, Wings Ltd., Hotels in Spain.
La Manga de Mar Menor, Costa Calida	Intasun, Lancaster, Thomson Holidays, Tailor Made Holidays, Hotels in Spain, HCI.
Leon	Hotels in Spain.
Lloret de Mar	Carousel, Cosmos, Enterprise, Flair, Global, Horizon, Hourmont, Intasun, Lancaster, Panorama, Portland, Saga, Sunstart, Thomson Holidays, Wings Ltd., Sunflight.
Logrono	Iberotravel, Hotels in Spain.
Madrid, Inland Spain	Global, Iberotravel, Mundi Color, Sovereign, Saga, Hotels in Spain.
Malaga, Costa del Sol	Allegro, Cadogan Travel, Bath Travel, Horizon, Iberotravel, Intasun, Mundi Color, Panorama, Saga, Wings Ltd., Hotels in Spain, Falcon.
Malgrat de Mar, Costa Dorada	Cosmos, Global, Iberotravel, Intasun, Lancaster, Panorama, Thomson Holidays, Flair, Airtours, Carousel, Sunflight.

Marbella, Costa del Sol   Allegro, Bath Travel, Cadogan Travel, Cosmos, Enterprise, Falcon, Global, Horizon, Intasun, Lancaster, Martin Rooks, Mundi Color, Paloma, Sovereign, Sunstart, Tailor Made Holidays, Thomas Cook, Thomson Holidays, Wings Ltd., Hotels in Spain.

Martinet, Pyrenees   Mundi Color.

Matalascanas   Saga.

Mijas, Costa del Sol   Allegro, Horizon, Sovereign, Tailor Made Holidays, Thomas Cook, Wings Ltd., Cadogan Travel.

Mojacar, Costa de Almería   Horizon, Intasun, Lancaster, HCI, Hotels in Spain.

Nerja, Costa del Sol   Allegro, Horizon, Mundi Color, Wings Ltd., Hotels in Spain

Nueva Andalucía   Paloma, Tailor Made Holidays, Sovereign, Wings Ltd., Hotels in Spain.

Peñíscola, Costa del Azahar   Horizon, Lancaster, Intasun, Global, Martin Rooks, Saga.

Pineda del Mar, Costa Dorada   Flair, Intasun, Lancaster, Panorama, Thomson Holidays, Sunflight.

Pontevedra, Galicia   Hotels in Spain.

Playa de Aro, Costa Brava   Thomson Holidays, Horizon, Nat Holidays.

Puerto de Santa Maria, Costa de la Luz   Mundi Color.

Ronda, Inland Andalucía   Mundi Color, Lancaster.

Roquetas de Mar, Costa de Almería   Intasun, Lancaster, Saga, Horizon, Global, Airtours, Portland, Hotels in Spain, Thomson.

Rosas, Costa Brava	Cosmos, Martin Rooks, Intasun, Horizon, Enterprise.
Saler (el)	Hotels in Spain.
Salou, Costa Dorada	Hotels in Spain, Cosmos, Enterprise, Flair, Falcon, Global, Horizon, Intasun, Lancaster, Martin Rooks, Portland, Saga, Thomson Holidays, Tjaereborg, Wings Ltd., Airtours.
San Lucar de Barrameda, Costa de la Luz	Mundi Color.
San Pedro, Costa del Sol	Cadogan Travel, Intasun, Paloma, Tailor Made Holidays, Sovereign, HCI.
Santa Cristina de Aro, Costa Brava	Mundi Color.
Santa Susana, Costa Dorada	Cosmos, Enterprise, Global, Intasun, Lancaster, Thomson Holidays, Sunflight.
Santiago de Compostela, Galicia	Mundi Color, Iberotravel, Hotels in Spain.
Santo Domingo de la Calzada	
Segovia, Inland Spain	Mundi Color, Hotels in Spain.
Seville, Inland Andalucía	Iberotravel, Mundi Color, Saga, Enterprise, Sovereign, Hotels in Spain.
Siguenza, Inland Spain	Mundi Color, Hotels in Spain.
Sitges, Costa Dorada	Arrowsmith, Falcon, Global, Horizon, Mundi Color, Panorama, Thomson Holidays.

Sotogrande, Costa de le   Cadogan Travel.
Luz

Tarragona, Costa Dorada   Mundi Color.

Toledo, Inland Spain   Mundi Color, Enterprise, Sovereign,
Hotels in Spain.

Torremolinos   Allegro, Arrowsmith, Bath Travel,
Cosmos, Enterprise, Flair, Global,
Horizon, Intasun, Lancaster, Marsans,
Martin Rooks, Mundi Color, Saga,
Sunstart, Tailor Made Holidays,
Twentys Holidays, Thomas Cook,
Thomson Holidays, Tjaereborg, Wings
Ltd., Airtours, Sunflight, HCI,
Portland, Hourmont Tours, Hotels in
Spain.

Torrevieja, Costa Brava   Intasun, Martin Rooks, Mundi Color.

Tossa de Mar, Costa   Cosmos, Lancaster, Intasun, Martin
Brava   Rooks, Portland, Panorama, Thomson
Holidays.

Valencia   Iberotravel, Saga, Hotels in Spain.

Verin, Galicia   Mundi Color.
Vich, Pyrenees   Mundi Color, Hotels in Spain.

Zaragoza   Iberotravel, Hotels in Spain.

BALEARIC ISLANDS
MAJORCA

Alcudia   Arrowsmith, Cosmos, Global,
Horizon, Intasun, Lancaster, Martin
Rooks, Panorama, Portland, Thomson
Holidays, Enterprise, Tjaereborg,
Wings Ltd., Flair, Sunflight.

Arenal	Cosmos, Airtours, Twentys Holidays, Allegro, Carousel, Enterprise, Flair, Global, Intasun, Lancaster, Saga, Sunstart, Thomson Holidays, Horizon, Martin Rooks, Iberotravel, Wings Ltd.
Aucanada	Panorama, Sunflight.
Banalbufar	Castaways, Mundi Color.
Barcaret	Cosmos.
Bendinat	Castaways.
Cala Bona	Cosmos, Global, Horizon, Portland, Thomson Holidays, Wings Ltd., Flair.
Cala d'Or	Intasun, Carousel, Cosmos, Enterprise, Falcon, Global, Horizon, Lancaster, Panorama, Portland, Sunstart, Thomas Cook, Thomson Holidays, Tjaereborg, Wings Ltd., Airtours.
Cala Ferrera	Carousel, Cosmos, Falcon, Global, Lancaster, Martin Rooks, Saga, Wings Ltd., Airtours.
Cala Fornels	Global, Holiday Islands, Horizon, Enterprise, Mundi Color, Intasun.
Cala Marsal	Intasun.
Cala Mayor	Allegro, Carousel, Horizon, Intasun, Martin Rooks, Mundi Color, Airtours, Sunflight.
Cala Millor	Carousel, Cosmos, Enterprise, Flair, Falcon, Global, Horizon, Intasun, Lancaster, Martin Rooks, Portland, Thomson Holidays, Wings Ltd., Sunflight.
Cala Mondrago	Enterprise.
Cala Moreya	Intasun.

Cala Ratjada	Castaways, Intasun, Thomson Holidays, HCI.
Cala San Vicente	Enterprise, Intasun, Martin Rooks, Mundi Color, Intasun, Thomas Cook, Thomson Holidays, Wings Ltd., The Travel Club of Upminster.
Cala Santañyi	Castaways.
Cala Viñas	Allegro, Enterprise, Intasun.
Calas de Mallorca	Cosmos, Enterprise, Flair, Global, Horizon, Intasun, Martin Rooks, Thomson Holidays, Lancaster, Airtours, Carousel, Hotels in Spain, Falcon, Sunflight.
Camp de Mar	Global, Thomson Holidays.
Can Pastilla	Allegro, Bath Travel, Carousel, Cosmos, Enterprise, Flair, Horizon, Intasun, Lancaster, Martin Rooks, Saga, Sunstart, Thomson Holidays, Wings Ltd., Horizon, Hotels in Spain.
Can Picafort	Cosmos, Enterprise, Flair, Global, Intasun, Lancaster, Portland, Thomson Holidays, Wings Ltd., Airtours, Carousel, Horizon, Sunflight, Hotels in Spain.
Cas Catala	Allegro, Castaways, Enterprise, Mundi Color, Sovereign, Thomas Cook, Wings Ltd.
Costa de los Pinos	Cosmos, Castaways.
Deya	Allegro, Castaways, Mundi Color, Sovereign, Wings Ltd.
Estellenchs	Mundi Color.
Formentor	Allegro, Castaways, Sovereign, Saga.

Illetas	Allegro, Bath Travel, Cosmos, Enterprise, Global, Horizon, Intasun, Mundi Color, Sovereign, Thomson Holidays, Wings Ltd., Hotels in Spain.
Inca	Saga.
Lluc Alcari	Castaways.
Magaluf	Allegro, Arrowsmith, Bath Travel, Carousel, Cosmos, Enterprise, Falcon, Flair, Global, Horizon, Hourmont, Intasun, Lancaster, Martin Rooks, Mundi Color, Portland, Panorama, Thomson Holidays, Tjaereborg, Wings Ltd., Airtours, Saga, Hotels in Spain.
Orient	Castaways, Sovereign.
Paguera	Allegro, Bath Travel, Cosmos, Enterprise, Global, Horizon, Intasun, Martin Rooks, Sunflight, Mundi Color, Panorama, Thomas Cook, Thomson Holidays, Wings Ltd.
Palma	Allegro, Arrowsmith, Bath Travel, Carousel, Castaways, Cosmos, Enterprise, Global, Horizon, Intasun, Lancaster, Mundi Color, Thomas Cook, Thomson Holidays, Flair, Martin Rooks, Wings Ltd., Sunflight.
Palma Nova	Allegro, Arrowsmith, Bath Travel, Cosmos, Sunflight, Enterprise, Hotels in Spain, Falcon, Flair, Horizon, Hourmont, Intasun, Lancaster, Mundi Color, Portland, Sunstart, Thomas Cook, Thomson Holidays, Tjaereborg, Wings Ltd., Iberotravel, Airtours, Hotels in Spain, Twentys Holidays.

Playa de Alcudia Global, Martin Rooks, Wings Ltd., Enterprise, Horizon, Sunflight.

Playa de Palma Allegro, Carousel, Cosmos, Enterprise, Falcon, Global, Horizon, Iberotravel, Intasun, Martin Rooks, Lancaster, Panorama, Thomas Cook, Thomson Holidays, Wings Ltd., Sunflight, Hotels in Spain.

Playa de Calobra Mundi Color.

Portals Nous Saga, Allegro, Enterprise, Global, Intasun, Lancaster, Thomson Holidays, Airtours, Carousel.

Porto Colom Lancaster, Thomson Holidays, Portland, Falcon.

Porto Cristo Sunflight, Enterprise, Horizon, Lancaster, Mundi Color, Wings Ltd., HCI.

Porto Petro Enterprise, Wings Ltd., Horizon.

Puerto Andraitx Allegro, Bath Travel, Castaways, Wings Ltd.

Puerto Alcudia Horizon, Saga, Carousel, Martin Rooks, Wings Ltd., Airtours.

Puerto Pollensa Allegro, Bath Travel, Castaways, Enterprise, Falcon, Flair, Global, Horizon, Intasun, Lancaster, Martin Rooks, Mundi Color, Thomas Cook, The Travel Club of Upminster, Wings Ltd., Sunflight, Lancaster.

Puerto Sóller Mundi Color, Thomson Holidays, Enterprise, Tjaereborg.

San Agustin Carousel, Panorama, Thomson Holidays, Airtours, Sunflight.

Santa Ponsa	Allegro, Bath Travel, Carousel, Cosmos, Enterprise, Global, Intasun, Hourmont, Lancaster, Martin Rooks, Panorama, Saga, Thomson Holidays, Wings Ltd., Hotels in Spain, Airtours, Horizon, Sunflight.
Sa Coma	Airtours, Carousel, Horizon, Thomson Holidays, Intasun.
S'Illot	Sunflight, Carousel, Enterprise, Flair, Horizon, Intasun, Lancaster, Thomson Holidays.
Sóller	Saga.
Vall de Mosa	Saga.

MENORCA

Arenal d'en Castell	Enterprise, Global, Horizon, Intasun, Lancaster, Mundi Color, Thomson Holidays, Wings Ltd.
Biniancola	Martin Rooks.
Binibeca Vell	Enterprise, Global, Saga, Wings Ltd., Hotels in Spain.
Binisafua	Carousel, Airtours.
Cala Alcaufar	Horizon.
Cala Galdana	Cosmos, Enterprise, Global, Horizon, Intasun, Mundi Color, Thomas Cook, Thomson Holidays, Tjaereborg, Wings Ltd., Flair, Hotels in Spain.
Cala S'Algar	Global, Horizon, Mundi Color, Thomas Cook, Tjaereborg, Falcon.
Cala Blanca	Airtours, Thomas Cook.
Cala'n Bosch	Intasun.

Cala'n Forcat   Carousel, Cosmos, Global, Intasun, Lancaster, Portland, Thomson Holidays, Tjaereborg, Wings Ltd., Airtours, Horizon.

Cala'n Porter   Enterprise, Flair, Global, Horizon, Lancaster, Portland, Wings Ltd., Airtours, Sunflight.

Ciudadela   Cosmos, Intasun, Martin Rooks, Saga, Wings Ltd., Flair, Airtours, Carousel, Horizon, Hotels in Spain, Falcon, Family.

Cala Blanca   Martin Rooks, Horizon, Wings.

Cala Blanes   Martin Rooks, Horizon, Wings, Sunflight.

Cala'n Bosh   Global, Cosmos, Martin Rooks, Wings Ltd., Horizon, Thomson Holidays, Falcon.

Cala'n Morell   Carousel, Airtours.

Fornells   Saga, Airtours, Carousel.

Mahón   Flair, Horizon, Saga, Thomson Holidays, Iberotravel, Wings Ltd., Intasun.

Mercadal   Horizon.

Punta Prima   Carousel, Cosmos, Flair, Global, Intasun, Panorama, Portland, Airtours.

S'Algar   Carousel, Enterprise, Global, Horizon, Mundi Color, Portland, Thomson Holidays, Tjaereborg, Wings Ltd.

San Luis   Carousel, Enterprise, Tjaereborg, Horizon, Thomson Holidays.

San Jaime	Enterprise, Wings Ltd., Horizon.
Santo Tomas	Horizon, Intasun, Martin Rooks, Mundi Color, Thomson Holidays, Hotels in Spain.
Shangri-La	Wings Ltd., Hotels in Spain.
Son Bou	Cosmos, Enterprise, Horizon, Falcon, Tjaereborg, Flair.
Son Park Beach	Global.
Son Parc	Enterprise, Horizon, Wings Ltd., Intasun.
Villa Carlos	Carousel, Horizon, Intasun, Mundi Color, Panorama, Saga, Sovereign, Thomas Cook, Wings Ltd., Airtours.

IBIZA

Cala d'en Bossa	Cosmos, Global, Horizon, Wings Ltd.
Cala Leña	Intasun, Lancaster, HCI.
Cala Llonga	Arrowsmith, Cosmos, Enterprise, Horizon, Martin Rooks, Portland, Thomson Holidays, Tjaereborg, Wings Ltd.
Cala Tarida	Intasun, Wings, Thomson Holidays.
Cala San Vicente	Portland.
Cala Vadella	Intasun, Wings Ltd., HCI.
Es Cana	Sunflight, Arrowsmith, Cosmos, Enterprise, Flair, Global, Horizon, Intasun, Lancaster, Martin Rooks, Panorama, Portland, Thomson Holidays, Tjaereborg.
Figueretas	Sunflight, Cosmos, Global, Intasun, Lancaster, Sunstart, Hotels in Spain, Tjaereborg.

Ibiza	Iberotravel, Horizon, Intasun.
Playa d'en Bossa	Carousel, Cosmos, Enterprise, Global, Horizon, Intasun, Lancaster, Portland, Thomson Holidays, Wings Ltd., Flair, Airtours, Falcon.
Portinatx	Carousel, Lancaster, Martin Rooks, Portland, Thomson Holidays, Wings Ltd., Airtours, HCI.
S'Argamassa	Intasun, Thomson Holidays, Wings Ltd., HCI, Hotels in Spain.
San Antonio Abad	Sunflight, Arrowsmith, Carousel, Cosmos, Enterprise, Flair, Global, Horizon, Intasun, HCI, Lancaster, Martin Rooks, Mundi Color, Panorama, Portland, Sunstart, Thomson Holidays, Tjaereborg, Twentys, Wings Ltd., Airtours, Hotels in Spain.
San Miguel	Intasun, Mundi Color, Portland, Sovereign, Thomson Holidays, Airtours, Carousel, Thomas Cook.
Santa Eulalia	Arrowsmith, Cosmos, Enterprise, Flair, Global, Horizon, Intasun, Martin Rooks, Panorama, Portland, Thomas Cook, Thomson Holidays, Wings Ltd., Airtours, Carousel, Sunflight.
Talamanca	Enterprise, Flair, Intasun, Lancaster, Thomson Holidays, Wings Ltd., Airtours, Carousel, Horizon.

FORMENTERA

Es Pujols	Global, Lancaster, Horizon, Wings Ltd.

Mitjorn	Horizon, Thomson Holidays, Wings Ltd.
La Sabina	Intasun, Lancaster.
Las Salinas	Horizon, Wings Ltd.
San Francisco Javier	Thomson Holidays, Wings Ltd.

CANARY ISLANDS

GRAN CANARIA

Bahis Feliz	Wings Ltd.
Islas Bonifas	Saga.
Las Palmas	Arrowsmith, Carousel, Horizon, Iberotravel, Lancaster, Mundi Color, Thomson Holidays, Wings Ltd., Saga, Hotels in Spain.
Las Canteras	Saga, Iberotravel.
Maspalomas	Cosmos, Horizon, Iberotravel, Mundi Color, Thomas Cook, Wings Ltd., Airtours, Carousel, Inghams.
Playa del Ingles	Arrowsmith, Carousel, Cosmos, Enterprise, Global, Falcon, Horizon, Intasun, Lancaster, Martin Rooks, Mundi Color, Portland, Saga, Sunstart, Thomas Cook, Thomson Holidays, Tjaereborg, Twentys, Wings Ltd., Flair, HCI, Airtours, Sunflight, Hotels in Spain, Inghams.
Playa de Trajadillo	Mundi Color, Sunflight.

Puerto Rico   Arrowsmith, Carousel, Enterprise,
                                   Global, Lancaster, Portland, Thomson
                                   Holidays, Tjaereborg, Martin Rooks,
                                   Wings Ltd., Flair, Airtours, Thomas
                                   Cook, HCI, Horizon, Sunflight, Hotels
                                   in Spain.

San Agustín   Arrowsmith, Cosmos, Enterprise,
                                   Global, Horizon, Iberotravel,
                                   Lancaster, Mundi Color, Portland,
                                   Thomas Cook, Thomson Holidays,
                                   Sunstart, Tailor Made Holidays,
                                   Wings Ltd., Martin Rooks, Sunflight,
                                   Hotels in Spain, Inghams, Falcon.

FUERTEVENTURA

Caleta de Fuste   Horizon, Intasun.

Playa de Corralejo   Horizon, Intasun, Lancaster,
                                   Lanzarote Villas.

Playa Barca   Horizon, Hotels in Spain.

LANZAROTE

Arrecife   Arrowsmith, Iberotravel, Lancaster,
                                   Lanzarote Villas, Paloma, Wings Ltd.,
                                   Thomson Holidays.

Costa Teguise   Cosmos, Holiday Islands, Lancaster,
                                   Lanzarote Villas, Lanzotic Travel,
                                   Thomas Cook, Wings Ltd.,
                                   Iberotravel, Airtours, HCI, Hotels in
                                   Spain, Intasun.

Matagordos   Inghams, Horizon.

Playa Blanca	Cosmos, Lanzotic Travel, Intasun, Horizon, Martin Rooks, Lanzarote Villas, Thomson Holidays.
Playa de los Pocillos	Arrowsmith, Enterprise, Lanzotic Travel, Paloma, Tjaereborg, Wings Ltd., Lanzarote Villas, Holiday Islands, Thomson Holidays, Falcon.
Puerto del Carmen	Arrowsmith, Carousel, Cosmos, Enterprise, Global, Holiday Islands, Horizon, Intasun, Lancaster, Lanzarote Villas, Lanzotic Travel, Martin Rooks, Paloma, Portland, Sunstart, Thomas Cook, Thomson Holidays, Tjaereborg, Wings Ltd., Flair, Airtours, Hotels in Spain, Inghams, Falcon.

TENERIFE

Costa del Silencio	Carousel, Enterprise, Airtours, Hotels in Spain.
El Medano	Horizon, Wings Ltd.
Las Galletas	Global, HCI, Hotels in Spain.
Los Cristianos	Allegro, Arrowsmith, Bath Travel, Carousel, Cosmos, Enterprise, Global, Holiday Islands, Horizon, Intasun, Lancaster, Mundi Color, Tailor Made Holidays, Thomson Holidays, Sunstart, Wings Ltd., Airtours, Sunflight, Hotels in Spain, Falcon.
Los Gigantes	Arrowsmith, Thomas Cook, Lanzarote Villas, Wings Ltd., Flair, Horizon, Hotels in Spain.
Los Realejos	Lancaster, Saga.

Playa de las Americas   Allegro, Arrowsmith, Bath Travel, Carousel, Cosmos, Falcon, Enterprise, Global, Holiday Islands, Horizon, Intasun, Lancaster, Martin Rooks, Mundi Color, Portland, Sunstart, Tailor Made Holidays, Thomas Cook, Thomson Holidays, Tjaereborg, Wings Ltd., Flair, Airtours, Sunflight, Hotels in Spain.

Playa Paraiso   Allegro, Wings Ltd., Hotels in Spain, Thomson Holidays.

Puerto de la Cruz   Allegro, Arrowsmith, Bath Travel, Carousel, Cosmos, Enterprise, Flair, Global, Horizon, Iberotravel, Intasun, Lancaster, Martin Rooks, Mundi Color, Portland, Saga, Tailor Made Holidays, Thomas Cook, Thomson Holidays, Tjaereborg, Wings Ltd., Airtours, Sunflight, Hotels in Spain, Inghams, Falcon.

Puerto de Santiago   Arrowsmith, Enterprise, Horizon, Mundi Color, Wings Ltd., Hotels in Spain, Thomson Holidays.

Santa Cruz de Tenerife   Thomson Holidays, Hotels in Spain, Iberotravel.

LA PALMA

Santa Cruz   Hotels in Spain.

LA GOMERA   Hotels in Spain.

HIERRO   Hotels in Spain.

On the following pages are the names, addresses, telephone numbers and details of all British tour operators who run holidays to Spain. Some of these firms are relatively obscure and their brochures will not be widely available but if they specialize in the type of holiday you're after, give them a ring and request a brochure. The major specialists in the different areas are listed separately on pages 83-92. Every effort has been made to ensure this list of operators is comprehensive and accurate, but please remember that in the fluctuating world of the travel business, tour companies spring up and go bust with amazing regularity. Contact the Spanish Tourist Office in London for an updated version if you bought this guide after February 1989.

*AIRTOURS,
Helm Shore, Rossendale, Lancs. BB4 4NB
Tel. 0706 26 0000

*ALLEGRO HOLIDAYS,
15a Church Street, Reigate, Surrey RH2 0AA
Tel. 0737 221323

*ARROWSMITH HOLIDAYS,
Royal Buildings, 2, Mosley Street, Piccadilly, Manchester M2 3AB
Tel. 061-236 2361

*BATH TRAVEL PALMAIR,
Space House, Albert Road, Bournemouth BH1 1BY
Tel. 0202 299299

*CADOGAN TRAVEL LTD.,
Cadogan House, 9-10 Portland Street, Southampton SO9 1ZP
Tel. 0703 332661

*CAROUSEL HOLIDAYS LTD.,
45 New Street, Birmingham B2 4LL
Tel. 021-643 7737

*CASTAWAYS,
Carew House, Wallington, Surrey SM6 0DQ
Tel. 0177 32616

*COSMOS LTD.,
Tourama House, 17 Homesdale Road, Bromley, Kent BR2 9LX
Tel. 01-464 3400

*ENTERPRISE HOLIDAYS,
PO Box 100, 17-27 High Street, Hounslow, Middx. TW3 1TB
Tel. 01-699 8833

*FALCON HOLIDAYS,
33 Notting Hill Gate, London W11 3JQ
Tel. 01-221 6298

*FLAIR HOLIDAYS,
4-6 Manor Mount, London SE2 3PZ
Tel. 01-291 7979

*GLOBAL AIR HOLIDAYS,
26 Elmfield Road, Bromley, Kent BR1 1LR
Tel. 01-464 7515

*HCI,
Broadway, Edgbaston Five Ways, Birmingham B15 1BB
Tel. 021-643 2727

*HOLIDAY ISLANDS,
Suite 2, Rayleigh House, Admirals Way, London E14 9SN
Tel. 01-538 5544

*HORIZON HOLIDAYS LTD.,
Broadway, Edgbaston Five Ways, Birmingham B15 1BB
Tel. 021-643 2727

*HOTELS IN SPAIN,
310 London House, 26/40 Kensington House, London W8 4PF
Tel. 01-938 3792

*HOURMONT LTD.,
Brunel House, Newfoundland Road, Bristol BS2 9LU
Tel. 0272 426961

*IBEROTRAVEL,
Palladium House, 1st floor, 1/4 Argyll Street, London W1V 1AD
Tel. 01-437 6996

*INGHAMS,
Holiday House, 329 Putney Bridge Road, London SW15 2PL
Tel. 01-789 6555

*INTASUN HOLIDAYS LTD.,
Intasun House, 2 Cromwell Avenue, Bromley, Kent BR2 9AQ
Tel. 01-290 1900

*LANCASTER HOLIDAYS LTD.,
Tetley Street, Bradford, Yorks. BD1 2SA
Tel. 0274 736644

*LANZAROTE VILLAS,
Springfield Road, Horsham, Sussex RH12 2PJ
Tel. 0403 51304

*LANZOTIC TRAVEL,
Sundial House, 3a Brook Road, Redhill, Surrey RH1 6DL
Tel. 0737 66311

*MARTIN ROOKS HOLIDAYS,
204 Edbury Street, London SW1W 8UU
Tel. 01-730 0808

*MUNDI COLOR TRAVEL LTD.,
276 Vauxhall Bridge Road, London SW1V 1BE
Tel. 01-828 6021

*PALOMA,
Drayton House, Drayton, Chichester, Sussex PO20 6EW
Tel. 0243 778181

*PALOMA HOLIDAYS LTD.,
6 Farncombe, Worthing, Sussex BN11 2BE
Tel. 0903 820710

*PANORAMA HOLIDAYS,
Panorama House, Church Road, Hove, Sussex BN3 2BA
Tel. 0273 206531

*PORTLAND HOLIDAYS LTD.,
218 Great Portland Street, London W1N 5HG
Tel. 01-388 5111

*SAGA HOLIDAYS PLC,
The Saga Building, Middlesburg Square, Folkestone, Kent
CT20 1AZ
Tel. 0303 47000

*SOVEREIGN,
PO Box 100, Hodford House, 17-27 High Street, Hounslow, Middx.
TW3 1TB
Tel. 01-572 7373

*SUNFLIGHT,
Broadway, Edgbaston Five Ways, Birmingham B15 1BB
Tel. 021-643 2727

*SUNSTART HOLIDAYS,
33 Notting Hill Gate, London W11 3JQ
Tel. 01-328 5642

*TAILOR MADE HOLIDAYS,
35 Eyre Street, London EC1 5ET
Tel. 01-833 3751

*THE TRAVEL CLUB OF UPMINSTER,
Station Road, Upminster, Essex RM14 2TT
Tel. 040 222 5000

*THOMAS COOK HOLIDAYS,
Thorpe Wood, Peterborough PE3 6SB
Tel. 0733 502200

*THOMSON HOLIDAYS,
Greater London House, Hampstead Road, London NW1 7SD
Tel. 01-387 8484

*TJAEREBORG LTD.,
194 Camden Hill Road, London W8 7TH
Tel. 01-727 2680

*TWENTYS HOLIDAYS,
33 Notting Hill Gate, London W11 3JQ
Tel. 01-221 5018

*WINGS LTD.,
Travel House, Broxbourne, Herts. EN10 7JD
Tel. 0992 87211

*ABTA (Association of British Travel Agents).

General Tour Operators

With so many tour operators going to Spain, obviously not all of them are targeted towards certain areas of the customer market, such as golf-packages, parador holidays (in state-owned buildings, located in places of scenic or historic interest), etc. Many are general operators offering a standard flight, transfer and hotel arrangements. Of the many on offer we have tested the vast majority and from our personal findings we highlight the following as having something exceptional to offer:

In the lower price bracket, **Martin Rooks, Portland** or **Tjaereborg** are well worth looking at. Their 'no frills' approach keeps costs well down, but all are large enough companies to ensure a professional service is given and back-ups in terms of couriers and accommodation are available. This is an important service if you get to your destination only to find you are badly disappointed by the hotel and you find your courier less than helpful. In some small companies no alternative will be available.

In terms of good quality all-rounders **Horizon, Thomas Cook, Thomson's, Enterprise** and **Intasun** are worth checking out. The market share taken up by these five companies is substantial, but it is clear why: they are all large companies of long standing, who cannot afford to let their standards drop as they have so many repeat customers, year after year. They are middle of the price range, with a wide family appeal. All offer good child discounts and they give genuine value in terms of the standard of their accommodation, professionalism of reps and flight efficiency.

Horizon trades as Horizon, Wings, OSL, Blue Sky, Holiday Club International and Sunflight. It sells around 1.5 million holidays per year and is one of the big boys of the package trade. Its products range from the very low-cost Sunflight packages to all the major Spanish resorts, through to luxury villas with pools in Menorca, Majorca and Ibiza, offered through OSL's 'Villas with Pools' brochure. In between lie hotels, self-catering and small pensions in virtually every coastal resort of Spain. It flies from twelve regional airports, using its sister company Orion Airways on 60% of its charters. It is one of Britain's more reliable operators, with a firm hold on the Spanish market, helped by the fact that it owns travel agents in Spain who efficiently handle all its ground arrangement.

Redwing Holidays is the parent company of Sunmed, Sovereign, Enterprise, **Martin Rooks** and Flair. With the advantage of reliable British Airtours flights, these companies range from the economical direct-sell prices of Rooks through to the top of the range hotels and villas and conveniently timed flights of **Sovereign,** which is well worth considering for up-market fly/drives and singles holidays with no Club 18-30 overtones whatsoever.

Enterprise offers good value deals for holidays to most of the major resorts on the mainland and islands. For those who want to see a bit more of the country, but can't afford to do a fly/drive deal, its competitively priced coach tour takes in most of the interesting sights and famous cities of southern Spain.

Thomson, which operates as Thomson, Skytours, Portland and Freestyle, has a comprehensive range of holidays, which includes coach tours to the cities in Castile and Andalucía as well as special options for those who favour accommodation in small hotels or *pensiones*. The range of standard packages focuses on the large coastal resorts, well priced for family holidays. It is the UK's largest tour operator with 30% of the British market, and owns the **Lunn Poly** travel agency and Britannia Airways.

Thomas Cook's packages tend to be a bit more expensive, but the standards of service and accommodation which this company gives its clients is also above average. You have the added advantage of dealing not just with a tour operator, but a major travel agent with all the additional expertise and knowledge that goes with this. Thomas Cook offers packages to high-quality accommodation in the main resorts in Spain as well as the Balearics and Canary Islands. The Thomas Cook Group operates as Company Tours, Inter-Church, Rankin Kuhn and Thomas Cook.

Intasun offers packages which are particularly attractive to families with young children. Child discounts, free holidays for children and kiddies' clubs in specific hotels are a few aspects of Intasun's packages which account for its popularity among cost-conscious parents with some energetic offspring to keep occupied for a two-week holiday. It is part of the I.L.G. organization – the second biggest operator after Thomson. Its brand names include Intasun, Global, Lancaster, Select, Club 18-30 and Hourmont, and it is linked with the Air Europe airline.

There are a few other major tour companies whose brochures are worth scanning for a standard package to Spain. **Cosmos** has established a reputation for good value and efficient service, while at the bottom end of the price-scale, Sky-Tours offers low-price tours to the major Spanish holiday destinations.

WHO SPECIALIZES IN WHAT

Self-Catering

Most of the large tour companies operate special self-catering programmes in addition to their standard package tours: **Thomson's,**

Thomas Cook, American Express and **Enterprise** are just a few of the well-known companies that come into this category.

For self-catering specialists in Spain, **Interhome** is hard to beat. It offers packages to over 123 inland and coastal destinations in Spain, and this amounts to over 3,000 properties for you to choose from. The type of accommodation covers a wide price range – from a simple apartment in a huge complex to a secluded villa in the middle of the Spanish countryside. The service given to customers is generally good and, despite the number of properties dealt with, the villas and apartments are maintained to reasonable standards.

Other companies which specialize in particular areas are **Lanzarote Villas** which operates an extensive programme of self-catering packages mainly to Lanzarote but also to other destinations in the Canary Islands, and the **Travel Club of Upminster** which deals exclusively with Majorca in Spain, and has a long-established reputation for quality, 'value-for-money' holidays.

Rainbow Sunshiners represents another alternative to holiday-makers. It operates a compromise between a package holiday and independent travel by offering accommodation-only packages and leaving the flights and travel arrangements up to you. The advantage of this is that you are not tied down to the fixed two-week period of a standard package holiday and can stay as long as you like in your chosen accommodation.

Other companies which are worth considering are **Arrow Holidays** which has a variety of self-catering packages to Spain especially suited to healthy types and the provision of sporting facilities, **Meon Villas and Apartments** which specializes in up-market, high-quality self-catering facilities, and **Beach Villas** and **Villaseekers** who both operate packages to a considerable number of Spanish destinations.

Cost-Conscious Holidays

It pays to shop around for holidays which offer good value for money. Very often, tour companies use the same hotels as their competitors, but prices may vary dramatically from operator to operator for an identical package, depending on the type of customer each firm is trying to attract. Similarly, the cheapest prices may not always represent best value for money. Don't be fooled by the cost – check out precisely what is included in the price of your accommodation and what facilities are available at your hotel. Remember, you more or less get what you pay for and often the extra £30 companies like Thomson or Horizon charge will result in a higher quality hotel.

For a standard two-week beach-based holiday, it is the major tour operators, such as **Cosmos, Enterprise, Intasun** and **Skytours**, which are the most competitively priced. Among the smaller companies, **Flair** (part of British Airways Holidays) and **Wings** offer good family holidays at a reasonable cost.

Among the most cost-conscious deals available are the packages based on coach travel to and from Spain. **Cosmos Express** does a very good deal for those wanting a low-cost break which includes hotel or apartment accommodation in one of the major resorts on the Costa Brava/Dorada. **Wallace Arnold** does a similar deal to Benidorm on the Costa Blanca, as well as destinations on the Costa Brava. Alternatively, a number of companies operate coach tours which incorporate the major sights and attractions in Spain. These are usually less expensive than a standard package holiday and worth considering if you are interested in discovering the historical and scenic parts of the country (see 'Coach Tours' on page 86). The cheapest option of all is a two-week camping holiday in the south of Spain which may be arranged through one of the camping specialists (see 'Camping' on page 87).

Sunscene Holidays offers very low-priced, inclusive holidays by express coach to de-luxe tents, mobile homes, caravans, tents and apartments in the Costas Brava, Dorada and Azahar. You can make considerable savings as it is a direct-sell company. What's more, its Beach Clubs and children's entertainments make it a good choice for families keen to cut costs.

Another way to cut costs is to holiday out of season and take advantage of the price cuts and freebies which companies offer in a bid to attract customers. Otherwise, cheap holidays may be obtained by booking at the last minute and taking pot luck on where you end up. The Air Travel Advisory Bureau on 01-636 5000 or 061-832 2000 provides information on the best last-minute flight deals, plus villas, apartments and hotels, and its service is free.

Coach Tours

Coach tours are undoubtedly one of the cheapest ways to spend a fortnight abroad, but they do tend to have a bit of an OAP image and to a large extent that is deserved – the average age on a coach party is rarely less than fifty. Nevertheless, coach holidays are a good way to take a whistle-stop tour of the major sights of a country – something you might not have much opportunity to do if you took a standard 'sun, surf and sea' package to one of the major resorts on coastal Spain.

For tours which deal entirely with Spain, **Thomson's** operates a number of programmes to different parts of the country. Its three tours – the cities of Castile, the Pilgrim's Way to Santiago, and the cities of Andalucía – have varied and comprehensive itineraries and are accompanied by an escort throughout. For those on the tour of Andalucía, there is the additional option of staying a further four or seven nights in a resort on the Costa del Sol. Spanish travel agents **Marsans** do a five-, seven- or nine-day trip to Andalucía, the Costa del Sol or the north of Spain respectively. The cost of flights is not included in the packages but may be arranged on request. **Mundi Color** operates a fairly exhaustive tour of Andalucía which takes in lesser-known areas as well as the famous sights of Granada, Seville and Córdoba. Alternatively, the company operates a longer tour which visits Portugal as well as locations in the south of Spain. **Enterprise** also offers a good value eight-day tour to Andalucía, following a varied and interesting itinerary.

For coach tours which include Spain among other countries, **Cosmos Tourama** does a two-week Grand Tour of Spain and Portugal, which spends five or six days in Spain and goes as far south as the historic centres of Seville and Córdoba. This company also offers a tour of southern Spain, Portugal and Morocco which visits Granada, Seville and Alicante among other destinations. **Insight** operates a two-week tour of Spain, Gibraltar, Morocco and Portugal. **Global Continental** offers a fourteen-day Portugal and Spain tour, which includes coach travel to and from Britain, or it also offers a week-long air-coach tour to the major cities and sights of the country.

Driving Holidays

For those who wish to have the security of taking a package holiday, but don't want to be stuck in one resort for two weeks, then a fly/drive option is worth considering. This combines the advantage of a cheap flight with the freedom of a self-drive car at the other end. Unfortunately, while many of the larger tour companies do offer car hire as a standard feature of their packages to Spain, only a few deal specifically in fly/drive.

Sovereign, Mundi Color and **Cadogan** are the most notable of these. Sovereign arranges a touring itinerary of Andalucía, with accommodation booked en route, while Mundi Colour offers several fly/drive tours to various parts of the country with overnight accommodation in paradors. Cadogan operates a Gibraltar fly/drive programme which makes the southern coast of the mainland, as well as Gibraltar itself, easily accessible to travellers.

Another alternative is offered by **NAT Holidays**. If you want to drive from Britain to your Spanish resort, then NAT will arrange ferry crossings, accommodation en route and maps to facilitate your drive through the continent.

Camping

There are a number of companies specializing in camping holidays. **Club Cantrabrica** offers the widest choice of destinations, with packages operated to around half a dozen camps in the south of Spain. The sites, which are well equipped and maintained to high standards, may be reached by coach or air connections from Britain. If you choose to go by coach then there is no additional charge for joining the coach at your local departure point and travelling to London.

If you are planning to do a motoring/camping holiday, then undoubtedly **Eurocamp** is the best option. This company provides an excellent back-up service prior to leaving Britain, with a comprehensive pack of road-maps, local guide-books, and essential information leaflets issued free of charge to customers. It also has a Junior Eurocampers Club for children, and a motorrail facility for those who wish to avoid the drive through France.

Other tour operators to consider for camping holidays are **Tentrek** or **NAT Holidays** who operate to a more limited range of Spanish destinations.

Private Accommodation/Small Hotels

Horizon and **Thomson** both offer this type of holiday and for those who prefer the friendly atmosphere and personal service of a family-run establishment, then this is an alternative worth considering.

Several of the large tour operators have recently introduced separate programmes. In Thomson's case, for example, there is one called 'Simply Spain', and it deals specifically with pension/small hotel accommodation throughout the country. There are no shortcuts on the service – the standard features of car hire, low prices and two-centre holiday option still remain. There is also a special pound-savers deal which is particularly good for those who are working on a low budget; this operates by the customer choosing his or her holiday location and board arrangement, and leaving the final arrangement of resort and accommodation up to the company. Horizon, in their 'Small Hotels' programme, offers a good selection of Spanish destinations, and like Thomson, maintains the standards of service which have come to be expected of this major company.

Two-Centre Holidays

A number of tour operators offer two-centre holidays to Spain. These tend to focus on the islands where distances travelled are relatively short and enable the tour companies to keep transfer costs low. Even so, two-centre breaks are a bit more pricey than a standard package holiday, but they do have the advantage of allowing you to sample a bit more of Spain without having to go to the expense of choosing the car hire or fly-drive options.

Sovereign operates a two-centre holiday in Majorca where one week may be spent in the peaceful surroundings of the north of the island, and the other week in the lively environs of the south. **Horizon** and **Thomas Cook** offer a similar package for Tenerife, while **Lanzarote Villas** combines two centres on Lanzarote and Fuerteventura as well as Tenerife.

For a holiday split between two islands, **Lanzarote Villas** also does twin centre packages to Fuerteventura and Lanzarote, or **Mundi Travel** operates two/three island holidays to Tenerife, Gran Canaria and Lanzarote. For holidays incorporating the mainland, **Cadogan** and **Enterprise** offer one week in Gibraltar and one week in resorts in the south of Spain.

Parador Holidays

At present there are around eighty paradors to be found throughout Spain but such is the demand for this type of holiday accommodation, that there are several more being built or in the planning stage.

It is not difficult to see why parador holidays are popular among visitors – the buildings (often renovated castles or monasteries) give you the opportunity to experience at first hand the most beautiful or historic areas of Spain. However, British tour operators seem to have lagged behind in introducing this option into their regular programmes, and there are only a limited number of companies which will organize all-inclusive parador holidays – but those that do are acknowledged specialists in their field.

Mundi Color will put together a package, inclusive of accommodation and flights, which will suit your individual needs. It also does some very helpful introductory material which gives a short resumé of the facilities offered by some of the larger paradors. **Marsans** offers either a tailor-made holiday, according to your specifications, or a seven-day parador package which includes car hire and suggested itinerary for tours of Catalonia and Andalucía.

For British-based companies, **Hartland Travel** gives a good service, offering a number of flexible tours which cover the north as well as the south of Spain.

It should be noted that parador holidays are not particularly cheap. This is chiefly because parador accommodation is usually regarded as equivalent to a four- or five-star luxury hotel. However, if money isn't a problem, then without doubt, this type of holiday represents a unique and enjoyable way to explore one of Europe's most fascinating countries.

Activity Holidays

Most major resorts have a wide range of leisure facilities, so if you take a standard package there will be an ample choice of sporting amenities such as windsurfing, golf, swimming, etc. When you are deciding on your resort and tour operator, check out the details given in the brochures to see what sort of activities are on offer at each resort and what provision of sporting amenities individual hotels have available for residents.

Arrow Holidays are especially orientated to sporting types. They can arrange pre-booking of courts and rinks for sports, and may also arrange tuition at some of the larger sporting complexes. If you are interested in an activity holiday in the Canaries, **Lanzarote Villas** provides some useful information about availability of equipment, current prices of court hire and contact addresses to get in touch with when you arrive.

Golf and Tennis Holidays

A few operators specialize in golf or tennis holidays to customers. If you are an enthusiast, these options are well worth considering, as you will have the opportunity to use top-class facilities in addition to paying cheaper prices than could be obtained if you were playing independently.

Enterprise offers special packages to two destinations on the Spanish mainland, and details can be found in their tennis holidays leaflet which is available on request. For an additional fee, **Arrow Holidays** will arrange for participation in tennis-playing programmes at selected locations along the coastline. Arrow also offers a similar facility for golf players.

Longshot Holidays and **Sovereign Golf** deal exclusively with golf holidays, and among the features they offer to clients are reduced green fees, guaranteed tee-off times and the use of Spain's premier courses.

Sailing and Windsurfing Holidays

Learning how to sail or windsurf properly with the help of professional tuition is an increasingly popular option among those looking for a holiday with a difference. Once you've mastered the basic skills, there are few things more enjoyable than a day afloat in the warm seas of the Mediterranean.

Top Deck Travel, Minorca Sailing Holidays and **Lagoon Windsurf** organize packages suitable for either complete beginners or old hands who want to extend their range of skills a bit. Top Deck Travel and Minorca Sailing Holidays have facilities for both sailing or windsurf enthusiasts, while Lagoon Windsurf concentrates exclusively on windsurfing holidays.

Walking/Natural-Interest Holidays

Ramblers, acknowledged expert in its field, offers several interesting walking tours to Spain including walking on Majorca and bird-watching on Menorca. **Waymark** organizes tours to Majorca as well as to scenic locations in the centre and north of Spain. **Cox and Kings** operates botany, ornithological and painting holidays to parts of Majorca and Andalucía as well as to the Pyrenees in the North.

For ornithologists, **Mundi Color** runs special tours to the famous Doñana Bird Sanctuary and Wildlife Park while **Ornitholidays** offer natural-interest and bird-watching holidays to destinations in the Pyrenees, Majorca and the coast of Andalucía.

For natural interest of a different kind, **Peng Travel,** a leading tour operator in naturist holidays, offers packages to newly developed naturist resorts on the Costa del Sol a few miles from Marbella.

Cruises

There are no cruises which deal only with Spain – the Spanish ports of call are usually just one part of a much larger programme. Most of the large shipping lines have cruises which incorporate Spanish ports, and the most usual points of call are at Gibraltar, Barcelona, Menorca, Majorca in the Balearics, Tenerife and Lanzarote in the Canaries. The *Canberra* from **P&O**, the *Queen Elizabeth 2* from **Cunard**, the *Leonid Brezhnev* from **CTC** and the *Black Prince* from **Fred Olson** all operate Mediterranean or Iberian Island cruises and their brochures are readily available in most travel agents. Some tour operators offer cruising programmes and the main ones to consider here are **The Travel Club of Upminster, Fourwinds** and **Saga.**

SUMMING UP

To sum up, then, the package-holiday scene in Spain offers good value and a wide range of choice to suit your interests and your pocket! Some companies aim for good quality and an 'exclusive' approach while others concentrate on keeping costs down and providing an adequate, all-round service. The young, good-time set are also catered for – **Thomson's Freestyle** and **Club 18–30** are the main ones to consider in this respect, while **Sovereign** is clearly pitched towards the 'Yuppie' market.

There is also a substantial number of tour companies geared towards people with specialist interests, such as golf, sailing or tennis. It is worth remembering, however, that most major resorts have a wide range of sporting facilities and it is not necessary to travel with a specialist unless you want non-stop coaching or well-above-average facilities.

The outlook is also bright for those who want to break out of the standard package-holiday mould. The parador holidays are an attractive alternative for those who wish to see a bit more of the country, while the fly/drive option combines the freedom of independent travel with the security and inexpense of a package holiday.

However, it is the standard 'sun, sea and sand' break which makes up the bulk of the package holiday in Spain. Overall, this represents very good value and you'd be hard pressed to find anywhere else in the Mediterranean with the same range of resorts and amenities at similar prices.

One final point – it really is worth taking the trouble to shop around and collect as many brochures as you can. That way you can obtain a package which is best-suited to your interests and price-range.

CHECKLIST

As a final reminder to anyone taking a package holiday anywhere, check the following points before booking:

(1) Is your travel agent competent? Unfortunately many are not, and all too often it's the large chains of High Street agents who give the worst service and advice. Try to avoid the obvious trainees when you

go into the shop and have a list of questions prepared so that you don't end up having to make several trips when one would do.

(2) Is your travel agent a member of ABTA? If not, think seriously about finding one that is. There are plenty of them that are, and membership could make a big difference to you if things start to go wrong.

(3) Having chosen your country of destination, do you really know about all the packages available on the market? Many of the smaller tour operators do not get their brochures into the High Street travel agents but that does not mean their holidays aren't reliable or worth checking out. Check against the list on page 58 and phone for a brochure from any likely looking company.

(4) If the travel agent can't book the holiday you finally selected, don't necessarily accept his/her substitute recommendation. Have your second and third options sorted out beforehand, or if there really is no substitute, leave the whole idea and consider something completely different. Remember that travel agents are in the business of selling holidays for commissions – unscrupulous agents often don't much care what they sell, but they do like to clinch a sale before you leave the shop.

(5) As for the holiday itself, check the following before paying your deposit:

(i)   Does the holiday price include all airport or port taxes and security charges (for both the UK and abroad)?

(ii) Does it include meals on the journey?

(iii) Is it extra for a weekend flight or a day-time departure?

(iv) Is transfer between the point of arrival and your hotel included?

(v)   Be sure you know on what basis you are booked in at your hotel, i.e. full/half board/B&B.

(vi) Are you clear about supplementary charges made for single rooms/balcony/sea view/private bathroom, etc.?

(vii)   Is the insurance sufficient for you? Does it cover pregnant women/disabled people/people going on sports holidays? Is the limit on personal baggage high enough to cover all you are taking? Does it include a clause on delayed departure for your return journey? What provisions does it make for cancellations? Finally, check you're clear about the procedure in case a theft or loss does occur – often these matters have to be reported within a specified time limit and a police report procured.

(6) And finally, before handing over your money, ask:

(i)   What is the position on cancellations (from both parties' point of view)?

(ii)   What happens if your holiday needs to be altered significantly? Under the ABTA code you must be told and given the choice of accepting either the new hotel/resort/flight etc. or a full refund. (Alterations caused by bad weather or industrial disputes will only be covered by your insurance.)

(iii)   What's the score on overbooking? Is there a 'disturbance' compensation to be paid (there should be under the ABTA code): will the alternative accommodation be of an equally high standard (it must be under the ABTA code.)

Once you have gone through all these points you should have a clear understanding of the contract you are signing, and your travel agent will undoubtedly be in such awe of your intimate knowledge of the travel industry that you will receive preferential treatment all the way!

If, despite all this good groundwork, you still have cause for complaint, ABTA's address is 55-57 Newman Street, London W1N 4AH. Write to them with full details of your complaint and enclose copies of all your correspondence with the travel agent or tour operator.

Independent Travel

THE OPTIONS

Finding accommodation in Spain is not usually a problem as even the smallest resort is likely to have one or two hotels, hostels or *residencials* to house visitors. Difficulties do arise, however, if you are heading for some of the busiest resorts during July and August without pre-booking. There is no question that you will be able to find accommodation *somewhere* – but you may end up having to take a humble pension in the back streets rather than a comfortable hotel in the town centre.

Hotels are graded from one to five stars, while hostels are ranked on a one- to three-star basis. Those looking for a good quality hotel in a popular resort should consider the SOL network of hotels – Spain's largest. They have reliable international standards with many extras such as the 'family floors' now in twenty-two of their hotels. These offer parents a baby-patrolling service and range of facilities and entertainments for the children. Telephone (0800) 282210 for free brochure and reservations.

At the lower end of the scale, the hostel categories become somewhat meaningless as it is not uncommon to find a three-star hostel more comfortable and better run than a one-star hotel. *Residencials* differ from hotels and hostels, because they have no dining-room facilities, although breakfast will still be served, and a café may be available as a substitute.

There are numerous family-run *pensiones* throughout Spain, and they are likely to be the only form of accommodation available in small, rural towns away from the main tourist centres. *Pensiones* generally offer bed-and-breakfast board only and the cost is around £6 or £7 per night.

Bookings for hotels or *pensiones* can be made through the local tourist office for a small commission. If you want to book before you go, contact the Spanish National Tourist Office, 57-58 St James's Street, London SW1. They will supply you with lists of hotels which you may then write to personally or book through a travel agent. Preferably, letters requesting reservations should be written in Spanish, although three- to five-star hotels may be contacted in English.

If you are keen to go it alone in self-catering, the listings in the Sunday papers are your best bet. These contain details of flats and villas to be let by private arrangement. Renting accommodation abroad this way is obviously more risky than a standard package holiday, as there is no legal back-up if things fail to come up to your expectations. It is strongly advised, therefore, that people in this type of accommodation should obtain a full inventory, a recent photograph and as much information as possible about the accommodation before they commit themselves to anything.

Another alternative which is popular among holiday-makers is the Spanish parador, which is a state-owned building, located in a place of scenic or historic interest. The paradors are a marvellous way to discover more about the cultural side of Spain as both the architecture and the food which is served reflect the traditions of the area you are based in. All the modern conveniences that you'd expect from a luxury hotel are available too: swimming pools, tennis courts, garages in built-up areas. Considering the quality of these establishments, costs are reasonable: a double room and breakfast for two is likely to cost around £50. For more information concerning the location and costs of paradors, contact the Spanish Tourist Office in London. For reservations, contact the paradors' UK representative at Keytel International, 402 Edgware Road, London W2. Tel: (01) 402 8182.

As for camping, there are numerous sites along the coastline, usually costing around £1.50 to £2.00 per person. A camping carnet (obtainable from UK camping associations) is advisable, although this is no longer obligatory in many places. The Spanish Tourist Office in London will be able to supply you with camping maps which detail the locations of most of the sites. Off-site camping is permitted but not on crowded tourist beaches or built-up urban areas. Advance bookings may be made through ANCE, Gran Via 88 10-8, Madrid-28013. If you prefer a roof over your head, then there are over ninety youth hostels in the country, many of which can be found in large tourist resorts both on the mainland and the Balearic Islands.

Overall, the accommodation scene for the independent traveller is good. There are plenty of different types to choose from, depending on your individual specifications, although you might feel the squeeze in the big resorts during peak season.

So much for the independent accommodation scene. Now let's turn our attentions to the ways of travelling to Spain.

BY AIR

There are two main alternatives open to the independent traveller – either take a scheduled flight with one of the big airlines or a chartered flight through a main tour operator.

Spain's national airlines operating flights to Britain are **Aviaco** (Tel: (01) 247 9005) and **Iberia** (Tel: (01) 437 5622). Iberia is the larger of the two and is well worth considering as an alternative to the major British airlines. It runs frequent and efficient services between Spanish airports and Britain, and we have had very favourable reports regarding in-flight comfort and hospitality. Moreover, as Iberia is Spain's national airline, scheduled flights operate frequently to all airports in Spain – not simply the major tourist destinations. Most of the major British airlines run services to destinations in Spain. Airports are located at Alicante, Barcelona, Málaga and Valencia on the mainland and Palma de Mallorca on the Balearics. The Canaries are well-equipped to handle international flights, with one terminal at Las Palmas on Gran Canaria and two airports on Tenerife – Tenerife-Norte Los Rodeos and Tenerife-Sur Reina Sofia. Iberia and Aviaco airlines operate services between the mainland and the Balearic and Canary Islands, while Iberia also runs internal flights to all the islands in the Canary archipelago, with the exception of Gomera.

Scheduled flights to Spain generally work out more expensive than chartered flights, although costs depend on what day you are travelling (mid-week is cheaper than weekends) and what kind of fare you buy. Both SUPER-PEX fares and excursion fares are operative to Spain. A SUPER-PEX fare does not need to be purchased in advance but there is limited availability, so it is advisable to book early. The fare entitles you to a maximum stay of one month but the dates you prescribe may not be changed and cancellation costs up to the full amount of the fare may be charged. An excursion fare is more expensive, but this allows you up to six months in the country, dates are flexible within that period of time and there is no charge for cancellation. The price of a return air-flight to the south of Spain ranges from £165 (mid-week SUPER-PEX) to £240 (mid-week excursion).

Charter flights usually represent better value for the holiday-maker, although in fact this depends on your location in the country. Most chartered flights leave from London airports and when you start adding up the cost of train journeys and perhaps overnight accommodation if you're booked onto an early morning flight, you'll soon begin to realize that fares on scheduled flights aren't as uncompetitive as they might seem. It is also worth remembering that on scheduled flights, you can choose your date of departure and what airport you want to fly to in Spain, rather than having to organize your holiday plans around the limited departure dates and destinations which chartered flights represent.

However, for the majority of people living near to major airports, chartered flights represent the cheapest and quickest way to get to Spain. The prices of chartered flights vary, depending on what time of year you are travelling and what company you are travelling with, but even at peak season you should be able to make savings of around £40 per person, compared to the price of scheduled flights. Most of the major tour operators offer charter deals, although smaller companies are increasingly offering this alternative to holiday-makers. It is worth noting, however, that flight delays are not uncommon on aircraft chartered by tour operators, and if anything goes wrong with the agreement between the airline and the tour operator, it is the passengers who suffer by being stranded in a foreign airport until the matter is cleared up. As a consequence, holiday-makers who travel with an established tour operator, such as Horizon or Thomson, may well get better service at the end of the day than those who simply choose the cheapest charter flight.

Students or young people under twenty-five get a good deal from USIT, who offer very competitive rates on flights to Barcelona, Bilbao and Madrid in Spain. If you fall into either of these two categories, it is worth checking out USIT's pricings, as they can work out cheaper than taking a peak-season flight on a chartered aircraft. For more information, contact your local Student Travel Office or telephone USIT at (01) 730 3402.

Chartered flights usually include some form of basic accommodation (i.e. dormitory beds in hostels) to get round the law on the sale of inclusive air holidays to Europe. What this actually means is that on paper at least, some very basic accommodation is included in the price of your flight (so the company can legally claim that it is selling you a package holiday consisting of travel and accommodation). It's up to you whether you want to use this accommodation or not, although tour companies do not usually include travel facilities from the airport to your accommodation, or even guarantee it will be in the same town the airport is located in!

The only other way to get a cheap flight is to scout around bucket shops, or scan the columns of the Sunday newspapers – but remember to read the small print. You're unlikely to come up with a cheaper way of going than the tour-operator charter flight anyway.

BY RAIL

It costs around £290 (plus £15 if you want an overnight sleeper) for a second-class return from Britain to the south of Spain. Travelling by train is *not* a cheap option – in fact for the cost of a rail fare, it is possible to get a cheap package holiday, inclusive of flights, accommodation and half board. Undoubtedly, it is better to be under twenty-six and still eligible to buy an Interrail pass or a BIJ ticket (available from Transalpino or Eurotrain) which will get you there for half the price of the standard rail tariff.

If money isn't your primary consideration, then travelling to Spain by train is one of the most scenic ways to reach your holiday destination. The Pyrenees in northern Spain can be quite spectacular if you get fine weather and are a startling contrast to the vast, arid plateau (*meseta*) of central Spain.

The quickest direct route to take to the south of Spain is a train to Folkestone arriving at Boulogne, then a connecting service to Paris. In Paris you change stations from Paris Nord to Austerlitz and pick up a sleeper, which will take you down to Port Bou on the French/Spanish border, arriving at around 8 am. From there, it's a straight run down, arriving at Alicante in the early evening. There are no buffet facilities on this train so pre-packed food and drink for the journey are essential.

If you're planning to travel extensively by train, or if you want to plan your journey in detail before you go, then *Thomas Cook's Continental Timetable* is a good buy. This is issued monthly and contains timetables for train services throughout the continent. Once you've worked out how to read it (it looks complicated but, in fact, is very simple) this is an indispensable guide to have on hand, although you'd still be advised to check train times in local stations. Another excellent guide for the train-traveller is *Europe by Train*. Published by Fontana, this book gives you all the information you need to know about the Spanish rail network, as well as details about what to see and do in places you travel to.

Whichever route you opt for, seat and sleeping reservations for the journey are strongly advised.

BY BUS

Spending thirty-six hours on a bus – which is the time it takes to get to the south of Spain – is a pretty gruelling experience, and this option is most popular among the young back-packing brigade with not much money and plenty of stamina. Costs are cheap – around £70 for a single and £120 for a return – but it's worth remembering that last-minute bookings on charter flights (or USIT fares if you're a student) are often around the same price.

Two companies operate services from London to Spain. Euroways (Tel: (01) 730 8235) runs through Barcelona, Valencia and Alicante, stopping at most coastal towns en route. Supabus (Tel: (01) 730 0202) goes further south to the Costa del Sol destinations, taking in Málaga, Marbella, Torremolinos and Algeciras. Tickets may be booked through National Express depots or travel agents.

BY CAR/CAMPERVAN

Whichever way you look at it, it's a long drive to the south of Spain. If you're driving straight there, the journey will take around three days with two overnight stops to complete. However, on the plus side, travelling by car can be relatively cheap if you're going with a group of friends and sharing the cost of petrol and motorway tolls.

Obviously the route you take depends on what you want to see before you get to Spain, but the most direct way to go is to take the motorway from Paris via Toulouse, Narbonne, Perpignan, crossing the border to Spain, and from then on the road goes straight down the coastline, passing through, or near to, most of the major tourist resorts en route. Remember to time your journey so that you are crossing the border during the day-time (between 8 am and 11 pm) as most frontier posts close for the night.

French railways run a Motorrail facility which cuts out the long drive through France. Services connect up the channel ports of Boulogne and Calais with Narbonne, close to the French/Spanish border. A second-class return fare will cost around £340 for the car and driver, plus £80 or so for each additional adult and £45 for children. On the surface, these prices may seem expensive, but the tariffs for additional adults and children do represent considerable reductions on the standard return fares. Also, by the time you have paid for motorway tolls, petrol and arranged accommodation for the journey, you may find that it would have been only marginally more expensive to travel in comfort by Motorrail. More details can be obtained from French Railways, 179 Piccadilly, London W1 (Tel: (01) 499 9333).

Another alternative is a twice-weekly car ferry from Plymouth to Santander in north Spain. The sailing takes twenty-four hours and cuts off approximately 600 miles of motoring. Prices vary according to the type of car you are taking and the time of year you are going, but the approximate cost for a Fiat-Uno-type car in high season is £110 – £120, with £57 extra for each adult travelling. For more details apply to Brittany Ferries (Tel: (0752) 221321).

Most roadways in Spain are maintained to reasonable standards, suitable for high-speed travelling and well able to cope with the huge influx of holiday traffic during peak season. One exception to this is the notorious south-coast road, which is said to be the busiest and most dangerous road in Europe! Driving on this can be quite a hair-raising experience – but take comfort, trying to cross it is even worse! Cars seem to pull in front of oncoming vehicles with apparent disregard for safety or lives and the problem is increased by the lack of lane markings on the road which results in traffic weaving about at a breakneck pace. Unfortunately, as this is the main road along the south coast, drivers do not have much option but to use it – the best advice that can be offered is to keep alert and be prepared!

Those taking campervans or caravans into Spain should stick to the major routes, especially when crossing the Pyrenees, as some of the minor roads have some rather daunting hair-pin bends to negotiate. In case of a serious accident, motorways have special telephones which may be used to contact the emergency services by dialling 091.

The rule of the road is to give way and drive on the right. Any exceptions to this rule are indicated at road junctions by the sign 'Ceda el Paso' (Give Way).

Speed limits in built-up areas are indicated by numbers in round signs with a black rim. On other roads, the limits are 62mph (100kph), and on motorways 75mph (120kph). Speed limits in Spain are quoted in kilometres per hour.

To drive in Spain, you need the following documentation:

An international driving licence
GB stickers
Car registration document
'Green Card' (International motor-insurance certificate)

It is also advisable to take out a 'bail bond', obtainable through insurance companies, which acts as extra cover in case of an accident involving personal injury to a third party. Seat belts are required to be worn on all roads outside towns, but are not obligatory within towns themselves. Children under the age of fourteen are forbidden to sit in front seats of motor vehicles.

Both petrol and diesel may be bought. There are two grades of petrol available, 97 octane (super) and 92 octane (normal), which are equivalent to Britain's 4- and 2-star petrol.

In case of breakdown, drivers are advised to take some basic spare parts (spark plugs, bulbs, etc.) with them, as replacements may be difficult to find abroad. The AA motoring organization has a reciprocal agreement with its Spanish equivalent RACE, which provides basic patrol service for breakdown, although garage costs are not covered. Travellers are strongly advised to have a suitable insurance policy to cover driving abroad. Both the AA and RAC have policies especially for car travel in Europe, and details may be obtained from local branch offices.

Everyone has their own preference when it comes to a driving holiday, but speaking as someone who has driven on the continent in everything from a Daimler limousine to a battered old Mini, I feel it's worth putting in a word here about what to look for when choosing a car to drive abroad in. Obviously luggage capacity is an important consideration. Fuel economy, spare parts and comfort are the other major considerations. Don't try to squeeze too many people into a car, and remember, you'll return with more than you set out with. When we were researching this section of the guide we used our Vauxhall Carlton 2LGL Saloon, which over any other car we'd tried gave us the best in terms of comfort, room and efficiency. It's worth bearing in mind if you intend doing a lot of holiday motoring, or if you're in a position to hire one. A car with a bit of extra power is well worth having on long journeys – and safer.

HITCH-HIKING

Hiking down to the south of Spain through France can be an unrewarding experience, unless you're lucky and manage to get a long-distance lift from one of the channel ports. In France itself, drivers don't look favourably on hitch-hikers, and in Spain, the situation is even worse along the busy coastal routes, where you might find yourself hanging about for hours waiting for a decent lift. However, if you manage to reach Spain, the good news is that bus and train travel is relatively cheap, so it makes sense to travel by public transport rather than take the risks of hitching.

BY SEA

The only direct sea-route between Britain and Spain is the twice-weekly ferry service to Santander in northern Spain, run by Brittany Ferries (*see* 'By Car/Campervan' on page 100). Otherwise, the majority of cruises to the Mediterranean or North Africa stop off at Barcelona, the Balearics or Canary Islands for a few days. (*See* 'Cruises' on page 91).

USEFUL INFORMATION

Time

Spanish time is one hour ahead of British time, five hours ahead of New York time (USA East Coast) in the summer and six hours in the winter.

Electricity

Voltage in most places is 220 volts AC, although power points for electric shavers may be 110 volts. Most plug sockets are two-pin, but this problem may be overcome by taking a small travel adaptor with you.

Water

Officially, water is safe to drink anywhere in Spain, but if you have a delicate stomach you'd be better to drink bottled mineral water, especially if you're travelling to the most popular tourist areas.

Part Three

WHEN YOU'RE THERE

TOURIST INFORMATION

In Spain, tourists offices (*turismos*) can be found in all major towns and resorts. Brochures, maps, timetables and details of boat or bus tours can be obtained from these offices. The literature, written in English, is usually adequate, although it tends to be region-based, and doesn't really tell you much about other parts of the country. If you are doing a lot of travelling and want more general information, write off to the Spanish National Tourist board (57-58 St James's Street, London SW1A 1LD) before you go to obtain more details of what the country has to offer. Often the tourist offices in busy areas run out of certain leaflets in peak season, and you may find that German or French versions are the only alternatives.

Staff in *turismos* usually speak English and will be able to help with any enquiries you might have. They can point out the main areas to look for accommodation or, for a small commission, find you a place for the night in a guest-house or hotel within their area. Opening hours are 9/10am – 1/1.30pm and from 3/3.30pm – 7.30/8.00pm.

Apart from *turismos*, information and tickets for sightseeing trips, boat or air journeys can often be obtained from Spanish travel agents (*viajes*). Some of the larger tourist agents to look out for are **Iberia**; **Interopa**; **Iberotravel**; **Iberojet**; **Meliá**; **Politor**; **Internacional Expreso** and **Marsans**.

SIGHTSEEING

There are some wonderful sights waiting to be discovered by visitors to Spain. Historic centres such as Barcelona or Valencia provide plenty in the way of famous buildings and galleries to visit, while the islands offer some beautiful, and occasionally spectacular, scenery. All the pain and hassle of organizing special day-trips is alleviated for you, as there are plenty of buses running from coastal resorts to the most popular sightseeing destinations. All-inclusive coach tours are another option which is open to holidays-makers. Usually lasting a day or a half-day, these are whistle-stop trips which give you a flavour of the history and scenery of the area you're based in. Details of tours are usually prominently displayed in travel agents' windows. Car hire is another possibility for those keen to see a lot of the country. Having your own transport certainly dispenses with the problem of having to stick to the times and locations of a bus tour, and there are many enchanting Spanish villages to be discovered off the tourist track. However, this can be an expensive way to move around the country if you are working on a tight budget, and given the volume of traffic on the main coastal routes, driving for long periods in hot weather can be rather uncomfortable and stressful. For more details about car hire abroad, and how to go about it, turn to page 114.

Museums and galleries are open Monday to Saturday. There appear to be no fixed opening hours, but most places take a siesta between 2 and 4pm. Larger establishments, such as the Picasso Museum in Barcelona, usually open on Sunday mornings.

For more details on specific sights, see individual sections or 'The Sightseer' (p 14).

SHOPPING

Shops are open from 9/10am – 1/1.30pm and from 3/3.30pm – 7.30/8.00pm (Monday – Saturday).

Large supermarkets and general stores can be found in most tourist resorts and are generally open all day from 10am to 8pm. The majority of towns and resorts have a weekly market (sometimes twice weekly) where typical souvenirs may be bought. Most of the larger centres have fashionable shopping areas, selling high-quality clothes, leather and china goods. Busy resorts also attract their fair share of street-sellers, and it is often worth checking out their goods, as prices are generally lower than the marked-up tariffs in 'tourist' shops.

Good buys in Spain are the colourful blue, hand-painted pottery items, leather goods (which are especially cheap in Majorca), lace from the Canary Islands, cloths embroidered in traditional styles, sherry and Spanish wine (*see* 'Customs' for regulations on page 30). Spanish fashions can be remarkably stylish, but tend to be quite expensive, as do the beautiful gold and silver hand-worked jewellery items.

FOOD AND DRINK

With Spanish cuisine, the emphasis is on hearty and filling meals rather than *haute cuisine*. Eating-places abound, ranging from quick stop-off *tapa* bars to open-air restaurants where a three-course meal can be enjoyed *al fresco*.

Dining out is relatively cheap and often a seemingly seedy restaurant in the back streets can offer some wonderful traditional Spanish fare. For those who fight shy of trying out foreign food, many hotels have 'international' menus while restaurants in busy resorts offer simple dishes such as fried fish and chips or roast chicken to cater for holiday-makers.

The usual start to the day, either in a hotel or café, is a continental breakfast (*desayuno*) consisting of a crusty bread roll, butter, jam and either tea or coffee. Most hotels serve breakfast from 8 to 11am. Lunch (*almuerzo*) is from 1 to 4pm and you have the choice of a three-course meal in a restaurant or a snack in one of the numerous *tapa* bars. Traditionally, *tapas* are simply an entrée to a main meal. However, for many people, a combination of two or three of these snacks is ideal as a light lunch. There are a wide variety of *tapas* to choose from, ranging from a straightforward sandwich or omelette to the more substantial fried fish or *chorizos* (spicy sausages). The selection of food on offer is usually arrayed either along the top of the bar or in a glass-fronted case underneath, so if your Spanish isn't too good, you can simply point. Some of the tastiest *tapas* are *tortilla*, a filling potato omelette served hot or cold in a sandwich, *huevos a la flamenca*, a delicious dish of baked eggs, ham and asparagus or *calamares* (squid) crisply fried in batter. Price-wise, tapas are reasonably cheap: a lunch consisting of an omelette, bread and a small carafe of cheap wine will cost around £1.50 in towns; £2-ish in resorts where prices are *always* inflated. If you prefer to take your family to lunch at a restaurant, look out for the *menú del día* (menu of the day) as these invariably offer better value than the à la carte menu. With the *menú del día*, you can have a three-course meal (occasionally wine and bread are included) for a fixed price of around £3 a head. Another saver is the *platos combinados*, a selection of foods on a single plate, costing about £2.

Dinner (*cena*) is served relatively late in the evening, starting around 8.30pm and continuing to 11 or 12 midnight. Spanish restaurants are officially graded from one fork to five forks, according to the excellence and food on offer. If you're not looking for anything fancy, stick to the two or three fork establishments and you will be served with perfectly adequate meals for around £4.50 for a three-course dinner. Restaurants with four or five forks have exquisite food, but also charge prices which are beyond most people's holiday budgets.

Afternoon tea, as such, is not usually served in Spain. However, there is no shortage of *tapa* bars, *heladerías* (ice-cream parlours) or *pastelerías* which serve coffee and food throughout the day. Coffee is normally strong and black; if you want milky coffee ask for *café con leche*. Although the Spanish are not great tea-drinkers, most places in busy resorts keep a packet or two on hand especially for thirsty Brits.

As far as the food itself goes, most dishes use olive oil and garlic as staple ingredients. The result is not heavy as might be expected, and there are some internationally renowned dishes which are quite delicious when cooked in the authentic Spanish manner. Foremost of these is *paella*, a tangy rice-based dish using a selection of mussels, prawns, eel and ham. *Gazpacho* is another great favourite with both tourists and locals. A refreshing soup, it is made from tomatoes, onions and garlic and chilled until ice-cold. *Cocido español* (Spanish stew), made from meat, pulses and vegetables is also a popular choice, with the liquid of the stew often served as an appetizer for the main meat and vegetable course.

Spanish puddings are not very elaborate and are usually confined to *helado* (ice-cream), yogurt or *flan* (crème caramel). The sugary little pastries found in *pastelerías* are a better bet for those with a sweet tooth. Delightful sweets such as *alfajores* (for dipping in hot chocolate) *tortas* (oil cakes) and sugared chestnuts are often made by Spanish nuns and prepared to traditional Arabic recipes.

Although the dishes listed above are equivalent to Spain's national cuisine, as is to be expected from such a diverse country, each region has its own distinctive dishes and specialities. In Barcelona and the Costa Brava, you can sample the unique *fideos a la cazuela*, a tasty noodle-dish incorporating spare-ribs, bacon and ham. The Costa del Sol offers dishes such as young fried anchovies, *moujarres* (fish stew), and *las halbas a la granadine* (ham seasoned with mint, parsley and bay leaves). In the Canaries, cooking centres around the two main agricultural products, the tomato and the banana, while the Balearics offer a number of specialities including *el tumbet* (a kind of potato cake), the wonderful *caldereta de lagost* (lobster flavoured with garlic, onion and herb liqueur) and *coque*, a savoury snack full of diced vegetables. And, of course, if you are on Majorca, don't forget to sample its most famous recipe – mayonnaise, made the original way!

Wherever you go in Spain, sea food dishes will feature heavily on the menu. Eating houses called *marisquerías* serve exclusively fish and sea food. Dishes involving squid, mullet, tunny and mussels are reasonably priced, costing between £1 and £5 for one course. Fresh lobster, prawns and swordfish are more expensive and if you require an elaborate *paella* or lobster dish you may have to inform the restaurant a day in advance. Fish is sold by weight – always ask the price first or you could be in for a nasty shock!

Spanish wine is cheap and there are numerous varieties to choose from. You won't break the bank by paying £1.50 for a decent bottle from the local wine store (*bodegas*). Red wine is *vino tinto*, white wine *vino blanco*, and rosé is *vino rosado*. Among the vast array of wines to choose from, look out for *Marqués de Riscal* from the main wine-producing area of Rioja, *El Priorato* and the sparkling *Rosal* from the Costa Brava. In average one- or two-fork restaurants, don't expect extensive wine lists – usually only a house red or a house white is available, and it's pot luck whether it's good or bad

For a lighter, more refreshing drink try *sangría*, which is red wine mixed with fruit juice and slices of orange and lemon. Otherwise, *horchata* made from earth almonds is light and sweet, and makes a pleasant change from tea or coffee. *Cavas*, the Spanish equivalent to champagne, is cheaper than the real stuff, and highly successful in Spain's domestic drinks market. All the usual brands of soft drinks and mineral waters are widely available. The beer (*cerveza*) is light and drinkable, suitable for quenching mid-day thirst.

For apéritifs, Spain is *the* main sherry-producing country in the world. Made in the province of Cádiz, around 130 million litres are produced each year, and these are loosely categorized as *fino* (dry), *amontillado* (medium) and *oloroso* (heavy). There are literally hundreds of varieties to choose from, so you are sure to find one which suits your taste as well as your pocket. For after-dinner drinks, Spanish cognacs (*Osborne* and *Fundador*) are widely drunk while *moscatel* is an exceptionally good sweet raisin wine.

NIGHTLIFE

The nightlife scene in Spain is lively and varied. As is to be expected from such a hugely popular holiday destination, there is entertainment to suit everyone: for the young ones there are sophisticated nightclubs playing the latest sounds; for older couples, large hotels often host cabaret and old-time dance nights. Other entertainments on offer include flamenco shows (*see* 'The Socialite' on page 17) and live folk music and jazz in bars and restaurants.

Obviously the larger the resort, the better the range of nightclubs and eating places to choose from. However, it is not impossible to combine the quiet pleasures of a small resort with the night-time buzz of a larger place. Because of the built-up nature of the coastline, small developments are only a mile or so away from big resorts. Many people, therefore, take a taxi into town for an evening out – taxi fares are low and a two-mile journey is likely to cost around £2.

Wherever you go in Spain, the chances are that there is a local fiesta going on somewhere in the locality. Do make the effort to go and see one of these at night: the dancing, feasting and celebrating are particularly infectious and enjoyable by torchlight. Details of local fiestas can be obtained from the local tourist offices, or before you go, from the Spanish Tourist Office in London.

COMMUNICATIONS

There are no problems keeping in touch from Spain. International telephone calls can be made direct from most telephone kiosks and it is equally possible to telegraph, write or telex Britain from Spain.

Post Offices

Post offices (*correos*) are open from 8-12 noon and from 5 – 7.30pm.

The mail service between Spain and Britain is *reasonably* efficient: the delivery time varies from a week to ten days. As for prices, it will cost about 20p to send a postcard to Britain, and around 23p to send a letter.

Nearly all the main post offices operate *Poste Restante* facilities, and mail should be addressed to the *Lista de Correos* (*Poste Restante*) in the town and province where you are staying. Remember, you may be required to produce your passport as proof of your identity before mail may be collected.

Telephones

International telephone calls can be made from most public telephone kiosks in major cities or from special telephone exchange bureaux (*central de teléfonos*). Cabins accept 50 peseta, 25 peseta and 5 peseta coins.

There are direct dialling links between Britain and Spain, so to dial home, first place a 50 peseta coin in the slot, and dial 07 for an international line. Wait for a higher tone, then dial the country code – for Britain this is 44 – followed by the area code (minus the initial 0). So if, for example, you were phoning London the full code would be 07 44 1.

Emergency services in Spain may be reached by dialling 091.

MOVING AROUND THE COUNTRY

There are a number of ways to move about the country. Train, local bus services, coach tours and car hire are all possible modes of travel for those who want to see a bit more of Spain.

If it is a sightseeing trip to one of the major attractions you're interested in, then there are plenty of bus companies taking visitors to and fro on day trips. Information and tickets can usually be obtained from travel agents. Otherwise, local buses are a good way to travel if you're based in a coastal resort but want to visit one of the inland market towns.

The train network on the mainland criss-crosses the country extensively. There are usually express trains linking larger centres along the coast with important cities, such as Barcelona or Seville, or for shorter jaunts to neighbouring villages, the provincial trains stop at practically every small town on the track.

Car hire is another option, albeit a rather expensive one, unless there is a group of you sharing the costs of hire and petrol. Roads along the southern coast of the mainland are poor, considering the volume of traffic which thunders along them during the summer months, but the good news is that extensive upgrading is currently in operation. Things get better when you join the motorway at Murcia on the Costa Blanca, and from then on it's a straight run along the coast, through Barcelona and to the French/Spanish border.

Car-Hire

There are many local car-hire firms in Spain itself, but it usually works out cheaper – and safer – to book before you go either through one of the international car-hire firms or your tour operator. If you hire in this country in advance of your holiday, you will be paying a fixed price which is not dependent upon currency fluctuations. By waiting until you get to Spain, you'll soon find that prices (especially during peak season) will be high and subject to change. Reserving ahead also means a car is assured when you arrive in Spain, whereas by waiting until you get there, you may well find that, during peak season, the car-hire firms are busy and no cars are available.

If you're hiring ahead in this country, there are two options open to you – to go through your tour operator, or to book ahead with a large car-hire company, such as Hertz, Budget or Avis. Most of the major tour operators now offer car-hire facilities. Often the prices quoted are at specially negotiated rates with local car-hire firms, and are much cheaper than could be obtained if you were shopping around by yourself. Usually the cost of car hire through tour companies includes local taxes, unlimited mileage, delivery and collection to and from your hotel, and some kind of insurance policy. The disadvantage of booking with tour operators is that this facility is inflexible; you often have to reserve your car either when you book your holiday or at least a month in advance of arriving in the country.

By contrast, major car-hire companies only require bookings of up to seven days in advance before supplying you with a car in Spain. Car hire generally works out more expensive with a major car-hire firm – primarily because their prices exclude local tax charges. However, on the plus side, you do have the back-up and facilities of an international company. Obviously the rates and services available differ from firm to firm, but usually, if you hire through one of the international firms, you get unlimited mileage, third-party insurance and an emergency break-down service. There is normally no charge for delivering cars to a different town, as long as the car-hire firm operates there, otherwise you will be expected to pay collection expenses (usually about 10p a mile from the nearest depot). As with tour-company car hire, petrol and fines for driving offences are the driver's own responsibility.

If you are thinking about hiring through one of the major agencies, Avis is the largest car-hire company in Europe and also, in our experience, one of the best. It operates in ninety-three countries, its prices are among the most competitive, and its service is hard to beat. If you hire your car before you go, you get a guaranteed price which cannot be altered whatever happens to exchange rates, and you also have much more of a come-back if things go wrong. You can book either through your travel agent or through an Avis office.

For those of you who do not want to commit yourself to car hire until you see the resort, or more importantly, find out what the weather is doing once you're there, Avis operates a scheme called 'Driveaway Cheques'. This allows you to buy cheques in the UK, on a no-commission basis, and to choose car rental on the days you want, paying with these cheques. All the paperwork and hanging around is done in the UK, so no time is wasted when abroad, and you are entitled to all the same conditions of rental as if you had hired the car in advance: guaranteed price, unlimited mileage, etc.

If you choose not to hire a car after all, the vouchers can simply be traded back in the UK at face value, so no money is lost. For flexibility and value this scheme makes a lot of sense, though obviously if you are going to a busy resort in peak season you would still be better advised to make a definite booking in advance, as there can be no guarantee that the car you want will be there on the day you want it.

At regards documentation, an international driving licence is necessary and can be obtained from the AA or RAC motoring organizations. In practice your British licence may suffice. The minimum age for driving a hired car is twenty-one and you must have held a driving licence for a minimum of one year (two years in Majorca and Ibiza). Third-party insurance is compulsory for driving in Spain. Rates that are offered by tour companies are usually inclusive of third-party insurance, local taxes and a collision damage waiver. If you're freelancing with a local Spanish firm, make sure you know what kind of insurance cover is included in the basic price. Car-hire companies in Spain normally ask for a refundable deposit to be paid in advance.

There are two grades of petrol available: 97 octane (super) and 92 octane (normal). Expect to pay about 50p per litre for super, and 40p per litre for normal. Diesel can also be purchased at around 30p per litre.

Trains

There is an assortment of different trains to choose from in Spain, depending on the length of your journey and how much money you have to spend.

For long-haul journeys, the best advice is to stick to the expresses (*Talgos*, TER and ELT). These trains are the most expensive to travel on, but for comfort and luxury they rival the best that France has to offer. Other alternatives are the ordinary *rápidos*, or the provincial *correos* and *tranvías* which crawl along at an excruciatingly slow pace.

Trains get very crowded and busy during the summer months, so if you are planning to go to a major tourist attraction (e.g. Barcelona), it is advisable to play safe and book a seat in advance. Reservations are obligatory anyway for all express trains.

Buses

The bus network is extensive, linking up hill villages and market towns which are not otherwise served by public transport. Prices are reasonable, ranging from 20p for city routes to £1.50 for trips of around ten to twenty miles.

Details about services may be obtained from bus stations or tourist offices, although in small places hand-written timetables outside a bus shelter or bus stop may be your only source of reliable information. Remember that most services are reduced or cease altogether on Sundays.

Taxis

Taxis (distinguished by their black and white colour) are cheap: a journey of two or three miles to a neighbouring resort is likely to be £2 – £4, while a trip within town usually costs less than £1.

Extras are charged for large amounts of luggage, for trips outside town limits (especially to airports) and for late-night journeys.

Most taxis are metered, and when free have a *libre* sign displayed during the day-time, and a green light illuminated at night. In larger places there are usually ranks, otherwise taxis may be hailed from the street. Even the smallest resort is likely to have two or three taxis, and these can usually be found in the main square or along the seafront.

PROBLEMS/EMERGENCIES

Medical

If it's a minor problem, head for a chemist. There should be at least one all-night chemist in town, and *farmacias* usually have the name and address of this displayed clearly in their windows. If it's more serious, go to the nearest hospital or phone an ambulance (dial 091).

Police

The police (*la policía*) must be contacted if any of your belongings have been stolen. Insist on a copy of your statement – insurance companies often require this as proof of theft before they will reimburse you. It is also a good idea to inform your travel rep. Telephone 091 in emergencies.

Embassies and Consulates

The British Embassy in Madrid is at Cala de Fernando el Santo (Tel: 341 419020).

The British Consulate in **Algeciras** is at Avenida de las Fuerzas Armadas 11; **Málaga** at Duquesa de Parcent 4; **Alicante** at Plaza Calvo Sotelo 1 – 2; **Tarragona** at Santián 4; **Barcelona** at Diagonal

477; **Palma de Mallorca (Majorca)** at Plaza Mayor 3D; **Eivissa (Ibiza)** at Avenida Isidoro Macabich 45.

Work

There are not many openings for long-term work in Spain. Teaching English is an option, but a TEFL or equivalent qualification is usually necessary for procuring a reasonably well-paid and reputable job. Au-pair work is another possibility, and vacancies are advertised in the columns of newspapers and magazines in this country as well as English newspapers for ex-patriates in Spain. If you speak fluent Spanish, British travel firms sometimes hire seasonal couriers. Similarly, people with a particular sporting skill (such as a qualified sailing instructor) can often find a summer job with a tour operator that specializes in activity holidays. Otherwise, the usual range of over-worked, underpaid jobs are available in bars and restaurants around the major holiday resorts on the Mediterranean.

Women

Spanish resorts and towns are fairly cosmopolitan, and there are no real problems about wandering around in shorts and T-shirts during the day. If you're going out at night, the usual warnings apply: stick to well-lit areas and take a taxi in preference to walking home alone. If any trouble develops, make as much noise as you can.

A few Spanish resorts have a bad reputation for petty theft and bag-snatching. To minimize risks, don't wander around with your handbag slung over your shoulder – wear it crossed over your chest, as the locals do, and under no circumstances leave any sort of bags unattended.

A Potted History of Spain

The colourful and turbulent history of Spain begins fairly inaus-
piciously in 14000BC, when Palæolithic men lived and hunted in the
north of the country. The traces of these tribes may be seen in
colourful cave paintings and monolithic monuments which can still be
seen in Basque territory today. After the Palæolithic period, a
succession of peoples drifted into the peninsula – firstly the Iberians,
who migrated from North Africa and settled round the coastal area of
Almería, then the Celts who came from the heartland of central
Europe to establish strongholds throughout the country.

Civilization proper began with the arrival of the sea-faring Phoenicians, around the twelfth century BC, and there began the establishment of maritime trading posts along the Spanish coastline, the
most important of which was Cádiz, on the Costa de la Luz. Because
of its strategic position on the western edge of Europe, Spain played
an important part in the dynasties and empires of the ancient world
with the Carthaginians, the Greeks and the Romans all holding sway
over the Iberian peninsula at some point during their histories.
However, it was under the auspices of the Romans that Spain
particularly flourished. The country became the largest outpost of the
Roman empire, and the remains of splendid Roman monuments and
buildings can still be seen in modern-day Spain, most notably at
Córdoba and Tarragona. The collapse of the Roman empire in the
Iberian peninsula was heralded by the incursions of the Huns and
Visigoths in the fourth century AD although it was not until the
Muslim conquest began in the eighth century that the dominance of
the ancient world began to wane.

Under Moorish rule, Spain became a centre of education and
enlightenment at a time when most of northern Europe was still
submerged in the Dark Ages. Agriculture, architecture and schol-
arship flourished, and a sample of the incredible achievements of
Moorish craftsmen may be seen in the remarkable monuments at
Córdoba and Granada. However, five centuries of relative prosperity
and civilization drew to an end in the thirteenth century when the

reconquest of Spain began to gain ground, spearheaded by the Christian kings of Léon, Castile, Aragon and Navarre. By 1242, the Moorish kingdom was reduced to a remnant, centring around the stronghold of Granada. The rest of the peninsula was carved up into the four great Spanish kingdoms, which continued to remain administratively and politically independent for a hundred years after the reconquest. The first significant step towards unification of the peninsula came in the fourteenth century, when two of Spain's largest and most powerful kingdoms, Castile and Aragon, were joined together through the influential marriage of Ferdinand of Castile and Isabelle of Aragon.

Under the rule of Ferdinand and Isabelle, religious fervour was renewed in the shape of the Inquisition which sought to drive out heretics – especially Jews and Muslims – from the country. In 1492, the reconquest of Granada took place and within a few years, the remaining Moors had either been expelled or converted to Christianity. The year 1492 was significant for events abroad, as well as at home. The historical discovery of the Americas was made by Christopher Columbus and so began a period of Spanish colonization, which was to last for two centuries. In 1517 Ferdinand died and was succeeded by his son Charles I.

Under Charles' rule, the Golden Age of Spain began. Wealth flowed into the country from colonies rich in mineral and natural resources. At home, the Spanish empire was extended when Charles succeeded to the Hapsburg throne, thus gaining control of the Netherlands, Germany and Austria. However, despite the wealth and power of the Roman church in Europe, the teachings of Martin Luther in Germany soon spread throughout Europe, forcing Charles to concede some degree of religious freedom. In 1556, Philip II succeeded his father and as a fanatically devout Catholic, rigorously defended the religion against the Protestants' heresy. The Counter-Reformation was launched and the Inquisition re-instated, within a few years of the sovereign coming to the throne. In 1558, after a period of political intrigue and physical intimidation, Philip took the Portuguese throne – a prize which had been much coveted by Spanish kings for many years. A further attempt for Catholic supremacy was made in 1588 when the Armada sailed to overthrow the Protestant monarch, Elizabeth I, in England. The humiliating defeat which the fleet suffered at the hands of the Protestant forces has become a milestone in English naval history.

The beginning of the seventeenth century marked the decline of Spain as a world power. Costly wars were waged as more and more colonies revolted against colonial rule, putting a severe financial drain on the monarch's resources. The decline was further hastened at the beginning of a ten-year War of Spanish Succession, which the country could ill afford to finance. Conflicting claims to the throne were lodged by Philip V of Spain and Archduke Charles of Austria, who had the backing of British troops. By the end of the war, the British had successfully seized Gibraltar and Philip was stripped of territories in Belgium, Luxembourg and Italy.

Spain's involvement with the Napoleonic Wars led to further defeat, most notably by the British at Trafalgar in 1807. A period of political intrigue and confusion ensued, which ended when Napoleon's brother, Joseph, was installed on the throne. Popular outrage at this move initiated an allegiance between Britain and Spain, which resulted in a series of successful campaigns, until Wellington finally defeated the French at the battle of Vitoria in 1813.

The first signs of the democratic spirit also emerged in the nineteenth century when the *Cortes* (parliament) was set up with a chamber of democratically elected representatives. However, when Philip V was established on the throne he moved swiftly to stamp out the *Cortes*, which he rightly saw as a threat to the monarch's right to rule. The abolition of the *Cortes* had far-reaching effects and over the next fifty years there were to be many bitter, and sometimes bloody, clashes between the liberals, who favoured democratic government, and the monarchists who stoutly defended the sovereign's autocratic powers.

In the lead-up to the First World War, popular unrest was germinating among the lower echelons of Spanish society. Denied of any say in government, the peasants and workers found themselves bearing the brunt of the worsening economic situation, while the wealthy continued to live in the style to which they were accustomed. Spain stayed neutral during the war, but afterwards, as all the western world felt the effects of the post-war depression, inflation soared to new heights and the nation entered into an ill-timed and costly war attempting to defend its territorial rights in Morocco.

In 1923, the disillusionment among the people was sufficient for a military coup to take place under the auspices of General Primo de Rivera. The right-wing dictatorship was short-lived. Although a brief period of prosperity ensued, the harsh restrictive practices which the administration pursued resulted in the exile of Primo de Rivera only seven years after the government's overthrow. Over the next five years, in the run-up to the Civil War, the country was in turmoil. Several new political parties emerged: the separatist movements in Basque, Catalonia and Galicia; the socialist and communist parties; and the right-wing Falangists headed by Primo de Rivera's son. In 1936, a left-wing coalition narrowly won the general election, but subsequently failed to carry out its election promises of agrarian or economic reform. Increasing militancy among low-paid workers resulted in crippling strikes, while right-wing anger was fomented by the imprisonment of the Falangists' leader and the murder of another leading right-winger. On 17 July 1936, General Franco led a military rebellion in Morocco, and the Civil War had begun.

The ensuing war between the nationalists and the republicans was one of the most violent and bloody that the world has seen. Indiscriminate slaughter took place as whole villages and towns were laid to waste in a war that tore the country apart. However, as the war dragged on over three years, it emerged that the nationalists, with the help of fascist Italy and Germany, were gaining the upper hand. The fall of Barcelona to the nationalists in January 1939 signalled the end of the bitter war, and Franco quickly established a dictatorship which was to last for thirty-six years. In the immediate aftermath of the war, there were terrifying repercussions for those who had fought on the side of the republicans: dissenters were mercilessly hunted down and executed, and concentration camps were established until all opposition to the dictatorship had been eliminated.

Ravaged by the effects of the Civil War, Spain again remained neutral during the Second World War. Economic reconstruction over the next fifteen years was painfully slow as the country was spurned by neighbouring, western democracies. It was not until 1953, when an agreement was reached with the United States to establish American air-bases on Spanish soil, that an upturn in the country's fortunes was indicated. The new prosperity brought with it the first signs of a fledgling tourist industry, as the first holiday-makers from northern Europe were able to enjoy the natural assets of Spain's beautiful coastline.

In the latter years of his dictatorship, Franco's reign was shaken in the revival of nationalist activity in the Basque area. Terrorist attacks began, and the disaffection which was felt throughout the country was articulated through major strikes which brought industrial activity to a halt. In an attempt to regain full control of the country, Franco once again exercised horrific repressive tactics, with the full-scale persecution and torture of Basque nationalists, which culminated in mass executions in August 1975.

Franco died six months later, on 20 November 1975, and King Juan Carlos was nominated as his successor. From the beginning, Juan Carlos met with renewed and persistent demands for democratic government. Recognizing the frailty of his right-wing dictatorship, the king bowed to popular pressure and set in motion political reforms.

The first free multi-party elections were held in July 1977, and the democratic system of election has continued in use up to the present day, the only crisis occurring in 1981 when an abortive right-wing coup was attempted. Today, the dominant figure in Spanish politics is Felipe Gonzalez, leader of the Socialist Workers' Party. Gonzalez, who has been in government since 1982, has had the difficult task of holding together a country which still feels the effect of severe political and economic divisions. The problem of Basque terrorism still remains, despite frequent negotiations to appease the separatists, while from an economic point of view, there has been the immense task of mass unemployment and raging inflation to tackle. Entry into the Common Market in 1986 was one positive step towards increased prosperity – the booming industry of tourism and the foreign wealth which it brings into the country is another.

Tourism is one of Spain's great success stories. Since the first package holiday-makers started arriving on its shores over thirty years ago, Spain has rapidly adapted to the demands of holiday-makers by offering a range of accommodation, top-class sporting facilities and entertainment provision at prices which are unrivalled by any of its Mediterranean competitors. But despite the development, the beauty of Spain's long, golden beaches and warm azure seas remains undimmed and it is this that draws back hundreds of thousands of people each year to discover afresh the charm and friendliness of Spanish climes.

Part Four

THE COUNTRY

The Balearic Islands

San Antonio Abad

Santa Eulalia del Río

IBIZA

FORMENTERA

BALEARIC ISLANDS

Inca

Lluchmayor

Felanitx

MALLORCA

Ciudadela

MENORCA

Mahon

MAJORCA

Introduction

Majorca, or Mallorca as it is known in Spanish, is the largest of the Balearic Islands and has been one of Europe's principal holiday destinations for a couple of decades now. It lies 112 miles south-east of Barcelona and the fact that the island measures nearly 1,500 square miles is a statistic many visitors find surprising. Majorca deserves its reputation as an outstanding all-round package-holiday destination, particularly as only a relatively small area of the island has been extensively developed for the package market. Parts of the inland remain completely untouched and there are even one or two small stretches of coast which visitors, with the appropriate transport, can escape to if they feel like a break from the packed hotel beaches.

Majorca is a fascinating island and offers a lot more than many people give it credit for. In this chapter, we begin our island tour in the capital Palma and the major resorts around Palma Bay, and then continue clockwise around the coast, concluding with a brief look at the relatively unspoiled interior.

History

Little evidence survives of Majorca's early history: prehistoric settlers are known to have lived on all three main Balearic islands but by far the best evidence of this survives on Menorca in the form of three distinctive varieties of stone monuments. The Moors occupied the island for several hundred years between the ninth and thirteenth centuries, although little evidence survives from this period. The impressive cathedral in Palma was started just after the Moorish occupation on the site of a magnificent mosque, and likewise the Almundaina Palace in Palma was originally a Moorish construction, but virtually all of the original medieval building has been rebuilt and altered since the thirteenth century.

By the nineteenth century, when the island was firmly in Spanish control, Majorca began to receive more and more visitors from further afield on more peaceful missions than the earlier Moors. Austro-Hungarian dukes, German princes, frustrated artists looking for inspiration and even great composers like Chopin found their way to the island's shores. Modern-style package-holiday tourism took off rapidly from the mid-sixties, and has flourished ever since. Unlike neighbouring Menorca, the Majorcans embraced the influx of foreign visitors and capital with open arms and the result today is many of the best-equipped, if rather over-developed, package resorts in Europe.

Getting There

Majorca has one airport, a reasonably large international, just outside Palma. Most visitors to the island are British, and nearly all arrive as part of a package holiday by air via Palma. Scheduled daily internal flights are possible to Madrid, Barcelona, Valencia and Ibiza. There are ferry connections between Palma and Barcelona and Valencia, both of which take between eight and nine hours depending on the weather. There are also inter-island connections between Palma and Ibiza Town (about five hours), and Alcudia and Ciudadela on the western side of Menorca.

Climate

In common with all the Balearic Islands, Majorca enjoys a long, hot summer with little wind and practically no rain, by British standards. By May the average temperature is up to around 22°C (72°F) reaching a peak in July and August around 29°C (84°F). The temperature varies from 14°C (57°F) to 18°C (65°F) between November and March. June and July are the best months for sunshine, with approximately eleven hours a day. October and November tend to be changeable and March is invariably the wettest month.

Culinary Specialities

As you might expect of an island with such a high turnover of foreign visitors, hotel and restaurant food has a very international flavour to it in order to appeal to as many tastes as possible. Majorcan specialities include *sopas mallorquinas* which are vegetables soaked in garlic and baked with bread beneath, to soak up the juices, and usually a piece of meat on top; and *fritos mallorquinos*, a filling and very rich fried dish made up of liver, kidney and potatoes. British-style food is widely available in the resorts.

Where to Go for What

The Sunlover and the Socialite will love Majorca. **Arenal** is the most commercialized resort on the island and offers superb possibilities for both these categories, together with the Sportsperson. A new Aqua Park, opened in 1987, is perfect for the kids. There are a number of excellent beach resorts and one or two of the best are **Cala Mesquida, Cala San Vicente** and **Alcudia. Callas de Mallorca** is perfect for Family Holidays, and the Recluse may enjoy any of the inland villages which are still relatively quiet and undeveloped.

The Coast

PALMA is best described as a small city. It has an unmistakable island feel (not least the large harbour) but it has the sights, sounds, population, and facilities which more than qualify it as one of Spain's smallest, but most vibrant, cities. The city is known as *Ciutat de Mallorca* in the local dialect and contains more than half the population of all the Balearic Islands combined. Palma was an important link in the medieval kingdom of Aragon, and enjoyed most influence between the thirteenth and sixteenth centuries. Many of the great Italianate mansions which you can still see in Palma date from this period of its history.

The city's port is by far the largest and busiest in the Balearics as, indeed, is its airport, a few miles outside the city. It doesn't have the largest natural harbour, though, as that honour belongs to the Menorcan capital of Mahón which has the second largest in the world, after Pearl Harbour in the United States.

Palma is a sightseer's paradise, an interesting city with a large collection of famous sights reflecting its history over the last thousand or so years. All the main attractions are located within a relatively short distance of the harbour and can be covered on foot or by using the impressive city bus network, making sightseeing a painless affair.

The best place to start your tour of the city is in the old town. The magnificent **cathedral** dominates the old town from a hill overlooking the seafront. There are too few superlatives to describe what is undoubtedly one of Spain's finest ecclesiastical buildings: few mainland cathedrals can rival this famous structure whose unique architecture evolved over a period of more than five centuries. The honey-coloured limestone building is essentially Gothic, with its huge flying buttresses and enormous pillars, and was built on the site of a grand mosque which had been the ecclesiastical centre of the Balearics during the centuries of Moorish occupation. One interesting feature of this fascinating building is the large canopy which hangs above the main altar. This was designed by Antonio Gaudí and completed in 1904; its twisted wrought-ironwork looks oddly suited for the cathedral.

There is a small **museum** in the adjoining chapterhouse. It is open daily from 10am – 1pm and 4pm – 6.30pm, and houses an interesting collection of pottery, silverware, coins and other items dating back to early Christian times, which are associated with the cathedral.

Directly opposite the cathedral is the **Palacio de la Almundaina**, one of Spain's most impressive Moorish buildings and the former home of both the Moorish *walis* and later Majorcan kings. Most of the building dates from between the thirteenth and fifteenth centuries. It is only possible to look round it on one of the frequent guided tours. These are conducted in three languages, including English, and it's worth mentioning that a substantial part of the palacio, which visitors aren't shown, is still in regular use as the island's official State Apartments. Once a year King Juan Carlos holds a ceremonial assembly here and, as you might expect, this is the central public event in the island calendar. The palacio is open from 9.30am – 12.30pm and again from 4pm – 6.30pm Monday to Saturday. The surrounding **gardens** are worth a look as well.

Just down from the gardens is the **Provincial Arts Museum**, an attractive building which used to be the city's old stock exchange in the days most towns and cities had their own money market, and modern-day international dealing was a distant dream. Admission is free and the museum is open from 9am – 1pm, and again from 5pm – 9pm. Until a few years ago Palma also had a fascinating maritime museum near the arts building. Unfortunately this has been closed for some time so don't be misled by information in older guide-books which recommend it.

After the cathedral, a good runner-up to the title of Majorca's finest ecclesiastical building is the **Basílica de San Francisco** in the Plaza San Francisco. Open daily from 9am – 1pm, this imposing Gothic building is reputed to have been built on the site of a Moorish soap factory! Most of the church dates from the 1300s, although its striking façade was added in the seventeenth century. Inside you can see one of the most remarkable cloisters in any Majorcan church, and also the tomb of the distinguished medieval theological philosopher Ramon Llull who died in 1315.

Another of Palma's older sights is the **Castillo de Bellver**, located on a hill in the Terreno district which overlooks most of the city and the harbour. The Castillo is a fourteenth-century fort, remarkably well preserved and with three striking circular towers and a large cylindrical keep. It is open most days from 9am until sunset, a time of day when the views are particularly spectacular. It is well worth the climb for the views alone.

Calle Morey was one of the main streets in old Palma, and it is still a good location in which to admire the architecture of many of the city's older buildings. Look out for the **Arco de la Almudaina** and further down, once the street opens out onto the Plaza Santa Eulalia, an attractive **Gothic church**. The city's main public building, the **Ayuntamiento**, sits on the left of the square and is another typically fine example of Renaissance architecture.

The city of Palma offers a superb range of nightlife. Most activity is concentrated around Palma Bay, which is one of the liveliest resorts in Europe, although there are a growing number of increasingly popular discos and nightclubs in the old town. These are concentrated in the Plaza Gomila, in the Terreno district. 'In' places vary from year to year but two of the most popular discos are **Club de Mar** and **Bar Bellver**. **El Hexagono** is much more exclusive, and a popular choice for young visitors is **Bésame Mucho**.

Eating out is one of the real pleasures of both the old capital and the adjoining Palma Bay. There is a remarkable range of cafés and restaurants, and this changes constantly as the number of visitors to the island continues to grow. **Pizzeria El Padrino** (Tel: 401 962) along Juan de Saridakis is a good choice for an informal bite to eat most hours of the day.

Three of Palma's best restaurants are **Le Bistrot** (Tel: 287 175), a French-style bistro along the Teodoro Llorente whose menu ranges from Burgundian snails to locally caught seafood served in a delicious selection of French sauces; **El Portalón** (Tel: 237 866) is a romantic old courtyard restaurant, at Bellver 9, specializing in *nouvelle cuisine* Majorcan style; and **Plat Pla** (Tel: 232 066) which is reckoned to be one of the island's most stylish (and expensive) restaurants with a good range of Italian dishes on the menu.

Finding somewhere to stay in Palma can be a real problem for the independent traveller. Among the better package hotels are the four-star **Palas Atenea Sol** (Tel: 281 400) situated on the Pasco Maritimo with commanding views of the harbour and wide bay. The

Palas is a very modern building, and has 370 rooms, all with private bathrooms and air-conditioning. Nearby, the three-star **Costa Azul** (Tel: 231 940) overlooks the marina. This relaxing building is just five minutes from the city centre and an interesting feature is its heated indoor swimming pool on the third floor well away from traffic noise. For a very luxurious break, however, you should consider staying at the five-star **Son Vida** (Tel: 451 011) built from a converted medieval castle about four miles outside the capital. The hotel is part of the worldwide Sheraton Hotel Group so you can expect typical Sheraton standards of comfort. There are 175 well-appointed bedrooms, and sports facilities are excellent.

A little way round the bay from the old capital is the first of several large resorts: **PLAYA DE PALMA.** Playa is bordered by two other major resorts, **C'AN PASTILLA** and **ARENAL**, and with each summer season that passes it becomes increasingly more difficult to tell them apart. The two main features all three resorts have in common is access to a superb beach, and an excellent range of large purpose-built package-holiday hotels.

All three resorts stretch down to a magnificent sandy stretch of coast which runs for over two miles around the Bay of Palma. A busy main road separates the beach from the hotels, but there are plenty of pelican crossings to ensure that holiday-makers can cross back and forwards as often and as safely as possible. The beach itself slopes gently so is ideal for children. It is dominated by regimented rows of parasols which will cost you a couple of hundred pesetas to sit under – so be warned! It is always busy: the number of visitors from the resorts alone would ensure that was always the case, but day-trippers from other resorts, and locals from the capital soon swell the number of toasting sunlovers.

The beach at **PLAYA DE PALMA** has a huge range of water-sports available: the enormous beach and idyllic bay location make it a perfect choice for the enthusiast, and any of the main hotels will have details of precisely what sports are available on any given day. Another obvious attraction of Playa as a resort is the short transfer time from the airport – just fifteen minutes compared with up to an hour and a half for resorts like Cala Millor and Cala Bona on the other side of the island.

There is a good selection of souvenir shops, cafés, bars and restaurants clustered around the centre of the resort. Even so, Playa de Palma is not Majorca's best resort, by any stretch of the imagination, for nightlife. What there is tends to be concentrated around the major hotels. This resort would be best suited for younger families, or perhaps the older holiday-maker who might appreciate the short transfer time, good beach and maybe the occasional opportunity to let their hair down in the evening.

There are at least three dozen hotels used by British tour operators in Playa de Palma. They are mostly three-star hotels, although a couple of slightly better four-star options do stand out. The **Garonda** (Tel: 262 200) is a very eye-catching modern building directly opposite the beach. It has 116 bedrooms, all with private bathrooms and balconies, and is ideal for older couples. Casual dress is not welcome and the regular programme of entertainment is unlikely to appeal to many younger visitors. The **Playa de Palma Sol** (Tel: 262 900) is the less comfortable of the two, but nevertheless offers typical standards of Sol Group comfort and entertainment. This four-star hotel has 125 bedrooms built over five floors and sits next to the three-star **Tropical Sol** (Tel: 262 150).

Among the three-star hotels, one of the best is the **Cristobal Colon** (Tel: 262 75) which is an extremely attractive hotel, opened in 1986, and situated in the most convenient part of Playa de Palma close to the beach and the resort centre. The Cristobal Colon has two wings of different heights giving this hotel a smarter than average exterior; inside, the hotel is bright and airy, and the style of decor and furnishings conveys a surprisingly authentic Spanish feel. The buffet-style evening meal, fire safety precautions and facilities for children and adults alike are superb.

Two other popular three-star hotels are the family-owned **Ayron Park** (Tel: 260 650), which sits a couple of minutes back from the sandy beach, and was one of the first modern hotels built on this part of the island when it opened nearly thirty years ago; and the **Bali** (Tel: 262 700) which has 264 rooms within ten minutes of the beach, and offers live music twice weekly and the occasional disco.

Little distinguishes Playa de Palma from next-door **ARENAL** (sometimes known as El Arenal). It shares the same two-mile stretch of beach, only all the hotels are naturally a little way further round the bay. There is still confusion about where one resort ends and another starts but that shouldn't affect your holiday in any way as facilities available in all the resorts around Palma Bay are pretty similar.

Arenal is easily the most commercialized resort on Majorca. It is wall-to-wall with large hotels, busy bars and cafés, crowded souvenir shops and young people having fun. It is an environment most visitors to Majorca love, but if you are unfortunate enough to arrive here expecting a relaxing couple of weeks on the beach, then forget it. Each summer, the place is virtually taken over by British and (increasingly) German holiday-makers; this is package travel at its most clichéd and you will either love it or hate it.

In its favour, of course, Arenal offers some fine nightlife, excellent beach facilities, and it is well connected (by road and rail) to the rest of the island, so excursions are not a problem. All the major tour operators will have an organized programme of day trips available at your hotel if you prefer not to explore the island independently.

A large number of the older hotels are concentrated around the eastern end of the resort, close to a small fishing harbour which survives as a gentle reminder of the bay's main industry before tourism developed on a large scale. The newer hotels have largely been built along the back of the main resort. Rather surprisingly, the range of hotels is more limited than in the slightly smaller resort of Playa de Palma.

The best hotel is probably the four-star **Delta** (Tel: 264 754), part of an impressive new development about six miles out of Arenal. A full range of facilities and evening entertainment is available, and all 288 bedrooms have private bathrooms and either a forest or garden view. A quality three-star hotel in a quieter part of the main resort is the **Copacabana** (Tel: 261 766). It has an impressive programme of lively entertainment, perfect for young singles. Its one drawback is the fifteen minute trek to the sandy beach.

Two other popular two-star hotels in Arenal are the **Bahamas** (Tel: 263 200) and the **Torre Arenal** (Tel: 263 850). The Bahamas is one of the best value hotels in the resort, situated on high ground in the Son Veri part of the town. It is a member of the Barcelo group, and has 259 bedrooms, all with private bathroom and balcony. The Torre

Arenal has a lively atmosphere and a popular sun terrace roof. It has 115 rooms on eleven narrow floors, and is located within five or six minutes' walk from the beach.

Continuing along the large beach from Playa de Palma and Arenal, the resort of **C'AN PASTILLA** has grown up. It lies near the main flight-path leading into Palma airport and, although the noise is seldom obtrusive, the constant sight of charter jets landing and taking off might be. The stretch of beach nearest the main hotels in C'an Pastilla is clean, wide and ideal for children. Nearly all the big hotels have excellent facilities for looking after and entertaining children so if you have a young family this would be an ideal resort to consider.

An attractive little harbour adjoins the main beach, and there are plenty of cafés, bars, small restaurants and souvenir shops. Most of the popular hotels have some form of organized evening entertainment, although that could be anything from a fancy dress 'theme' evening to a lively disco.

Like its neighbouring resorts around this wide bay, C'an Pastilla has a wide selection of hotel accommodation available. It is virtually impossible to find anywhere here during the summer months which has not been pre-booked by the large tour operators, so independent travellers looking for somewhere to stay should steer well clear of the whole area.

The hotel rated highest by the Spanish tourist authorities is the four-star **Alexandra Sol** (Tel: 262 350), a very attractive six-storey building with 164 twin bedrooms and an excellent programme of regular entertainment. The hotel is well furnished, and certainly not lacking in either character or atmosphere.

Los Almendros (Tel: 260 462) is a pleasant three-star hotel which is still family-run and offers relatively peaceful accommodation in its 91 bedrooms. It is in the heart of the resort, and just two minutes away from the beach. Another popular three-star hotel is the **Oasis** (Tel: 260 150) which sits directly opposite the beach, on the other side of a busy main road. This 110-room hotel is recommended for visitors without children as although the convenience of the sandy beach is an attractive feature, the close proximity of a major road should be taken into consideration.

Among the numerous two-star hotels, two worth considering are the **Cisne** (Tel: 261 400) quite close to the beach (although care is needed in the swimming pool as the shallow end shelves suddenly with no obvious warning signs) and the **Apollo** (Tel: 262 500) which has 151 twin bedrooms in a quiet location overlooking the entire bay. A live band plays regularly in the Apollo (you may find some brochures spelling the name of this hotel with just one 'l'.)

Continuing round the bay, in a clockwise direction after Palma, you will again come across another group of three resorts closely bunched together immediately before you reach Palma Nova and Magaluf, two more of Spain's premier resorts which have developed around Palma Bay. CALA MAYOR, SAN AUGUSTIN and C'AS CATALA have grown up near to the old Palma-to-Andraitx coast road and, of the three, Cala Mayor is the largest resort with about a dozen British tour companies offering holidays there each summer.

None of the three has a separate identity, and it is only fair to say that there is no obvious dividing line between them. All three have a good selection of shops, cafés and restaurants to suit most tastes: the local traders recognize the high percentage of British holiday-makers who come here and, consequently, you can expect most shopkeepers to speak good English, and most cafés and restaurants to offer dishes that will appeal to the unadventurous British palate. The three resorts overlook a narrow stretch of sandy beach. It is safe for children but very popular so expect it to be crowded. The area generally considered to be San Augustin occupies arguably the finest location of the three resorts as it overlooks the coast road, and many of the hotels offer commanding views across the beach and out to sea. There is a regular bus service from all three resorts into the centre of Palma which is about four or five miles away, depending which end of the development you are staying in.

One of the best known hotels in Cala Mayor is the rather old-fashioned-looking four-star **Nixe Palace** (Tel: 403 811) which has an excellent beach location but the disadvantage of sitting quite close to the noisy main road. It has 132 bedrooms, all with private bathrooms, balcony and sea views, and a small swimming pool surrounded by sun beds for those who prefer not to make the short walk down to the beach.

Most of the other hotels in Cala Mayor are smaller two- and three-star hotels. Two of the better ones, both favourites with a number of tour operators, are the clean two-star **Los Leones** (Tel: 401 413) and the reasonable three-star **Atlas/Rimini** which is actually a tiny complex of two hotels (Tel: 400 812 for Atlas and 400 262 for Rimini).

Los Leones is a well-laid-out hotel, with 75 bedrooms, about ten minutes' walk from a strip of rocky beach. There is a good-sized swimming pool and, in the evenings, live music and discos are occasionally organized. Bedrooms' views are mediocre: those at the front face onto a noisy street and those at the rear look out across the swimming pool. The Atlas/Rimini complex has a total of less than 100 bedrooms, but it is a reasonably quiet hotel more suitable for holiday-makers without a young family (although there is a children's playground available on a separate level from the main outside public area).

Accommodation at nearby San Augustin is much more limited. The best hotel, and easily the most striking on the skyline, is the enormous ten-floor **Belvedere Park** (Tel: 401 411), a 414-bedroom three-star hotel which used to be known as the Jumbo Park Hotel. Facilities are excellent for holiday-makers of all ages who are not looking for a particularly quiet, or 'away-from-it-all' holiday. The beach is a steep fifteen-minute climb away, but you are just ten minutes from the centre of the resort where the shops, nightlife and most popular cafés and bars are located. Try to get a room at the front of the hotel (overlooking the bay) as rear views are limited.

Two other recommended hotels are both modern two-star buildings: the **Cesar** (Tel: 402 362) and **Gran Mallorca** (Tel: 403 261). The Cesar has ten floors, but just 100 bedrooms, so you might find its narrow profile disconcerting at first glance! There are a number of reasonable shops nearby, and the impressive range of entertainment facilities throughout the week makes it ideal for all classes of holiday-makers except young families: The Gran Mallorca, on the other hand, does not really cater for young singles. It has 130 bedrooms over eleven floors, and the views from the upper floors across the bay are spectacular on a clear day. This is a quality hotel for its two-star Spanish tourist-authority grading.

There are very few places to stay in C'as Catala, and this is certainly not a resort to consider if you are looking for much in the way of nightlife or a variety of places to eat out. The best hotel is undoubtedly the old four-star **Maricel** (Tel: 402 712), which has 56 bedrooms overlooking the bay, and sits close to the main stretch of beach. It is a little way from the resort centre but there is an occasional programme of organized entertainment. This hotel would best suit retired holiday-makers or couples looking for a more relaxing holiday within reach of both the capital and a good stretch of beach.

The enormous resorts of **PALMA NOVA** and **MAGALUF** are virtually identical copies of each other. In both cases, a tiny local settlement has been completely engulfed and taken over by tourist development. The end result is effectively one enormous resort offering every conceivable facility and service to the package holiday-maker. Nightlife, watersports, good restaurants and vast stretches of golden sand are the best-known features of both Palma Nova and Magaluf.

The skyline is dominated by dozens of enormous modern hotel buildings offering accommodation to suit all tastes and budgets, with the significant exception of independent travellers working on low finances. Cheap accommodation anywhere in the Palma Bay area is a luxury which has long since gone, so be warned.

Both resorts are extremely lively and you will have no difficulty whatsoever finding a busy disco or swinging nightspot if that is what you are looking for. Practically all the main hotels have a regular programme of organized entertainment, so more often than not you will need to look no further than your hotel lounge for a sample of the cosmopolitan nightlife which Majorca is rightly famous for.

The beach at Palma Nova is a beautiful, long, narrow strip of sand which is flanked by many of the larger hotels. It is one of the most popular stretches of beach in Spain and, as you might expect, is absolutely packed throughout the late spring, summer, and early autumn months. Magaluf's beach follows on from Palma Nova's, and is a long man-made stretch which blends well with the rest of Palma Bay. Both Palma Nova and Magaluf are popular year-round resorts, although it's worth remembering that the weather in Majorca during the British winter months is seldom warm enough to sunbathe or swim comfortably.

Palma Nova and Magaluf offer everything a top package-holiday destination should: nightlife, year-round sunshine (if not year-round sunbathing!), cheap bar prices and virtually non-existent bar hours, and above all a superb range of accommodation options. Choosing who to book with from the two dozen or so British tour operators who offer holidays to either resort will be your most difficult decision, once you've settled on the prospect of holidaying in this part of Spain.

Prices can vary alarmingly for identical holidays – travelling on the same day, from the same airport, to the same hotel – so you must check *all* the brochures you can find and, if necessary, go into two or three travel agents to make sure you've got as complete a 'set' as possible before making a final decision. This advice applies to all holidays, but particularly those in the most popular destinations like Palma Nova and Magaluf.

In this chapter, rather than attempt an objective summary of all the major hotels in both resorts, we've selected have a dozen of the better ones in Palma Nova and Magaluf which will give you a few ideas of those to look out for when you are scanning next summer's brochures.

Two good four-star hotels are the **Comodoro Sol** (Tel: 680 200) and the **Cala Blanca Sol** (Tel: 680 150). The Comodoro Sol occupies a superb position overlooking the beach and has 85 twin or double rooms, each with a private bathroom, sun terrace and sea view. Another advantage is its prime location within a few minutes' walk of the nightlife and shopping centres of both Palma Nova and Magaluf. The Cala Blanca Sol is another of Majorca's very popular Sol hotels, and it also has a great location, close to both the beach and the centre of the resort. It has 180 bedrooms, all with private facilities, and its high standards of furnishing and comfort make it a keen choice with older couples who might spend a little more time relaxing in their hotel rather than letting their hair down.

In the three-star bracket, the **Hotel 33 (Treinta Y Tres)** (Tel: 681 470) and the **Santa Lucia** (Tel: 681 358) are both popular and well recommended. The Hotel 33 is a favourite with young people, as it offers a superb range of water-sports and entertainment for them. It is a bright, modern building with 272 bedrooms, and it's worth pointing out that the hotel is restricted to young people looking for an active, fun-filled holiday.

The Santa Lucia, on the other hand, is more than suitable for most age groups although it is particularly popular with young families because of the excellent child-minding and children's entertainment which is laid on throughout the summer. The 332-room hotel has a commanding location overlooking the beach and is within a short walk of the resort centre.

Both the **Don Bigote** (Tel: 681 162) and the **Dulcinea** (Tel: 680 700) are worthy two-star hotels. The Don Bigote has the edge, primarily because of its location within five minutes of the resort centre. Both hotels are popular with British visitors and offer basic, but comfortable accommodation, with none of the frills you might expect from a hotel in the Spanish tourist authorities' higher rating.

Virtually all the main hotels in Magaluf are either three- or four-star modern buildings. Right on the beach at Magaluf is the four-star **Atlantic** (Tel: 680 208), a popular family-owned hotel with 80 twin bedrooms and perfectly located for you to enjoy the local nightlife, which is just as well as there is no organized entertainment within the hotel. The **Cora Playa Sol** (Tel: 680 562) is yet another fine four-star hotel occupying an outstanding location on the headland between Magaluf and Palma Nova. It has 185 rooms (including, unusually, half a dozen singles) and is well recommended for all types of holiday-maker. In addition to a daily programme of organized games, there is a weekly disco and a live band for the rest of the week.

A final four-star recommendation is the **Magaluf Playa Sol** (Tel: 681 050). From the exterior, it is a rather clumsy-looking modern building in two sections, reaching seven floors on one side, twelve on the other. Inside, though, it is extremely well appointed. There are 317 bedrooms and a lively (if noisy) programme of organized entertainments throughout the day and evening.

Among the various three-star hotels, the **Guadalupe Sol** (Tel: 681 958) is certainly one of Majorca's largest with 488 bedrooms over nine storeys. It is close to a number of shops and bars, but a good ten minutes' walk from the beach. Two other three-star hotels worth noting are the **Playa Marina Sol** (Tel: 402 500) which overlooks the sea and has a good collection of shops within a short walk, and the **Barracuda** (Tel: 681 258) which is simply furnished but offers all the main amenities with none of the extras. This 254-bedroom hotel would be an ideal choice for a couple or young family travelling on a tight budget.

A little way around the headland which marks the end of Palma Bay, and within a couple of miles of Magaluf, are the rapidly growing twin resorts of SANTA PONSA and COSTA DE LA CALMA. These form a picturesque part of the island and most of the resort overlooks a long, clean stretch of sandy beach which is backed by lush pine woods. Although it offers little in the way of shops or nightlife, it has a number of reasonable restaurants and a host of hotels. Bus services into Palma are frequent and efficient, and water-sports are available in abundance for the enthusiast. The beach is invariably crowded, but seldom as packed as those around the bay proper. Even if you're not staying in either of the resorts, it is a good beach to visit for a morning or afternoon excursion.

Two excellent three-star hotels in Santa Ponsa are the **Bahai del Sol** (Tel: 691 161) and the **Rey Don Jaime** (Tel: 690 011). The Bahai del Sol caters for all groups of holiday-makers with the notable exception of young singles looking for the proverbial 'good time'. It has 160 bedrooms and an excellent selection of leisure facilities for residents to enjoy. In addition to two swimming pools, there is a jacuzzi (an uncommon facility in Spanish package hotels), solarium and sauna. The atmosphere is relaxed and friendly, and there is an organized programme of nightly entertainment throughout the summer.

The Rey Don Jaime, on the other hand, is an enormous, fat-looking building with over 400 bedrooms on six floors. Inside, it is well furnished and the atmosphere is relaxed and informal. It has a large swimming pool which is bordered by a lovely sun terrace, and one obvious advantage of the hotel as a whole is its prime location within a few minutes' walk of both the beach and the resort centre.

A couple of other good hotels, both two-star graded, in Santa Ponsa are the **Playa de Majorca** (Tel: 680 400) which has 215 bedrooms over four floors, and the **Casablanca** (Tel: 690 361). Of the two, the Casablanca occupies a noticeably more isolated position. It has 85 bedrooms which all offer excellent views across either the surrounding hills, to the back of the building, or out to sea from rooms at the front. Facilities for chidlren are good, and this would be a sensible choice of hotel for older couples, or even young families who might be looking for a bit of peace and quiet whilst on holiday.

From here, the coast sweeps round sharply past PUERTO ANDRAITX and SAN TELMO before leading into the relatively straight western side of the island. Many visitors to Majorca venture no further than the bright nightspots around Palma Bay and, sadly, miss so much of the real beauty of this green and fertile island. The west coast has a number of sleepy little villages which are perfect for the Recluse, or anyone simply wanting to have a completely peaceful, relaxing break. The contrast with the large Palma Bay resorts could not be more striking.

PRIVATE.
Keep Out

ESTELLENCHS and **BANALBUFAR** are two such secluded villages. Estellenchs is visited by at least one British tour operator. This tiny hamlet sits high up on a hillside looking far out to sea. Facilities are negligible; the nearest town of any size is *Andraitx* a few miles south on a winding mountain road. It is a steep hike down to the small beach nearest the village, but you have the consolation of relative privacy once you get there.

The only place of note where you can stay in Estellenchs is the two-star, family-owned hostel **Maristel** (Tel: 610 282) right at the edge of the village. Each of the 40 bedrooms has a private bathroom, and a number have fine views across the rolling green countryside all around. If you can't face the trek down to the beach, the hostel has a small L-shaped swimming pool.

One or two more tour operators also offer nearby Banalbufar in their summer brochure. The village is similar to Estellenchs, although there are one or two more shops and bars for visitors to explore. The beach is even smaller and more inaccessible than the one at Estellenchs so you'd be well advised to take a bus to one of the more popular beaches around Palma Bay, or else go further east. The undulating scenery around Banalbufar is probably the most striking on Majorca, and the principal attraction of an otherwise unassuming little resort.

Just about the only place where you can stay in Banalbufar is the very pleasant three-star **Mar Y Vent** hostel (Tel: 610 000). It has only 15 bedrooms, all with private bathrooms and balconies offering distant sea views, but advance booking is essential, particularly if you are travelling independently, as it quickly fills up with package tourists.

    ★ ★ ★

A little way up the coast, the fishing village of **PUERTO SÓLLER** is slightly more developed than either Banalbufar or Estellenchs. It is dominated by the picturesque backdrop of hills which surround it on three sides and, as you might imagine, it is a popular spot with day visitors who often make the crowded three-mile tram ride down from the small town of Sóller.

The main attraction of Puerto Sóller is the extremely attractive sandy beach, although in recent years the water has had a reputation for smelling rather foul. It is one of the best of several similar-sized gently curving bays on the island, and this resort is becoming annually more popular with the 18–30 set because of its 'away-from-it-all' beach atmosphere.

Nightlife is reasonable, and there is a good selection of shops and restaurants. One superb restaurant worth looking out is the family-run **El Guía** (Tel: 630 227) which specializes in Majorcan seafood delicacies. Slightly cheaper, but no less impressive, is the food which can be enjoyed at **Balear**, next door to one of the resort's better nightspots, **Bar Pirata**. For an excursion, it's worth remembering that a bus service operates four times daily to Palma, via both Deya and Vall De Mosa.

One of the resort's most unusual hotels is the **Atalaya Club** (Tel: 631 403) which occupies a rather isolated position on high ground overlooking the whole area. It is self-contained, with 150 comfortable bedrooms, all with private bathrooms, sun terrace and great sea views, and offers a good programme of organized entertainment. One obvious drawback is the very steep thirty-minute hike straight down to the sandy beach. To reach the resort centre, you can look forward to the same downward climb. The hotel is ideal for active people of all ages but not suitable for young families or elderly visitors (unless very fit!).

The **Es Port** (Tel: 631 650) began life as a large farmhouse which has been converted and extended into a bright, three-star hotel with 95 bedrooms. Views are limited, but it is located right in the resort centre and is only five minutes' walk from the beach. Nearby, the **Eden** (Tel: 631 600) is another three-star building standing eight floors high and looking across to its sister hotel, the **Eden Park**. Live music is available most evenings, and, overall, this place offers a relaxed, informal atmosphere ideal for older couples and retired holiday-makers.

For visitors on a more limited budget, two very good one-star hotels are the **Brisas** (Tel: 631 352) overlooking the entire bay, and the **Costa Brava** (Tel: 631 550) which is one of the best value bases in Puerto Sóller, provided you plan to spend as little time as possible in the hotel itself.

The inland town of Sóller is considerably more dull than the port of the same name, and this is partly because it hasn't developed at all as a resort. It has retained a certain quaint feel which you might appreciate as a contrast to many of the busy, built-up beach resorts, but there are few sights other than the **municipal museum** which is open most days during the summer and has been lovingly restored over the last decade. **El Guia** (Tel: 630 227) is a modest little hotel, close to the railway station, which attracts many independent visitors each summer. The sole railway line on the Balearics connects Sóller with Palma.

To the east of Sóller, the village of DEYA is worth a visit by those who remember the carefree hippy days of the 1960s. This peculiarly British village is best known as the former home of the poet and writer Robert Graves, but in the heyday of hippy activity it was an international gathering place for hippy bands. Both Robert Wyatt and the cult 'Soft Machine' were regulars in Deya. There's little to see now, of course, although one or two ageing human relics of the hippy era still live here and make frequent appearances in one or two of the local nightspots. **Upper Bar** is considered one of the best if you want to sample what remains of the hippy reputation Deya once had. There is a small stretch of rocky beach here, reached only after a steep downward climb.

North of Puerto Sóller, the coast is rugged and completely undeveloped except for CALA SAN VICENTE. This resort offers an excellent destination for those looking for a quiet beach holiday, although there are few shops and restaurants to speak of. The main attraction is a very picturesque sandy beach overlooking a picture-postcard bay. Most water-sports are also available.

A couple of suggestions for where to stay, from a limited selection, are the medium-sized, three-star **Don Pedro** (Tel: 530 050) and another three-star hotel, the **Cala San Vicente** (Tel: 530 250). The Don Pedro has 136 bedrooms and sits in a good position overlooking the beach. It has a bright green exterior which you cannot miss and although facilities for children are reasonable, this is not the best resort for families. The Hotel Cala San Vicente is a very attractive hotel, with just 50 bedrooms, all with private facilities, terrace and the unusual extra of a telephone. It offers little in the way of organized entertainment.

From here, the main road winds through dense orchards of fruit trees, olive groves and undulating countryside for a few miles before you arrive at the large village of **POLLENSA**. This place has little to offer the visitor other than basic amenities like a chemist, post office and a few shops. One sight of note is the enormous **Shrine of Calvary** which totally dominates the town, and can only be reached after a lengthy climb of nearly 400 steps.

Whilst you're climbing up to the summit of this great religious monument, you might see the spectacle of a devout pilgrim making the climb on his or her knees. Whatever way you decide to reach the top (and there's no reason why you shouldn't emulate the pilgrims!) the views over the surrounding coast, and across the village, are spectacular. By foot you can also reach the northernmost tip of the island, marked by a lighthouse at Cabo FORMENTOR.

Pollensa is better known as Puerto de Pollensa, the stretch of sandy coast around which a large resort has grown up. The hotels are well dispersed and set against a wide backdrop of green hills. Car hire is recommended as Puerto de Pollensa's northern location makes it an excellent base for exploring the island as a whole. There is a varied collection of walks and hikes in and around Puerto de Pollensa which makes a healthy alternative to lying on the clean, but rather narrow beach. The resort has a number of good restaurants and a handful of shops and cafés, but there is little nightlife to speak of, so it might be better suited to older couples keen to avoid the larger resorts around Palma Bay.

There is a good spread of hotels and hostels in Puerto de Pollensa, although it would be fair to say that most of them are in the lower categories in terms of price and quality. Two of the better hotels are both reasonable three-star establishments: the **Pollentia** (Tel: 531 200) and the **Pollensa Park** (Tel: 531 350) which are situated near the main beach area. The Pollentia is a relatively small hotel, with just 70 rooms, but it is clean and comfortable, and has plenty of facilities (sun chairs, baby-minding service, attractive garden areas) for visitors who want to do nothing more energetic than sit back and relax under the sun.

The Pollensa Park, on the other hand, has a nightly disco and impressive range of sporting facilities so is clearly better suited to younger holiday-makers or visitors looking for a bit of activity during their stay. It is a much larger hotel than the Pollentia, with over 300 bedrooms and two swimming pools including a safe children's pool. The hotel has a number of rooms specially adapted to meet the needs of disabled visitors.

One other hotel well worth considering is the three-star Illa D'Or (Tel: 531 100) which is an impressive old building, heavily renovated in recent years, and actually one of the oldest 'package'-type hotels on the Balearics. It was built in 1929 and retains much of the elegance and character you'd associate with a building of this age. There are 120 bedrooms with private bathroom facilities, and a further 8 very well-appointed suites with large balconies. There is a disco, and live music at least twice a week, but this hotel is better suited to holiday-makers of all ages who are looking for a more relaxed holiday destination.

Nearby is the isolated resort of FORMENTOR which has grown up around a small fishing village of the same name. It is dominated by an enormous luxury hotel and an extremely attractive strip of clean, sandy beach. Several British tour operators offer holidays to this attractive part of Majorca. There is little to do in Formentor, although there is a wealth of scenic coast and countryside to explore all around. There are no shops or restaurants away from the main hotel, but even if you're not actually staying here you will probably find this idyllic resort is a favourite for day visits from the larger, more crowded resorts at the opposite end of the island. Facilities are limited but this is an ideal resort for a comfortable 'away-from-it-all' holiday. It's not recommended for children, though, as there is little to keep them occupied during the day or in the early evening once they tire of the beach.

The only hotel of note is the de luxe **Hotel Formentor** (Tel: 531 300) which occupies a quiet location close to the beach. It has 131 bedrooms, all with private facilities and air conditioning. The entire hotel is very well appointed and the attractive mansion-like exterior helps make this one of the best hotels in the Balearic group. All the public rooms are bright and airy, including the superb dining room, and extremely well furnished. A good feature is the enormous landscaped gardens which slope down about 200 yards towards a private beach.

The next resort round the point of Cabo del Pinar is **ALCUDIA**, at the head of the wide Bahia de Alcudia. Although this is one of Majorca's larger resorts, it is also, unfortunately, one of the island's most disappointing. The village of Alcudia is a faceless, rather ugly place which still retains some of its original character but, as an inevitable result of the developing tourist industry, that is slowly being eroded. It centres around two old harbours: one serves an enormous (and very obtrusive) power station, and the other functions as a bustling yacht harbour surrounded by small restaurants and crowded cafés.

In its favour, of course, Alcudia has one of the largest beaches on Majorca, and an excellent range of hotels geared almost exclusively for the needs of the package-holiday market. The beach is a vast stretch of sand which sweeps right the way around the gently curving bay to the resort of CALA PICAFORT. The further along the beach from the village you go, the cleaner and softer the sand becomes: nearest the harbour, it is a grubby grey but this becomes gradually more golden as you continue along.

Take care if swimming a reasonable distance from the shore, as parts of the bay are known to shelve. One advantage for the sportsperson is the excellent variety of water-sports available near here; the sheltered bay is an ideal location for windsurfing and pedaloes and you'll find few better locations to experiment if you're a complete novice! Ask at your hotel reception for details of lessons if you're keen.

One sight worth looking out for is the remains of what is reckoned to have been Spain's smallest **Roman theatre**, to your left as you approach Alcudia town on the main road. There's little left to see now, unfortunately, but it is effectively a miniature copy of many similar

Roman theatres which you can still see on the Spanish mainland. The **Tourist Information Office** in the town centre offers enthusiastic assistance and information, in English, about what there is to see and do in the immediate area as well as up-to-date bus and ferry times.

An interesting day trip from Alcudia is by ferry across to Ciudadela (*see* page 175), the second largest town on the neighbouring island of Menorca. Ciudadela is a good shopping centre and has a handful of tourist attractions worth visiting. Crossings are regular throughout the week and usually take no more than a couple of hours. The ferries leave at 9am and an early start is essential to avoid arriving on Menorca in the middle of the afternoon siesta when NOTHING is open!

The main beach at Alcudia runs parallel to a major road which separates it from the hotels and restaurants. Care must be taken, particularly with children, when crossing. The best hotels are large, modern three-star tower blocks, and one of the most typical is the **Bahai de Alcudia** (Tel: 545 800) which lies a couple of minutes' walk from the beach. It has 205 bedrooms, all with private facilities and balconies (take care with young children, as some have large gaps). There is a good entertainment programme throughout the summer, and one of the brightest public rooms in the hotel is the large, airy dining room. Many of the guests tend to be German, and the à la carte dinner menu reflects this.

Two other good three-star hotels are the immaculate **Platja d'Or** (Tel: 548 085) and the **Martimo** (Tel: 546 562). The Platja combines an attractive location, in a peaceful little cul-de-sac, with a convenient stretch of beach directly opposite. There are 232 good-sized rooms: the upper floor ones have superb seaviews and all have balconies. The public areas are spotlessly clean and tastefully furnished, making this one of the most obviously appealing hotels in the resort.

The Martimo is an enormous new building, with 249 bedrooms over seven floors. It was opened at the start of the summer season in 1987 so the furnishings and décor are bright and rather garishly modern. Service is friendly and efficient, and various forms of evening entertainment are organized during the week; bingo is an occasional feature. The only obvious criticism is the number of polished marble floors – dangerously slippy if you run with wet feet, and extremely hard on little heads!

Two other good hotels in Alcudia are the three-star **Condesa de la**

Bahai (Tel: 545 316) some five minutes out of the main resort centre by car, and the attractive two-star **Condesa de Alcudia** (Tel: 545 920). The former hotel is a massive building, with nearly 500 bedrooms and large public areas. It is almost totally self-contained, even allowing for its isolated position, and the range of organized entertainments is one of the best of any hotel on this part of the island. There are organized kids' events too, and a wide playground (with a sensible sand base) is available all day. An obvious choice for families and young couples who don't object to the short distance from the resort centre.

The Condesa de Alcudia, on the other hand, is a cheerful, busy hotel lying about five minutes from the beach behind a small shopping precinct. There are 238 bedrooms, all with private facilities and balconies, although few of the rooms have exceptional views. Facilities for children are again excellent, and although there are occasional discos and live music evenings, this is not an ideal hotel for young singles.

A couple of suggestions for the independent traveller are **Fonda Llabres** (Tel: 545 000) a small, modest pension in Alcudia town's main square, and the **Vista Alegre** (Tel: 545 439) in Puerto Alcudia. Ideally, you should try and book accommodation in advance, but if this has not been possible then the Tourist Information Office in town is generally quite helpful with suggestions about where to stay. Options are limited, though, particularly in the peak summer months, so you may find yourself on the beach yet!

The beach at Alcudia extends right round the wide bay to the resort town of CALA PICAFORT. Until relatively recently the town had the reputation of offering little more than a sprinkling of ugly, concrete tower blocks and a handful of souvenir shops. Many of the shabby tower blocks are still there, but thankfully this well-spread-out resort is changing its image for the better. There are, for instance, a number of newish discos and restaurants in the resort centre, but most of the entertainment in what is still essentially quite a quiet resort is concentrated in the large hotels. The beach is long and clean: busy but seldom completely crowded because of its length. As with the neighbouring resort of Alcudia, water-sports are available in abundance.

Among the hotels in Cala Picafort, one of the most popular is the three-star **Janeiro** (Tel: 527 125) which is a large, well-maintained building about two minutes' walk up from a rocky stretch of beach. The Janeiro has 210 rooms, all with balcony, private facilities and cots. Entertainment is limited to a weekly disco and occasionally live music.

Most of the other hotels are respectable one- and two-star establishments. From the crop of two-star hotels, the **Sarah** (Tel: 527 388) and **Gran Playa** (Tel: 527 226) are the most readily recommendable. The Sarah sits in a quiet position in the Son Boulo area, about twenty minutes from the main resort. Nevertheless, this relatively isolated position is one of its positive attractions and the facilities available are more than worthy of a two-star hotel. It is a well-maintained building, both inside and out, and has 110 bedrooms on four floors.

The Gran Playa is a medium-sized building, with 156 bedrooms and an excellent location close to both the beach and main shopping area. It isn't too large, either, having been built on just four floors, and it underwent a major refit before the start of the 1988 summer season. One further hotel of note is the **Vista Park** (Tel: 527 300), a large two-star hotel in a quiet location and ideal for families. It was the overall winner in Thomson Holidays 1987 Gold Awards as 'Best TT Summer Sun Hotel'.

Beyond the large Alcudia Bay the scenery becomes much more rugged and beautiful. Stark cliffs dominate the coastline except for a few attractive stretches of golden sand which have been developed into flourishing resorts over the last twenty years. The only one right on the north-eastern tip of the island is CALA MESQUIDA – a clean, modern development dominated by the Holiday Club International complex. Various forms of evening entertainment are organized during the week, but the only obvious day-time activity is lying by the pool or enjoying the sun and sea on the attractive little beach. Two possible excursions are to the old town of Capdepera, or to the larger resort of Cala Ratjada. Hiring a car is strongly recommended if you are staying in this part of Majorca and plan to explore the island fully.

Virtually next door to Cala Mesquida is the expanding resort town of CALA RATJADA. Only a handful of operators offer tours here, but it is an increasingly popular spot with British holiday-makers. There is a reasonable selection of shops and restaurants; better than average for what is still a relatively small resort.

The most obvious attraction is the large sandy beach at Son Moll, and here, again, an excellent day trip is to the old town of Capdepera where you can walk up to a magnificent fourteenth-century castle and enjoy spectacular views over the whole area.

One drawback of all the resorts on this northern part of the island is the transfer time from the airport to your hotel. On average, the coach from Palma Airport (about fifty miles away) takes around 105 minutes. Very occasionally, with an older coach and/or a slow driver, the connection can take nearly as long as your flight from London!

From the small collection of two- and three-star hotels in Cala Ratjada, all offer reasonable accommodation for their given grading, but none are outstanding. The three-star **Son Moll** has the best location, directly opposite the beach and ten minutes from the resort centre. It is a tall, narrow tower block with 118 bedrooms over ten floors. Most of the rooms have good views across the beach and out to sea.

Two other hotels of note are the **Lux Sol** and the **Carolina** (Tel: 563 158). The Lux Sol is a relatively modern three-star hotel with 236 bedrooms on seven floors. It offers standard Sol Hotel comfort and facilities and a very comprehensive programme of entertainment for all the family. This hotel is ideal for all age groups, and the added feature of a weekly Gala Dinner is very popular with residents.

The Carolina, on the other hand, is a very attractive two-star hotel, with 180 bedrooms, which occupies an isolated location about three miles out of the resort proper. The public areas, both inside and out, are extremely comfortable. The hotel has its own entertainments manager and residents are unlikely to be disappointed with the range of games and organized activities available. In addition, a bus runs twice daily into the resort proper and, on Mondays, to the local market.

Continuing down the coast from Cala Ratjada, a string of popular summer resorts dominates the island's eastern coast. COSTA DE LOS PINOS is a small, purpose-built resort set against a backdrop of sweeping hills. It is essentially a modern villa development which has been built up behind a small, narrow stretch of beach made up of a number of rock or shingle inlets.

This is an excellent destination for sports enthusiasts as there is a superb range of water-sports available. At the time of publication only one British tour operator, Cosmos, offered tours directly to Costa de Los Pinos although it is easily accessible as a day-trip option from anywhere else on the island.

The enormous four-star **Eurotel Golf Punta Rotja** (Tel: 567 600) is a popular, self-contained hotel and apartment complex, and the only hotel to speak of in the resort. One or two operators to nearby resorts of Cala Bona and Cala Millor (both ten minutes away by car) offer accommodation here so bear this in mind if you don't want to spend your holiday in a relatively isolated location. Practically next door is the little harbour town of CALA BONA which is fast being taken over by the expanding resort of **CALA MILLOR**. The town is dominated by its small harbour and man-made beach, and there are a number of reasonable shops and restaurants. Cala Bona is noticeably quieter than Cala Millor, although the two resorts adjoin one another and it is quite easy to walk from one to the other.

Of the two, Cala Millor has easily the larger and better selection of hotels with facilities for all age groups. Cala Bona has a clutter of one- and two-star hotels, most of which are best suited to people (of all age groups) looking for a reasonably quiet holiday within easy reach of a good beach and some nightlife if they feel like letting their hair down one evening.

Two of Cala Bona's best hotels are the two-star **Levante Park** (Tel: 585 015), which sits directly opposite its two-star sister hotel, the significantly more noisy **Levante**, close to the beach. The Levante was a winner of a 1987 Thomson Holidays Gold Award in its 'Young at Heart' category. The Levante Park, though, has 105 bedrooms, all with private facilities, balcony and seaview. There is an occasional disco and live music, and activities for all age groups are good. The **Consul** (Tel: 585 971) is an attractive, modern two-star hotel with 78 twin or double rooms. It offers a friendly atmosphere and a clean, busy interior. The basement **Paradis Disco** is reckoned to be one of the better nightspots in Cala Bona.

Cala Millor is a large resort dominated by an enormous sandy beach. The beach is easily one of Majorca's best, and understandably a popular choice for families and sunlovers alike. German, French and Dutch visitors dominate the resort, although there is an ever-increasing British contingent arriving through more than a dozen of the main tour operators. One local sight worth checking out near Cala Millor is the **Cuevas de Arta**, arguably the best collection of caves on Majorca's eastern coast. They have been formed high up on the cliffside and groups are guided in parties daily throughout the summer between 9.30am and 7pm.

Cala Millor has a host of good hotels: overall, the standards offered by hotels in this resort are above average and one of the best has to be the large three-star **Borneo** (Tel: 585 511). A former winner of Hogg Robinson Travel's 'Family Hotel of the Year Award', the Borneo has 200 bedrooms and offers a very lively atmosphere and excellent facilities for holiday-makers of all ages. This well-appointed hotel comes highly recommended, and lies just a few yards from the main beach.

The **Sumba** (Tel: 585 061) is another quality three-star hotel and, with 280 bedrooms, is one of the largest in Cala Millor. It is the sister hotel to the **Borneo** and lies at the end of Cala Millor Bay. It is essentially a bright, modern hotel, well furnished but still not managing to lose the rather anonymous character associated with large hotels. One popular feature is the full (and noisy) programme of evening entertainment which makes it a favourite choice for young singles. This is a great hotel, but not one for a quiet holiday.

Two very good two-star hotels are the T-shaped **Alicia** (Tel: 585 600) and the **Osiris** (Tel: 567 325). The Alicia sits opposite a rocky stretch of beach and about ten minutes' walk away from the resort centre. There are 166 bedrooms, all with private facilities and balconies, and most have a seaview. The rooms that do not have seaviews are noticeably more gloomy so it would be worth your while specifically requesting a room with a view if you have a strong preference.

The Osiris has an unattractive exterior but, inside, furnishings and facilities which would have been commendable in a three-star hotel. It has a lively atmosphere inside which is more than enhanced by the disco and weekly live music sessions. The enormous dining room is one of the most appealing features of the Osiris, and there are usually at least three choices for each of the four courses at dinner.

Continuing down the coast, **PORTO CRISTO** is a spread-out resort which has grown up around an old fishing village. The town centre is a busy place, with a handful of useful shops and a few bars and restaurants. Porto Cristo's beach is long and sandy: water-sports are limited, but it is a clean, safe beach for all the family.

In town, the **old harbour** is worth a stroll, but the most popular attractions in the surrounding area are the **Caves of Drach and Ham**. Although the caves have their similarities, Drach is the more popular and the more attractive: it is a favourite venue for concerts during the summer months (generally classical music) and excursions are widely available through the main hotels.

Another local attraction is the small **safari park** on the same road as the Caves of Drach. The collection of wildlife is limited, but much more fascinating is the **aquarium** where a vast collection of rare and exotic fish swim about in large magnified glass tanks. Children will be fascinated by the surprisingly inoffensive-looking piranha fish and the great stinging eels!

Porto Cristo has no large luxury hotels. It has, however, a good selection of more modest one- and two-star establishments which are ideal for the budget traveller who might be looking for an economical holiday destination.

The **Drach** (Tel: 570 025) is arguably the resort's best hotel, and offers two-star accommodation within about fifteen minutes' walk from the beach. It has 52 bedrooms, most of which have sun terraces and a reasonable view across the sea-front. There is practically nothing in the way of organized entertainment other than dancing once a week, and overall visitors might find this budget hotel a little disappointing. It certainly qualifies as an ideal hotel for middle-aged or retired visitors.

Small, family-run hotels are typical of the sort of accommodation you can expect in Puerto Cristo. Two of the best such (one-star) hotels are the central **Residencia Bini** (Tel: 570 033) and the **Perello** (Tel: 570 004) in the main town square opposite the busy bus terminal. Both offer comfortable, but modest, accommodation and, of the two, the former is the more popular with younger visitors. One further suggestion is the **Hostal Sol Y Vida** (Tel: 570 298) next door to the fascinating Caves of Drach. It has 22 rooms and sits ten minutes from the beach. Despite its name, it is not to be confused with one of the many excellent Sol Group hotels on the island!

CALAS DE MALLORCA is another of the island's purpose-built resorts a few miles down the relatively straight stretch of eastern coastline from Porto Cristo. It still has a relatively bright, fresh look about it and is a particular favourite for water-sports enthusiasts and family holidays. In addition, it is well connected with the rest of Majorca, so makes an ideal base if you're looking for a well-appointed hotel in a fairly lively, good value all-round resort.

There are only a few hotels, all of which are fairly well dispersed. The main beach is a clean, if unremarkable, strip of sand although within a short walk you can reach a number of smaller (and generally quieter) rocky beaches. Entertainment, shops and restaurants are limited mainly to the hotels. There is a small shopping precinct, but many visitors wisely prefer to wait until they can visit Palma (about seventy minutes' drive away) before doing their main souvenir shopping. One interesting sight is a semi-permanent **parrot show** which opened in summer 1987 and is already one of Majorca's most interesting attractions – particularly if you hadn't previously given parrots much thought!

Accommodation in Calas de Mallorca is generally very good. Nearly all the dozen or so British operators who offer tours here use large three- or four-star hotels. Two huge four-star Sol Group hotels, **Los Mastines Sol** (Tel: 573 125) and **Los Chihuahas Sol** (Tel: 573 250) occupy superb locations close to both the beach and the resort centre. Both are extremely well appointed with approximately 250 bedrooms each. A buffet-style international dinner menu is available in each hotel in the evening and there is no shortage of organized entertainments to keep all types of holiday-makers, up to and including early middle age, more than amused throughout the day and evening. Well-laid-out gardens, sun terraces and a large swimming pool are shared between the two hotels.

Two highly recommended three-star hotels are the **Maria Eugenia** (Tel: 573 277) and the **Balmoral Sol** (Tel: 573 102). The Maria Eugenia has 330 bedrooms, all with balcony and most with a seaview. Entertainments are well organized and a keen favourite is the terrace disco which takes place most evenings. The hotel has a wide selection of amenities, including a hairdresser, gift shop, table-tennis, electronic games, football and card tables, and even a mini-cinema. Easily one of the best value all-round family hotels in Majorca.

The Balmoral Sol is another popular Sol family hotel which underwent a massive programme of renovation work in 1987. The entire building gives an impression of space, particularly in the comfortable, well-laid-out dining room. A new glass roof above the public lounge areas is a nice touch. In all, there are 277 bedrooms, many of which offer an outstanding seaview which helps make the transformation from a good to an excellent hotel.

A little way further down, still on the south-eastern corner of the island, is the large and extremely popular resort of **CALA D'OR**. This is one of the largest resorts on the Balearics, with approximately twenty major tour operators choosing to include it in their annual summer selection of European holiday destinations. The resort is a pleasing combination of smaller, older hotels and the inevitable faceless modern tower blocks. That said, it is well spread out and can be recommended for a relatively quiet holiday as it is somewhat isolated and very self-contained. As pointed out earlier in this chapter, virtually all the loud, noisy resorts are concentrated in and around the Palma Bay area.

The resort of Cala D'Or can be neatly divided into four distinct areas, and there's a fair chance that any one of the four might be listed separately as a holiday destination. In effect, CALA FERRARA, the village of CALA D'OR, CALA EGOS and CALA ES FORTI are all the same place. The resort is concentrated around a long stretch of clean, if rather rocky, beach where water-sports are a popular attraction should you tire of sunbathing. There is a reasonable selection of shops and restaurants around the resort centre.

Most of the hotels in Cala D'Or are two- or three-star tower blocks. Three of the better ones are the elegant **Hotel Cala D'Or** (Tel: 657 249), the older **Cala Gran** (Tel: 657 100) and the very attractive **Rocador** (Tel: 657 076). The Cala D'Or is an unusual-looking hotel as it has been built on more than one level against a backdrop of pine trees. The only drawback is a number of unusually low corridor ceilings, but this is a small complaint about an otherwise excellent hotel for couples without a young family.

The Cala Gran, on the other hand, is an older building with 77 bedrooms across five floors. It is ideally situated for the beach and resort centre and offers a clean, inviting environment to all types of holiday-maker except the young single. Entertainment is limited to dancing occasionally, and the inevitable games machines in one or two of the public areas.

The Rocador has a superb location, just a few yards from a sandy stretch of beach and minutes from the resort centre. It is a popular hotel, but remains surprisingly uncrowded throughout the season. Young families and singles will enjoy its relaxed informality most. All the bedrooms have good views across either the sea-front or the pool area.

Virtually next door to Cala D'Or is PORTO PETRO, a very small, quiet village which offers peaceful holidays through one or two keen British operators. It is generally likened to a smaller, quieter version of Porto Colom. Don't come here expecting anything in the way of nightlife, points of interest or much else to do except sit back and soak up the peace and quiet.

Accommodation is limited to a handful of small hotels. A couple of suggestions are the one-star **Hotel Porto Petro** (Tel: 657 002), a basic hotel a few minutes' walk from the bay and the harbour, or the hostel **Roca Blanca** (Tel: 657 002) with 14 sparsely furnished but comfortable rooms in an annexe of the Hotel Porto Petro (and close to its pool). Another suggestion, for the independent traveller, is the one-star **Hostal Nerida** (Tel: 657 223) which may have a few rooms available.

Running into one another beyond Porto Petro are CALA MONDRAGO and CALA FIGUERA, two small resorts built up round an old fishing village in a rocky creek. Figuera attracts more day trippers than residents and, despite this large influx of people each summer, it retains much of its original charm. There is no beach to speak of at Cala Figuera, but swimming is possible, if care is taken of the rocks.

There is a very fine strip of sandy beach at Cala Mondrago, and nearby there are two sandy coves at CALA SANTAÑYI and CALA

LLOMBARTS which still remain relatively undeveloped, except for a few private apartments. The area round the coves is reckoned to be one of the best spots on the island for camping. Two modest suggestions for accommodation are the **Hotel Condemar** (Tel: 657 756) and the **Residencia Playa Mondrago**. Both are small, independent, one-star establishments suitable for all age groups, apart from young singles, who are not looking for much in the way of entertainment beyond good company and the beach.

The remaining south-eastern part of Majorca, leading right back round to Palma Bay, is the least developed part of the island. For years a Spanish banking boss has owned this part of the island and preserved most of it as an enormous nature reserve. As more and more holiday-makers choose to visit Majorca, of course, pressure to develop this southern coast becomes more acute. Already there are apartment-dominated resorts growing up around COLONIA DE SAN JORDI, ARENAL DE LA RAPITA and CALA PI.

Arenal de la Rapita, incidentally, has an outstanding beach and may well be a prime target for hotel development in later years. As yet, though, there is nothing apart from apartments and no British tour operators offer holidays to this relatively unknown part of Majorca or, indeed, any part of the southern coast east of Palma Bay.

Inland

The inland part of Majorca is surprisingly undeveloped and offers a glimpse of the true character of the island which very few of the large beach resorts can even begin to. One of the closest towns to the capital, Palma, is ANDRAITX, a dull little place which appears to remain almost completely untouched by the extensive tourist development along the coast around it. It is a good base to go hiking in the nearby hills, and the Tourist Office in Palma should be able to give you some guidelines about where to go. One obvious target is the old ruined **Castle of San Telmo**.

The village of ALGAIDA, a few miles from Palma in the opposite direction from Andraitx, offers more opportunities for hiking, and a popular route will take you across country a few miles to the even smaller village of RANDA where, if you're fit, you can join the path to hike up to the highest peak on the island – PUIG RANDA. There is an active **monastery** on the summit which occasionally welcomes visitors; whether or not you stay, the views are out of this world.

If you are keen to explore more of Majorca's many monasteries, most tourist maps will give you a reasonable indication about which ones are still inhabited and which are not. Be careful not to confuse monastery symbols with those for filling stations (and vice versa if you are running short of petrol) as they look alarmingly similar on one or two of the more basic maps!

The railway line to Sóller (*see* page 145) is an enjoyable journey through fine mountainous scenery. One place definitely worth visiting near Sóller is VALL DE MOSA. This former monastery is now a museum, and many of the rooms contain memorabilia of the composer Chopin and his mistress George Sand, when they stayed on the island in the early nineteenth century. The **Palacio Rey Sancho**, next door, has a modest collection of paintings and furniture. Near ESPORELS, **La Granja** is a large country house with a famous terrace overlooking fountains, gardens and rich vineyards. Most afternoons (except Tuesdays when it is closed) you can see traditional folk dancing, and an added advantage is the opportunity to sample traditional Majorcan food and drink for a modest charge. Near the Palma to Sóller railway line, the **Alfabia Gardens** are a popular attraction surrounding a luxuriant old palace. The gardens were heavily influenced by Moorish designs and have stood for centuries.

The **Monastery of Lluch** is an obvious excursion from Pollensa and the resorts around the northern edge of the island. It is easily the largest monastic complex on the island, and is dominated by a huge thirteenth-century statue of the Virgin Mary. It is very commercialized now: there is a small museum, souvenir shop and a bar/restaurant open most days during the summer.

Other inland towns include INCA, famous for its leather factories and its excellent Thursday-morning market. It has a railway link with Palma. MANACOR, on the east of the island, is Majorca's second population centre and, frankly, the contrast couldn't be more striking. It is an unappealing, colourless settlement known only for its numerous **pearl factories** which are heavily advertised on enormous hoardings in and around the town. The **Gordiola glassworks** on the main road to Palma are worth a visit.

FELANITX, on the south-eastern corner of the island, is a prosperous little town producing bottled wines, colourful ceramics and pearl goods. Apart from these local industries, two obvious attractions are the thirteenth-century **Monastery of San Salvador** and the remains of the **Castillo de Santueri**.

MENORCA

Introduction

Menorca is the second largest of the Balearics and probably the best of the three main islands to opt for if you are travelling with young children or looking for a quieter beach holiday. As a tourist destination it developed later than either Majorca or Ibiza: the Menorcans clung stubbornly to their traditional independent spirit for decades and consequently missed out on a lot of General Franco's 'benevolence' when he decided to push Spain towards the forefront of the European package-holiday market in the 1960s. As a direct result, Menorca was relatively unknown as a tourist resort until the early 1970s. It was a popular excursion from Majorca, and paradise for a secluded 'away-from-it-all' break in the sun, but the tower-block package development never had a chance to take off and, as a result, Menorca today has very few large pockets of modern hotels or apartments such as you find all over neighbouring Majorca.

In this chapter we begin our look at the island of Menorca in the capital of Mahón and then follow the coast round in a clockwise direction.

History

Paradoxically, least is known about the earliest phase of Menorca's history, yet, of the three main Balearics there is more surviving evidence of prehistoric civilization on this island than anywhere else. Three distinct types of prehistoric monument can be seen on

Menorca: *talayots* are the most common – these rocky mounds are believed to have been burial chambers or watchtowers; *navetas*, which look like upside-down boats and are thought to have been communal burial chambers; and *taulas* which are unique to Menorca. These huge stone constructions often measure as much as twelve to fifteen feet in a curious T-shape. Taulas have no obvious function, other than decoration, and are invariably found alongside a talayot.

In more recent centuries, Menorca has played a not insignificant role in European history. After Pearl Harbour in the United States, the island's capital of Mahón has the largest natural harbour in the world. During the Spanish War of Succession, in the eighteenth century, the British gained control of the island and held it for most of that century. For hundreds of years until then the capital of the island had been at Ciudadela in the North, but the British made Mahón their main base. Evidence of Georgian architecture can still be seen in Mahón's older buildings, but the main legacy from seven decades of British occupation was the recipe for the island's famous gin. You will hear more about that later!

Getting There

Virtually all Menorca's international visitors arrive as part of a package holiday at the island's only airport, a small international just outside Mahón. It exists almost exclusively to serve the British package holiday charter market although there are regular internal flights to and from Barcelona on the Spanish mainland and Majorca. Daily during the summer, and less frequently between October and March, you can make the nine-hour ferry journey from Barcelona to Mahón, and also the four-hour journey from Palma (on Majorca) to Mahón. Less frequently, ferries make the two-hour crossing from Ciudadela, on the opposite end of the island from Mahón, to Alcudia on Majorca.

Climate

By British standards, Menorca enjoys a long, hot summer. By mid-May it is warm enough (just) to sunbathe and have a paddle in the sea as the temperature generally reaches 21°C (70°F). This rises gradually until July when the average is up to 30°C (in the low eighties Fahrenheit). The October temperature is similar to what you'll find in May, but this is also the island's wettest month. The winter average ranges from 14-18°C (54-65°F) during the day but it can get much colder in the evenings, and there is usually a sharp breeze blowing as well.

Culinary Specialities

Among the many delightful speciality dishes you can expect on Menorca, look out for *gazpacho*, a chilled and highly flavoured soup made from chopped tomatoes, peppers, cucumber, onions and croûtons. *Cochinillo* is the local roast suckling pig, and *parcillada* is a popular mixed grill (which can be either meat or fish based) served with tomatoes or potatoes. For a special meal, try *langosta a la catalana*, a unique dish of fried lobster with assorted chopped vegetables, white wine and Cayenne pepper.

Where to Go for What

Sightseers should head for Mahón or Ciudadela but, frankly, Menorca is not a sightseer's island and all the main attractions in either main town can be seen in an afternoon. Sun Worshippers will adore Son Bou with its two miles of golden beach, and also the idyllic Cala Galdana which is probably the most attractive beach in the Balearics. Socialites should also head for Cala Galdana, but nightlife in most resorts is restricted to the hotels. Other resorts mostly offer quieter holidays within striking distance of a good beach. Es Grau is a small resort near the salt marshes of S'Albufera which is perfect for the Nature Lover because of its rich collection of migrant bird life.

Three miles from the sea, **MAHÓN**, the capital of Menorca, lies at the end of a wide inlet which forms the second largest natural harbour in the world. Admiral Lord Nelson once said, 'The best harbours in the world are July, August and Mahón.' Rather surprisingly, though, the area surrounding the harbour has not been heavily industrialized and you are more likely to see a luxury cruise liner making a brief call than a procession of tankers and freight carriers.

The fierce independence of the Menorcans has been known for centuries, and today you are still likely to see most of the road signs with the name MAHÓN obliterated and replaced with the word MAO which is how the island capital is known in the native Menorcan language. To really see the island of Menorca at its best you will need to walk, and nowhere is this more true than in Mahón. The town has a population of around 25,000 and during the summer this expands dramatically; the traffic is chaotic, so taking a taxi or hire car round the town centre is not recommended.

The old town of Mahón is built on a huge cliff-top looking out across the harbour. Although there are new developments on the outskirts of the town, Mahón remains essentially a rambling Georgian settlement which grew up during the time of the British occupation in the eighteenth century. The occupation didn't finally end until the Treaty of Amiens was signed in 1802; its most obvious reminder is the large casement windows which you can see on many of the older buildings instead of shutters.

Slowly, but unmistakably, the town has been taken over by the influence of more modern Spanish architecture. Even so, the Georgian architecture is one of the first things which will strike you about Mahón. Several of the older streets will give you a good idea of what the town looked like when Admiral Lord Nelson made his one brief visit to the island in 1799. The **Calle Isabel II** is a good starting point for any tour of the capital as it has the best collection of these Georgian-style buildings. Alternatively, you may prefer to start your tour of the town from the water-front. The views across the harbour and back up towards the town from here are outstanding. Boat trips around the harbour start from here, and one feature of the water-front is the bustling Xoiriguer **gin distillery**.

The distillery is open to the public, at no charge, from 9.30am (just the time for gin!) till 1pm, and again from 4.30pm until 8pm. Most tour buses to Mahón include a brief stop here but it is invariably in the morning, when you least feel like knocking back several sharp nips of sweet gin. Tiny little sample glasses stand in regimented rows beside a half-barrel filled with water: the idea is to use one glass per sample and then deposit the glass, bottoms down, in the barrel. Naturally there is no obligation to buy, but a full bottle of this famous

Menorcan fire-water is the perfect souvenir and will set you back only a few pounds. A favourite is the honey-coloured banana gin, but remember not to get too carried away since the gin will count as spirits towards your duty-free allowance. You are welcome to sample as many of the hundred or so varieties on offer as you like so why not come here independently at a more respectable hour for tasting spirits?

Mahón has a number of fascinating old churches. The most impressive is the **Church of Santa Maria** in the Plaza de la Conquista, which was constructed during the British occupation, between 1748 and 1772. The present structure was modified from an existing thirteenth-century church founded by Alfonso III. Inside, the church is deathly quiet and surprisingly chilly, which makes the contrast of its dark exterior all the more striking as you enter from the sweltering street.

The church's most interesting feature is an enormous **monumental organ**, with more than 3,000 pipes and no less than four keyboards. It was built in Austria in 1810 and there is a free recital every Tuesday and Thursday at 6pm throughout the summer. There is also a small **archaeological museum** and a small **tourist information office** in the Plaza de la Conquista where English is spoken and very good free maps of the island, which include a street plan of Mahón showing the main sights, are available.

Also in the Plaza de la Conquista you can visit the **casa de cultura** which combines the services of a museum, art gallery, historical archive and library together with an extensive document archive. The *casa* houses a large collection of sixteenth- and seventeenth-century decorative ceramics. The building is open every morning from 10am until 12 noon, although the library is also open from 5pm until 8pm.

There is a rather less elaborate **Carmelite church** in the Plaza del Carmen. It serves a double function, as the town's vibrant morning market is held here throughout the year, and if you follow any of the winding side streets leading up to the left from here, you'll come to the oldest parts of the town, from where the views are outstanding.

The town's main public building is the **Ayuntamiento** (town hall) which is round the corner from the Plaza del Carmen in the Plaza del Generalissimo Franco. Curiously, Mahón and Ciudadela are among the very few Spanish towns which still have streets or public squares

named after the country's fascist dictator who died in 1975. The
Ayuntamiento has an attractive Georgian-style arcaded façade that
was completely restored in 1788. A large English clock, presented by
the island's first British governor, was added at the same time.

You can visit another fine church, the **Church of San Francisco**, if
you follow Calle Isabel II. Its elegant twisted pillars were crafted by
Francisco Herrera who later went on to become the principal
stonemason at Palma Cathedral on Majorca. The town's main square
is **Plaza Explanada**, alive with tame pigeons and housing another
tourist information office. The main shopping centres on the island
are in the streets of Mahón's main square, notably the Calle Doctor
Orfila, Calle Hannover and Calle General Goded.

There is no shortage of good places to eat out in Mahón, but don't
be put off by the fact that the town was the birthplace of mayonnaise,
as surprisingly few cafés and restaurants have dishes featuring the
popular salad dressing on their menus! One of the best restaurants is
El Greco (Tel: 364 367) at 49, Doctor Orfila. Despite the rather
non-Spanish name, this marvellous old place serves some of Mahón's
finest seafood and prime-cut steaks.

Rocamer (Tel: 365 601) at 32 Fonduco is probably the best
restaurant on the island for seafood alone but if you would prefer,
instead, a really meaty steak, then head for **Chez Gaston** (Tel: 360
044) along the Conde de Cifuentes. There are many small cafés and
restaurants scattered around the central area of Mahón, and one or
two more suggestions for somewhere comfortable and relatively
inexpensive would have to include **Comidas Economicas** at Calle
Rosario 27, and **Kelly's** (Tel: 35 04 57) along San Sebastián.
Nightlife in Mahón, other than eating out, is limited, but one or two
discos worth looking out for are **Si** in town and either **Lui** or **Tonic** on
the road from Mahón to Villa Carlos.

The Menorcan capital is not a package resort as such, and
consequently there are virtually no large package hotels or apartments
in the town of Mahón itself. For the independent traveller, the local
tourist office will point you in the direction of private rooms and small
pensions which may or may not have a free room. Finding somewhere
to stay is a real problem on all the Balearic Islands if you have not
booked in advance so don't be surprised if you can't automatically find
somewhere to stay in the middle of July after a nine-hour ferry journey

from Barcelona! A couple of respectable pensions which are worth trying are **Pension Tito** (Tel: 36 22 67) or **Pension Company** which are both located on the small street linking the Plaza Bastion to the Plaza Franco.

Two miles east of the capital lies VILLA CARLOS, an attractive little suburb of Mahón which was originally built by the British during their occupation in the eighteenth century. The streets are laid out in a grid pattern and the attractive central **square** still has an army barracks around it. **Cala Fons** is the centre of the modern resort, beside the picturesque little harbour. The quay is lined with a sprinkling of small shops, bars and cafés which are invariably bustling with a marvellous mixture of visitors and locals alike.

There are no beaches near Villa Carlos, but swimming is possible from a small jetty and off the surrounding rocks. The rocks are smooth, although the slippery plant-life covering them just below the waterline requires caution and really makes them unsuitable for small children. For careful swimmers, the water is crystal clear and spotlessly clean so ideal for snorkelling enthusiasts. Views from the surrounding hillside are excellent – although the novelty of watching (and hearing) the frequent jumbo jets making their final approach to Mahón Airport soon wears off.

The best accommodation in Villa Carlos is in two three-star hotels: the **Rey Carlos III** (Tel: 363 100) which is ten minutes' walk from the harbour area, and the **Agamemnon** (Tel: 362 150) which is a slightly smaller hotel overlooking Mahón Bay. Both hotels are popular with British visitors and have medium-sized swimming pools with shaded poolside bars. More basic accommodation is available in the five-storey **Hamilton** (Tel: 362 050) or the one-star **Del Almirante** (Tel: 362 700) which has a rather isolated position a mile from both Villa Carlos and Mahón but is one of the most charming buildings in the area, having once been the eighteenth-century home of Lord Collingwood.

Just down the coast from Villa Carlos is S'ALGAR, a very quiet resort which is dominated by two large hotels and a collection of residential and holiday apartments. There is little to see here and its rather isolated location will appeal more to retired visitors who might be looking for a more 'away from it all' break. There are only a few general shops and no beach to speak of other than a rocky stretch from where you can swim in relative safety. Not a resort which is ideally suited to children, or young people looking for any nightlife.

Accommodation in S'Algar, apart from self-catering apartments, is limited to the **Hotel S'Algar** (Tel: 361 700) and the **San Luis** (Tel: 361 750). Both are three-star hotels although the San Luis is about twice the size of the Hotel S'Algar, with 228 bedrooms. Facilities at the San Luis are better in terms of electronic games, mini-golf, table tennis and so on and both hotels offer an international buffet-style menu for half-board residents.

Nearby, the tiny resort of CALA ALCAUFAR has a very small sandy beach overlooked by a few apartments and a small hostel. The **Hostal Xuroy** (Tel: 36 18 20) is a two-star hostel with 44 rooms ideal for couples in the twenty-five – sixty age group. The bar and its terrace enjoy good views across the bay.

Inland a little from both Cala Alcaufar and the somewhat larger resort of **PUNTA PRIMA** is the small town of SAN LUIS. It has one central square, a modest white church, and nothing else to recommend a detour apart from a post office and a couple of reasonable general stores. Few of the tour buses even bother to go through San Luis.

Punta Prima, on the other hand, is an equally small but more established resort on the extreme south-western tip of the island, about six miles from Mahón. The beach is a reasonable stretch of sandy coast with plenty of water-sports available. Just around the corner, there is a very pleasant cove at BINIANCOLLA. There are usually a number of fishing boats here and the cove provides an interesting contrast to the rest of the resort.

Accommodation is mainly limited to apartment complexes, but there is a reasonable one-star **Hotel Xaloc** (Tel: 36 19 22) within five minutes' walk of the beach area at Punta Prima. There's also a children's playground and a small, circular pool for residents to enjoy. Another hotel option is the **Hotel Sur Menorca** (Tel: 361 812), a large, modern, one-star hotel in a rather secluded position within ten minutes' walk from the beach.

The next small resort is BINEBECA, sometimes known as *Cala Torret* as its eastern end is called. You will find mainly apartments leading down to a central service complex around Binebeca and Cala Torret, but there are a good number of bars and restaurants catering for residents and day trippers alike. The beach here is a magnificent strip of sand stretching between Binebeca and Cala Torret. It does get quickly crowded, but if you fancy a rest from the scorching summer sun then the main beach bar here has an excellent reputation for traditional Spanish *paella*. Such is the popularity of this place that advance booking is sometimes necessary! This is a good beach for children, and pedaloes are among the various beach facilities available.

Two large apartment complexes, **Binebeca Vell** and **Pueblo de Pescadores** are constructed in a style which resembles many of the traditional little hamlets and villages you can see near the coast in Menorca. There is no beach to speak of near either complex, and swimming is only really practical from a concrete platform.

The town of SAN CLEMENTE, inland a little from Binebeca, has nothing to offer beyond a few shops and an early Christian **basilica** which may be of interest to the sightseer.

Arguably the two least impressive developments on this stretch of coast, BINISAFUA and CAP D'EN FONT, come next. The 'beach' areas are rather ugly and the smell (and sight) of tons of seaweed, which is constantly being washed ashore, is a real disappointment. Apart from one small company, none of the major package operators offer accommodation near this part of the south-west coast and it is best avoided.

A reasonably good contrast is CALA'N PORTER a little way further along the coast. This is not a large resort, but it is expanding fast around a fragmented old fishing village and an excellent stretch of golden beach. There is a good choice of bars and restaurants but little else to see or do beyond the beach and a number of short scenic walks around the surrounding hillside. The beach is gently sloped and ideal for families with young children.

Probably the best nightspot on Menorca is the **Cave of Xoroi** at Cala'n Porter. All the major tour operators offer excursions to this breathtaking nightclub which really is a converted cave. It is cleverly illuminated to offer just the right level of intimacy, and visitors can enjoy a first-class meal, combined with some truly breathtaking sea-views, before dancing the night away to the best modern music.

Among a slowly increasing number of hotels in Cala'n Porter are a couple of comfortable, if rather basic, hotels which overlook the beach. The **Aquarium** (Tel: 36 64 15) is ten minutes from the resort centre and although it sits near an area of scrubland and marsh, it has nearly 60 rooms on three floors and is ideal for couples sufficiently past their first flush of youth for the absence of an energetic nightlife not to discourage them. The **Playa Azul** (Tel: 36 70 67) is the rather plainer sister hotel to the Aquarium and about twice the size.

 Continuing along the coast, the twin resorts of **SAN JAIME** (pronounced *San Hi-may*) and **SON BOU** lay claim to the longest stretch of uninterrupted beach on the island. San Jaime is almost exclusively made up of spacious and comfortable self-catering apartments to which a number of British operators, including Beach Villas and Villa Seekers, organize packages each summer. San Jaime has a handful of small shops and a small water-slide which, for a modest charge, can be enjoyed by children of all ages. There's also a large outdoor swimming pool nearby and the secluded lawn is favoured by topless bathers who can't bear the five-minute stroll down to the beach.

The resort of Son Bou is one of the most popular on Menorca, and virtually all the main British tour operators, including Tjaereborg, Cosmos, Horizon and Thomson, offer summer packages here. Against a scenic backdrop of narrow hills, two identical modern twelve-storey hotels dominate the skyline. Any more than two and this gorgeous stretch of coast would have been destroyed completely, but thankfully the Spanish authorities recognized the potential scenic disaster and authorized the building of no more than two towers.

The beach at Son Bou is nearly two miles long and the soft, white sand stretches all the way along to the next resort of Santo Tomàs. The beach and water shelve gently, so this resort is extremely popular with families bringing young children. Water-sports are available in abundance but be aware of those tempting fixed parasols on the beach and the sun loungers lying about all over the place, which cost a couple of hundred pesetas each to hire for a day. Facilities and entertainments for children are superb, and there is an organized programme of theme nights – talent shows, fancy dress, Tarzan nights and so on – for mums and dads. Like nearly all of Menorca, neither Son Bou nor San Jaime are young persons' resorts.

Los Milanos Sol (Tel: 371 175) and **Los Pinguinos Sol** (Tel: 371 075) are the two identical sister hotels at Son Bou. Both sit right on the beach, all the rooms have private balconies and most of the 594 (total) bedrooms have superb views across the beach and out to sea. The atmosphere is busy and functional and both hotels offer a fine self-service buffet for residents each evening: the spread of food is varied and ranges from succulent, lean pork cooked in Spanish style to traditional British favourites like fish, chicken and chips. Dinner is served over a three-hour period, from 6pm until 9pm, and the selection is as large at 9pm as it is at 6pm. Whenever you choose to dine, you are unlikely to leave hungry.

SANTO TOMÀS has a narrow, clean beach. This modern resort is a well-thought-out combination of hotels, apartments and residential villas. There is little in the way of nightlife other than that organized by the hotels and, like San Jaime and Son Bou, the hotels are almost directly on the beach with the apartment complexes built on the gently sloping hillside behind.

This is an ideal resort for the beach lover as the marvellous, long stretch of white sand is divided into three quite distinct areas: **Playa Santo Tomàs**, which is nearest the hotels and offers the widest stretch of sand (and also the busiest) and a host of extras such as sun-beds, pedaloes, limited water-sports and so on; **San Aldeodato** at the western end of the development, which tends to be much less crowded but the beach area and, particularly, the water's edge is quite rocky; finally there is the popular nudist beach at **Playa de Binigaus** further west still.

Many visitors make the lengthy walk from Son Bou to Santo Tomàs (about two miles although on a roasting summer's afternoon the heavy sand makes it feel like twenty) and are rather surprised to discover a veritable nudist colony as they wander through this relatively isolated stretch of coast. Theoretically, this part of the beach is quite secluded, as there are no direct roads to it and only a wearisome hike along the beach in one direction or another will get you here. But every week literally dozens of surprised tourists stumble on Playa de Binigaus quite innocently and, in an instant, find themselves with their central topic of conversation for the rest of the week! Thankfully the nudists are quite immune to these unsuspecting voyeurs, as most quickly pass with a perplexed shake of the head, but if you are one of the many planning to walk along from Son Bou to Santo Tomàs, then be prepared to disguise your surprise for the few minutes it will take you to cross this narrow strip – or else strip completely and blend into the surroundings!

Package accommodation in Santo Tomàs centres around three large, modern hotels. The largest is **Los Condores Sol** (Tel: 370 050) which is a fine three-star hotel with an attractive façade for such a modern building. It has a total of 188 bedrooms, all with private bathroom and balcony and most have excellent seaviews; those that don't, overlook the surrounding hills. There is a full programme of entertainment here and, of the three hotels in the resort, this one has the best stocked shop, although expect to pay slightly over the odds for most things, particularly fresh food.

The **Hotel Santo Tomàs** (Tel: 370 025) is a four-star hotel opposite the sandy beach and close to the centre of the resort. It is much smaller, relatively quieter and has a more limited programme of entertainment and range of facilities available for residents. The **Lord Nelson** (Tel: 370 125) is an average large package hotel, in need of some refurbishment, but offering most basic hotel facilities. It has a large, clean swimming pool and a smaller one for children.

The next resort is **CALA GALDANA**, probably the most attractive bay in Menorca and rapidly establishing itself as the island's premier resort. Two smaller bays are divided by a striking rocky promontory: white limestone cliffs, worn smooth by eons of natural erosion, form the natural boundaries of the beautifully curved main beach, and natural pinewoods create the perfect backdrop to the whole scene.

Cala Galdana's beach gets quickly crowded with both resort residents and day trippers alike as it is a mandatory stop on virtually all island tours. The best vantage point from which to admire the bay in all its glory is high on the cliff-top above Los Gavilanes Sol hotel. A picnic area and small car park have been made here, and the opportunity to take some truly spectacular photographs shouldn't be missed. It is not the best place to take children, though, as there are no barriers at the cliff edge – and there is a sheer drop of at least a couple of hundred feet into the sea.

Overall, though, Cala Galdana, with such a safe beach, is a superb resort for children. The sand is spotless, sheltered, and gently slopes down towards the water's edge for at least a hundred yards or so out to sea. There are a number of small shops on the beach selling cold drinks (at inflated prices), British newspapers, sun lotion and popular souvenirs. The resort also offers a reasonable amount of nightlife in the three large hotels, but Cala Galdana's main attraction is its outstanding beach.

El Gallo, just outside the resort, has an excellent reputation for charcoal-grilled steaks. Among the numerous cafés and informal restaurants clustered near the beach are the **Oasis** (another grill specialist), and the **Tobogan** which serves a particularly commendable squid and chips, a variation on traditional British fish and chips you are unlikely to regret. All the waiting staff at **Bar Maseo** speak some English, but they sensibly provide foreign guests with a picture menu which makes life so much more simple when trying to order a light lunch or evening meal at this café.

The premier hotel in Cala Galdana is **Los Gavilanes Sol** (Tel: 373 175). It is an impressive modern tower block perched halfway up a cliffside with spectacular views across the bay. A private lift connects the hotel to the beach. The hotel has every popular facility, English-speaking staff and an excellent programme of organized entertainment. As you might expect, this is arguably the most popular hotel in the most popular resort on Menorca, so early booking is *essential*. Many visitors to Menorca staying anywhere else on the island make up their mind to return the following year to this particular hotel and Tjaereborg, for example, urges people wanting to stay here next summer to get their booking forms in on 'the first day the new brochure comes out' to avoid disappointment.

Both the other large hotels, the two-star **Hotel Cala Galdana** (Tel: 373 000) and the **Audax** (Tel: 373 125) have a reasonable range of facilities within minutes of the beach. Of the two, the Audax is the better hotel, although it is a relatively old building as package hotels go and its rather gloomy corridors and public rooms could certainly do with some refurbishment. Both have swimming pools, but the Audax pool has no depth markings, so take extreme care with children.

The last resort along the popular southern coast of the island is **CALA'N BOSCH**, still relatively undeveloped but likely to mushroom in coming years. There are a number of public beaches between Cala Galdana and Cala'n Bosch which are only really accessible if you hire a car (easily the best way to see Menorca). MACARELLA is a half-hour walk from Cala Galdana and is a rather dull little beach with plenty of muddy sand and a small café. Much more impressive is CALA TURQUETA, although access is only really feasible down a steep rough track. CALA D'ES TALAIER is idyllic, although there are no facilities and the small sandy beach can get quite crowded.

Cala'n Bosch itself is quite small, with only a handful of shops and absolutely nothing in the way of nightlife or entertainment. Most of the accommodation is in the form of villa complexes but one or two hotels have started to appear and at least four or five British tour operators, including Global and Cosmos, visit this resort. There are two beaches: one stretch of fine white sand, and an attractive little cove which offers an excellent range of water-sports.

Until 1987, the only hotel in this resort was the impressive three-star **Hotel Cala'n Bosch** (Tel: 380 600) with a very good location, right on the sandy beach. All 180 rooms have private bathrooms and views to the front over the resort and marina, and to the rear over the beach and sea. This hotel is ideal for all types of holiday-makers except young singles who are likely to find the resort as a whole much too quiet.

In 1987 a new low-rise complex, made up of a main hotel building and several bungalow-style apartment blocks, was opened. The **Club Falco Sol** (Tel: 384 623) has a total of 447 twin bedrooms, all with bright modern bathrooms, and a superb range of leisure activities to keep guests of all ages amused. There is a number of wide sun terraces and three reasonably large pools including a shallow one for children. The organized entertainment programme at the Club Falco Sol is one of the best on Menorca.

A few miles up the coast, the development of CALA BLANCA overlooks a rocky inlet and a small stretch of white sandy beach. It is not yet a sizeable resort as accommodation is restricted mainly to private apartments, but one very pleasant hotel does stand out: the **Hotel Cala Blanca** (Tel: 380 450), a medium-sized three-star hotel with 147 bedrooms which at least one British tour company operates to. The hotel has a clean swimming pool and a separate children's pool, and offers a reasonably quiet location in an atmosphere of relatively self-contained comfort which might suit retired visitors more than any other age group. Nearby, CALA SANTANDRIA is an unappealing villa development overlooking another small stretch of sandy beach. Pedaloes are the only facility available on the beach.

Four miles up the coast from Cala Santandria is **CIUDADELA**, the second-largest town on Menorca, and for centuries the capital of the island until the British, during their occupation in the eighteenth century, decided to move it down nearer the wide harbour at Mahón. The British had no interest in Ciudadela (pronounced *th-eea-dadela*) and consequently made virtually no contribution to the architecture of the town.

Ciudadela has a long history behind it, and in the sixteenth century was known as 'Medina Minurka' whilst the island was under Muslim rule. Much of the town was destroyed in 1558 when the Turks invaded, but it was slowly rebuilt in the centuries that followed, and traces of its early history can still be seen around some of the older public buildings. Today the town is a very popular retirement destination for wealthy Spaniards and, interestingly, a flat in Ciudadela will cost you more than a comparable apartment in Madrid.

The best place to start a tour of the town is in the main square, **Plaza d'es Borne** (formerly the Plaza Generalissimo), which is dominated by a large **ornamental obelisk** commemorating the islanders' unsuccessful defence against the sixteenth-century Turkish invasion. The square is surrounded by olive trees and an impressive collection of old eighteenth-century mansions, two of which have been converted into the main **post office** and **tourist information office** and **police station**.

The lower floor of the police station is a fascinating **museum** of local history which appears to have been organized in the most haphazard manner: everything from century-old city keys to medieval human bones are on display. Among the more interesting exhibits are a good selection of old street signs dating back over the last few generations. From here it is only a short walk down to the town's quaint little **harbour** which usually has a colourful collection of small yachts bobbing up and down. A stroll in the opposite direction, from the main square, will take you into the main shopping streets of Ciudadela. For a superb selection of fine leather goods for gents and ladies, have a look round the **Modus Avalon** showroom along San Antonio M. Clarat.

Other points of interest in the town include several distinguished old churches. The magnificent **cathedral** was constructed from honey-coloured stone during the reign of Alfonso III, on the site of an ancient mosque, and resembles a fortress. It is probably the coolest place in town to visit on a scorching summer's afternoon and some of the ornately decorated small chapels are exquisite. Two further churches of note are the **Church of San Francisco**, a bright fourteenth-century Gothic building dominating one corner of the main square, and the nineteenth-century **Palacio de Torre-Saura**.

Although nightlife is rather restricted in Ciudadela, the town has a good range of places to eat out. **El Horto**, just off the northern corner of the main square, specializes in local seafood; **Es Calin** is renowned for its selection of barbecued and charcoaled meats; and **Casa Manolo** (Tel: 380 003) at Marina 103 is reckoned to be *the* place in town for fish and crustaceans, either grilled or served in stews or soup.

About half a dozen British tour operators organize tours directly to Ciudadela, although the range of accommodation options is surprisingly limited. Independent travellers may care to try **Pension España** (Tel: 380 288) on Calvo Sotelo for clean, basic accommodation. The three-star **Hotel Esmerelda** (Tel: 380 250) is a more modern building favoured by package companies and occupying a splendid location overlooking the sea from both the front and the rear. It is about ten minutes' walk from the centre of town, and has 135 bedrooms, all with private facilities, and nearly all enjoy a magnificent seaview. There is a medium-sized swimming pool, with an area for children, and one or two nice sun terraces where guests can relax and enjoy their siesta or pre-dinner drink.

A mile or two from Ciudadela proper is the developing holiday complex of CALA N'FORCAT. It is still an extremely quiet choice of resort, although as developers realize the potential of this attractive site, with its sheltered sandy cove fringed by striking rocky headlands, that will undoubtedly change. The beach itself is extremely small: still large enough to cope with the limited demand from the resort at present, but the addition of day trippers from nearby Ciudadela quickly crowds it. Be cautious of brochure descriptions of Cala N'Forcat which describe it as 'a relaxing family spot' or a 'tranquil' location, as they mean precisely that! Besides apartment accommodation, the two most popular package hotels are the three-star **Almirante Farragut** (Tel: 382 850) and the less impressive two-star **Los Delfines** (Tel: 382 445 or 450). The Almirante Farragut is an enormous hotel: nearly 500 bedrooms make it quite possibly the largest on the island. It takes its name from an American admiral who stayed here during the last century, although the present building is an entirely modern construction which the old admiral would not recognize today. It is situated within five minutes of the beach and most of the rooms look out in this direction. The town of Ciudadela is quite a lengthy hike round to the other side of the bay.

Los Delfines, on the other hand, has nearly 100 rooms on four floors and seems to have been constantly undergoing some sort of building work or refurbishment over the last few years. The work is not obtrusive, but guests are constantly aware that it is going on: as the cliché goes, it will be nice when it is finished. Meantime, facilities are basic but the staff friendly and considerate to minor British grumbles. Children are made particularly welcome.

The last coastal resort of any size is Arenal d'en Castell, the only major resort on the northern coast of Menorca. Before you reach there, though, you will come across the delightful little village of FORNELLS. The building of a massive resort complex, **Playa de Fornells**, is just getting under way outside the village and promises to be one of Menorca's major tourist centres in a few years' time. For now, though, visitors to the island shouldn't miss the opportunity to see this famous old fishing village which itself remains remarkably untouched by tourist development.

Virtually all the village spills down to the seafront and lines the quay like an enormous procession of little houses, cafés, restaurants and shops. This place is heaven for windsurfers because of its shallow, sheltered harbour: there's even a residential windsurfing school offering one- or two-week courses in the sport.

Some of Menorca's best restaurants can be found along the Fornells water-front, and this is the village's principal attraction. You will find none better than **Es Pla**, a bright modern building right on the water-front, which is a regular haunt of Juan Carlos, the King of Spain, when one of his frequent yachting excursions brings him as far as Menorca. Lobster is the king's favourite dish, and naturally most of the restaurants in Fornells include it on their menu, in the hope of attracting the royal custom, but expect little change from £30 for a main course alone. Two other restaurants worth looking out for along the harbour-front are **Es Port** and **San Cora** which both have excellent seafood specialities.

ARENAL D'EN CASTELL is one of Menorca's quietest resorts: the adjective 'quiet' can be applied to most of the island's popular resorts but this one deserves it more than most. Although it is just fourteen miles from Mahón, the road is narrow and wearisome, with barren green fields all around the peak of Monte Toro rising to your left. Facilities in the resort are limited to what is available through your hotel reception and the essential 'all-round' grocery store. Similarly nightlife is strictly limited to the hotel, although occasionally it can be quite entertaining.

A few apartments and a number of large hotels dominate the hillside which looks down onto a wide horseshoe bay. The beach is wide and clean, suitable for children and has one or two water-sports available for the more energetic visitor. Nearly a dozen British tour operators visit Arenal d'en Castell, almost exclusively using one of three large, modern, tower-block hotels.

The **Aguamarina** (Tel: 371 275) is a cheery-looking three-star hotel within five minutes of the heart of the resort. Most of the 248 rooms have good views across the bay, and there are about fifty steps to climb down to reach the bay. There is a good swimming pool and an excellent programme of children's entertainment available. Next door, the **Topacio** (Tel: 371 300) is a 276-bedroom two-star hotel offering basic comfort and more limited views. Of the three main hotels, this one has the drabbest exterior and the least impressive facilities for residents.

The **Castell Playa** (Tel: 371 450) is a very impressive four-star hotel, one of Menorca's best, slightly more comfortably furnished than the previous two but requiring a slightly longer hike down to the beach. The public areas are spacious and air-conditioned and, for those that want to make a bit of noise, there is a nightly disco.

A wide range of possibilities for excursions is on offer from any of the coastal resorts, not only to the obvious destinations like Mahón, Ciudadela and some of the more isolated beaches and coves, but also to see something of the interior of Menorca. The road network is particularly good for an island less than thirty-one miles long and nine miles wide. A busy two-lane road runs between the two main towns (called, incidentally, the M1, and with an accident record per mile equally grim as its British namesake), and car hire is available from all the main resorts. It is *essential* that you think seriously about booking a hire car from anyone other than your package-tour representative as, sadly, there is no shortage of unscrupulous operators throughout Europe's busiest tourist destinations keen to give you a shaky deal in terms of dubious insurance or unforeseen 'compulsory taxes' and so on.

None of the inland towns or villages really merits a special trip but you may be keen to explore a few of the more isolated beaches or spend an hour or two in an appealing little café or restaurant which you could spot away from the main tourist routes. ALAYOR will be the first town you come to if you are driving from Mahón towards Ciudadela. It is a typical rural Spanish town with narrow winding streets and dominated by a large church overlooking the town.

Some of Spain's best icecream is made in Alayor and it is difficult to believe that such a quiet-looking little town held, for many years, the record for the highest birthrate per head of population anywhere in Spain. That might explain why, as many a tour guide is known to comment, you seldom see much sign of life in Alayor! There is a **chemist** in town near the Plaza Franco. For somewhere to eat in Alayor, **Es Plans** serves good local food, and the enthusiastic proprietor speaks excellent English.

The large village of FERRERIAS is unattractive and not worth a stop unless you are keen to see one of the numerous leather factories on the island which is situated just outside the town. Of slightly more interest is the last inland town of any size, MERCADAL, which is a cramped old market town at the foot of MONTE TORO, Menorca's highest point. The town has two particularly good restaurants, specializing in local food, which are well worth seeking out: **Es Moli d'es Raco** (Tel: 375 392) and **C'an N'Aquedet**.

Menorca is a relatively barren, flat island and the soil is not good enough for much intensive agriculture. It was so poor in the past that the dead were entombed in above-ground concrete catacombs rather than buried. Monte Toro is the single peak of any significance on the island. The view from the summit of this single 1,180-foot peak is breathtaking on a clear day, but then it has no competition. It is possible to make the three-mile hike up to the summit by foot, but the only access route is a narrow public road which is always busy with hire cars and coach tours. Half an hour is alloted to the peak on virtually all island tours and, frankly, this is easily the best way of seeing the view.

Most days from the summit you can see almost the whole outline of the island. On rare occasions the distant haze on the horizon lifts to the extent that you can even see Majorca – but locals point out that if you can see Menorca's larger sister island then this is invariably a sign that the fine weather is about to break in favour of a torrential downpour, so don't look *too* hard!

On the summit, there is an enormous statue of Christ, arms outstretched, which was built fifty years ago to commemorate the island's dead in the bloody Civil War of 1936. For centuries a monastery also flourished on top of the peak but this eventually gave way to a convent which is still very much alive. Indeed, the nuns run a prosperous little souvenir shop (easily the cheapest place on the island to buy postcards!) and refreshments are available in a large, shaded café next door. There is an extremely cool chapel where visitors can enter and draw breath for a few minutes if they are careful to respect the sanctity of the place. The nuns make no charge for this resting place, or for the opportunity for visitors to photograph their magnificent gilt altar, but a small donation is always appreciated.

IBIZA

Introduction

Although it is the smallest of the three large Balearics, Ibiza is second only to Majorca in terms of volume of visitors who reach its busy coastal resorts each year. The island measures twenty-two miles long by sixteen wide and you can still see some of the famous pine forests which earned it the name *pitiousa* – the pine island – from the early Greeks. The popularity of this bustling little island has rocketed over the last few years, and it has gained the reputation of being very much a young person's island. Most of the resorts are on the west coast and those which aren't are the quieter ones which will appeal more to those looking for a relaxing holiday destination.

In this chapter we begin our tour of Ibiza in the capital, Ibiza Town, before looking at each of the major resorts in turn, beginning with Figueretas and Talamanca, and following the coast of the island anti-clockwise from the capital.

History

Although there is little evidence of it outside the capital, Ibiza has been known to many great civilizations since the earliest days of antiquity. The first known settlers, in the tenth century BC, were Phoenician traders, although the Carthaginians and the Romans followed over the next few hundred years. The Moors took over the island in the eighth century, and despite various Christian civilizations gaining control of Ibiza for varying lengths of time, it was always known by a name derived from a stem meaning 'white isle': indeed, its modern Spanish name, Eivissa, means just that

By the late 1960s, Ibiza began to receive increasing numbers of overflow visitors from neighbouring Majorca. Gradually the trickle of day trippers became a flood of regular package tourists and many of the peaceful coastal resorts rapidly became some of the fastest growing holiday destinations in Spain.

Getting There

Most visitors to Ibiza arrive through the only airport on the island, the small international a few miles outside Ibiza Town. There are regular internal flights to Barcelona, Madrid and Valencia, and also to Palma on Majorca. Daily ferries operate the ten-hour crossing between Barcelona and Ibiza. About three times a week a ferry crosses from Valencia to the island capital and there is also a daily service (except

Tuesdays) from Denia. Three ferries a week make the five-hour journey from Ibiza Town to Palma.

Climate

Ibiza's climate is similar to that of both Majorca and Menorca, with a long, hot summer lasting from May until early October. The weather usually breaks around November when it can get quite chilly in the evenings. August is the best month with the average temperature about 30°C (86°F) although you can expect superb weather any time from June to September. If you visit Ibiza between May and August you are likely to receive up to eleven hours of sunshine, but this drops to about eight in September and just five from November to January.

Culinary Specialities

Ibiza has a few good local specialities, although seafood is as plentiful (and expensive) as on both Majorca and Menorca. *Parillada de pescado* is a particularly popular mixed fish grill which is available throughout the main resorts and *tumbet*, the Spanish version of ratatouille, is worth trying.

Where to Go for What

Sightseers should stray no further than Ibiza Town: there is practically nothing to see beyond the capital other than modern resorts and woodland. Sunlovers and Sportsmen should head for Cala Vedella or Portinatx. Puerto San Miguel is another option for the Sportsman. The Socialite must head for San Antonio, although Es Cana and Portinatx are more modest options. The Recluse should avoid the Balearics altogether, but parts of inland Ibiza can be very secluded.

The only historic town on Ibiza is its imposing capital, **IBIZA TOWN**, which has occupied a position of strategic importance for centuries: it rises steeply from the sea and clings to the rocky hillside. The overwhelming impression which will strike you about Ibiza Town is just how brilliantly white everything appears. This is the dominant colour throughout the Mediterranean for houses and buildings because of its reflective qualities, but, with the very odd exception and brilliant dashes of colour from the dense array of flowers and shrubs which adorn many side walls, you will find it difficult not to be struck by the whiteness which has distinguished the capital for hundreds of years.

The remains of the oldest part of the town are enclosed by the old **town walls**, and Ibiza Town is just about the only place left in Europe where the medieval walls survive intact. Wherever you are staying on the island, you will have the chance to take a day trip to the capital. It is an opportunity which shouldn't be missed, primarily because there really is nowhere else with much to offer the sightseer on the island, but also because a day in Ibiza Town is likely to give you a glimpse into the history of the Balearic Islands as a whole.

The town walls are as good a place as any to start a tour of the town. The Old Town behind the walls is known as the 'Dalt Vila'. There are just three entrances to the walled town including the main gate, the **Portal de las Tablas**, which is a one-way entrance for cars that then have to leave by the **Portal Nou**. Most pedestrians, though, enter and leave through the **Bastion of San Juan**, at the western corner of the town.

Ancient buildings, quaint back-streets, street markets and arched alleys are appealing features of the old town which you can expect to come across in the Dalt Vila. The central square in the old town is the **Plaza Desamparados** and it is always covered by enthusiastic street sellers offering everything from locally made jewellery to the usual tourist goods like mugs, belts and colourful ornaments.

The **Museo de Arte Contemporaneo** is just off the square and it is open daily from 10.30am – 1pm, and again from 6 – 8.30pm. For a small admission charge you can see (and also buy) some of the best paintings, sketches and sculptures from up-and-coming Spanish artists and their contemporaries throughout Europe and the rest of the world.

The main street in the old town is **Sa Carossa**, lined with quaint little shops and offering the best access route to the top of the town walls. Caution is required at all times if you decide to investigate the walls, but you will be rewarded by some outstanding views. The higher up you go in the old town, the less commercialized your surroundings become; by the time you reach the cathedral square you would almost think time had stood still.

As you might expect, Ibiza Town's **cathedral** stands in the cathedral square and it is probably the most fascinating of the many churches on Ibiza. It is a wonderful old eighteenth-century building, with a distinctive square bell tower which dates back over five hundred years, and a whitewashed interior. Although rather simply furnished for a major ecclesiastical building, it is well worth a visit. A small **cathedral museum** adjoins and features a wide range of relics associated with the building, including a wall display charting the Christian conquest of the island from the Moors. The cathedral is open daily from 10am – 1pm, and again from 4 – 6.30pm except when a service is in progress.

In the Plaza de España you can visit another striking church, the **Church of San Domingo**, which was built in the sixteenth century and stands next to a former monastery that was converted into the **town hall** in 1838. For a small admission charge, you can visit the **archaeological museum** which is just a couple of minutes' walk from the cathedral. Among the exhibits are some pre-Christian bones found on the island of Formentera and a good selection of Roman artefacts found at various sites across Ibiza.

Lying between the Dalt Vila and the harbour is the old fishermen's quarter, known as **Le Peña**, which is a veritable maze of tiny passages, alleyways, and cramped nineteenth-century houses. The quay is a wonderful place to be in the evenings if you really want to soak up something of the atmosphere of the real Ibiza: there are countless little bars and cafés for you to blend discreetly into the general atmosphere and just watch the world go by from this enviable vantage point. The daily market takes place around the **Plaza de la Constitucion** and that, too, is always a fascinating place to wander through.

Le Peña has little in the way of tourist attractions but most of the best bars, restaurants and shops are in this part of the town. The **Puig des Molins Museum** (open daily from 4 – 7pm) is in Le Peña and many of the archaeological finds from the necropolis can be seen here. A disproportionately high number of burial sites have been found on

Ibiza over the last few centuries and, for many years, it was believed that ancient civilizations had looked upon the island as some sort of sanctified burial place. However, the sheer logistics of the ancients endlessly transporting even their most important dead to the island eventually convinced historians that this was probably not the case. Nevertheless, the Puig des Molins Museum has a fascinating collection of burial artefacts, clay figures, and pottery fragments that deserve to be seen. Your admission ticket for the main archaeological museum in the Old Town is also valid for this museum.

The last part of Ibiza Town is the new town, a relatively unattractive area containing what limited industry there is in the island's capital and a good range of shops. It centres around the **Paseo Varo del Rey**, but the only tourist sight of note is the **Church of El Salvador** in the Plaza Canalejas. This modern ecclesiastical building has an unusual pine sculpture of Christ looking, as one guide described it, 'like Roger Moore in discreet sauna wrap and 1965 haircut'.

Nightlife in Ibiza Town can be as lively or as subdued as you want it. This really is one of Europe's premier resorts for the socialite but, frankly, it is geared much more towards the under-thirty market rather than package holiday-makers as a whole. Most of the bars and discos are located in the port area, as mentioned already, and you will find a good selection in and around Calle Major. Such is the competition between rival discos and clubs in Ibiza Town that you are likely to be accosted by enthusiastic youngsters thrusting leaflets or stickers into your hands and telling you how 'absolutely wonderful' their chosen establishment is!

Little happens before midnight but when Ibiza Town starts to swing, it really swings. **Pacha** and **Ku** are two of the best nightspots in Ibiza, with the latter probably having the edge, despite an entrance charge of over £10. At least two or three evenings a week are devoted to special theme evenings, so if you're game enough to visit this place then don't be surprised to find yourself dancing till dawn around the outdoor swimming pool with a grass skirt round your waist. It's probably worth mentioning that Ibiza no longer has its rather exaggerated reputation as the gay centre of Europe, a label which, for years, attracted as many visitors as it put off. There is still something of a gay scene on the island although **Anfora's** in the upper part of the Old Town is the only exclusively gay disco left in Ibiza Town.

Wherever you turn in Ibiza Town you are sure to find at least one or two small restaurants and cafés, so you are unlikely to be stuck for a good range of places to choose to eat out. Very few are really bad, most are reasonable, and only a handful are exceptional. Three of the best we found were **El Brasero** (Tel: 307 168) at Barcelona 4, a bright, cheerful, modern restaurant with an above average menu which offers local specialities in an impressive range of styles; **El Sausalito** in the Plaza Garijo which is a more upmarket restaurant, with more upmarket prices, offering sumptuous seafood dishes with a delicious international flavour; and **Los Pasajeros** along Calle Vicente Sóller which is a bit more difficult to find than the other two, but its elegant first-floor location makes the effort all the more worthwhile.

Ibiza Town isn't really a package-holiday destination in itself: only Iberotravel operates tours specifically to the island capital, so accommodation is limited. Most of the hotels are restricted to the resorts of Figueretas and Playa d'en Bossa just south of the capital which we will be looking at next, but the main **tourist office** at Vara de Rey 13 (near the Iberia airline office) should be able to give you a few ideas of basic accommodation available in town. A couple of options for the independent traveller are **Hostal Sol Paris** (Tel: 301 000) on Calle Vicente Cuervo, and **Hostal Juanita** (Tel: 301 910) along Calle Juan de Austria.

Virtually on the outskirts of Ibiza Town lies FIGUERETAS, a built-up resort concentrated around a small bay. Half a dozen British tour operators visit Figueretas, and the resort's main attraction is undoubtedly its close proximity to the island capital. There are a few shops and a number of reasonable cafés and restaurants around the large hotels but many visitors prefer to go into town for a meal or entertainment in the evenings.

The beach at Figueretas is divided into several small areas: the sum total is really still much too small for this expanding resort, when you add in the inevitable day trippers and locals from Ibiza Town who flock here at siesta time and at weekends. There's not a lot of sand and most bathing is from large rocks, which means this isn't the best place for comfortable sunbathing or children.

One of the better hotels in Figueretas is **Los Molinos** (Tel: 302 250) at 60 Ramón Muntaner. This attractive four-star hotel has 147 rooms spread over six floors. Most of the rooms are at the front of the hotel with good sea views. Make sure you ask for a front room when you book if you don't want the alternative dull rear view. The **Nautico Ebesco** (Tel: 302 300) is an airy, two-star hotel within easy reach of Ibiza Town. Its quiet daytime atmosphere and limited nightlife appeal more to middle-aged and retired holiday-makers, and one or two operators do offer good value packages to it. A reasonable hotel for young singles is the modern **Cenit** (Tel: 301 404). Always busy, this 62 room hotel is a steep climb from the beach and has a wide annexe-roof perfect for sunbathing.

PLAYA D'EN BOSSA lies three miles away from Ibiza Town and is one of the island's fastest growing resorts. Playa began its resort life as a popular day retreat for town dwellers in the island capital, but its magnificent beach quickly established it as a major resort. Nearly all the major British operators run tours here, including Cosmos, Global, Horizon, Intasun, Lancaster and Thomson Holidays.

Playa's best attraction is undoubtedly its beach: an enormous long sandy stretch which is always busy but seldom absolutely packed, even at the height of summer. Most guides and holiday brochures claim this is Ibiza's best beach, a bold claim, but it would be difficult to find one that's better. It is ideal for children and, for the sporting enthusiast, water-sport facilities are superb. Like neighbouring Figueretas, the resort as a whole has a good range of cafés and small restaurants but many visitors prefer to make the short journey (buses are regular) into Ibiza Town. One of Ibiza's best, and newest, discos, **Space**, is well worth checking out in Playa.

The one real disadvantage of Playa d'en Bossa is its close proximity to the airport. Although your transfer time will be under fifteen minutes, you will see and hear all the frequent arrivals and departures (mostly British charters) throughout the day. Although it's never deafening, the noise is irritating and in the evenings can be a real nuisance.

Playa d'en Bossa has a wide range of large, modern hotels from which to choose. The only one which the Spanish Tourist Authorities award four stars to is the **Torre del Mar** (Tel: 303 050) which occupies a commanding position overlooking a part of the beach that is pretty but not perfect for bathing. Bedroom views from its seven floors are excellent, though, and there is a good selection of facilities for children and most age groups apart from young singles.

The three-star sister hotels of **Goleta** (Tel: 302 158) and **Carbela** are popular with British visitors. Facilities are shared and include a large swimming pool with a section for children and an excellent programme of entertainment throughout the summer. Both hotels are located on the beach overlooking a small marina and, for the sports enthusiast, there is a reasonable choice of water-sports available.

One or two hotels have been reported as suffering particularly badly from aircraft noise. These include the three-star **Playa d'en Bossa Fiesta** (Tel: 302 100), and its near-namesake the **Club Bahamas Fiesta** (Tel: 301 716).

Continuing east again, in the opposite direction, the resort of **TALAMANCA** is a collection of small, narrow strips of sand to the south of Ibiza Town proper. Most of the main beach forms an arc shape which would be quite attractive were it not for large seaweed deposits and, at the height of summer, quite a bit of litter as well. A few larger tour companies visit this otherwise cheerful suburb of Ibiza Town although there is a noticeable sameness about the half dozen or so large hotels which dominate the area behind the beach.

The best hotel in Talamanca is the three-star **El Corso** (Tel: 302 062) which sits on a magnificent headland overlooking a small man-made beach. All 178 rooms have private bathrooms and fine views across the beach or towards the harbour at Ibiza Town. Another three-star hotel, the **Simbad** (Tel: 302 262) sits opposite a small stretch of rather untidy, rocky beach. It has a good-sized swimming pool, with a very pleasant sun-terrace around it, but has little in the way of organized entertainment. The **Victoria** (Tel: 302 512) is a clean two-star hotel at the edge of the resort. It is just a few minutes from an average beach, although an obvious attraction is its enormous (Olympic-size) swimming pool. The public areas are informal and relaxing, and there is a good play area for children, with a sandy base, near the swimming pool.

Continuing along the coast, the next resort is **CALA LLONGA**, another modern development eight miles north of Ibiza Town. Cala

Llonga has grown up in recent years around a medium-sized sandy beach and is set against a very pleasant backdrop of pine-clad hills. The main beach is a wide stretch of sand in an attractive horseshoe bay which is reckoned to be one of the safest beaches on the island because of the way it shelves gently into the water. There is a reasonable collection of shops and bars here but most of the entertainment and nightlife centres around the large hotels.

The hotel which occupies the most attractive location is the three-star **Cala Llonga Fiesta** (Tel: 330 887). The modern 163-bedroom building stands on a superb elevated position overlooking the long beach and curving bay. All the rooms have private bathrooms and either sea views or views across the surrounding hillside. Parents with young children should take extreme care with the large, open windows in the public rooms on the first and second floors.

Two other hotels in Cala Llonga are the **Playa Imperial** (Tel: 330 287) and the **Playa Dorada** (Tel: 330 010), two sister hotels occupying adjacent positions overlooking the bay. Both hotels have more than 250 near identical rooms, all with private bathrooms and sea or hill views. The range of organized events for children is most impressive, and a baby-minding service allows mums and dads to relax for a few hours and enjoy the buffet-style international dinner menu, or maybe even let their hair down at one of the Playa Dorada's regular discos.

Ten miles north of Ibiza Town, the resort of **SANTA EULALIA** has mushroomed in the last decade to become Ibiza's number three package-holiday destination after San Antonio Abad on the opposite side of the island and Es Can further up the coast. Compared with Ibiza's other resorts, it is a large settlement which has grown up around a small town. Santa Eulalia has the distinction of being located on the only river in the Balearic Islands.

One of the few tourist attractions of any consequence for miles around is the crumbling remains of a **Roman aqueduct** near the Hotel S'Argamassa (a modest hotel which may be of interest to the independent traveller). Another site worth looking out for if you fancy a change from the beach, is the town's whitewashed **church**. You can't miss it, as its hilltop location dominates the bustling main streets of Santa Eulalia. A small **museum** adjoins the church but its opening hours are erratic so you'd better ask locally if you're keen to see inside.

The main beach of Santa Eulalia is a medium-length curve of golden sand which is another beach that is always busy but seldom too crowded. It has a reputation for having a bit of a seaweed problem, but this tends to be exaggerated by one or two travel guides; it is a potential threat to the island's tourist ecomony which the authorities are painfully aware of. Water-skiing and windsurfing are two of the more popular leisure activities available here.

Apart from the restaurants in the larger hotels, Santa Eulalia has a number of reasonable places to eat out. **El Naranjo** on Calle San José specializes in local dishes and has a very attractive patio surrounded by highly perfumed orange blossoms. Two other restaurants of note in the centre of town are **La Posada**, and the slightly more expensive **Owl and the Pussycat**. 'In' nightspots vary from season to season, but a couple of consistently good ones are **Mozart** and **Harlequin**.

Accommodation in Eulalia centres around a range of one- to four-star modern hotels which cater almost exclusively for package visitors. The best hotel in the resort is the **Fenicia** (Tel: 330 101) which is a relatively new four-star hotel opened as part of a La Siesta development on the river estuary. The 199-room hotel is constructed over eight floors and sits within a hundred yards of the sandy beach. One of the best all-round hotels is the three-star **S'Argàmassa Sol** (Tel: 330 051), a typical Sol hotel with a wide choice of organized activities for visitors in most age groups. Most of its 230 balconied bedrooms have good sea views.

A little way up the coast lies **ES CANA**, probably the fastest expanding of all the growing Ibizan resorts. Es Cana is one of the best all-round resorts for young singles and the young at heart looking for some decent nightlife. There are many busy little cafés, bars and restaurants in the centre of the resort and by the water-front. Look out for the 'hippy' market which operates most days on the outskirts of the resort.

 Es Cana's main attraction, though, is its superb sandy beach, gently curving and wide enough to accommodate the hundreds of visitors which flock to it every day throughout the long summer months. Water-sports facilities are excellent and it is a particularly safe beach for families with young children. Es Cana is also a reasonably good shopping centre, although Santa Eulalia four miles away definitely has the edge with a much wider stock of goods available. One of the most popular excursions from here is across to the island of *Formentera* (see page 196) and there are frequent services on the short crossing.

There is a varied collection of large package hotels in Es Cana, all of which are neatly spread out along the shoreline. Pine forests reach down almost to the edge of the beach and all the popular hotels offer magnificent views across the beach of the pine forest. One of the resort's best hotels is the very popular two-star **Cala Nova Fiesta** (Tel: 330 300) which, although about a mile and a half from the resort centre, sits right on the sandy beach. It caters for all age groups and has a swinging nightlife which centres on a very popular hotel disco. All 305 bedrooms have private bathrooms, balcony and a sea view.

Another two hotels in Es Cana which are worthy of special mention are the **Miami** (Tel: 330 201) which is a more upmarket three-star hotel, with 370 bedrooms, and occupies a quieter situation which might appeal more to an older age group; and the **Coral Playa** (Tel: 330 177) which is a slightly smaller two-star hotel within a few minutes' walk of the resort centre. The Coral Playa's nightly disco can be rather loud so this hotel is likely to appeal more to younger holiday-makers.

There are a couple of reasonable beaches near Es Cana which you might want to seek out: **Cala Nova** is a medium-sized beach divided into natural sections by rocky intrusions in the golden sand. Horse riding is available near here. **Cala Lefia** is a much more popular sandy beach. It's not really bigger than Cala Nova but it has a very attractive red-cliff backdrop and a host of water-sports, making it one of the most popular day-trip options on this side of the island.

S'ARGAMASSA is a small, rather away-from-it-all-type resort quite close to Es Cana. It has a superb beach which, occasionally, can be surprisingly quiet. S'Argamassa is more popularly associated with the larger resort of Santa Eulalia and is a popular spot for water-sports enthusiasts. All the main sports are available for reasonable charges.

The north-east coast of the island has no developed resorts and only a couple of small stretches of sand which could possibly pass as beaches.

There is a small town, FIGUERAL, which for years was one of the most popular places for the hundreds of hippy visitors to Ibiza. There is a large number of apartments here but no British operator visits the town and its only obvious attraction is a couple of larger shops and a noisy disco. **Es Alocs** offer simple accommodation close to the beach for the independent traveller, but don't gamble on finding an empty room at the height of summer.

A little way further round the northern headland, CALA SAN VICENTE looks set to become one of Ibiza's newest 'in' resorts in a few years' time. At the moment there is just a handful of hotels, and only one British company, Portland, runs tours here. The beach is exceptionally attractive but can get quickly crowded.

The next resort of any size is PORTINATX on the north-west coast. It is surrounded by some of the most picturesque countryside around any resort on Ibiza and has three superb beaches which are favourites for water-sports enthusiasts. There is a good selection of small supermarkets, souvenir shops, bars, cafés and restaurants scattered mainly around the beach area. Most of the large hotels have discos or a programme of organized entertainments for residents to enjoy. One point of interest in Portinatx is the old stone **watchtower** from which you can enjoy a breathtaking panorama of the harbour and resort. It is a brisk climb, but one many visitors enjoy.

One of the most popular choices for accommodation in Portinatx is **Club Portinatx** (Tel: 333 077), a medium-sized bungalow-style hotel complex with 120 rooms. Children under seventeen are not allowed. In addition to a small private beach and boisterous range of entertainments, the complex lies within ten minutes' walk of a much larger sandy beach. Other good hotels in this resort include the three-star **El Greco** (Tel: 333 048), which sits right on the beach within ten minutes of the resort centre; and its sister hotel, the **Presidente Playa** (Tel: 333 014). Between them, the two hotels have over 500 rooms and the friendly, English-speaking staff help sustain a wide range of activities for children. Both hotels have swimming pools which include separate sections for children.

The small inland village of San Miguel is worth a short visit, although its old port is now much better known than the town as the resort of **PUERTO SAN MIGUEL**. The village itself sits on top of a small hill overlooking some of the best natural scenery on the

Balearics: acres of olive trees whose layout has changed little since pre-Roman times. Puerto San Miguel is a relatively small resort, used by just half a dozen tour operators including Thomson, Sovercign and Intasun, and has only three hotels of any size to accommodate visitors.

Its main attraction, the beach, is an extremely picturesque sandy bay which is sheltered and perfectly safe for family holidays. The sand is rather coarse compared with other resorts on Ibiza but this is a small problem. There is no nightlife to speak of, apart from a couple of hotel discos and occasional theme nights, and nowhere to eat out other than one or two small cafés near the beach.

Of the three hotels, two of them have been built into the side of a cliff which overlooks the beach: the **Cartago** (Tel: 333 024) is a sister hotel to the neighbouring **Galeon** (Tel: 333 019) and both have nearly 200 rooms with private bathrooms and sea views. Both hotels have a lively atmosphere, but the Galeon has a larger swimming pool, tidier public rooms and definitely the edge all round. The Galeon's nightly **Cartago** disco is reckoned to be the best 'nightspot' in Puerto San Miguel.

The only other hotel of note is the **Club San Miguel** (Tel: 333 041) which is classified as a medium-size two-star hostel. It sits almost right on the sandy beach and has 110 rooms, mostly with sea views. Entertainment is organized most evenings and there is a wide range of common facilities (barbecue area, sunterrace etc.) near the rectangular swimming pool.

Ibiza's largest resort, by a long way, is **SAN ANTONIO ABAD** which lies further down the west coast of the island. The place is chock-a-block with large, modern, tower-block hotels: indeed, there are more hotels in this one resort than there are in all the other resorts on the island added together. You will quickly discover that San Antonio is the resort which gives Ibiza its reputation as a young persons' island. The island as a whole doesn't really deserve to be labelled in such sweeping terms, but San Antonio as a resort certainly does, and realistically, unless you are looking for an energetic, fun holiday surrounded by young people enjoying themselves (i.e. getting drunk) then you would be well advised to consider another holiday destination, whether on Ibiza or elsewhere in Spain.

The modern resort has grown out of the remains of the run-down coastal fishing village of San Antonio. Not a lot of the original town has survived the package developer's bulldozer, but traces of the history of San Antonio in earlier centuries have survived. It is known that the Romans called San Antonio *portus magnus* – literally 'great port' – and even today the harbour is always full of tiny boats bobbing up and down with the current.

There is an excellent collection of shops in the resort, the best selection on Ibiza outside the capital. In the evening the place comes alive with street traders and, if you're prepared to look disinterested and haggle, you can often pick up a bargain souvenir to take home.

There are plenty of discos and vibrant nightspots which come alive after midnight: life in San Antonio generally starts after the siesta and seldom winds down much before dawn. 'British pubs' are a mandatory feature of a resort like San Antonio. They survive because of the vast package-holiday market from the UK. Most of them offer a surprisingly good range of British beers, which is a pleasant side-effect of the ruthless competition between the Spanish owners.

You shouldn't be stuck for somewhere to eat out in San Antonio, but a couple of recommended establishments are **Grill San Antonio** along the Calle Obispo Torres, and **Rias Baixas** on Calle Ignacio Riquer.

As you might expect, the principal attractions of San Antonio are the nightlife and the beach. It is worth mentioning that San Antonio itself is reckoned to have easily the worst beach of any major resort in the Mediterranean. The one stretch of natural sandy beach which lies directly in front of many hotels advertising themselves as 'within a hundred yards of the beach' is seriously overcrowded, invariably covered with decaying seaweed (which has an incredibly arid stench in the hot summer sun) and often quite seriously polluted, which not only makes it unpleasant but also dangerous to swim here. The Spanish authorities are forever trying to improve the situation, but it really seems to be a losing battle.

Having painted this less than enthusiastic picture of San Antonio, it is only fair to say that there are a number of man-made beaches carved out of the bay surrounding the resort. Apart from being frequently overcrowded, these are all generally clean, safe and have a host of water-sports, beach bars and beach accessories for you to enjoy. If you tire of the beaches for an afternoon, there is a host of leisurely strolls and walks up to the surrounding hills which you can enjoy. Take plenty to drink with you (bottled mineral water is cheap and effective), as you'll find yourself dehydrating much more quickly if you're walking, no matter how slowly, than if you were lying on the beach.

In 1988 nearly two dozen British tour operators used over sixty different hotels in San Antonio. Few were outstandingly good or outstandingly bad, but we list below a selection of the better ones which is representative of the quality of all the large hotels in San Antonio. There are only two hotels in the four-star bracket: the **Nautilis Fiesta** (Tel: 340 400) and the **Palymra Fiesta** (Tel: 340 354). The Nautilis has a secluded position, but to reach the main resort centre you need to take a short boat journey – a common feature with many of the resort's hotels. Inside, it is extremely well furnished, and, although all 156 bedrooms have private bathrooms, not all have sea views. The Palymra is a similar size and has a more central location in terms of getting to and from the resort centre. It sits on a narrow strip of man-made beach adjacent to the **Hotel Arenal**. The spacious public rooms are furnished in a mixture of old and new styles and, for the time being at least, the result is tasteful.

Two of the best three-star hotels are the **Bergantin** (Tel: 340 950) and the **Helios II** (Tel: 340 500) which is a sister to another three-star hotel, **Helios I** (Tel: 340 750) just across the road. The Bergantin is 1.5 miles from the resort centre and ten minutes' walk from a decent beach. It has 200 well-furnished rooms and places a strict limit on the number of children it accepts each week, so think ahead if this six-floor hotel appeals to you. Helios II was opened in 1987 and is substantially better furnished than its namesake Helios I. It has a particularly good swimming pool which kids will love: three interconnecting pools, on two levels, with flowing water and non-slip green surround. It is a bright, busy, friendly hotel offering just about the best all-round value of any hotel in its price bracket in San Antonio.

Two of the best two-star hotels are the **S'Amfora** (Tel: 340 700) and the **Riviera** (Tel: 340 812). Both are located within a few minutes' walk of one of the stretches of sandy beach, although the Riviera is another hotel where guests will need to take a short boat trip to reach the resort centre. It is the larger of the two, with 168 rooms, and a good range of organized events for kids and parents alike. The S'Amfora is more suitable for young singles: it has a busy and popular bar and a wide variety of events organized by the tour companies which visit this hotel.

The most popular excursions from resorts on Ibiza will take you on a complete island tour, or a day trip to the capital Ibiza Town. Inland, Ibiza has very little worth a special trip. Most of the island is covered with acres of olive trees and dense scrubland which are extremely attractive to drive through but offer little, beyond the occasional dusty village, if you decide to stop. SAN JOSÉ and SAN RAFAEL are typical of the inland villages, although if you follow the narrow road down to the coast from San José there is a peaceful little beach at **Cala Yondal**. An interesting side-trip from anywhere near the capital is down to the **Covas Santa** (the Holy Caves) which are open most days throughout the main summer season from 9am – 1.30pm and again from 3 – 7pm. The caves are over fifty feet underground and represent what is probably the most spectacular natural phenomenon on the Balearics. Most of the dripping stalactites and protruding stalagmites have been fascinating visitors to Ibiza for hundreds of years.

FORMENTERA

Introduction

As the smallest inhabited island in the Balearic group, Formentera is one of the few remaining 'get-away-from-it-all' destinations in Spain. Only one hour's ferry ride away from Ibiza, the island could not be a more startling contrast to its bigger neighbour: tourist development is confined to one or two smallish resorts and Formentera's glorious, white beaches remain relatively quiet, even during the summer months.

Historically the island's strategic position – 100 miles off the Spanish coastline – meant it was a convenient stopping place for many travellers of the ancient world. However, it was not until the growth of the Roman Empire that Formentera became colonized and cultivated. The Romans turned the island into a major wheat-producing area, and indeed, the name 'Formentera' means 'Isle of the Wheat'.

Today corn is the main agricultural product, and the windmills which are dotted around the island continue to operate, grinding the grain into flour. Geographically Formentera is rather flat, and outside the main cultivated areas, very arid. It is the shortage of water which has put a constraint on the level and rate of tourist development on the island. Only 10,000 people live permanently on Formentera, and the traditional ways of life have changed very little with the advent of tourism.

Accommodation is adequate, but not exactly plentiful. Independent travellers who are coming to Formentera without pre-booking may find some of the best places already full of package holiday-makers.

Similarly, there are no fancy restaurants to eat out in – the usual assortment of local bars or restaurants are in the larger resorts, although in the more remote spots, hotel restaurants may be the only eating-places available.

In the summer months there is a once-hourly ferry from Ibiza. The picturesque town of **LA SABINA**, surrounded by salt-pans, is the island's only port and from here local buses may be taken to the main resorts and towns. Bikes are the most popular way to get about Formentera, and a number of moped-hire and car-rental agencies can be found along La Sabina's sea-front. Be wary of hiring a car – road surfaces are generally poor and ill-maintained. Lack of clear signposting may also present problems during your first few days, although there is scarcely any chance of getting lost on an island measuring ten miles by one and a half.

La Sabina itself is a charming little port with an easy-going atmosphere. There are a couple of bars and a few shops, otherwise the main activity is watching the hourly arrival of boats from Ibiza. The beaches tend to a mixture of shingle and sand, although there are better stretches only twenty minutes' walk away. Accommodation is not plentiful, and your best bet is the **Hostal La Sabina** (Tel: 320 094) close to the town centre, which is clean and friendly, if somewhat austere.

Eight kilometres away on the east side of the island, is Formentera's largest resort of **ES PUJOLS**. A relatively new development, this town boasts a clutch of bars/restaurants, shops and a couple of late-night discos. The beach, which rates as one of the best on the island, is a long stretch of fine white sand. Windsurfing, water-skiing and sailing may be pursued in the calm waters of the bay. Nearby, where the coastline gets rockier, there are some superb, crystal-clear waters for snorkelling, diving and fishing. Walking into the hills behind the resort, there are some lovely views looking eastwards to Ibiza and other islands in the Balearic group.

The holiday-club complex **Club Punta Prima** (Tel: 320 366), perched on cliff-tops some twenty minutes away from Es Pujols, is a good accommodation choice for those with younger children. A wide range of activities is on offer, including tennis instruction, organized games and a variety of water-sports. Discos are held regularly and occasionally feature live music. **Hostal Los Rosales** (Tel: 320 123) is an adequate one-star hotel, located in the town centre and within four minutes of the beach, while **Hostal Ca Mari** (Tel: 320 180) is a small, comfortable hostel a bit further out of town, in a quiet, secluded location.

A mile or so above Es Pujols is the small town of *San Fernando*. A few bars, restaurants and a nightclub are available to holiday-makers who stray out of Es Pujols for the day. Guided tours of the D'en Xeroni Caves (about two miles away) leave from the town centre.

Almost directly opposite Es Pujols on the western side of the island is **PLAYA MITJORN**. Generally a quiet resort, Playa Mitjorn has a beautiful three-mile stretch of sand which is increasingly popular with holiday-makers day tripping from Ibiza. However, there is not much in the way of nightlife or places to eat out, and generally, much of what's on offer tends to be built as part of a holiday-complex – the main source of entertainment in the area. The four-star **Club La Mola** (Tel: 200 011) is one of the best and busiest holiday complexes on the island. A special programme for children, as well as nightly discos and water-sport facilities are just a few of the activities available to visitors. One word of warning – such is Club La Mola's popularity among package holiday-makers that independent travellers are strongly advised to book well in advance.

Another slightly cheaper possibility is the three-star Hotel **Formentera Playa** (Tel: 320 000). Surrounded by pine trees, this hotel fronts onto the sea and is an ideal location for those who anticipate spending a lot of time on the beach. **Club-Mary-y-Land** (Tel: 320 046), a two-star complex, offers a good range of sporting and entertainment amenities. It is not suitable for older couples, however, as the complex is spread out on a steep slope and it's a ten-minute walk downhill to reach the main entertainment area.

Located halfway between Es Pujols and Playa Mitjorn is the island's capital **SAN FRANCISCO JAVIER**. An unremarkable little town, its main attractions are a local open-air market and two fairly uninspired nineteenth-century churches. Nevertheless, on the practical side of things, it's a useful stopping place as it has two banks and a tourist information office, located opposite the church in Casa Consistorial. Cheap accommodation may be found in the family-run *pensiones* around the town centre – **Casa Rafael** (Tel: 320 227) near the church offers decent rooms at reasonable prices.

About four kilometres to the south-east of the capital is the small development of **ES CALÓ**. The village consists of a few scattered hostels, a couple of bars and shops. This is practically the last chance you have of obtaining food and board, as the countryside further east is covered in uninhabited pine forests. **Hostal Entre Pines** (Tel: 320 023) at Es Caló is a good value, three-star hostel in a very secluded spot, only five minutes away from the sea.

Continuing eastwards, the road takes you to the highest point on the island, La Mola (192m). This is the one place on the island which it is worth making the trek to see, as there are some magnificent views of Ibiza and a lighthouse perched out on the point.

On the west coast, about five kilometres south-west of the capital, is the idyllic spot of **CALA SAHONA**. This tiny resort is located in one of the most secluded and picturesque parts of the island. The approach road isn't too good, but once you arrive, there are a few bars and a local restaurant as well as the clean and reasonably priced **Cala Sahona** (Tel: 320 030) to stay in. The main resort of Es Pujols is a fifteen-minute drive away, so some kind of rented transport (bikes, mopeds, cars) is advisable.

Atlantic Beaches

Not all of Spain's resorts are to be found along the Mediterranean. The southern and northern Atlantic coastal areas also offer a number of small, relatively undeveloped places, whose chief recommendation is their excellent, unspoilt beaches of fine sands, washed clean by the ocean surf. From the Ría Bajas, butting up to the Portuguese border, to the Basque Coast, this area has a great deal to attract the beach-lover – especially the sporting type in search of surf as well as sun and sand.

Perhaps the only real disadvantage of the Galician, Cantabrian, and Basque coasts and of the Costa Verde, is the climate. Naturally the climate here is cool – as low as 3°C (36°F) in winter, and it is also much wetter than the Mediterranean resort areas – almost half the year Galicia sees rain falling. But summer is still warm, with temperatures reaching 22°C (72°F) in August and the sun shines often enough to make sunbathing feasible. This is certainly a region of Spain which the beach lover should consider seriously.

RÍA BAJAS AND RÍA ALTAS – THE GALICIAN COASTLINE

Galicia, an autonomous region of Spain taking in the provinces of Pontevedra, La Coruña, and Lugo, lies in the north-west corner of the country bordered by Portugal and the Atlantic. It is Spain's wettest and probably its most fertile area with a climate not unlike that of south-east England in many respects.

The Ría Bajas and Ría Altas are the coastal areas of this land, fjord-like estuaries which offer some beaches of high quality, though the weather is a problem for visitors planning to take advantage of these, and they are therefore not the principal attraction of this area.

The Ría Bajas lies to the south of Santiago de Compostela, famous for its pilgrims' cathedral, and is the less steep of these estuary areas. The first of the Ría Bajas beach resort areas is **BAYONA**, just north of the Portuguese border. It's a colourful little place with cobbled streets and there are small beaches of fine sand at Concheira, Playa de Barbeira and Playa de Burgo.

To the north is **VIGO**, a major port and fishing centre. Although the town itself is essentially industrial there are some good beaches, surprisingly untouched by serious pollution. These include **Playa América** and **Playa Bayona**, but the best of the beaches here are on CIES ISLAND, to which you can take a ferry for a reasonable charge. There are few sights in the town, but you may want to see the two castles around which the town is built – the **Castillo de San Sebastían** and the **Castillo del Castro** – there are good views from both. The **Old Town** and the fishing quarter known as **Berbés** are also both colourful and worth a wander through if nothing else.

Across the Ría from Vigo is **CANGAS** with the reasonable quality **Playa de Rodeira** beach. Around the town there are a number of other easily accessible beaches: the **Playas de Mednudiña, de Pitens**, and **Area Brava**. The latter has probably the best sand.

Continuing north, via the pleasant but unremarkable provincial capital of Pontevedra, we reach **SANGENGO** which has found great popularity with the Spanish during the summer season. There are excellent beaches of fine sand, the **Playas de Silgar** and **Panadeira**.

EL GROVE, a little way around the headland, situated on a small peninsula, has some beautiful and some not so beautiful beaches on the Ría de Arosa. The town is principally commercial, but there is an expanding tourist trade and also a **casino**.

CAMBADOS, across the bay, is a small fishing town where you can enjoy delicious seafood. The beaches are nothing special, but the town is picturesque and there is a Gothic-style **church** worth visiting.

VILLAGARCÍA DE AROSA, is another place to enjoy seafood, and is a pleasant port and increasingly popular resort on a small scale. The beach, **Playa de Compostela**, is again of good quality, as are those to the north at **Oleiros** and **Noya**.

Northwards, is the very edge of Europe and the point which was once thought to be the edge of the world, FINISTERRE. Not far from here there are a number of good, sheltered beaches, and there is another just to the east around the cape, at CORCUBIÓN.

Around the remainder of the coast of La Coruña province, there are a few small villages and fishing ports and all offer more fine beaches, among them those at CAMARIÑAS, LAXE, MALPICA and CAYÓN. These are the first of the beaches of the Ría Altas, areas which are more rocky and much steeper than the Ría Bajas to the south.

LA CORUÑA itself offers a second-rate, polluted beach, and is not really notable as a city of much interest to the sightseer.

The coast of Lugo province has 'resorts' of sorts at RIBADEO, which is rather dull and unimpressive, and at VIVERO, an attractive town, and the beaches in both are excellent – Ribadeo's is particularly beautiful. There are also good beaches in the small towns and villages of SAN CIPRÍAN, BURELLA, FOZ and BARREIROS, though some of the places themselves are not up to much.

THE COSTA VERDE

The Costa Verde – which should not be confused with the developed tourist area in Portugal which shares the same name – is the coast of the principality of Asturias, a fertile and mountainous area of Spain. There are a number of delightful little fishing villages and some really good beaches too. Starting at the western edge of the costa, GIJON is an industrial town and also a resort of sorts. It's not really an attractive place but the beaches aren't bad – though the danger of pollution looms large.

VILLAVICIOSA is set at the end of a long estuary and the beaches here are quite beautiful – much more so than the town itself, which is mediocre if not actually unattractive. RIBADESELLA, some distance on, is a small port with a few hotels and the horseshoe-shaped beach Playa de Santa Marina on the Ría de Sella – which is great. Not far from the town you can see the Palaeolithic cave paintings of the Tito Bustillo caves. Eastwards is LLANES , another fishing port with as many as thirty small beaches of good quality arranged under cliffs. There's a good cliff walk too. More good beaches are to be found at COLUNGA and at LA ISLA.

THE CANTABRIAN COAST

The Costa Cantabria is not a name that is generally part of the vocabulary of the average Spanish holiday-maker, but this is an area which offers some excellent potential for beach lovers. Situated on the northern coast of Spain, east of the Basque lands, and centred around the city of Santander, the beaches of Cantabria offer unspoilt, fine sands, and some excellent surf – though naturally the water is colder than that of the Mediterranean.

The first place of interest on this coast is SAN VICENTE DE LAS BARQUERA, lying on a triangle of land jutting in to the Atlantic and surrounded by the sea – a dramatic location. It's an increasingly popular resort with more and more in the way of modern developments, but it still retains a little of its old character. The excellent **beach** is of fine, white sand and is a good size. In the town itself there are some really good fish restaurants.

A little way along the coast is COMILLAS, a quiet resort with some attractive older areas. The Playa Comillas beach is again of fine, white sand and slopes gently down to the sea. Nearby, the **Oyambre Beach** is of similar quality but is much longer and less busy than its neighbour.

Above Comillas there are a number of interesting palaces and buildings – the resort is still popular with the Spanish aristocracy. Amongst the sights is the massive, splendid **Jesuit College** in Gothic style and **El Capricho**, a small and highly unusual palace designed by the famous Spanish architect Gaudí.

Continuing to the east we come to SUANCES around which there are three beaches. **Playa de Cuchia** offers around 800 metres of fine white sands, fringed by dunes. Opposite, **Playa de la Concha** is a similarly sized beach set against a pinewood. A little way to the west is the less impressive **Playa de los Locos.**

SANTANDER is a major city, lying at the centre of this stretch of coast, a university town which is a popular holiday destination with the Spanish. The beaches here are excellent. The first of them, and the most popular, is **El Sardinero**, a long, well-serviced stretch of fine sand where the ocean rolls in with some force. The surrounding resort area has an elegant, old-fashioned air. The **Playa de Magdalena** is another long stretch of fine yellow sand on the edge of the wooded headland, which boasts a **windsurfing school**. Above the beach is a Tudor-style palace built for King Alfonso XIII. Other beaches around Santander include the very long **Playa de Castañeda, Puntal de la Bahia**, and the **Playa de Mataleñas**, in a very picturesque bay.

Among the sights of Santander – and there's not a vast selection – are an interesting **Museo Provincial de Prehistoria**, an archaeological collection of great importance, which includes remains from the surrounding area dating from 13,000 BC! The museum can be found on Calle Casimiro Sainz and opens Monday-Friday 9am-2pm, Saturday 9am-noon. Free admission. Other sights of the city include a rather dull **Museo de Bellas Artes** – there are a few Goyas but not much else. There's a reasonable amount of nightlife in Santander – certainly more than you will find in many of the rather quiet resorts along the Costa Cantabria.

East of Santander are NOJA and SANTOÑA, small, attractive resorts, both with good beaches – Santoña's is particularly long. Right next door to Santoña is LAREDO, with a beautiful beach of fine sand stretching out for more than three miles and shelving gently down to the ocean; it may well be the best of the Cantabrian beaches – it's certainly amongst the best. The resort is very busy in summer, when it is especially popular with French visitors. The town itself is not unappealing, particularly its older areas, and for the socialite there are a fair number of **bars and discos**.

The last of our Cantabrian resorts is CASTRO URDIALES, halfway between Laredo and the city of Bilbao. It's a small, picturesque fishing port, still relatively uncommercialized with two very good beaches, **Playa de Brazomar** and **Playa de Oriñón**, which get quite busy at weekends with crowds of Spaniards from Bilbao.

THE BASQUE COAST

From the edge of the Costa Cantabria on the west, to the French border on the east, is the Basque coast, the very edge of an area of pleasant, verdant countryside, whose people are renowned for their independent streak. Unfortunately, that urge for independence has been taken to violent extremes by the notorious Basque terrorist movement ETA, though this shouldn't deter you from visiting the area and taking advantage of some excellent beaches, as the media tends to over exaggerate the problem. All the beaches along this coast are of a fine golden or white sand and, with few exceptions, are clean and unpolluted.

The first of the Basque Coast resorts is ALGORTA, just north of

Bilbao, with two very good beaches and an attractive old quarter appealing to sightseers. Not much further on is PLENCIA, another small resort and fishing port with a smallish beach of good, soft sand. Eastwards, there are a number of small villages and towns with more beaches of the same fine sand, including BAQUIO, which has some tourist development on a small scale, and PEDERNALES.

Some distance on, past Cape Machichaco, are LEQUEITIO and ONDÁRRAO, set amongst hills clothed in pine trees. There's an attractive harbour area in both places and small beaches.

DEVA, midway along the Bay of Biscay, is a small resort at the mouth of a river with a beach of fine, golden sand. If you visit Deva, take the opportunity to see the remarkably beautiful **Church of Nuestra Señora de la Asuncíon** which dates from the thirteenth century and is now a national monument. Further east is ZUMAYA, a picturesque fishing town and small resort with two beaches, the **Playa de San Telmo** and the **Playa de Santiago**, both excellent. ZARAUZ, around ten miles from San Sebastián, is another attractive beach resort on quite a large scale, by the standards of this area.

And so to SAN SEBASTIÁN, which the Basques call Donostia. Situated only twelve miles from the French border on the mouth of the River Uremea, and around the Bahía de la Concha, San Sebastián is a large, fashionable resort, popular with the Spanish and French – and deservedly so. The marvellous **beaches** are of high-quality golden sand and the town itself is extremely pleasant, with an atmospheric old quarter and a new town area of wide, tree-lined boulevards and quite tasteful modern architecture. Among the sights of the town are the sixteenth-century Gothic **Church of San Vicente**, and the eighteenth-century Baroque **Church of Santa María**, both particularly attractive. Also worth seeing is the **City Museum**, housed in what was once the Convent of San Telmo, which offers a superb collection of pictures by Spanish masters. From the nearby hills of **Monte Ulia** and **Monte Igueldo** there are magnificent views across the town and the surrounding countryside, and the latter also has an amusement park.

Beyond San Sebastián, right on the border with France and not far from Biarritz, is FUENTERRABÍA, a popular resort town with a good beach and picturesque streets. The **Castillo de Carlos V** has been turned into a parador and offers some fine views as well as superb accommodation.

Mediterranean Beaches

Costa Brava

INTRODUCTION

The area reaching about forty miles north-east of Barcelona to the border town of Port Bou is known as the Costa Brava, literally the 'Wild Coast'. This was one of the first parts of Spain to become heavily developed by the package market, and is still a popular destination for road or rail travellers visiting Spain independently. For such a relatively small stretch of coast, the Costa Brava has a wide range of natural scenery from long, golden beaches to breath-taking mountains. Inland, there is plenty to see as well, including the famous old city of Gerona and the great monasteries and vineyards east of Barcelona.

The Costa Brava forms part of the Spanish region of Catalonia, traditionally one of the most fiercely independent areas of the country. It is a fascinating region which, in many respects, offers a greater diversity of natural beauty and history than the larger coastal areas of Costa Blanca or Costa del Sol. In this chapter, we begin our tour of the region at the Spanish border and work south through the main resorts until we reach Barcelona. Where possible, we have made suggestions about possible day excursions from the main resorts and conclude with some suggestions about the best inland excursions.

HISTORY

Much of Spain's eastern coastline is distinguished by countless tiny harbours and, as you might imagine, many of these became flourishing ports which played a significant part in the region's history. One after the other, the Phoenicians, Greeks and Romans all settled here and were conquered. Although the Moors held most of the Iberian peninsula for many generations, they occupied the Costa Brava for only a relatively short period as Christian resistance was strong. The reconquest was among the most straightforward of any region in Spain, and ultimately the Costa Brava formed part of the Catalonian/Aragonese kingdom.

The War of Succession was a difficult period as the Catalonians sided with Archduke Charles of Austria, the eventual loser. The region did no better in the early nineteenth century during the War of Independence, because of its close proximity to the territory of the invading French. Things cooled considerably in the wake of the Spanish Civil War earlier this century, and by the late 1950s the region was being heavily promoted as one of Spain's first large-scale holiday destinations. Today, of course, the legacy of the Costa Brava's history is some fine sights and many places of interest for the visitor who might be tiring of the beaches for a day or so.

GETTING THERE

The majority of visitors arrive on a charter flight to the region's main airport at Gerona. Over a million passengers a year are handled, mostly British tourists and domestic air travellers. There is a second airstrip, suitable only for private aircraft, at Ampuriabrava on Rosas Bay. Rail links with major Spanish destinations and the rest of Europe are excellent: the main line crosses the border at Port Bou and winds inland through Figueras and Gerona before continuing south to Barcelona and beyond. There are regular ferry links from Barcelona to Majorca, Ibiza and Menorca but nothing to speak of from ports further north.

CLIMATE

The Costa Brava is not one of the warmest parts of Spain. The peak month for temperature is July when the average is around 27°C (80°F), with around ten hours of sunshine. This slips gradually down to about 21°C (70°F) by the end of October, and then drops sharply to between 14° and 18°C (57°-65°F) from November until April. By June, the average is back up to 23°C (74°F). October is the wettest month, with an average of seven rainy days.

CULINARY SPECIALITIES

If you look beyond the international menus offered by most of the large hotels, you will find some of Spain's best cuisine in the Costa Brava. A delicious trout dish is *truchas à la navarra*, although the rabbit-based *conejo con alo-oh* is likely to be a more common sight. Many dishes are made more lively by the addition of *picada*, a speciality Catalan sauce made from garlic, parsley, toasted almonds and chopped pine seeds. To was it all down, look out for *El Priorato*, a thick, mild red wine peculiar to this region.

WHERE TO GO FOR WHAT

To most people, the Costa Brava means no more than the large resort of Lloret de Mar. This bustling, cosmopolitan destination is perfect for the Sunlover, Socialite and Family Holidays. The Socialite will also be interested in the growing resort of Blanes. Gerona is a must for the Sightseer, and the Sportsperson is likely to be attracted to the wide range of water-sports available at Playa D'Aro.

THE COAST

Right on the border with Spain, the small town of PORT BOU will be your first sight of the Costa Brava and Spain itself if you enter the region by rail. The town has just over 2,000 inhabitants and is a popular stop-over destination with independent travellers heading north or south. Until the start of this century, it used to be a popular haven, with smugglers making the same journey. There are one or two beaches nearby, including **Cala Petita** and **Playa Farella,** but the sand is coarse and realistically this is not the best place to bathe with so many better beaches further down the coast.

The port of LLANSÁ is slightly more lively, and already it is a small self-catering resort for at least one British tour operator. Llansa once had a thriving marble industry but, like so many little towns and villages on Spain's eastern coast, it is looking more and more towards the tourist industry to provide the mainstay of its income. The beaches near here tend to be quiet and clean compared with many further south.

Five miles down the coast PUERTO DE LA SELVA (meaning literally 'the Port of the Woods') is one of the chilliest places to be in Spain during the winter months; even in summer it can quickly get very cool in the evenings, though a backdrop of round hills gives it some protection against the elements and regular finds of prehistoric knives, bones and other artefacts have proven that this was one of the earliest human settlements on this part of Spain.

The **Monastery of Sant Pere de Roda** is a tough two hours' walk away from the port, but one of the most rewarding sights for miles around. It is located at the top of Mount Vedera, one of the highest peaks in the region, and an outstanding vantage point for the whole northern coast. The origins of the monastery date from the tenth century, although it fell into disuse by the eighteenth century and has been undergoing major restoration work for a number of years now. For the geologists, Mount Vedera is the last of the Pyrenean foothills to reach the coast.

The only village of note on the isolated Cap de Creus peninsula is CADAQUÉS, one of the most peaceful and picturesque spots on the northern coastline. It has not been developed as a resort of any description and, clearly, that is one of its obvious charms. Much of its local colour and character has been preserved, and a great many famous writers and artists have chosen to live in or near here. Perhaps the greatest surrealist artist ever, the ailing Salvador Dali, still lives near the village, and once described it as somewhere where the 'mornings are of a savage and bitter gaiety and the evenings often tinged with a morbid melancholy'.

Almost certainly, Dali was recalling the village's troubled past; for such a peaceful village, Cadaqués has had a colourful history. In the late thirteenth century it was first sacked by French invaders and, three centuries later, the great pirate Barbarossa burned the church, killed many of the residents and almost destroyed the little village. The great architect Pau Costa was responsible, in the seventeenth century, for rebuilding the **church** in fine Baroque style as you can see it today.

All the major resorts on the Costa Brava are clustered a good way further down the coast, with the notable exception of **ROSAS**, on the southern side of the Cap de Creus. This is the beginning of the 'real' Costa Brava, the beautiful 'Wild Coast', with its beaches and large hotels, so often associated with this part of Spain. Rosas, or 'Roses' as it is often spelt in English, is one of several towns on the Costa Brava which have undergone considerable development with the onset of a growing tourist industry: in the space of a couple of decades, the once sleepy village has turned into a resort which now has a population of nearly 10,000.

The town has a long history: it is known the ancient Greeks settled here and some historians reckon that the unusual name Rosas came from the Greeks as a derivation of Rhodes. At the peak of Catalonia's power and influence, a great fleet sailed from Rosas in the mid-fourteenth century to quell a rebellion in Sardinia.

The most obvious monument to the town's former glory is a magnificent **fortress** which Charles I built in 1543. La Ciutadella was one of the most heavily fortified buildings in Spain at the time it was built, yet the French still managed to capture it during the Peninsular

War. Today, the peaceful ruins belie its troubled past and make a very interesting spot to visit.

Rosas remains an important fishing port: the fleet arrive back on most evenings at around 6pm and it is no exaggeration to say that the fish in just about any of the restaurants in the town are among the best anywhere on the Costa Brava. The town is a reasonable shopping centre, and a traffic ban in the main street makes things a lot safer for visitors. There is a **Tourist Information Office** (Tel: 257 331) on the Avenida Rodas. There are also several excellent beaches near Rosas, all set against a marvellous backdrop of low Pyrenean foothills. The coastal area round about here is a favourite for residents of the northern coast to visit during the warm summer siestas.

Continuing down the Costa Brava, there is little to interrupt the coastline until you reach L'Escala. There is a tiny, developing apartment resort close to a good beach at EMPURIA BRAVA, but the only other village of note is SAN PEDRO PESCADOR. San Pedro is one of the coast's many unremarkable fishing villages, although this one is a little bit unusual simply because it sits two miles inland, on the banks of the River Fluviá. Three or four miles inland again, the remarkable eleventh-century Romanesque church at SAN MIGUEL DE FLUVIÁ might make a more rewarding visit.

L'ESCALA lies at the southern end of the Gulf of Rosas, and its name means literally 'the Stopping Place'. An ever-increasing number of visitors does just that in the growing fishing village which is best known for its canning industry. The village itself has very little to merit a stop, but nearby the beaches of **Portichol, Riella** and **Montagó** are worth a visit if you feel like getting away from your resort for a day. Unfortunately, these more northerly beaches are no longer a well-kept secret, so don't be surprised if a few hundred of your fellow holiday-makers have the same idea as you if you do decide to visit.

A couple of miles outside L'Escala are the most significant archaeological remains on the Costa Brava at **AMPU-RIAS.** Lying close to the beach, these considerable remains bear witness to two of the greatest European civilizations, the Greeks and the Romans, who built a major settlement on this site. Much of the site has been excavated, and it is now known that it was founded around 550 BC by Phoenician merchants. The Romans occupied it in the third century BC and, in turn, they were replaced by the Visigoths and eventually the Normans.

Ampurias began life as the Greek town of Emporion, and is a truly fascinating place easily recognized as one of Spain's most important archaeological sites. One of the large temples has a striking replica third century BC statue of the Greek healing god Asklepios. Other remains include the original town gate, a couple of magnificent villas (complete with mosaic floors), and the Roman market place.

The site was first excavated in 1908 and most of it can now be visited. It is open daily from 10am – 2pm, and again from 3 – 7pm. The **Greek Crown Emporium** and an **archaeological museum** record the detailed history and show some of the best artefacts from this fascinating site. Ampurias is a good 'two-in-one' destination, as there is over half a mile of long sandy beach for you to relax on once you have seen the remains – and it is a perfect place to spend the hour from 2 – 3pm when it closes for the afternoon siesta.

ESTARTIT lies at the head of the long Bay of Pals, and is the most northerly package-holiday resort on Spain's eastern coastline. It lies twenty-seven miles east of Gerona, and only one road leads in and out of it. The native population is under 1,000, and little remains of the original fishing hamlet as a result of the booming tourist industry which has settled on the Costa Brava over the last couple of decades.

The resort is dominated by a backdrop of pine-clad hills and, although it is a resort whose popularity increases annually, it remains a relatively peaceful destination. It is the most popular resort with UK-based self-catering tour operators, and last year a dozen or so offered holidays to this part of the coast.

Estartit has a wide, sandy beach which shelves gently into the sea and is reputed to be the best on the Costa Brava. It is located close to the resort centre and is extremely safe for children, although, as with all the Costa Brava's beaches, caution against unexpected tall waves is always needed. The easy pace of life in Estartit means it is tailor-made for young families looking for a quiet, relaxing beach holiday.

One of the most popular activities in this resort is the boat trips to the MEDAS ISLES, a handful of tiny islands about a mile and a quarter from the main beach. Once there, you can see a very attractive underwater **fauna preserve**. For snorkelling enthusiasts, this is reckoned to be one of the best spots on the Costa Brava.

The largest island, MEDA GRAN, claims to have a genuine pirates' lair, from where raids on the nearby coast were launched. A monastery was erected in the fifteenth century but, since the end of the last century, the island has been virtually uninhabited apart from tourists and a lighthouse keeper.

Estartit has a good range of shops, including a surprising collection of exclusive ones, and a number of reasonable bars and restaurants. Monday is market day and the best time to see the resort 'in action'. Nightlife is limited to a few bars around the harbour and one or two modest discos. Day excursions to the ancient town of Ampurias and the city of Gerona (see 'Inland' section at the end of this chapter) are strongly recommended, and it is possible to visit independently or as part of an organized group through your tour-company courier. The **Tourist Information Office** (Tel: 758 910) is at Rocamaura, 29.

There is a reasonable sprinkling of accommodation in Estartit, although the emphasis is on value-for-money comfort rather than luxury. The best hotels are a handful of mainly two-star establishments which mostly retain a surprising amount of character and charm for a growing resort.

Arguably the best hotel is the **Miramar** (Tel: 758 628), a very appealing hotel made up of three large blocks which are all connected by well-tended gardens. It has 80 bedrooms, sits close to the beach, and about ten minutes' walk from the resort centre. Leisure facilities include a small swimming pool, occasional live music and water-sports from the nearby beach. Ideal for most holiday-makers except young singles; a description which fits the resort as a whole quite neatly. The largest hotel is the 160-roomed **Panorama** (Tel: 758 092) which is actually a budget one-star place, just a few steps away from the beach and about twenty minutes from the resort centre. There is a regular 'Flamingo Show' for residents to enjoy, and although the quality and standards of furnishing are pretty basic, this is a good, all-round family hotel for anyone who isn't expecting any frills from where they stay.

A little way inland, TORROELLA DE MONTGRÍ is an interesting village to visit for an afternoon or even to take a small detour to on your journey further north or south. Torroella was a flourishing port in early times: indeed, the largest ships of the day used to sail regularly up the River Ter as late as the thirteenth century but, since then, the estuary has silted up to the extent that the village now lies totally inland.

Among the points of interest in Torroella are a partly finished **castle**, started shortly before the estuary began irrevocably to silt up by the great warlord King Jaime II. At that time, Torroella was a favourite royal hunting area, but its popularity diminished in the following century when most of the population was wiped out by a devastating plague. The unlucky village had recovered most of its strength by the sixteenth century when it was repeatedly hit by foreign invaders and pirates. Its exposed coastal position, despite the silted estuary, made it a popular target and, without the protection of a large fortress (remember, the castle was never actually finished), it was unable to defend itself adequately.

Further down the coast, BAGUR is a small self-catering resort with a population of around two and a half thousand. Like so many ancient coastal towns and villages, it has mushroomed out from the old **castle** which still stands over it. Narrow, white-washed streets echo the receding rural charm which countless little resorts like Bagur are slowly sacrificing as the package-holiday market continues to expand.

Four or five good beaches cluster round the town. The five beaches are: **Aiguablava**, so named because of its intense blue water, **Cala Fornells, Cala de Sa Tuna, Sa Riera**, and **Aiguafreda**, and all are beautiful. In the words of the Spanish Tourist Authority, 'They rival each other in perfection, beauty and tranquility.' They certainly are beautiful, but slowly the tourist market is developing round them, to say nothing of the hordes of day visitors who arrive here all summer, so they are far from tranquil. Aiguablava has an excellent marina for either the sailing enthusiast or the sightseer to enjoy. One of nearly a hundred magnificent paradors throughout Spain (and, incidentally, the only one on the Costa Brava) is also located near Aiguablava – ideally situated for you to moor your yacht at the marina and stroll up the hill for dinner . . .

Practically next door to Aiguablava, LLAFRANCH is a small village, formed by a group of white houses descending from the mountains to the sea, and one of the larger self-catering resorts on the 'Wild Coast'. Llanfranch is dominated by a fantastic bay, with a long promenade on one side looking down onto the long, golden beach which stretches round the coast for nearly three-quarters of a mile. On the other side, you can see the **mountains, lighthouse** and **Shrine of San Sebastian** at the other end of the beach. From here you can stand back and enjoy the best views along the coast.

Nearby, TAMARIU and **CALELLA DE PALAFRUGELL** are small, secluded resorts. Tamaria is an unassuming self-catering resort and less impressive than Calella. Calella, incidentally, should not be confused with another Calella, on the Costa Dorada, as there is a considerable difference in the facilities available. The resort is remarkably compact, and spills out from an old whitewashed fishing village; the net result is one of the most charming, characteristic destinations on the Costa Brava.

There are a number of bars, cafés and small restaurants in this resort, but shopping facilities are limited and, clearly, this is not one of the reasons why you come to a small resort like this. A key attraction is the numerous small beaches round about it, although it has to be said that, on the whole, these tend to be extremely small with limited facilities. The best known are **Port Bou, El Golfet, Canderell** and **Mela Espina**. Without exception, they are all extremely picturesque but the sand is coarse and swimming is limited due to an alarming number of rocks just beneath the water level. They are totally unsuitable for families or keen swimmers of any age.

A couple of miles inland, you can visit the slightly larger village of PALAFRUGELL proper, although the only attraction is the fifteenth-century **Church of Saint Martin** with its imposing Gothic façade. This is a good place to pick up one or two bargains if you are interested in either local pottery or leather goods, two handicraft specialities of the Costa Brava.

Accommodation in Calella de Palafrugell is limited. The best place to stay is a four-star *residencial*, **Residencia Alga** (Tel: 300 058) which has 54 small rooms located about five minutes from one of the better stretches of sandy beach. Facilities for children are good, and there is a delightful cellar bar – De L'Alga – which has live entertainment four nights a week. A useful feature is the large swimming pool, considering how poor beach swimming is.

One other place to look out for is the two-star **Hotel Gelpi** (Tel: 300 154) which has 34 straightforward bedrooms and an unusual location on top of a narrow hill in the centre of the resort. Just walking here will give you a glimpse of some narrow, typically Spanish back-streets. Inside, the atmosphere is informal and relaxed: ideal for all age groups except young singles looking for nightlife.

A very traditional old two-star hotel is the **San Roc** (Tel: 300 500), with 50 (small) bedrooms, set in an extremely attractive location on a large rocky headland overlooking the resort centre. It is quite a steep climb down to the beach, so visitors should bear this in mind. The dining room is probably the most attractive public room, and the three-course/three-choice evening menu is most impressive. No organized entertainment, but no shortage of genuine Spanish charm and hospitality.

The town of **PALAMÓS** lies at the geographic centre of the Costa Brava, and almost exactly halfway between Calella and the next resort of any size, Playa de Aro. Palamós will strike you as a busy place: it is constantly bustling with visitors and locals alike, and many of the 12,000 inhabitants are sustained by the fishing industry. The wide harbour has played an important part in the town's long history, and it was from here, in 1299, that the Catalonian fleet set out to conquer the Turks who had occupied the island of Sicily.

One of the most popular sights in Palamós is the **fishing harbour** from where the fleet leaves each morning at dawn and returns by late afternoon to commence the daily auction of its catches. The fast-talking auctioneer still uses native Catalan, and is reckoned to pack in up to four or five hundred words a minute.

The harbour also acts as one of the best marinas on the Costa Brava, and several hundred small crafts can usually be seen bobbing about in the clear water. One place of note in Palamós is the small **museum,** in the centre of town, which has a remarkable collection of modern paintings, local ceramics and natural history artefacts which include a number of cases full of stuffed Costa Blanca mollusks. It's worth a visit, but don't expect it to be the highlight of your trip!

Water-sports on the surrounding beaches are superb. The best stretch of golden sand reaches round the coast to SAN ANTONIO DE CALONGE. San Antonio itself is an attractive small village which is expanding rapidly; all around, the water is an amazing turquoise blue and there is considerable villa development all around this area.

PLAYA DE ARO is the next coastal resort, and it spills down from the town of CASTILLO DE ARO a couple of miles inland. Castillo is the communications centre of the region, and a singularly unremarkable place were it not for its fine coastal namesake. Playa de Aro is still growing, and will strike you as an essentially modern resort. The neatly tree-lined streets are well laid out, and this purpose-built development is fast evolving as one of the Costa Brava's most fashionable destinations.

In its favour, Playa de Aro is a very good shopping centre for a resort of its size. In addition to the usual range of souvenir shops, there is a reasonable selection of more upmarket boutiques. Locally made leather goods are a particularly good buy throughout the Costa Brava. Nightlife is good, although the larger resorts further down the coast offer more variety for the serious Socialite, and there are a number of popular restaurants in the harbour area where you can try some of the best fish from local catches. There is a **Tourist Information Office** (Tel: 817 284) at Jacinto Verdaguer, 11.

Playa de Aro is primarily a self-catering/apartment resort, like many on the Costa Brava, and consequently has very little hotel or *residencial* accommodation available. One notable exception is the relatively new, functional, three-star **Hotel Monterray** (Tel: 819 613) which was opened in 1986. It has 112 bedrooms, all with private bathroom facilities and balcony, and it lies about seventy yards from a reasonable stretch of (coarse) sandy beach. Entertainment facilities for all the family are superb, with a nightly disco and weekly live music programme. Although there's plenty to do, young singles might feel a little suffocated by the happy family atmosphere which prevails.

Just down the coast is S'AGARO, a small town started from scratch in the 1920s and now a charming coastal settlement overlooking a good stretch of sandy coast which is backed by a green curtain of heavily scented pine trees. Well-planned, deluxe apartments in a near identical style are the most obvious feature of S'Agaro.

SAN FELIU DE GUIXOLS, on the other hand, has a longer history. This industrial town has nearly 16,000 inhabitants and is one of Spain's most important cork-producers. It has little to merit a visit unless you are keen to see some reasonable examples of early twentieth-century Spanish architecture, or perhaps visit its small **museum** which will give you a clearer idea of the town's origins. Nightlife is reasonable as there are a number of good bars, restaurants and discotheques which have sprung up in the last few years.

Legend has it that the great Iberian King Brago ordered a massive fortress to be built overlooking the bay here, which he felt was easy to defend. Whether or not he ever did build his castle will probably never be known for certain, but a large structure was destroyed by the Moors, in medieval times, and what they built in its place can still be seen today as a **monastery**. The oldest part is the **Porta Ferrada**, an eleventh-century tower which was restored shortly before the Spanish Civil War.

San Feliu de Guixols is already a small self-catering resort, although the hotel industry has yet to take off. That will surely follow in a few years' time as resorts on either side of it continue to expand. The nearest beach, incidentally, is an unspecial stretch of crowded sand near the fishermen's berthing jetty; it's not bad but, frankly, there are plenty of better places within easy reach of the larger resorts on the Costa Brava.

A much better beach is a couple of miles away, at **San Pol**. There are a good number of water-sports available, including windsurfing, sailing, hire of pedaloes, dinghies and so on. The sand is no less coarse, but the water is cleaner and the beach slightly less crowded. An obvious advantage is the selection of beach bars and cafés which lines the back of the beach.

The Costa Brava has only three resorts of any size which cater for more than just self-catering/apartment holiday-makers. They are all clustered down at the southern end of the region, and the first of these is **TOSSA DE MAR**. Like so many idyllic little coastal towns, Tossa was a haven for artists and writers from across Europe for generations before the package boom started in the late 1960s.

The town has a population of just over 3,000, and its strategic importance in earlier centuries is instantly obvious. It sits right on the coast, yet is surrounded on three sides by steep, pine-clad hills; the fourth side is protected by a **medieval wall** which was built in the twelfth century and much of which remains as a popular tourist attraction today. You can visit some of the original guardhouses and dog kennels.

By the seventeenth century, the town was relatively safe from invaders, and it slowly began to expand outside the wall. Around this time a new **church** was built between the wall and the beach, and this attractive old building is worth a visit. One feature of the original wall was four huge **towers** to guard against invaders trying to scale it. One had to be demolished when a lighthouse was built earlier this century, but three of the original towers can still be seen. In the centre of the town, you will be able to see remains of even older settlers in the shape of the old **Roman square**. The Old Quarter (Vila Viele) has been largely excavated, and many of the artefacts are now on display in the town museum.

The town itself is distinguished by its long, narrow streets and a good assortment of bars, restaurants and souvenir shops. Tossa has a lively nightlife which, in recent years, has moved away from the hotels into the town centre. An added attraction is the regular ferry-boat service to the two other large resorts on the southern coast, Lloret de Mar and Blanes. Tossa's **Tourist Information Office** (Tel: 340 108) is at Cruce Ctra.

Tossa was one of Spain's earliest resorts but, thankfully, development was stopped before the old character was completely destroyed by mile after mile of tower-block hotels. All round, Tossa is an excellent choice of resort. It offers facilities for all the family, plenty of nightlife and the sightseer won't be disappointed either. The Sun-Worshipper will delight in the long sand and shingle beach; at long last, the sand starts to get significantly finer from here down the coast.

The choice of accommodation in Tossa de Mar is good. The best hotel is the four-star **Hotel Reymar** (Tel: 340 312) which lies within fifteen minutes' walk of the main resort centre and opposite the Menuda stretch of sand/shingle beach. The Hotel has 156 bedrooms, including a number of family rooms, and all have private facilities, a balcony, and a good sea view. Overall, this is a quiet, relaxing hotel but, for those who want a bit of action in the evening, there is a nightly disco during the peak summer season.

The **Costa Brava** (Tel: 340 224) is a tidy, clean hotel with 150 bedrooms and a good location, close to the resort centre. The Spanish Tourist Authorities officially grade it a three-star hotel, but it is only fair to say this rather characterless hotel has had little work done on it in the last few years and, accordingly, will disappoint visitors who have ever stayed in a smarter, more representative, Spanish three-star hotel before.

An alternative might be the **Oasis Tossa** (Tel: 340 750), a large three-star hotel with over 200 bedrooms which opened only in 1984. The Thomson Group operates this clean, modern building, so its UK outlets might have a tendency to oversell it. The Oasis Tossa is situated in a residential part of the resort, fifteen minutes from the beach and an isolated ten-minute walk from the centre of the resort.

If you plan to visit the Costa Brava with children, then you will find few better destinations than the two-star **Son Eloy** (Tel: 340 453), a popular hotel complex about a mile and a half from the resort centre. The location is superb, provided you don't mind the short bus journey into Tossa whenever you want to visit the shops or the beach. There are nearly eighty apartments, plus a further fifteen studios, and leisure facilities include a large swimming pool, live and/or disco music most evenings, organized games and 'theme' evenings, and a variety of sports including tennis, table tennis and minigolf. It is definitely aimed at the under thirties, both with children and without.

A bleak stretch of coast separates Tossa de Mar from **LLORET DE MAR**, an extremely popular Spanish resort and easily the largest on the Costa Brava. More British tour operators offer Lloret than any other destination on Spain's northern coastline, although only a handful use self-catering/apartment accommodation. If you arrive in Lloret for the first time from Tossa de Mar, you cannot fail to be struck by the total contrast from leisurely relaxation (although, inevitably, that is changing) to complete, undisguised, commercialization.

The tourist industry has caused Lloret to mushroom into a substantial town, with nearly 12,000 inhabitants, and it makes no secret of the importance of tourism to its continued prosperity. One travel guide called Lloret de Mar 'the most extreme resort in Spain' because of the rate the tourist industry has swallowed up this one, small part of the Spanish coast, and it is no exaggeration to say that it has become so faceless and cosmopolitan that it is difficult to believe there was ever an authentic Spanish town here before the package boom started.

Not surprisingly, little remains of the old town for the visitor to explore. The most obvious attraction is **Sant Romà**, a sixteenth-century church, decorated with colourful minarets. A common sight on the long summer evenings is a group of locals dancing beneath this strange, mosque-like building. A few remains of the old **Roman town** can still be seen, and for the bloodthirsty, the resort has one of the Costa Brava's most 'popular' bullrings.

The town's most famous former resident was Saint Christine, a young Italian martyr who lived here for a number of years in medieval times. For her religious beliefs, she was thrown into the sea from the high cliffs overlooking the beach, with a huge rock tied to her feet. Weeks later fishermen found her pathetic little body perfectly intact and, in later years, a **hermitage** was built in her memory close to where her body came ashore. **San Cristina Cove**, two miles from the main beach, is named after her and is the object of a colourful floating fiesta on 24 July each summer. Lloret de Mar has a good **Tourist Information Office** (Tel: 364 735) at the Plaza de la Vila, and a second, smaller, office at the main bus station.

Like most major resorts, Lloret de Mar is a very good shopping centre. A labyrinth of tiny streets converge on the tree-lined Passeig Verdaguer in the centre of the resort. Practically every form of shop is represented in some way or another in Lloret de Mar. Almost as numerous as the countless souvenir and gift shops are the bars and cafés: most offer a bland variety of 'international' cuisine geared very much towards the British palate – 'egg and chips', 'bacon and egg' and so on. The big chains, Wimpy and McDonalds, have already moved in, and with their cheerful, reliable burgers, manage to obscure yet another fragment of the real Spain which, to many people, has already long since lost the battle against relentless tourist development.

The most obvious attraction of a large, popular resort like Lloret de Mar is its beach but, frankly, the overcrowded stretch of coast which Lloret can call its own is by no means the best beach on the Costa Brava. In its favour, it is clean, picturesque and close to most of the better hotels. It is wide but not excessively long: about three-quarters of a mile at its most generous. Like so many of the Costa Brava's better known beaches, the sand is not entirely fine and golden but made up of many tiny pebbles which are not ideal for lying on to read or sunbathe, nor the most comfortable surface for young children to run about on.

The main beach slopes quite steeply and this is another reason why families should consider an alternative resort: inexperienced swimmers venturing further than waist-high are likely to find themselves quickly out of their depth – so don't risk it. **Fanals** is a smaller, more attractive beach just beyond a rocky headland at Lloret but, like the larger stretch, gets extremely crowded during the peak months.

Lloret de Mar has several large hotels, most of which are reputable, modern buildings representing good value for money. The few that don't are reasonably small one- and two-star establishments which seldom make their way into a tour operator's brochure. In this section, we have selected eight of the resort's better hotels: the first three are four-star graded, and the remaining five are three-star hotels.

The **Gran Hotel Monterrey** (Tel: 364 050) is one of the best hotels on the Costa Brava. It occupies a commanding position within fifteen minutes' walk from the main beach, and about ten from the resort centre. Views from most of the 228 well-appointed bedrooms, over nine floors, mainly look over to the resort centre. The inside of the hotel is bright and spacious, and there is a large garden to either stroll in or let the children run around. There is also an occasional disco, and resort nightlife is only a few minutes' walk away; close enough to be practical but far enough to make sure you can't hear the noise!

A much more unusual option is the **Rigat Park** (Tel: 365 200) which has been built in the style of a very traditional old Spanish hotel. Its 99 bedrooms are furnished in a comfortable period style. The **Gran Hotel Reymar** (Tel: 340 312), on the other hand, is a lively, modern hotel with 156 bedrooms overlooking the Menuda Beach. Facilities for all the family are good, although it is quite a steep climb down to the sandy/shingle beach. One attractive feature is the large, split-level dining room which overlooks the sea. Jackets are required for dinner but it is worth the effort as four courses, each with three choices, are generally offered.

The best of the three-star hotels is probably the **Cluamarsol** (Tel:

365 750) which is in a superb location, overlooking the long promenade. It stands eight floors high but has just 87 rooms, all a good size with private bathroom facilities, balcony and sea view, and, unusually, a television. Views from the rooftop swimming pool are fantastic, and a friendly, relaxed atmosphere prevails throughout the hotel. Worthy of a higher star rating.

You will not miss the **Don Quixote** (Tel: 365 860) as its striking blue exterior acts like a beacon from a considerable distance. It lies in the Fanals part of the resort, so expect the beach to be pretty crowded all summer. It has 374 bedrooms and a very well-organized programme of children's entertainment. The **Flamingo** (Tel: 364 358) is a noisy, popular hotel tailor-made for the fast turnover of the package-holiday market. It has 287 bedrooms and lies close to the beach and the resort centre. This hotel is an improvement on its sister hotel, the Frigola, which adjoins.

The **Gran Garbi** (Tel: 367 704) is an appealing, modern building with 270 bedrooms on seven floors. There is a ten-minute (uphill) walk to the crowded beach, and views from bedroom windows are limited, but this bright hotel remains popular with British visitors and has a good programme of entertainment for all the family.

The **Rosamar** (Tel: 364 658) sits at the end of the promenade facing the beach. It is a friendly, above average three-star hotel with little to make it stand out from the crowd. Close to both the beach and resort centre.

The last resort on the Costa Brava is **BLANES**, an interesting combination of a prosperous industrial town, a popular fishing port and a growing tourist resort. If you travel south of Blanes you come into the Costa Dorada. With over 21,000 inhabitants it is easily the largest coastal town in the region and, as such, is well connected with Barcelona and the rest of Spain by both road and rail. More than a quarter of the population is still employed in the local nylon industry, although the demands of employment in the tourist trade are eating into that impressive statistic.

Various scattered ruins in and around Blanes testify to a long history, although little of any importance has survived. The exception is the oldest building of note, the **Parish Church of Santa**

Maria, which is a fine building reputed to date back to the fourteenth century, although it was seriously damaged during the Spanish Civil War earlier this century.

Inside the church you should look out for the great vault keystones as they bear the arms of the Cabrera family who once owned most of what is now the Costa Brava region. They used to live in a magnificent **palace** which adjoined the parish church, but over the centuries it fell into disuse and eventually crumbled to practically nothing. A few stones and parts of medieval walls behind the church, believe it or not, are all that remain of the palace apart from the large fifteenth-century **fountain** which was known to serve the noble household. Quite why the fountain has survived when the substantial structure of the old palace has crumbled to oblivion is not quite so obvious, but what remains is worth a look all the same.

Other sights of note in Blanes are the impressive **aquarium**, and the daily **fish market** near the harbour if your interest in fish is more basic! The market gives a fascinating insight into daily life as it was on this coast long before tourism, and if you are self-catering you might be lucky to pick up a bargain or two. Tempting as many of the fruits of the sea might seem at one of these markets, they certainly won't keep long enough to be brought home again so enjoy them while you're here. One final 'must' is the **Murimurta Gardens**, landscaped in 1928 by Carlos Faust and one of the most popular attractions of the town ever since. There is a **Tourist Information Office** (Tel: 330 248) at Passeig de Dintre, 29.

Blanes has a reasonable shopping area, and is one of the fastest growing centres of nightlife on the Costa Brava. Many younger holiday-makers are finding nearby Lloret de Mar a little 'clichéd' year after year, so are looking towards Blanes as an alternative. Whether you want an intimate candelit dinner for two, or a wild disco to dance the night (or morning) away, then you are likely to find it in Blanes. Many of the discos stay open until 5 or 6am, just in time for a champagne breakfast back at your hotel . . .

If, incidentally, you are *not* looking for a good time socially, or more to the point, cannot stand the noise of other people having a good time, then you'd be well advised to get a hotel as far away from the centre of the resort as possible. This is sound advice which applies equally to all larger resorts, but noise seems to travel unusually far in Blanes particularly.

The range of accommodation is not brilliant, and easily the best is the excellent three-star **Beverley Park** (Tel: 336 762) which was opened only in 1987. It is an extremely attractive modern building, thoughtfully constructed with the most up-to-date facilities: an immaculate, if oddly shaped, pool; pink and white blinds in the public areas; 170 smart bedrooms with functional private facilities and a balcony. Live music is available most evenings and the hotel is located just a couple of minutes' walk from the sandy beach.

Two other simple, but comfortable establishments, both one-star *residencials*: the **San Antonio** (Tel: 331 150) has 150 surprisingly well-appointed bedrooms for its one star; all the rooms, for example, have a shower or private bath. Views to the front overlook the promenade and harbour. The **Mar-Ski** (Tel: 330 334) has 98 rooms across seven floors, many of which overlook the harbour and seafront. This place is popular with European holiday-makers of all nationalities.

INLAND

Easily the most popular inland excursion is to the marvellous old city of GERONA. Many centuries before Christ, the city was founded where the rivers Ter and Onyar met, although the Onyar is more readily associated with Gerona because it neatly divides the city in two. Gerona is only a small resort so far as British tour operators are concerned and, as a result, you are much more likely to spend no more than a day, or even just an afternoon, in the city rather than a week or two. Consequently, we will not go into great details about where to stay or what to do in the evenings, but instead concentrate on the main points of interest recommended for even the shortest visit. Gerona stands on a wide hill: in earlier centuries this elevated position played a crucial role in the defence of the city. One of the oldest sights is the **Arab baths** which are reckoned to have been built in the thirteenth century by late Moorish settlers, several hundred years after the main period of occupation ended. You can still visit the cold, warm and steam baths which are all modelled in the style of even earlier Roman baths. All three are open daily from 10am – 1pm, and again between 4 and 7pm.

The vast **cathedral** dates mainly from the fifteenth century although, inevitably, it was built on the site of a much older building which goes back several hundred years before then. The oldest parts of the main structure which you can still see date back to the early eleventh century; indeed, the high altar was consecrated in 1038. A total of thirty side chapels lead off from the main nave, and the outstanding stained-glass windows are among the finest in Spain. This is an exceptional building and even supposing you never see another church during your stay in Spain, do try and make the effort to see this one.

The city's **Museum of Art** is next door to the cathedral and it houses a remarkable little collection of works of religious art. One of the oldest exhibits is a tenth-century illuminated manuscript which came from the Monastery of Liébana. The museum is open daily, except Mondays, from 10am – 1pm and again from 4 – 7pm, and these opening hours also apply to the **Archaeological Museum** which you can visit on the other side of the river. The region's long history, from prehistoric times, is painstakingly charted here.

Accommodation for the independent traveller is very limited in Gerona. Conveniently, there are a number of cheap hostels and *residencials* round the station area, but your best bet is to enquire at the **Tourist Information Office** (Tel: 202 679) which you'll find in the Plaça del Vi. The Tourism Office of the Regional Government of Catalonia (Tel: 201 694) is located at Ciudadanos, 12.

PRIVATE. Keep Out   The rest of the region is rugged and picturesque; a part of the country which either the Recluse or the Nature Lover will appreciate from the point of view of just being able to drive on and on to take in the natural beauty of the place. North of Gerona, you run into the Pyrenees region proper, and a couple more inland towns worth heading for are Besula and Figueras. Of the two, Besula is the more attractive, and easily one of the most appealing of the many little towns in Catalonia.

Among the sights in BESULA are a twelfth-century **bridge**, dominated by the old **gatehouse** in the middle of it; and the amazing **Plaza Major** which is dominated by a number of remarkably well-preserved medieval buildings. Were it not for the telephone boxes and litter bins, the feeling of being caught in a time-warp would be complete. Look out, too, for the remains of the **Church of Santa Maria** which has the distinction of being one of Europe's shortest-lived cathedrals: from 1018 until 1020 it was the designated cathedral for the Bishopric of Basula, but the tiny see was swiftly swallowed up by the mighty Barcelona diocese.

FIGUERAS is the region's second largest town, after Gerona. It hasn't much to offer except the **Salvador Dali Museum** which was created by the artist himself in 1973 in a typically bizarre-looking circular building. An ancient Cadillac with the statue of a naked woman standing like an outsized bonnet mascot dominates the entrance to the museum dedicated to the world's greatest surrealist artist. Dali is someone whom *everbody* seems to have an opinion on: even if you happen to be one of the very few who don't, then a visit to this place is certain to be one of the most interesting experiences of your stay on the Costa Brava. It is open daily, except Mondays, from 11am – 12.30pm, and again from 4.30 – 7.30pm.

One or two more sights in Figueras are a seventeenth-century **castle**, one of the last outposts of the defeated Republicans during the Civil War. It is an enormous structure, and has a capacity for over 10,000 men and 5,000 horses. The **Museum of Empordà** is located in the old Rambles district of the town and is dedicated to the history of the region.

One final excursion worth making from anywhere on the Costa Brava is up to the tiny republic of ANDORRA. It proudly boasts that it is the biggest small country in Europe, which, of course, it is when viewed alongside the likes of Monaco, San Marino and even Liechtenstein. Entry formalities are a joke, but sadly this attractive little country, sandwiched in the Pyrenees between Spain and France, is no longer the great, tax-free shopping haven it once was. You can still pick up a few bargains, notably alcohol and, if you've a car, petrol; just about everything else is priced on a par with Spain and France. Pay a visit to the twelfth-century **cathedral** when there.

Costa Dorada

INTRODUCTION

Stretching down the Mediterranean coast from Calella in the north to Miami la Platja in the south, Spain's 'Golden Coast' is somewhat less scenic than its northern neighbour, the Costa Brava. However, although parts of the Costa Dorada are relatively uninspiring, it offers a number of excellent beaches and some pleasant resorts – in particular Sitges.

History is on offer too, notably in Tarragona, with its impressive range of Roman remains, and at the monasteries of Montserrat and Poblet.

And this Costa also offers Spain's proud second city, Barcelona, the capital of the independently minded region of Catalonia. Here you can sample the atmosphere of a great city, marvel at Gaudí's architectural style, stroll down the famous, tree-lined Ramblas, and enjoy the almost medieval character of the streets and buildings in the Gothic quarter.

GETTING THERE

There should be little difficulty with travel on the Costa Dorada. RENFE, the national rail network, provides as efficient a service here as elsewhere in Spain, with connections to all the main resorts. In Barcelona the Estacío Sants-Central is preferable to the Estacío França-Termino. The road network is, again, of the same quality as in the rest of developed Spain.

There are two principal airports – at Barcelona and Reus. The latter is, however, mainly concerned with charter flights. Barcelona Airport is connected to the city by both bus and rail links.

In Barcelona it is worthwhile making use of the excellent and economical Metro system. Taxis too are reasonably priced.

CLIMATE

The Costa Dorada has some of the most moderate weather conditions in Spain, with the best months being between May and September.

During this period temperatures range from an average of 21°C (70°F) to 28°C (82°F), with between eight and ten hours of sunshine expected on most days.

CULINARY SPECIALITIES

The Costa Dorada is scarcely the most notable of Spanish regions when it comes to cuisine but it does offer a number of local dishes and specialities.

Among these are barbecued chicken, the *butifarra* sausage, and *escudella* broth – which includes pasta and sausage amongst its ingredients. Other specialities include the *esqueixada* salad, made with cod, tomato and onions, and the Sitges variant of this, *Xato de Sitges*, which includes tuna and anchovies in an olive-oil based sauce.

Although it originates in Valencia, *paella* is also popular on the Costa Dorada.

Cakes and pastries are a Catalan favourite, and the bakeries in most towns offer a mouth-watering selection to tempt passers-by.

And wine too is produced. Notable are the pleasant white wines from Sitges – Malvasía sweet reds and whites from Tarragona; and the dry white, sparkling varieties from Panadés.

WHERE TO GO FOR WHAT

Most types of holiday-maker will find something – or somwhere – to interest them on the Costa Dorada.

The equable climate means, of course, that the Sun-Worshipper is well catered for, and there are numerous good beaches in the resorts – in particular at Sitges. This latter resort also has separate bathing beaches for naturists.

A number of resorts are good destinations for Family Holidays. Among the Costa's better offerings in this class are Salou and Calella.

The Sightseer has an excellent selection of places of interest to visit. Barcelona, Spain's second city, has numerous sights but amongst the best are the **Museu Picasso**, with a huge array of the artist's work; the **Sagrada Familia** – Gaudí's remarkable cathedral design; and for sheer atmosphere **Las Ramblas**. Elsewhere on the coast there are the Roman remains of Tarragona and, inland, the historic monasteries of Montserrat and Poblet.

For the Socialite, Sitges offers a lively nightscene, and Salou and Barcelona may also fit the bill.

Alternatively, for those seeking quiet, smaller resorts, Calafell and Miami Playa will suit the Recluse.

Travelling down the coast from the Costa Brava, one comes first to CALELLA DE LA COSTA, and the associated resorts of Malgrat and Pineda. These are rather unremarkable resorts and tend towards dullness.

Calella is the best of the three with a large, often crowded beach which lies across a railway that cuts the town in two. This limits access somewhat, and means that care should be taken with children. Nightlife during the season is fairly lively, but is often in the form of English pubs for English tourists and Bierkellers for the Germans.

Calella is principally a packaged resort in its pure form, though it is less commercialized than some of the larger resorts like Benidorm. It may be good value for a basic sun-and-surf family holiday. There are few sights in Calella, although there is a small **botanic garden** on Cabo Roig.

MALGRAT DE MAR, just north of Calella, is a similar type of resort and has expanded along the coast to absorb the adjoining area known as Santa Susana. With Calella, this resort has recently become popular with a number of UK coach operators.

PINEDA, which lies between Calella and Malgrat, and is really little more than an extension of the former, is unremarkable in the extreme – though the beach is of reasonable quality.

Not far down the coast from Calella is ARENYS DE MAR, a small and less developed resort with an attractive **marina**, which from time to time hosts sailing regattas.

South of Arenys, there is little or no tourist development and few places to visit. The road runs down the coast, skirting pleasant beaches interspersed with sprawling industrial towns such as Mataró and Badalona, until it reaches Barcelona.

Enlightened, confident, and independently minded, Spain's second city, **BARCELONA** – the capital of Catalonia – is a thriving commercial and cultural centre, with a unique atmosphere and a great deal to offer.

First developed as a Roman colony around 200 BC, the city subsequently fell under the rule of the Visigoths and the Moors. By the thirteenth century, its position on the Mediterranean coast had made it a leading centre for trade, but two centuries on, the discovery of America and the exclusion of Barcelona and the Catalonians from the New World signalled decline.

Barcelona recovered its prosperity in a great nineteenth-century renaissance, and the city expanded considerably in this period, with the construction of the geometrically perfect streets of the **Eixample**.

In the Spanish Civil War, the city became a Republican stronghold and Franco subsequently strove unsuccessfully to suppress the spirit of Catalan independence. With the *Generalissimo's* death in 1975 Catalonia was restored to semi-autonomy, and the *Generalitat* – the region's autonomous government – was re-established.

Today, Barcelonís are strong supporters of their region's independence and the visitor will notice the bilingual usage of Spanish and Catalan throughout the streets and public buildings.

Barcelona divides easily into distinct areas, making it relatively simple to find one's way around. From the harbour, the broad, leafy boulevard of **Las Ramblas** runs a straight mile to the city's hub – the **Plaça de Catalunya**

On the eastern side of Las Ramblas is the **Barrí Gotic**, a knot of narrow, medieval streets centred on the **cathedral**. The area is traversed north to south by the Via Laietana, towards the foot of which is one of the city's two main stations – **Estació França Termino**. Close by is the **Parc de la Ciutadella**.

On the opposite, western side of Las Ramblas is Barcelona's infamous red-light district, the **Barrí Xines**, bordered by the Avenida del Parallel, beyond which **Montjuic** rises to the south-west.

From Plaça de Catalunya, Passeig de Gràcia runs north through the nineteenth-century renaissance Eixample, bordered to the south by the vast avenue of Gran Via de les Corts Catalanes, and on the north by the appropriately named Avinguda Diagonal – the only street to break the right-angled conformity of the Eixample. This is prime territory in which to sample the unique art nouveau **architecture of Antoní Gaudí**.

Beyond the Eixample, the city extends though the Gràcia area to the hills of Tibidabo.

Las Ramblas are a part of Barcelona's unique flavour which you will find almost impossible to avoid – and you shouldn't try. A series of five short streets lined with plane trees, they are as essential a part of Barcelona as the Champs Elysées is of Paris, or Trafalgar Square is of London.

Lined with news-stands, open-air cafés, flower stalls, and fortune-tellers, an evening stroll down this street is a memorable experience. There are, of course, the usual tourist-inflated prices, and you should be prepared to pay over the odds if you want to idle with a drink and watch the crowds go by.

Among the attractions of Las Ramblas is the **Palau de Virreina**, at number 99. It houses the **Museu d'Arts Decoratives** – an impressive collection from various periods, with a broad array of paintings by European masters including Botticelli, Goya, Titian, Van Dyck, El Greco and Gainsborough. The Palau is open Tuesday to Saturday 10am-2pm, 4.30-9pm; Sunday 10am-2pm. There is a small admission charge.

Further down from the Palau (coming from Plaça de Catalunya) is the city's opera house, the **Gran Teatre del Liceo**. Built in the mid-nineteenth century it is open for non-performance visits, but only between September and June, and only on a Monday or Friday!

The **Palau Güell** on Nou de la Rambla, further on, is a creation of Antoni Gaudí. Gaudí was a Catalan architect renowned for his unconventional art nouveau designs and his controversial use of the parabolic arch. The Güell is not one of the best examples of his work, but it also houses the **Museu de l'Art Espectacle**, an interesting collection of theatrical memories, principally concerned with the last two centuries. (Open Monday to Saturday, 11am-2pm, 5-8pm. Admission charged.)

At the harbour end of Las Ramblas, the sixty-metre column of the **Columbus Monument** rises over the water. For a limited view of the city, you can take an elevator to the top. (Tuesday to Sunday, 9.30am-1.30pm, 4.30-8.30pm.)

Nearby, is a small Maritime Museum (on Plaça de la Pau) and in the harbour you'll find the full-size reproduction of Columbus' flagship **Santa Maria** moored in the harbour. The ship can be boarded 9am-2pm, 3pm-sunset each day. (Admission charge.)

To the east of Las Ramblas is the Barrí Gotic, the Gothic Quarter of Barcelona. It is an area of narrow, atmospheric, medieval streets and buildings and one where many of the city's architectural attractions can be found.

Principal amongst the sights of the area is Barcelona's **cathedral**, standing on the Plaça de la Seu. The cathedral was begun in 1298, and mostly completed by 1448, but it was not until 1898 that the façade was finished. It is dedicated to Saint Eulalia, the city's patron saint, who lies entombed in the opulent crypt.

The building is in Catalan Gothic style on a grand scale. Around the walls are twenty-nine chapels of varying interest, including one dedicated to the Black Madonna of Montserrat (see below). The upper pews are adorned with coats of arms of European Kings who met here in 1519 for a meeting of the Order of the Golden Fleece.

Not far from the cathedral (just to the rear), is a collection of interesting museums around the historic Plaça del Rei. The first you reach from the cathedral is the **Museu Frederic Marés**. This houses an extensive collection of religious sculpture including a seemingly endless array of crucifixes which trace the development of this symbol through the centuries. There is also a worthwhile collection of miscellaneous memorabilia – Marés apparently being a fanatical collector. (Open Tuesday to Saturday, 9am-2pm, 4-7pm; Sunday, 9am-2pm. There is a small admission charge.)

Behind the Museu Marés – which stands in a pleasant courtyard – is the Plaça del Rei, a rather empty royal square in one corner of which is a flight of steps to the **Salon de Tinell**. Columbus was received here by King Ferdinand and Queen Isabella on his return from the New World. Also on the square is the **Palau del Lloctinent** (closed to the public), which houses medieval documents of world importance.

Off the Plaça del Rei, on Carrer del Veyer, is the entrance to the **Museu de la Història de la Ciudad** (City History Museum). Here you can wander through the excavated remains of the city's Roman past, which have been marvellously presented in a modern infrastructure of steel walkways and steps. Upstairs, you can see other aspects of Barcelona's history – including the remarkable Big Clock of Barcelona, a huge, primitive and now defunct town clock.

Another important and historic square in the Barri Gotic is the **Plaça Sant Jaume**, the centre of provincial and city government, and a crucial arena since Roman times. The town hall or **ajuntament** stands on one side facing the seat of Catalonia's semi-independent administration – the **Palau de la Generalitat**. The former shows a neoclassical façade to the square, and has a fine example of Gothic architecture in its façade on the Carrer de la Ciudad. Some modern sculpture can be seen in the courtyard off the main entrance. (Monday to Saturday, 9.30am–1.30pm, 4–7pm; Sunday 9.30–1.30pm. Free.)

To the south of the Barrí Gotic proper, is the area around the church of Santa Maria del Mar. The streets here have the same medieval feel as those to the north, but are perhaps less tourist-orientated.

The **Church of Santa Maria del Mar** itself dates from the fourteenth century and is in a Gothic style which is impressive for its economy of design and simple, clean lines. Inside, the church has a spacious, uncluttered interior.

Nearby, along Carrer Montcada is one of *the* key sights in this city, and indeed in Spain, the **Museu Picasso**. Housed in another building of conspicuous architectural value, the Palau Aguilar, the museum contains an extremely large and diverse collection of the great artist's work. There are examples of his sketches and drawings, sculpture and ceramics, and from all the main periods of his paintings. Included are works from his naturalistic Blue Period (1901-4) and Rose Period (1904-6), through his famous Cubist paintings to the later neoclassical works.

Some of the notable works you can view are the fifty-eight paintings in his *Maid of Honour* series, and *Harlequin*. A visit to the museum is a must for any art lover in Barcelona. (Open: Monday 4-8.30pm; Tuesday to Saturday 9.30am-1.30pm, 4-8.30pm; and Sunday 9.30-1.30pm. Admission charge, but students free.)

To the east of the Picasso Museum is the **Parc de la Ciutadella**. The park is large and among the attractions in this pleasant setting is the **Museu d'Art Modern**. Not all the art in this museum is modern, though, some being eighteenth and nineteenth century, but some twentieth-century works are included – including paintings by Dalí and Miró.

Also to be found in the park is the **Barcelona Zoo**, with a typical collection of animals plus the world's only albino gorilla, called Floc de Neu (Snowflake!) Open: 9.30am-8pm. Admission charge.

Across the city is the Eixample, or 'broadening', the product of Barcelona's nineteenth-century renaissance expansion. The streets of the Eixample follow a geometrically perfect pattern. The area is notable for its Gaudí architecture. Principal amongst Gaudí's buildings is the **Temple Expiatori de Sagrada Familia**. This uncompleted cathedral, a quite amazing sight, was begun in 1891. Gaudí worked on it for forty-three years before he was killed in a street accident. He believed his greatest work would have taken two hundred years to complete – and it is still unfinished. Each part of the vastly complex design has a symbolic meaning. The doors of the completed façade, for example, are supposed to symbolize faith, hope and charity.

The Sagrada Familia's most striking features are the eight spires rising to over three hundred feet. Four more were to have been added to complete the symbolism for the twelve apostles. You can ascend right to the top of some of these spires, with an elevator going some of the way. The views from the top – when you reach it – are magnificent though the vertigo may be overwhelming!

Back on ground level, there is a model of the finished church and various displays on Gaudí's work in what should be the crypt. The rest of the open-air interior bears a striking resemblance to a building site – and work *is* continuing, based on Gaudí's original plans.

Of all Barcelona's sights this is one of the most outstanding and is strongly recommended. The Sagrada Familia can be found on Carrer Marina, and there is a Metro station nearby. (Open: in summer, 8am-9pm; in winter, 8am-7pm. Admission charge.)

Other examples of Gaudí's work can be seen at **Parc Güell**, open from 10am-9pm. A remarkable house, with a striking Hall of Columns, and other examples of Gaudí's unique style can be seen here.

Further north from the Exiample is the mountain of **Tibidabo**. Here you can enjoy yet another marvellous view of the city. The name Tibidabo comes from Satan's challenge to Christ, 'All these things will I give thee, if thou wilt fall down and worship me,' in Latin, *Haec omnia tibi dabo si cadens adoraberis me*. That's how good the view is; on a clear day you can see the Pyrenees. There is not much else to see though – an unremarkable church and run-of-the-mill amusement park.

You can get to Tibidabo on the Metro. From the Avinguda del Tibidabo station there is a fairly strenuous walk or a tram to connect further up with a funicular to the summit. (Open 7.30am-9pm.)

The remaining area of Barcelona that should be seen by any visitor is **Montjuic**, the hill area standing to the south-west of the city. The **Palau Nacional**, standing at the end of Avinguda Reina with its cavernous exhibition halls, houses the **Museu d'Art Catalunya** and the **Museu de Céramica**. The former has some excellent Roman-esque works and a large number of twelfth-century frescoes. Both museums are open Tuesday to Sunday, 9am-2pm. Admission charge; students free. Close by the Palau Nacional is the **Museu Etnològico**, with a collection of international artefacts that takes in Turkey, Mexico, Japan and Africa, among others.

Poble Espanyol, a model town boasting examples of architectural styles from across Spain, is one of Montjuic's more unusual attractions. It is worth visiting but it's not quite in the Disneyland class! Open daily 9am-7pm.

Also worthwhile are the **Museu Arqueologic** (Archeological

Museum) on Carrer de Lleida, which includes some Carthaginian remains, and the **Fundació Miró**. The latter is a permanent collection of the works of Joan Miró, together with examples of Salvador Dalí's surrealist art. (Open Tuesday-Saturday, 11am-8pm, Sunday 11am-2.30pm.)

Montjuic's other attractions include the **Jardin Botánico** and the castle with its Military Museum (and another excellent **view**).

An enjoyable amusement park, with the usual sorts of entertainments, is also to be found on the hill. It costs around 200 pesetas to enter, or 1,000 pesetas to enter *and* use the rides.

Accommodation in Barcelona is plentiful, with a good choice in most price ranges. At the cheaper end of the market a good pension to try is the **Hotel-Residencia Lausanne** at no. 24 Avda Porta de l'Angel. Standing opposite a large department store it offers clean, comfortable rooms, of a basic type. Singles cost around 1,100 pesetas, doubles with shower around 1,600 pesetas.

A bit more expensive, but still good value in its price range, is the **Hostal-Residencia Monegal** on Carrer de Pelai. With an excellent location on the corner of Plaça de Catalunya, and recent redecoration, it is priced at around 2,500 pesetas per night for a single, and 3,400 pesetas for a double.

A notch up is the **Hotel San Agustín** at Plaza San Augustín, 3, in the older part of town. It has 74 tastefully decorated, comfortable rooms, with doubles costing around 4,300 pesetas.

A good three-star hotel, such as the pleasantly situated **Hotel Regencia Colón** on Calle Sagristáns near the cathedral, would cost around 6,300 pesetas for a double. All rooms here have a private bath and phone, and half have television.

Naturally in a city of this size there is also a good choice of restaurants. Many are, however, overpriced – especially those around the Rambles – but there are a number of excellent restaurants as well.

At the economical end of the range is **Nou Celler** at Princesa, 16, close by the Picasso Museum. A small, unpretentious restaurant it has an authentic Spanish feel, despite its tourist-trap location. Ideal for a simple lunch or cheap evening meal you can enjoy a set meal for around 750 pesetas or dine à la carte for about 1,650 pesetas.

Also cheap and cheerful is the **Restaurant Roma** on Plaza Real, where a set menu meal will cost you around 950 pesetas.

To dine a little more expensively, try the restaurant **El 7 Portes** at Paseo Isabel II, 14 (Tel: 319 39 46). A full meal here will cost you about 2,000 pesetas, and there is a good choice of Spanish and Catalonian cuisine available.

For a real splurge, dine out in style at **El Dorado Petit** where you can savour your selection from an imaginative menu, which includes Spanish *nouvelle cuisine* – if you want to pay a lot for a little! The restaurant is set in a villa at no. 51 Calle Dolors Monserdà, and on a pleasant night you can sit outside in a charming garden (Tel: 201 51 53).

Not too far from Barcelona is the renowned monastery at MONTSER-RAT – a popular day-trip destination from the city. The monastery, which is built on the slopes of the mountain of Montserrat, is most famous for the polychrome figure of the **Black Madonna**, La Moreneta, an important focus of the Catalans' devotion to the Catholic faith. In addition to the monastery and the Madonna, the mountain also offers magnificent views and a number of pleasant walks through the forested areas of its slopes.

The monastery itself is architecturally unremarkable, the original buildings dating from the eleventh century having been smashed by Napoleon's army in 1812. They now house fewer than one hundred Benedictine monks, who produce a herbal liqueur, *aromas de Montserrat*.

You can enter the **basilica** through a side door, and walk up to the glass-encased figure of the Madonna. (Open daily, 6-10.30am, noon – 6.30pm.) There is also a **museum** most notable for its paintings which include works by Carravaggio and El Greco.

As well as visiting the monastery, you can enjoy some of the walks and the beautiful scenery of the mountain, some of which lead to hermitages wth excellent views. **Sant Joan**, for example, is accessible by funicular, and **Sant Jeroni** at over 1,350 metres is even more spectacular.

To reach Montserrat from Barcelona, you can take a bus from Plaça de la Universidad or perhaps more interestingly take a local

Catalan train and cable car. There are five trains per day from Barcelona connecting with the cable car. Again, some of the views are marvellous.

SOUTH OF BARCELONA

Returning to the coast south of Barcelona we reach the resort of **CASTELLDEFELS**, just half an hour from the city. It has a large number of hotels, and a vast beach. Popular with Barcelonís, this is a pleasant beach resort worth visiting.

The best of the beach destinations on the Costa Dorada is, however, a little further south at **SITGES**. A deservedly popular destination, Sitges offers three miles of excellent beaches, a lively, sophisticated nightscene and a pleasant setting. Although commercialized in part, it has avoided some of the worst excesses of Spanish tourist development, and while it is hardly architecturally distinguished, it is considerably more attractive than some of the high-rise concrete blocks found in some of the larger resorts. A pleasant promenade runs along the sea-front, and there is windsurfing from the frequently congested beach.

At the quieter end of town there is also a **golf-course** on offer, as well as – a bit further on – the **nude-bathing beaches** of Playas del Muerto. The second of these is exclusively gay.

Among the more cultural offerings in Sitges are three museums, all in the old part of the town behind the local church which dominates one end of the promenade from an elevated position.

The **Museu Cau Ferrat** includes a Picasso and El Greco's *Tears of St Peter* as well as an assortment of Spanish metalwork and pottery and paintings by the Catalan artist Rusiñol. (Open Tuesday to Saturday, 10am-1pm, 4-6pm; Sunday, 10am-2pm.)

Immediately adjacent, the **Museu Mar i Cel de Mar** features religious art and sculptures from the medieval era.

The third and most unusual of the museums is the **Museu Romántico**. Housed in an elegant aristocrat's mansion it contains decorative art, furniture and other items from the eighteenth and nineteenth centuries. (Open Tuesday to Saturday, 10am-1pm, 5-7pm; Sunday, 10am-2pm. Admission charge.)

Sitges offers a number of reasonable one- and two-star hotels, together with six three-star and two four-star hotels. The 95-room **Hotel Subur**, on the seafront, is a good choice from amongst the two stars. A double with bath is around 2,500 pesetas plus taxes. Among the four-star hotels, the 209-room **Terramar** is a quiet, pleasant establishment suitable for families and for older holiday-makers.

In addition to the hotels, there is no shortage of places to eat, with a number of reasonable restaurants along the seafront. Naturally these tend to be somewhat tourist orientated – but then this is a tourist resort. Among these the **Santa Maria** is a good middle-range choice – although with a slight tendency towards the bland. A reasonable meal would cost around 1500 pesetas.

A few miles south of Sitges, is CALAFELL, a smaller tourist centre, with a couple of miles of sandy beach and CUNIT, a village of holiday villas with little commercial development.

Continuing on towards Tarragona we come to COMARRUGA, another increasingly popular beach resort with a few hotels, as well as sporting and **spa** facilities.

Not far on is the **Arco de Bará**, a triumphal arch dating from the second century AD and heralding the extensive Roman remains to be seen in Tarragona (*see* below.) Between the arch and Tarragona is TORREDEMBARRA, another growing resort centre with a reasonable beach, and a castle undergoing restoration work.

Although it is not a traditional 'resort', **TARRAGONA** is one of the most interesting places to visit on the Costa Dorada. Its origins lie in Roman times, when it was an important centre for the empire's expansion through the Iberian peninsula, as well as being favoured by emperors including Augustus and Hadrian. A large part of its appeal is the extensive remains from the Roman era that can still be seen – the whole place is steeped in history.

One of the principal Roman sites is the **amphitheatre**, in a small but pleasant park not far from the eastern end of **Rambla Nova**, the town's main street. The amphitheatre was excavated in 1952, and a combination of restoration and reconstruction have produced an interesting insight into the past.

A cross-section of history can be seen at the **Passeig Arqueologic**, near Via de L'Imperi Romà. Another pleasant park is the setting for a walk alongside the ancient city walls. Parts of the base of the wall, constructed from massive 'Cyclopean' stones, date from the third century BC and before, and above these foundations are medieval, Moorish and Catalan additions. The park around the wall is adorned with cannons, columns, pillars, and a statue of the Emperor Augustus. The walk is open in summer from Tuesday to Saturday, 9am-8pm; Sunday, 10am-1.30pm; and in winter from Tuesday to Saturday, 10.30am-1.30pm, and 3.30-5.30pm. Admission is charged.

One of the most striking things about Tarragona is the way in which, when walking down a contemporary street, one comes upon echoes of the past. One of these echoes is the **Local Forum**, a centre of provincial Roman administration. The remains of the forum are preserved in an older area of the town, a site split in two by a modern street. The ruins are well worth a visit. The entrance can be found on Carrer Lleida. (Open Tuesday to Saturday, 10am-1pm, 4-7pm; Sunday, 10am-1pm. Free admission.)

The older, **Provincial Forum** is not so well preserved, but can be seen at Plaça del Forum.

More morbid, and possibly more interesting remains from ancient times are to be found at the **Necròpolis** and the **Museu Paleocristià** on Passeig Independència. A huge burial site has been excavated to reveal both Christian and Pagan tombs, sarcophagi and other relics, and a museum has now been opened to display the most interesting of these. The site can be visited free; entry to the museum carries a small charge (free to students). Open: Tuesday to Saturday, 10am-1pm, 4.30-8pm; Sunday, 10am-1pm in summer. In winter, open Tuesday to Saturday, 4-7pm.

Moving on through history, we can wander through the older parts of the town centre, beyond Rambla Vella and up steep, narrow streets to the Gothic **Cathedral of Tarragona**. The façade is notable for its 'cut-off' effect: the top appears to be missing. One enters the cathedral through the cloisters and, surprisingly, one pays. Note the carvings on the capitals to the left of the church door – monsters stare down and *The Procession of Rats* conducts a cat's funeral.

Nineteen chapels surround the walls of the impressive interior. Of most interest are those dedicated to the Black Madonna of Montserrat, and to Saint Mary of the Tailors (*Santa María de los Sastres*). This latter chapel features some excellent sculpture.

In the east gallery of the cathedral is the **Museu Diocesà** which features religious art, Roman and Iberian ceramics and valuable tapestries. The cathedral can be visited every day except Sunday 10am-12.30pm, and 4-7.30pm.

Another museum close to the cathedral is the **Museu Arqueològic** which offers a collection of statues, mosaics, and other artefacts. Adjacent is the **Pretori Romà** – the seat of the Roman governors of Tarragona and reputed birthplace of Pontius Pilate.

The most inaccessible of Tarragona's historic sights is also one of the most worthwile. Off the road for Lleida, about three miles outside town, is the **Roman Aqueduct** locals call the Puente del Diablo – the Devil's Bridge. The substantial remains of the original twenty-mile construction stand in a peaceful forest setting and can be reached on the bus from Tarragona for San Salvador (every twenty minutes). Tell the driver where you are going and you will be dropped off at the right spot. To get back, walk into San Salvador and catch a return bus.

Nightlife in Tarragona is limited, but there are a number of reasonable bars, if no discos. This is not a typical tourist trap.

Restaurant prospects are also fairly limited. For a relatively cheap meal – around 600 pesetas for the menu – try the **Restaurant El Plata** at Carrer August, 20, in the pedestrian zone behind Rambla Nova. More expensive, and offering some excellent examples of regional dishes, is the **Sol Ric**, which can be found on Via Augusta, at no. 227.

Accommodation in the town is reasonably plentiful and good. Among the best-value hotels is the one-star **Hotel Espanya** at Rambla Nova, 49. Well-equipped, clean and modern rooms with private baths. Singles are good value at around 1,800 pesetas; doubles at around 3,000. Breakfast is an optional extra.

Forty-eight kilometres inland from Tarragona is a marvellous day-trip destination – **Poblet Monastery**. There are daily buses from Tarragona to Poblet and the one-hour journey is well worth making. Founded in the twelfth century, the monastery became immensely rich and powerful until, in 1835, it was decimated in a peasant revolt. Not until 1940 was its religious function revived by Cistercian monks, and some reconstruction undertaken.

Today, both the ruined and reconstructed areas of the complex are impressive and fascinating sights. Among the highlights are the Romanesque cloisters and the Gothic chapterhouse, as well as tombs of the Kings of Aragon.

From the historic, untouristed Tarragona to a purpose-built resort – **SALOU**, seven miles down the coast. Almost completely modern, Salou offers what you would expect from a purpose-built resort: large, busy hotels; tourist shops and souvenirs, and a lively frenetic nightlife during the season. Fortunately, it has escaped from excessive high-rise construction. There are good beaches, and this is probably a good destination for a **family holiday**.

Some of the best **hotels** in Salou are the large, two-star **Hotel San Francisco** which offers good general facilities to suit most people, and the three-star **Hotel Las Vegas**.

Virtually adjoining Salou is the fishing port of CAMBRILS, with no real beach, little holiday activity, but some excellent seafood restaurants.

PRIVATE.
Keep Out
The last of the Costa Dorada's main resort towns is MIAMI PLAYA. Basically a quiet, relatively undeveloped place, it offers a number of small, reasonable family hotels, and some pleasant scenery.

Costa del Azahar

INTRODUCTION

The Costa del Azahar is Spain's 'Orange-Blossom Coast', a long expanse of flat coastal plain with numerous beaches, which also takes in the nation's third largest city, Valencia. The coast takes its name from the many pleasant groves of orange trees which grow in the area's fertile, irrigated soil, thriving in the equable climate.

The climate, the beaches, and the often pleasant scenery have led to this coast's development as an important tourist destination, and the would-be visitor to this part of Spain is faced with a choice between some very inviting resorts. Amongst the best are Peñíscola, Cullera and Gandia. In addition, one can visit Valencia and take in the sights of a major city, including a visit to see the chalice alleged to be the Holy Grail itself.

The Costa del Azahar also has the advantage of being slightly less developed than its ever-popular rivals, the Costa Brava and the Costa Blanca, thereby offering quality resorts without some of the disadvantages of mass tourist development.

GETTING THERE

The Costa del Azahar is well-served by communications, being one of the more densely populated areas of Spain. The major national highway, the N3 from Barcelona to Valencia, runs along its length, and most other roads are of a high standard.

The population numbers also mean that there is a rail service as good as any RENFE, the national network, provides elsewhere in Spain.

The principal airports to the area are at Valencia and, on the Costa Blanca, at Alicante. Scheduled and charter flights fly to both these destinations.

CLIMATE

Like much of the eastern coast of Spain, the Costa del Azahar enjoys an equable climate throughout the year. Winters are mild and summers comfortably warm rather than excessively hot.

Temperatures in Valencia, for example, range from a low of 10°C (50°F) in winter (January) to 25°C (76°F) in August. Rainfall is also relatively low in this region with between 300 and 800mm per year – the area around Valencia is one of the drier parts of the Costa. Summer minimums of around 8mm (⅜″) in August can be expected.

Overall, the best climate conditions will be found between May and September, but winter visits are by no means a bad idea.

CULINARY SPECIALITIES

Undoubtedly this area's most notable speciality is *paella*, the delicious saffron-flavoured rice dish popular across all Spain, but with its roots in Valencia. Today, it is served with seafood, beans, meats, or even snails.

Other regional specialities include the dish *eel i pebre*: fried eels served in an oily sauce flavoured with garlic and spices, and *arros a banda*, another fish dish made with saffron, tomatoes, and garlic.

Orxata de chufa is a drink made from coconut-flavoured beans. Wine is also produced in the area – principally sweet reds. Among the wines available are Monóvar, Requena, and Albaida.

WHERE TO GO FOR WHAT

The Costa del Azahar is principally a holiday destination for the Sun Worshipper and for Family Holidays. There are a large number of resorts offering excellent beaches with good services, in pleasant towns. Among the best are Peñíscola, Benicasím, and Cullera, though most are fairly acceptable.

In other respects this Costa is somewhat limited – the resorts are quieter than the likes of Benidorm, Salou and Sitges and so may not suit the Socialite; nightlife is equally on the limited side in Spain's third largest city, Valencia. Tourist sites too are scarcely plentiful, though Valencia does have a number of places of historic or cultural interest.

The Recluse may find that one of the quieter resorts, such as Oliva, is to their taste.

The Nature Lover may find some points of interest – in particular at Albufera, the nation's largest lagoon and the home of many wildfowl.

The two northernmost resorts of the Costa del Azahar, VINAROZ and BENICARLO, are both small, bustling fishing towns with relatively limited tourist development, making them ideal for a quieter type of holiday.

In both resorts, the beaches are on the small side, perhaps explaining the lack of development, but they are nevertheless generally worth visiting, though watch out for the pollution at Vinaroz. Among the other attractions on offer are the excellent, locally caught fish, including Benicarlo's popular giant prawns.

Not far down the coast is the somewhat larger resort of **PEÑÍSCOLA**, an attractive town standing on a prominent peninsula which juts out into the Mediterranean. Approaching from the

North, the peninsula, topped with a **castle** constructed by the Knights Templar, is an impressive sight.

The castle is flanked by the town and by the pleasant, if crowded, beaches. The town itself has undergone a fair amount of commercialization, and is busy and modern with a large number of hotels, apartments, restaurants and tourist shops.

There are very few sites of interest, but the castle may be worth a visit having been partly restored and offering excellent views.

Among Peñíscola's better hotels in the middle price range is the **Papa Luna**, a large, modern establishment with over two hundred comfortable rooms. A swimming pool is included in the available facilities. For children, there is a paddling pool and playground area.

Another good choice in this range is the **Hotel Los Delfines**, a modern place virtually on the beach and right in the centre of town. Facilities are slightly more limited than at the Papa Luna; a new pool has recently been added and is shared with the adjoining apartment complex.

For a pleasant meal, try the **Casa Severino**, whose reasonably priced food can be enjoyed in the open air on an attractive terrace overlooking the Mediterranean waves.

From Peñíscola southwards there are no real resorts of any note for about thirty miles when one reaches **OROPESA**, which in itself is a smaller resort. Centred around another ruined castle, Oropesa is quiet and picturesque with **good beaches**. Nearby – about half a mile – is an ancient watch-tower, the **Torré del Rey**, together with another good beach.

Among the accommodation on offer here, try the **Hotel El Cid**, an economically priced place with a pool and tennis facilities, and good beach access.

South of Oropesa, and set against an attractive backdrop of pines and cypresses on the Desierto de las Palmas hills BENICASIM, with its excellent beaches, is deservedly an increasingly popular destination on the Costa del Azahar. The tranquil Carmelite monastery, about four miles from the resort, may make for a pleasant break from sun, sea and surf.

Continuing southwards, one passes by the limestone crags of Peña Golosa, through the rich groves of oranges and olives, to CASTELLÓN DE LA PLANA, centre of the local orange trade.

The town is largely modern and commercial and is not really the ideal holiday destination. There are very few sights, but if you do pause here, the **Fine Arts Museum** on C. Caballeros may be worth seeing. It houses a fine display of local ceramics and art of some merit.

The nearby port of EL GRAO DE CASTELLÓN has a huge beach, but is also a centre of the region's petro-chemical industry and, consequently, can't be recommended.

From Castellón southwards there is little or no tourist development along another long stretch of coast to **VALENCIA**, Spain's third largest city.

A modern and thriving place, Valencia is scarcely one of the world's most beautiful cities and poses little threat to Barcelona and Madrid as Spain's top destinations for city-lovers. Despite this, it is worth visiting. There are some very attractive areas and examples of good architecture, and Valencia is not without impressive museums, art and historical artefacts.

The hub of the city is the Plaza del Caudillo, a long, stretched-out square from which Valencia expands towards and across the Rio Turia river in the north, and towards the Mediterranean in the west. On the west side of the square is the **Casa de la Cuidad** (Town Hall). Behind the modern façade one can discover the municipal Library and the **Museu Historic**. This last is not especially remarkable, but includes the 30 kilogram shield of King Jaime I who captured the city from the Moors in 1238, ending their four-century domination of the city, which was only briefly interrupted by El Cid who held Valencia from 1094–1101. In the basement of the building is a helpful **Tourist Office**.

Not far from the square is a large bullfighting venue, the 18,000-seat **Plaza de Toros**, together with the **Museu Taurino**, an interesting museum of bullfighting's bloody history and practice.

To the north of the square, on Plaza del Mercado, is the **Central Market Building**, dating from 1928. A bustling place with about 1,300 stalls, it is exuberantly decorated with *azulejos*, the coloured tiles commonly used for decoration in Spain and Portugal.

Close by, one can view the impressive Gothic architecture of the **Llonja de Seda** (Silk Exchange). Built in the fifteenth century on Moorish foundations, it is notable for its lavish entrance decoration and for its gargoyles, grimacing down from above. Inside, a magnificent vaulted ceiling is supported on twisted columns, and from the tower one can take in a fine panorama of the city.

A short walk from the Llonja northwards brings one to the **Seu** (cathedral). This stately structure is principally Gothic in design but the façade is in the more flamboyant Baroque style. The cathedral's most notable attraction for the visitor is to be found in the **Capilla de Santo Cáliz** chapel. There one can view the Santo Cáliz, a holy chalice set with pearls and rubies, which, it is claimed, is the **Holy Grail** itself.

Whilst visiting the cathedral, don't miss the opportunity to climb the 200-foot high **Micalet** bell-tower at its south-west corner. The tower remains unfinished, but there are excellent views from the outlook platform close to the top. The bell in the tower was once used to regulate the irrigation of the surrounding fields. It opens Monday–Friday, 10.30am–1pm and 5–8pm. There is a small admission charge.

The **Museu de la Seu** (Cathedral Museum) is small, but of some interest. The two rooms feature a collection of religious art – paintings, polychrome figures and statues – and two particularly grim pictures showing beheaded men (for which there is no explanation). The museum opens Monday–Saturday, 10am–1pm and 4–7pm between June and September, and closes an hour earlier in the remaining months.

The **Museu Paleontológico**, just to the north of the cathedral, is not an especially remarkable collection of prehistoric animals' remains, mainly from South America.

Approaching the river, one comes to the **Torres de Serranos**, the old city gates dating from the late fourteenth century and restored in 1930. Another fine view can be had from atop the substantial towers.

Across the Rio Turia river is the **Museu de Bellas Artes** with a very good collection which includes works by Velázquez, El Greco, Goya and Murillo. Also on display are a number of Valencian 'primitives', a form of religious art popular between the fourteenth and sixteenth centuries. (Open Tuesday–Saturday, 10am–2pm, 4–6pm; Sunday 10am–2pm. Admission charge; students free.)

The adjacent **Jardins del Real** gardens include a small and slightly run-down **zoo** with a limited collection of species. (Open daily, 8am–sunset. Free.)

Other attractions in Valencia include the **Palacio de Marqués de Dos Aguas** and the **Colegio del Patriàrca**, both to the east of the Plaza del Caudillo.

The palacio is a remarkable piece of architecture inside, with decoration that includes an unco-ordinated jumble of marbles, *azulejos*, and rococo murals. It houses the **Museu Nacional de Ceramica**, with thousands of examples of ceramic arts and pottery – mainly from the local area.

The **Colegio** – an attractive Renaissance mansion house dating from the early seventeenth century – houses a valuable collection of Old Masters, including works by El Greco and Caravaggio. (Open daily from 11am–1pm in summer, winters on Saturday and Sunday only. Small admission charge.)

The **Church of Corpus Christi**, close by, is noted for the painting of the Last Supper, by Ribalta, which adorns the High Altar. During the Miserere Service held on Fridays, the painting vanishes, and a series of curtains are drawn back to reveal a giant illuminated crucifix. One may find this dramatic event rather kitsch, but the church seems to regard it as conveying the right mixture of inspiration and mysticism to the congregation.

The **beaches** around Valencia itself are not to be recommended – being close to a major city they have suffered from pollution, and are, also, crowded with the local population. The better alternative can be found at the nearby resort of EL SALER which is much more pleasant. There are a number of hotels, a golf course, and a parador providing high quality accommodation to the usual standard found in these places.

For accommodation in Valencia, try the **Hotel Inglés** on Marquesde Dos Aguas, close to the Ceramics Museum, or the **Llar**, at C. Colon, 46 (Tel: 96 352 8460). Both are medium sized, the former being slightly old-fashioned, the latter modern but with less atmosphere. In the cheaper range, the **Europa**, at Ribera, 4 (Tel: 96 352 0000) is a good bet.

For an expensive meal, try **Los Viveros** restaurant, pleasantly situated in the Jardins del Real (Tel: 369 9426). More moderately priced food can be found at a range of restaurants across the city, many of the best being in the older areas of town. Try the **Palacio de la Bellota** on C. Moisér Femades, or the **Restaurante La Taula** at Pascaul and Genis, 3 (Tel: 352 3649). The latter offers a number of good, local dishes, including, of course, paella.

From Valencia, the road southwards to Alicante runs through beautiful scenery, including Spain's largest lagoon at Albufera which may be of some interest to the Nature Lover, towards **CULLERA**, a relatively minor, but quite busy resort.

Cullera stands on the slopes of the Monte del Oro and stretches down the coast where high and unattractive concrete blocks circle the bay, detracting somewhat from its natural beauty. Good views of the bay, town and surrounding countryside can be enjoyed from the **Hermitage of El Santuario**, standing above the town. There is also an unremarkable castle.

Most of the accommodation in the resort is in the low to middle range. Among the better hotels is the **Sicanià**, on Playa del Raco (Tel: 96 152 0143). It's a large, unpretentious place which boasts a private area of beach.

A trip to the fairly costly **Les Mouettes Restaurant** may be a worthwhile splurge – a small, French place, it offers excellent cuisine and superb views to the sea.

Down the coast from Cullera is the similarly scaled resort of **GANDÍA**. The town itself is about two and a half miles inland from the coast, and, as in Cullera, the excellent beach – which gets very busy in peak season – is lined with high-rise blocks.

The town is a mixture of modern and restored buildings in pleasant, sometimes tree-lined streets. Among the attractions is the **Ducal Palace**, formerly the Palace of the Dukes of Gandía. Saint Francis Borja (1510–1572), the fourth Duke of Gandía, was born here and is the village's best known ancestor. Saint Francis renounced the trappings of his noble lifestyle, and became a devout Jesuit after the early death of his young wife. Today, the palace is a Jesuit college open to visitors. Guided tours are available most days during the summer. Look out for some fine floor tiling when you reach the saint's former private chapel.

Accommodation, as in Cullera, is, for the most part, in the lower grades. Try the **Safari** on Legazpi (Tel: 96 284 0400), with a pool and pleasant garden. Slightly more expensive is the **Tres Anclas** (Tel: 96 284 0566), a contemporary creation on the seafront.

PRIVATE. Keep Out | Not far from Gandía is the Costa del Azahar's last significant resort. OLIVA is a somewhat quieter and more relaxed place than Gandía, with a long, and fairly good beach. There are quite a few villas and apartment blocks, but this *is* a less busy place and may be a good destination for a quiet family holiday. There are no real sights worth seeing.

Costa Blanca

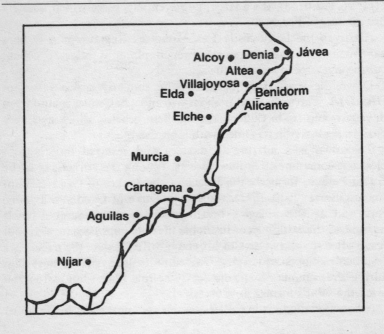

INTRODUCTION

The central stretch of Spain's eastern coastline is known as the Costa Blanca, literally meaning the 'White Coast'. Geographically it represents the Spanish district of Alicante, but for the last couple of decades it has been one of the best known holiday destinations for British package-tour operators. The Costa Blanca is generally reckoned to stretch from Denia in the North right down to Torrevieja in the South, a distance of more than 150 miles. As you might expect, much of this coastline is reasonable beach, and the really good stretches have long since been heavily developed into a number of Europe's best all-round package resorts. Easily the best known is Benidorm, a resort so famous that its unshakable appeal with British tourists has been the butt of comedians' jokes about package holidays for the best part of a generation!

Costa Blanca is lively, easily accessible from Britain, and offers some of the most cosmopolitan all-round resorts in Spain for all types of holiday-maker except, possibly, the Recluse. It is also an excellent base from which to explore much of the often neglected inland areas. In this chapter, we will introduce you to the half dozen or so main resorts in the region which British companies offer tours to, starting in the North with Denia, and continuing south past Benidorm and Alicante, and ending around Torrevieja. We conclude this chapter with a few suggestions for inland excursions, including a look at the towns of Alcoy and Elche.

HISTORY

Like practically every other corner of the Mediterranean, the Costa Blanca has had a troubled past. Long before the region first began to welcome the peaceful invasion of millions of British holiday-makers, various civilizations took control of Iberia's White Coast. The Phoenicians, Iberians and Greeks all settled in different parts of the region, mainly in the ports, and founded many of the settlements which remain today.

After the eighth century the area became part of the prosperous region of *al-Andalus* while in the hands of the Moors. By the thirteenth century the Costa Blanca was in Christian hands again, although the centuries which followed were far from peaceful as the crowns of Aragon and Castile continued to fight over sovereignty of the area.

In the eighteenth and nineteenth centuries, Alicante and Curia flourished and became prosperous ports. The first recorded tour coach arrived in 1868 when an enterprising businessman from Valencia offered 'medicinal' visits to the coast for members of the wealthy, overworked Spanish gentry. Even then, doctors recognized the health value of sunbathing and swimming in the warm Mediterranean waters. A century later, of course, advances in modern transport meant that the Costa Blanca was little more than a couple of hours away.

GETTING THERE

Virtually all visitors arrive by air to the international airport (El Altet) at Alicante. In addition to much charter traffic, it has regular scheduled flights to several other airports in Spain, including Palma and Madrid and most major European capitals. The transfer time to Benidorm is usually slightly under an hour. The main east-coast railway line runs from Valencia to Alicante, via La Encina, thus avoiding most of the resorts. There is, however, a narrow gauge line which connects Alicante with Denia and runs very close to the coast.

There is a regular boat service from Alicante Port to both Majorca and Menorca, and also to Orán in Algeria. Another service connects Denia with Ibiza. All the towns in the region are connected by excellent bus links with the rest of Spain and Europe.

CLIMATE

The summer months on the Costa Blanca are extremely hot by British standards. From April until early November the temperature is seldom less than 21°C (70°F). July and August are the hottest months, when the average is around 32°C (90°F) and rainfall practically non-existent. July is the peak month for sunshine, with an average of twelve hours daily. From mid-May until the start of September you can expect at least ten hours. The coolest months are December and January when the average is about 16°C (61°F).

CULINARY SPECIALITIES

You can reasonably expect international cuisine to be served in all the major hotels. One or two local specialities worth looking out for include *arroz con costra*, a rice dish particularly associated with Elche, which includes sausages and pork covered with a layer of eggs and baked in the oven. Among fish dishes in the region, prawn, red mullet and *sepionet* (squid) are favourites. *Morcillas* (blood sausages) are among the tastiest of several local sausage specialities and, to round off your meal, *turrones* is a form of nougat made in Jijona which is extremely enjoyable.

WHERE TO GO FOR WHAT

As mentioned in the Introduction to this chapter, the Costa Blanca has something for everyone, with the notable exception of the Recluse. The Sightseer should head for Alicante, although there will be plenty to see in Elche, and the Old Town part of Benidorm. The Sun Worshipper will be at home in most of the resorts as they all have good beaches. The four-mile stretch at Benidorm, though, takes some beating. Likewise neither the Sportsperson nor the Socialite are likely to be disappointed in any of the larger resorts, but, once again, Benidorm or Alicante are probably the best.

The ancient town of JÁVITA (often spelt with an 'X' on Spanish maps and roadsigns) is one of the oldest continuously inhabited settlements on the Costa Blanca, and was almost certainly founded by the Phoenicians more than two and a half thousand years ago. The Romans are known to have camped here around the time of the birth of Christ.

Jávita was once known as 'the city of a thousand fountains' and is an extremely beautiful place to visit. You will need to look very hard indeed to find somewhere offering a greater contrast to the Costa Blanca's large coastal resorts. The town itself is dominated by the remains of a fifteenth-century **castle**, and this should be your first stop when you arrive. The original castle on this site is reckoned to have been founded by Hannibal (of elephant fame) in the third century BC, and by the eleventh century AD this was one of the first places in Europe where paper was being manufactured in any sort of reasonable quantities.

Among the better-known former sons of Jávita were two popes, Calixtus III and the infamous Alexander VI. Both made a significant impact on Christianity as a whole during their reigns, not necessarily for the better, and today are remembered by their family name of Borgia. Both popes are best known for the illicit exploits in their private lives, the most harmless of which is the fact that both managed to father illegitimate children whilst still pope!

The first town of any size on the Costa Blanca is **DENIA**, a reasonable settlement dominated by an ancient ruined **castle**. This is one of the town's most interesting sights and, on a good day, the views are spectacular. Although Denia is a bustling resort, even during the cooler winter months when there are few visitors around, it offers few obvious attractions. The town has a long history as a port, and it is from here that a narrow gauge railway (locally called the Lemon Express because of the dense lemon groves by the side of the track) starts to wind its way slowly down the coast towards Alicante.

Denia's history dates back to Roman times, and it is known that the ancient town was a popular spot for the Roman legions to stop over as part of their long march north or south; arguably, they were the first real 'tourists'. Evidence of their stays remains, and you can still see what is left of an imposing **fort** perched high above the town with its obvious strategic location overlooking the harbour.

Another sight in town is the **Church of Santa Maria**, a seventeenth-century building which is an outstanding example of the architecture of that period. Denia's main (archaeological) **museum** is located in the castle, and a stroll round its corridors will give you a good insight into the chequered history of this part of the coast. The museum is open daily from 10am–2pm, and again from 5pm–8pm.

If you happen to visit Denia during the second week of July, you might be fortunate enough to see one of the Costa Blanca's most unusual local traditions being enacted. A bizarre bullfight, locally known as *boux del mar*, takes place, but unlike most Spanish bullfights, the unsuspecting animal is not slaughtered at the end of it. The climax of the ritual, which takes place on the beach, comes when the bull is symbolically submerged into the Mediterranean for a few moments.

Denia has a fine stretch of sandy beach: it shelves gently into the sea, so is a safe spot to bring children. It's worth remembering that the coast immediately on either side of Denia offers a few more beaches which are likely to be quieter than the stretch which the town leads directly down onto. On a clear day, you can see all the way to Ibiza from most of the beaches.

Seven or eight British tour companies include Denia in their brochures, but it is essentially a self-catering resort. Large operators like Falcon, Cosmos and Thomson feature Denia prominently as a self-catering destination. There is a vast number of apartments in and around the beach areas, and this is likely to be the type of accommodation most readily offered if you make an enquiry about the town.

There are only four officially designated hotels in the resort, although approximately a dozen smaller establishments offer simple, clean hostel/*residencial* type accommodation which is ideal for the independent traveller (preferably booking ahead) or those travelling on a tight budget. The best hotel is the three-star **Hotel Denia** (Tel: 781 212), along Partida Suertes del Mar. This large building has 280 beds, all with private facilities, and a central location. It is open from the start of April until the end of August, and additional features include facilities for tennis, swimming and hairdressing.

Two more modest options are the two-star **Los Angeles** (Tel: 780 458) along Playa de las Marinas, and the one-star **Costa Blanca** (Tel: 780 336). The Los Angeles has 60 bedrooms, all with bathrooms and telephone, and it is open from the start of April until the middle of October. The Costa Blanca has 53 bedrooms, again all with private facilities, and offers a similar grade of central accommodation with the added advantage of year-round opening.

Just a few miles south of Denia, right on the point of the coast, is CABO DE SAN ANTONIO, a ruggedly beautiful spot against a backdrop of the Montgó range of hills. The next resort is JÁVEA, lying about five miles south of Denia. This is a relatively small resort; just four tour operators visit here and there are only two or three good hotels. Nevertheless, it is reckoned to be the sunniest spot on the

Costa Blanca and it has been a traditionally peaceful destination where many retired visitors have chosen to spend a relaxing summer break, or even the best part of the winter, comparatively cheaply by British standards. One small thought worth keeping in mind when visiting Jávea is the fact that, about a decade ago, the World Health Organization declared the resort to be: 'environmentally near perfect'.

Jávea is a very picturesque place, but it really is little more than a large village. The fact that peaceful resorts like Jávea exist at all tends to get forgotten because of the bustling, lively reputation of much larger destinations like Benidorm or Alicante. There are two small beaches nearby, and Jávea Cove is an attractive, rocky inlet which heads a stretch of even more rocky coastline continuing right down to Cabo de la Nao.

One sight of note in Jávea is the old fortress-like **church**, with its imposing Gothic façade. The village has had an unremarkable history, and what survives can be seen in the tiny **Historic and Ethnological Museum**. The opening hours are, to say the least, haphazard, but it is generally open on Saturday afternoons and Sunday mornings.

Jávea's best hotel is the four-star **P.N. Costa Blanca** (Tel: 790 200), a well-appointed, centrally located hotel with 65 air-conditioned bedrooms, a busy restaurant, and large TV room, should you feel like sampling the delights of Spanish television! This popular hotel is open all year round.

Another reasonable establishment is the three-star **Toscamar** (Tel: 770 261), on the outskirts of the village, which is listed as a quality *residencial*. The Toscamar has 140 rooms and additional facilities including a swimming pool and well-tended garden. More modest accommodation options include the **Villa Naranjos** (Tel: 790 050), a large two-star hotel, with 147 bedrooms, which is open from the start of April until mid-October; and the 18-room one-star **Costa Mar** (Tel: 790 644).

Continuing down the coast, you may care to visit the CABO DE LA NOA, directly opposite the tiny island of Portichol. Fascinating natural **caves** have formed in the cliffs around here and, if you are keen to visit them, be prepared to negotiate one or two pretty precarious ladders. The caves really are amazing but should only be attempted after taking local advice or, preferably, accompanying a qualified guide. It's worth remembering their local name, *Pesqueras de la Muerte* or 'Fishing grounds for Death'.

The area inland from here is made up of vineyards and green fields, and you should be able to see a few examples of the *riu-rau* type of local dwelling which was the inspiration for many of the varieties of more modern villas that have been built recently.

The old fishing port of MORAIRA lies about nine miles south of Jávea. The village has little to recommend a special detour, although you might be interested to see the remains of the old **castle** and **watch-tower** which played a key role in the port's defence against pirates in more troubled times. Like many of the relatively undeveloped villages along Spain's eastern coast, Moraira has no hotels but does have a growing number of villa and apartment complexes. Three British operators, including Interhome and Private Villas, offer self-catering holidays to Moraira.

Seven miles south again, you will reach the busy resort of CALPE. You will almost certainly be struck by the sight of the enormous rock, known locally as *Peñon de Ifach*, which resembles the Rock of Gibraltar. The huge rock is one of the Costa Blanca's most striking natural features, and is joined to the mainland by a narrow isthmus. It features prominently on many local postcards and is well worth a look, if only to visit one of the two attractive little coves which have formed on either side of it.

Both beaches are safe and clean, and there is a reasonable range of popular water-sports available. You will notice quite a contrast between the two: the narrower is, by far, the easier to get to and is normally quite crowded during the peak summer months. The other one is broader but a good bit more rocky, which probably explains why it is invariably quieter: perhaps your best bet, though, if you just plan to sit back and read or soak up the sun, but not recommended for children.

As a holiday destination, you will find somewhere like Calpe is a total contrast to the mega-resorts further down the coast. It is still predominantly made up of villas and apartments, but its increasing popularity with British holiday-makers especially ensures that a number of hotels are springing up. Already three or four non-apartment tour operators offer Calpe in their summer brochures, as well as the half dozen or so self-catering specialists. In the evenings, there is a limited choice of bars and restaurants, and nightlife is restricted to what the hotels have to offer – and that is seldom much. If you want swinging nightlife, then stick to the bigger resorts.

For the sailing enthusiast, Calpe has a good port, although the maximum draught is only 2 metres whereas it is 4.5 metres at Jávea, and 5 metres at Altea. The resort also has a reasonable nine-hole golf course, located a couple of miles off the main Calpe-to-Moraira highway. It is open all year round and clubs can be hired for a moderate charge. For more information about these, and other attractions, the **Tourist Information Office** (Tel: 831 250) is along the Avenida Ejércitos Españoles.

Among the hotels in Calpe, easily the most impressive is **Aparthotel Galetamar** (Tel: 832 311), a very smart, three-star complex opened only in 1985. It is located in a secluded residential area about three miles from the centre of the small town, and has 117 very well-appointed bedrooms, all with private facilities, air conditioning, large balconies with a sea view, and comfortable soft-beds which are sensibly functional during the day if you so choose. Live music is occasionally available.

Two other hotels, both two-star establishments, are the **Paradero Ifach** (Tel: 830 300) along the Explanada del Puerto, and the **Porto Calpe** (Tel: 830 354) on the Avenida del Puerto. The Paradero Ifach is the smaller of the two, with just 29 bedrooms, but it has the added feature of an attractive garden, a television lounge and a tennis court. The Porto Calpe is significantly larger, with 60 rooms, and remains open all year round.

The busy coast road continues south, from Calpe, through the Mascarat Tunnel which crosses one of the rockiest foothills of the Bernia Sierra. If you've travelled this far by car, it is well worth pausing for a few minutes to admire the outstanding views far out across the rich blue sea from the Altea side of the tunnel. From here, the colour of the sea is particularly deep blue.

This is part of the district of Olla de Altea, a rural district which precedes the actual town of Altea. Near here, you can turn inland to visit Altea la Vieja (literally, 'Altea the Old') and Castell de Guadalest. This is one of the most picturesque excursions from this part of Spain, and one which we look at in more detail at the end of this chapter.

The modern town of **ALTEA** is not really a resort, except for a few relatively new villa developments on the outskirts, but it is a splendidly laid out town and well worth a visit to appreciate some of the views. The best local beach is the pebbly **Albir** just to the south of the town. In Altea itself, much of the style and character of the original Moorish village, from which the present town emerged, still remains.

Be prepared to do quite a bit of walking: the oldest quarter is a good 257 steps, not all of which you need to climb at once, but 257 steps all the same, reaching up from the town's main shopping street, the Avenida Fermín Sanz Orrio. If arriving by car, you'd be well advised to leave it (legally parked and locked, otherwise you can expect a nasty surprise) in any of the streets which branch off from the main road leading into town, and then prepare yourself for a long, leisurely stroll.

Altea has been built in layers: the oldest part of the town is also the highest, perched on top of a hill from which you can see for miles and enjoy some of the most spectacular views on the Costa Blanca. It is quite a keen hike to the summit, but you will pass through a fascinating collection of narrow side-streets which ultimately extend along the entire La Marina region of the town. Look out for the distinctive silhouette of the *Peñon de Ifach* on your left, and the Gelade range of hills in the opposite direction.

Right at the summit of the old town there is a tiny **parish church**, crowned with a tiled dome – a welcome retreat from the scorching summer sunshine. Lower down, there is no shortage of small cafés and bars if you are in need of liquid refreshment. For the golfer, Altea has a nine-hole golf club, open all year round, near the Old Town, where clubs can be rented. Altea has no other obvious attractions, and there isn't a tourist office in the town.

One recommended short excursion from Altea will take you four or five miles inland to the village of POLOP. This small settlement is surrounded by orchards and pine groves, and is a wonderfully picturesque spot to get away from the beach for an afternoon. A prominent hill, the **Via Crucis**, looks down on the village and offers excellent views towards the coast and further inland. Look out for the cool fountain in the centre of the village – irresistible on a hot, sticky summer's afternoon!

Back in Altea, there are only a limited number of options if you are looking for somewhere to stay, and it is fair to say that the independent traveller who isn't too fussy about the quality of his or her accommodation is likely to be the most easily satisfied. In the centre of town, the two-star **Altaya** (Tel: 840 800) has 24 rooms and is open all year round. It has a swimming pool, currency exchange facility, and private shower/WC for each bedroom. More modest, but no less central, accommodation is available at the one-star **Solymar** (Tel: 840 250) along the Avenida del Puerto. It has 17 rooms, each with en suite bathroom, and is open all year.

From Altea, or even Polop, there is nothing to interrupt your approach to **BENIDORM**, easily one of Spain's largest and best-known resorts. Over the next few pages, we will introduce you to the fascinating remains of the Old Town of Benidorm which existed for centuries before the package-holiday market invasion. We also offer a comprehensive introduction to this enormous, cosmopolitan resort, together with some detailed recommendations from Benidorm's extensive range of large hotels, many of which are fully-booked months in advance by the major British tour operators.

The resort of Benidorm is dominated by over four miles of golden beaches and one of the largest concentration of tower-block hotels anywhere in Spain. Today Benidorm has enough hotel rooms to look after the entire population of an average small town, and a variety of self-catering apartment accommodation from the superb to the dubious for a staggering half a million more. But the city hasn't always enjoyed this level of popularity, and even at the start of the last century, the then stagnant village of Benidorm had only a single, flea-ridden inn to welcome travellers.

The first 'package' tour to Benidorm arrived in 1868 when an enthusiastic businessman shuttled a few wealthy gentry by stagecoach from Valencia in order to sample the delights of the village's clear sea water and long, empty beach. A lot has changed since then, of course, but certainly there are few major resorts which can trace their package ancestry as far back as Benidorm can!

It is not entirely accurate, though, to assume that the village of Benidorm expanded uniformly to create the vast resort city which you will find today. On the contrary, the resort grew up around the postage-stamp village nucleus which, thankfully, still survives largely intact as a welcome contrast to mile upon mile of large, modern hotel blocks. The original **Benidorm village** hides away on the lengthy spur of land which divides the two main beaches.

A large fort, occupied by French troops, stood here until 1812, when combined British and Spanish forces blew it up during Spain's bloody War of Independence. The action certainly had the desired effect of driving the French out. Cynics have said ever since that the reason it took so long for Benidorm to build a better inn was because the French troops who survived the blast left without settling many outstanding room accounts at the one inhospitable flea-pit there was in 1812 – and the incentive to build a better one had gone!

Whatever you care to think, a stroll round the village makes a peaceful alternative to lying on the beach. On the site of the old fort you can visit the **observatory** which is known as the 'Balcony of the Mediterranean' because of the magnificent views it offers of the Levante and Poniente beaches, and the nearby island of Benidorm.

The **Isla de Benidorm** is a large chunk of rock lying a little way off the coast, distinguished by its wedge shape. It is uninhabited apart from occasional visiting tourists, a small café and the bird wardens who keep an eye on the large colony of sea birds which have made their home there. You can swim across to the island, but the water is deep and the distance should only be attempted by experienced swimmers. A more relaxing alternative is to take a boat trip from the beach. These informal little trips take about forty minutes in either direction, but do make sure you confirm your return journey before the Spanish boatman casts off back to the mainland!

As you wander through the narrow back streets and look in the tiny shops, you might just be able to summon up enough imagination to think what Benidorm looked like a generation ago before the package-holiday market really took off. For more information about what to do and see in and around Benidorm, visit the **Tourist Information Office** (Tel: 853 224) which you'll find along Martínez Alejos.

Benidorm can be proud of its two beaches. Many major resorts, including many large Spanish resorts, have a disappointingly small strip of sand which is woefully inadequate for the number of visitors the destination receives. Whatever other impressions you have of Benidorm, you will not be sorry about the size of the beaches. In total, there are just over four miles of golden coast, unevenly divided into the **Levante and Poniente Beaches**, although it's worth mentioning that most of the sand you'll see was originally shipped over from Morocco!

The Levante Beach stretches from the edge of the resort right up to the old village. This is slightly the larger of the two, although both curve smoothly and shelve gently into the crystal clear Mediterranean water. Despite the tens of thousands who flock here daily, you can always be assured of somewhere to drape your towel, and there is a surprising amount of space behind the inevitable fixed parasols (be warned: daily charge of a couple of hundred pesetas to sit under one of them!) for children to play safely.

Both beaches offer all the main water-sports, including sailing, snorkelling, windsurfing, the ever-popular pedaloes, and scuba-diving for those properly trained to enjoy this specialist activity. Should you tire of all this, or even of swimming or lying on the beach, there are innumerable beach bars just waiting to serve you that ice-cold drink. In short, Benidorm offers a superb beach for all the family, including the Sportsperson, so long as you don't mind the crowds.

A superb place for all the family to visit is the **Safari Park Vergel** which also has a dolphin park, restaurant, and children's amusement park. It is open throughout the year, 10am–7.30pm during the summer, and 10am–6pm in winter. Another option, right in the heart of Benidorm along the Avenida de Europa, is the **Europa Park Amusement Park**. This large complex is open every evening throughout the year and is popular with families and young singles. Opening hours, in June, are from 5pm–11pm; in July and August, 6pm–1am; and during the rest of the year, from 6pm–10pm.

One very popular excursion from Benidorm will take you a few miles inland to GUADALEST, a remarkable little town which has grown up inside the rocky remains of a huge old **castle**. Right on the summit of a massive, totally impregnable rock, it was originally built by the Moors more than twelve centuries ago. Many attempts to destroy it in more troubled times failed, although James I of Aragon did eventually capture it during one of the most bitter sieges of the thirteenth-century Wars of Reconquest. Today, the castle is a fascinating tourist attraction and, as you might imagine, the views from the summit are breathtaking. Don't miss the opportunity to glimpse this remarkable reminder of Spain's early history.

Nightlife in Benidorm swings. The resort has about eighty discos and nightclubs, plus dozens more if you add all the nightspots in the big hotels. As fashionable discos change from season to season, and frequently once or twice within seasons as well, it is impossible for us to make any realistic recommendations. Suffice to say, you will not be disappointed at the range of nightspots available in Benidorm, and you will find the largest concentration of discos along the highway leading north towards Valencia. Just follow the crowds . . .

One regular favourite, for those who can afford it, is the **Casino Costa Blanca** (Tel: 890 700) just outside Benidorm close to Villajoyosa. Among the attractions are French Roulette, American Roulette, Black Jack, Chemin de Fer and Punter. Opening hours are from 8pm–4am, and the casino is restricted to smartly dressed visitors over the age of twenty-one. Bring your passport to show at the door.

Benidorm has a huge collection of restaurants, ranging from the excellent to the mediocre. Preferences and standards vary from year to year (although seldom as quickly as what is and what isn't an 'in' disco!) and the following suggestions are among the resort's best places to eat.

El Hórreo (Tel: 857 471) is a favourite for the very best Spanish dishes, cooked to perfection and served in a traditional setting; **I Fratelli** (Tel: 853 979) is an expensive Italian-style restaurant, situated along Dr Orts Llorca. The décor is remarkable and creates an intimate, turn-of-the-century feel to the whole place. **Caserola** (Tel: 851 719), on the other hand, at Bruselas 7, is a more modern-looking, but no less comfortable, restaurant which specializes in fine French cuisine. It is the perfect place for that special meal, as dinner is served on the romantic, flower-covered sun terrace.

As you might expect of a resort the size of Benidorm, accommodation is available to suit every pocket. One or two older guides suggest that the independent budget traveller will be able to find somewhere to stay in the resort anytime except August. Although there are still a handful of flourishing one-star *hostals* and *residencials*, finding anywhere to stay independently in Benidorm between June and early September is likely to be a nightmare UNLESS you are travelling as part of an organized package group. Even then, it is all too easy to have settled on the notion of a holiday in a resort as well-known, and as large, as Benidorm without giving much thought to your choice of hotel beyond whether or not it has a pool.

The Spanish Tourist Board recognizes over 150 hotels in Benidorm. In the following section, we obviously cannot feature more than a representative sample, but we've chosen about a dozen of the (all-round) best-value hotels in Benidorm, from five-star luxury down to simple two-star comfort and value for money.

Benidorm has only one officially designated five-star hotel, the **Gran Delfin** (Tel: 853 400), which is an attractive, low-rise building with 150 air-conditioned bedrooms. All bedrooms and public rooms in the hotel are extremely well furnished, and overall you will find the Gran Delfin a quiet, peaceful choice of hotel. Wide sun terraces surround the large swimming pool and lead down to the beach. There is no organized entertainment, although additional leisure facilities include a tennis court and a small playground for the children.

Among the four-star hotels, the **Cimbel** (Tel: 852 100) is a very appealing hotel situated right opposite the larger Levante Beach. A ten-minute stroll along the sea-front will take you into the old village. The hotel has 144 bedrooms, mainly twins but with a few singles as well, and all have private facilities and a balcony. The rooms at the front have great seaviews, but those to the rear have disappointing vistas across yet more tower-block hotels. Live music and occasional floor shows are organized. This hotel would be ideal for all age groups apart from young singles.

The **Don Pancho** (Tel: 852 950) is one of Benidorm's tallest hotels, with 251 bedrooms spread out across a staggering eighteen floors. Bear this in mind when booking. Having said that, the Don Pancho is probably Benidorm's best four-star hotel and is no more than five minutes away from the Levante Beach. Entertainment facilities are excellent: some of Benidorm's best floor shows take place here, so befriend a resident if you're not staying in the hotel!

One more good four-star hotel is the **Selomar** (Tel: 855 278), a 246-room hotel over eight floors close to both the beach and town centre. Nightlife is excellent, and this hotel is ideal for young singles (or older holiday-makers looking for a bit of action). The roof-top pool is small for a hotel this size, but is nevertheless an extremely attractive feature of the Selomar. Views from the roof-top, and most of the front bedrooms, are excellent, although the street below can be noisy during the peak summer months – unless, of course, you are one of the revellers making the noise!

Among the many three-star hotels, which make up a large proportion of all the classes of accommodation available in Benidorm, four stand out as worthy of special recommendation. A lively hotel is the **Poseidon** (Tel: 850 200) which lies close to the main beach and opposite the popular **Stringfellows** disco. This large, modern building has nearly 250 bedrooms over eight floors and a nightly disco. The buffet-style evening meal represents very good value, although the informality of the self-service dinner might not appeal to older visitors. Definitely a young person's hotel.

Recently refurbished, the large **Presidente** (Tel: 853 950) has a first-class location close to both the main beach, and many of the best bars and restaurants in Benidorm. It is a good twenty minutes from the town centre, but is an attractive, self-contained hotel with a good range of activities for all the family. The Presidente has 228 bedrooms, including a number of four-bed rooms which are ideal for both families and groups of young people looking for good accommodation at relatively low prices. Audience participation 'fun' evenings are extremely popular, so be warned!

The **Didac** (Tel: 851 549) is a reasonable modern hotel, with 100 bedrooms and a convenient location about ten minutes from Pontiente Beach. There are regular floor shows and some form of musical entertainment in the evenings, although this is not the disco variety most likely to appeal to young singles. All the public rooms are comfortably furnished, and the hotel offers a relaxing atmosphere throughout the summer.

Les Dunes (Tel: 852 400) is popular with both German and British holiday-makers, and is one of the older three-star hotels in Benidorm. It has 110 bedrooms, mostly doubles with private facilities and a balcony, although the few singles there are tend to be on the cramped side and don't offer a balcony as standard. The hotel sits right in front of the Levante Beach and is ideal for older holiday-makers. Very little in the way of organized entertainment.

Among the two-star hotels, the seven floor **Rialto** (Tel: 853 450) is suitable for young families and older couples. It has about 100 rooms, all with private facilities and a balcony, and lies about fifteen minutes from the resort centre. It is a quiet hotel, comfortably furnished and no more than five minutes from the beach. It has no organized entertainment, although a weekly Gala Dinner is a popular feature.

The **Calypso** (Tel: 854 350) is one of Benidorm's largest hotels, with 364 bedrooms on twelve floors. You cannot fail to notice this hotel from a distance, as the outside looks as though it was decorated with army-green camouflage paint! The Calypso is a typical, lively, good-value family hotel close to the Levante Beach, but nearly half an hour's walk from the old village. The hotel is simply furnished, and has no pretences to be anything more than a value-for-money two-star establishment. Entertainment is regular and there is noisy fun for all the family.

The **Planesia** (Tel: 855 466) offers a bit more than your average two-star hotel as it is one of the smallest in the resort, with just 36 bedrooms. This generally means that guests are not aware of the impersonal atmosphere which prevails in larger hotels, particularly those with a high turnover of package-holiday visitors. The public areas are relatively newly furnished and surprisingly intimate for a

Benidorm hotel. It overlooks the Pontiente Beach, but be warned that there are seventy steps to climb down before you reach it. Entertainment is limited to a nightly piano player.

Six miles south of Benidorm lies **VILLAJOYOSA**, a modest little port where you can usually see a small fishing fleet lying at anchor. Among the things to look out for in the town are a number of remains from ancient Roman, Visigoth and Moorish settlements. During the last week of July, a large proportion of the town's 20,000 inhabitants dresses up in lavish costumes and re-enacts the defeat of the Algerian pirate Zala Arráez who tried to sack the town around dawn one morning in 1538. The culmination of the celebration is a noisy reconstruction of the attack itself, and if you can still hear yourself think by the end of it you might like to reflect that it was only a decade or so ago when this pageant was held at dawn rather than early evening! Two points of interest in the town are the enormous **Gothic church**, and a wonderful, long **esplanade** which is shaded by palm trees and flanked by the façades of old buildings. The combination of colours used to decorate the houses is an amazing sight.

Villajoyosa today remains a relatively small resort: the only British operators who offer trips to this part of the Costa Blanca are a handful of the better-known villa and self-catering apartment companies such as Falcon and Interhome. Despite this, there are one or two reasonable places to stay in town, although demand on the limited number of rooms available is considerable.

The best hotel is the four-star **Montiboli** (Tel: 890 250), a small luxury hotel with just 52 bedrooms along Partida Montiboli. It remains open all year, and among the excellent range of leisure facilities there is a good swimming pool for a hotel of this size, a tennis court, beauty salon and hairdresser, and a television lounge. Two more modest suggestions, for the independent traveller, are the two-star **El Pino** (Tel: 890 490) at Partida El Paraiso, and the one-star **Marina** (Tel: 890 094). Neither establishment has more than 20 rooms, but both offer good value, basic accommodation. Advance booking is strongly recommended.

Continuing down the coast, there is very little between Villajoyosa and the city of Alicante, although many of the inland turn-offs make interesting drives if you have the chance to hire a car. You will pass through the village of Busot shortly before the urbanization on the outskirts of Alicante begins, but it isn't worth lingering.

ALICANTE is almost certainly where you'll first set foot on the Costa Blanca. The busy international airport lies a few miles outside the city (transfer time about fifteen minutes) but surprisingly few visitors ever see much more than the outside of the airport terminal building if they consider Alicante at all.

The city has a number of excellent beaches on either side of it and, clearly, this is the main attraction to Alicante as a resort. Rather surprisingly, very few British tour operators offer trips directly to Alicante and, at the time of publication, only half a dozen companies offered either hotel or self-catering apartment holidays to the city.

Alicante has a long history. It was a popular holiday spot with both the Greeks and the Romans during their respective periods of occupation of the Costa Blanca. Unlike Benidorm, Alicante grew up as a commercial city rather than purely a tourist resort city and, consequently, there is a wealth of fascinating sights and good museums for visitors to explore, even if only for a day or an afternoon.

If you are lucky enough to visit the city on 24 June then you will see one of the Costa Blanca's best-known popular celebrations, the *Foqueras de Sant John* or the 'Bonfires of Saint John'. The symbolic importance of fire is central in most Spanish fiestas and traditions, and the marvellous celebration in Alicante is similar to the *Fallas* celebrated in Valencia. It is a noisy, fun evening in which visitors and locals alike invariably enjoy taking part.

The best starting point to explore the city is the **Castillo de Santa Bárbara** which sits 350 feet above the city on Mount Benacantil, and offers easily the best vantage point from which to see the Costa Blanca's principal settlement in all its glory. On a clear day, you can see as far as Santa Pola and Benidorm. The castle totally dominates the city. Its long history goes back to the third century BC when the Carthaginians first recognized the strategic importance of the mountain. The only time the castle has been stormed during its active history was in 1707, during the

Spanish War of Succession, when French forces managed to blow up a large part of the defending garrison.

You can reach the summit by car or on foot: there is a long, winding road up to the summit which is very steep and an extremely wearisome hike. The best way, though, is to take the lift which clings to the inside of the mountain as it climbs slowly towards the top. This option is not recommended if you don't have a head for heights but, as you might imagine, the lift is very popular, and you'll get access to it at one end of Calle Juan Bautista Lafora.

Lying between the Calle Mayor and the Calle Jorge Juan, in the city's old quarter, the **Church of Santa Maria** is one of Spain's finest surviving examples of a medieval Christian church built during the troubled decades when much of the Iberian peninsula was being reconquered from the Moors. Most of the church dates from the fourteenth century, and it is known that a great Moorish mosque stood on this site before the Christian church was built. Stand back for a few minutes and admire the magnificent façade, so typical of the Valencian Baroque style, before going inside.

Next door to the church you can visit Alicante's **Municipal Museum of Twentieth Century Art,** easily the best modern art collection in this part of Spain. Most major twentieth-century artists are represented in this remarkable collection, including Braque, Chagall and, naturally, one of the greatest Spanish artists ever, Pablo Picasso. The museum is open weekdays from 10am–1pm, and again from 5pm–8pm. During public holidays, it is generally open between 10am and 1.30pm although, in common with many public collections in Spain, it is closed on Mondays.

Near the museum, you can visit what little remains of the **Old Town**, known locally as the *Barrio de Santa Cruz*. The narrow streets and colourful little homes were typical of most Spanish towns until a few generations ago, but so many have now been overtaken by the pressures of twentieth-century living. Make a point of spending a leisurely hour or two rambling through this lovely reminder of Alicante town as it once was.

Near Calle Mayor, on Avenida General Sanjurjo, is the city's main ecclesiastical building, the **Catedral de San Nicolás Bari**. Much of it was destroyed during the Spanish Civil War earlier this century, but it has been lovingly restored since and is worth a visit – if only to see the outstanding ornamental façade and long nave which are among the finest examples of the work of architect Juan de Herrera. Herrera, incidentally, is also known for his work on the Escorial Palace just outside Madrid.

Close by, in the Plaza del Ayuntamiento, a large coin and stamp collectors' market is held most Sundays and on certain public holidays. It is an occasion which usually arouses considerable interest amongst visitors to Alicante. Whilst you are in the Plaza, make sure you have a good look at the very attractive eighteenth-century Baroque façade of the **Ayuntamiento** (town hall) itself. On the main staircase of this most appealing public building, look out for the large red-lettered marble plaque which represents a copy of the city's original charter, first granted by Ferdinand II of Aragon (who is perhaps better known for his association with, and encouragement of, explorer Christopher Columbus) in 1490. Inside the town hall, you can visit a small **picture gallery** and see the tiny chapel complete with tiles from one of the most important Venician tile centres at Manises.

Directly opposite Alicante's imposing castle, on the other side of the city, there stands a much smaller and lesser-known fortress, the **Castillo de San Fernando**. It is a modern building, as castles go, having been started as a defensive precaution during the Spanish War of Independence, a bloody six-year struggle which finally ended in 1814. The castle has seen little action but it makes an interesting stroll, particularly for the opportunity to sit in the **municipal park** where it is located. Ironically, it is one of the best places to go in order to get a really good view of the earlier Castillo de Santa Bárbara.

One more museum visitors to Alicante might enjoy visiting is the **Provincial Archaeological Museum** inside the Palacio de la Diputación (the Chamber of Deputies). A fascinating collection of traditional local ceramics, going back over two thousand years, is the key display. There are also a host of other related archaeological finds, including glassware, jewellery (including some amazing bone bracelets), and a number of Greek and Moorish carvings. The museum is open weekdays from 9am–2pm, except Mondays, and between 11am and 2pm on most public holidays.

Having seen just about all there is to see in Alicante, you will be delighted to know that there is a first-class collection of bars and restaurants in the city. Many are located in and around the Explanada de España, Alicante's main shopping area, or else up by the Barrio Santa Cruz. Below, we've selected a few of the better ones for you to consider.

El Delfin (Tel: 214 911), on the Explanada de España, is arguably the best-known restaurant in Alicante. If you go anywhere near the city's main thoroughfare, you cannot fail to spot its inviting collection of pavement tables, or smell the irresistible aromas coming from its kitchens. Seafood specialities dominate the menu, although less well-known Spanish dishes, including *solomillo Wellington*, an adventurous variation on beef Wellington where the steak is enclosed in a thick pastry envelope, are worth investigating.

Quo Venit (Tel. 216 660), on the other hand, is a much more informal, less sophisticated Spanish restaurant located in the Plaza Santísma Faz. The style of cooking, presentation, and jovial service is unashamedly Spanish. **Pizzeria Romana** (Tel: 260 602), on the other hand, is distinctly French, although you will find the occasional 'Mamma's speciality' pizza creeping into the menu. It is a bit of a trek to find though, being three or four miles out near Playa Albufereta, but the journey is well worth it when you see the menu and taste the result.

The sports fanatic is well catered for in Alicante as well. The yachting enthusiast can enjoy the facilities of the 'sports harbour' in the resort by contacting the **Real Club de Regattas de Alicante** (Tel: 223 442). The maximum draught in the port is 3 metres. Even supposing you don't own a yacht, you'll find that the harbour is a fascinating hive of activity, and a perfect place to spend an interesting (and inexpensive) afternoon admiring the comings and goings of some very fine crafts.

If golf is your sport, then there are two excellent clubs within a short drive of Alicante. The **Club de Golf Peñas Rojas** (Tel: 241 266) is located about ten or eleven miles out of the city, in the town of San Vicente del Raspeig on the Castalla highway. The attractive eighteen-hole course is open all year round and both clubs and golf carts can be hired. Slightly closer to Alicante, the **Club de Golf**

Almaina Park (Tel: 212 306) is a large, thirty-six hole course lying near to the San Juan beach.

Among the places to stay in Alicante, the best hotels are the four-star **Apartotel Melia Alicante** (Tel: 205 000) at Playa Postiguet, and another four-star, the **Gran Sol** (Tel: 203 000) along Avenida Méndez Núñez. The Apartotel is a massive building, with over 500 bedrooms and some great views from the top floor. Regular evening entertainment is available, and there are three restaurants, two swimming pools and a nightclub for residents to enjoy. The Apartotel Melia Alicante is open throughout the year.

The Gran Sol, on the other hand, is a much smaller establishment with 150 bedrooms. All rooms have private facilities, and the hotel has an attractive interior popular with families, although, unusually for a four-star hotel on the Costa Blanca, there is no swimming pool. One popular feature is the top-floor bar with its magnificent views across the harbour.

Among the three-star hotels, the largest is the **Estudio Hotel Alicante** (Tel: 212 011) at Poeta Vila y Blanco. This 493-room hotel has an excellent restaurant and a variety of entertainments organized throughout the summer. The **Maya** (Tel: 261 211), on Calle Penalva, has 200 bedrooms, all with en suite bathrooms, and a reasonable swimming pool. If you would prefer a smaller establishment offering similar standards of comfort, then the three-star **Palas** (Tel: 209 310), at Cervantes, Plaza del Mar, has just 48 well-appointed bedrooms and a smart, central location. All three are open all year round.

For the budget traveller, or the independent visitor to Alicante, then the following *residencials* are open all year round and offer good, clean, basic accommodation in the region's main population centre: the **Navas** (Tel: 204 011), with 40 bedrooms at Navas, 26; **San Remo** (Tel: 209 500), with 28 bedrooms nearby at Navas, 30; the **Alfonso El Sabio** (Tel: 203 144), which has 85 rooms and you'll find it along the street of the same name at Alfonso El Sabio, 18; and **Benacantil** (Tel: 207 422) with 47 bedrooms at San Telmo, 7. As always, though, do bear in mind that accommodation will be extremely difficult to find between June and September unless prebooked, and impossible during August. Think ahead.

*   *   *

The long stretch of coast from Alicante is virtually uninterrupted until you reach the fishing port of SANTA POLA, one of the main harbours for landing the famous local fishing catches. The scenery changes quite dramatically once you leave Alicante, from rugged terrain to relatively flat countryside. Much of the immediate area south of the city is an extension of salt deposits located close to miles of virtually uninterrupted beach.

There is an ancient medieval **castle** in Santa Pola itself, but the little town is not a resort as such and the only other attraction is the phenomenal range of bars and restaurants which line the seafront: a quite amazing collection for a relatively small place and, as you can imagine, they all specialize in fish dishes!

Look out for the morning fish market which has taken place near the harbour for generations and, if you're self-catering, you'll be hard pushed to find somewhere cheaper to try the local produce. Nearby, there are a few stretches of clean, white sandy beach at **Playa de Santa Pola** and **Playa de Pinet** which are perfect for a day trip away from one of the larger resorts further up the coast. A superb vantage point to view the whole stretch of coast is the **Cape of Santa Pola**, near the town. You get a great view of the island of Tabarca in the distance.

From here, the coast winds south past **GUARDAMAR**, a busy village standing out on a long stretch of beach which is surrounded by sand dunes and a dense backdrop of pine trees. Guardamar is one of the most important fishing centres on the Costa Blanca, and one of eastern Spain's principal lobster ports. Lobster is the speciality dish on the menu of most restaurants in the village and although it isn't a resort as such, there are one or two very small hotels which might suit the independent traveller.

The three-star **Meridional** (Tel: 728 340), at Dunas de Guardamar, is the best hotel, although its 11 rooms quickly fill during the summer months. Both **Las Dunas** (Tel: 728 110) and the **Oasis** (Tel: 728 860) are clean, simple, one-star hotels with around 40 bedrooms each. All three are only open from April until September, and the choice outside those months is even more limited. A good bet is the one-star **Bella Costa** (Tel: 728 835), which you'll find at Lepanto, 3. The Bella Costa has 16 rooms, all with private facilities and the additional feature of a television lounge for the darker winter evenings if you do decide to travel out of season.

The last resort of any size on the Costa Blanca is **TORREVIEJA**, about ten miles further south from Guardamar. The resort lies near vast salt deposits which, along with fishing, made up one of the main sources of income for the area before tourism really took off. The name Torrevieja means, literally, 'Old Tower', and you might reasonably expect to see some evidence of a crumbling old watch-tower standing guard over the village. Unfortunately the original **Old Tower** has long since crumbled into the sea but, ever resourceful, the people of this district have built a new 'Old Tower' which was funded from resources donated by former residents of Torrevieja keen to preserve part of the history of their home town.

Apart from the tower, the only sights of note are the **salt mountains**, the source of the salt crystals brightly covering the popular little ships which are on sale throughout the Costa Blanca. If you are keen to visit the salt deposits then you will need to get a pass. This is given freely from the local office of the salt company, the wonderfully named Nueva Compañia Arrendataria de las Salinas de Torrevieja which you will find at one end of the town's main square. This pass does not allow for photography, and if you do wish to take photographs, then you will need to get a second pass which is significantly more difficult to acquire – although it is issued by the same company office.

Close to the village, there are three stretches of beach where a substantial apartment development is starting to grow up. **Cabo Roig**, **La Zenia** and the **Dehesa de Campoamor** are attractive beaches, popular with day visitors, and any one of them will make an interesting alternative to the larger resort beaches further north on the Costa Blanca.

During August, the town comes alive for a few days during one of the Costa Blanca's many colourful fiestas. This is known as the *Habaneras* Festival, a term which originated in Bizet's classic opera, *Carmen*. During this pageant of colour, the nineteenth-century salt voyages are brought to life again. For further information about what to do and see in Torrevieja, there is a **Tourist Information Office** (Tel: 710 122) on the Avendia Libertad.

For the sportsperson, Torrevieja is an excellent destination to either bring your own yacht or see others in action. Three organizations oversee the port: **Puerto de la Dehesa de Campoamor** (Tel: 320 002) accepts a maximum draught of 3.5 metres, whereas both the **Club Náutico de Torrevieja** (Tel: 710 108) and the **Puerto Deportivo de Cabo** (Tel: 320 289) accept a maximum draught of 4 metres. For land-based sports enthusiasts, there is an eighteen-hole golf course a few miles outside the town, heading towards Cartagena. The **Club de Golf Villamartin** (Tel: 320 384) has been established for a number of years and is open all year round. Clubs are available for hire to visitors.

Torrevieja is developing quickly as a resort. Half a dozen British operators offer summer tours here, obviously attracted by the golden beaches on either side of the town and its relatively central position for exploring the rest of the region and further south into the Costa del Almería. The best hotel is a three-star establishment, the **Fontana** (Tel: 714 111) which has 156 bedrooms along Rambla Juan Mateo. Additional facilities include a swimming pool, television lounge and large garden.

A very good two-star hotel, with a similar range of facilities to the Fontana, is the **Berlin** (Tel: 711 537) on Torre del Moro. The Berlin has 50 bedrooms, all with en suite bathrooms and a reasonable resort location. A one-star hotel worthy of recommendation is the **Edén Roc** (Tel: 711 145) on Cala del Monjón. The Edén Roc has 30 bedrooms, and all three hotels are open throughout the year.

South of here, the Costa Blanca eventually merges into the Costa del Sol and Almería. Precisely where the definitive boundary appears is a matter of considerable contention: some travel books put it as far south as Mojácar, others as far north as Elche. Even the literature produced by the Spanish Tourist Authority offers various options! The consensus appears to make the break at Aguilas.

INLAND

The rolling inland countryside of the Costa Blanca is often ignored by holiday-makers who, more often than not, never stray further than the bars and beaches of the larger resorts during their stay in Spain. None of the towns and villages of inland Costa Blanca are big resorts: most are not even resorts at all, and the few which do receive visitors for anything more than a curiosity day trip have little more than self-catering or apartment accommodation to offer. Beginning at the northern end of the White Coast, the following section will give you an introduction to the inland districts and highlight a few of the best destinations for an excursion from any one of the coastal resorts.

The countryside surrounding the northernmost town of Denia offers the opportunity for a very enjoyable drive. This is an important agricultural region, specializing in rice and citrus fruit. The scenery is constantly changing, and you will pass a small **safari park** near the village of PEGO. Car hire is strongly recommended if you plan to explore much of the inland area, although the main towns and villages are well connected by bus links.

PLANES is about as far inland as you can reasonably go within the Costa Blanca area. The town sits on the wide slopes of a large hill, and the old **castle** perched on the top is a reminder of medieval town 'planning' when virtually all settlements had to have the protection of a castle above it. The remains of the old town reveal some fascinating architecture and, nearby, the late medieval **aqueduct**, with its distinctive ogival arches, is worth a visit.

AGRES, about ten miles from Planes, lies at the foot of the Sierra de Mariola and, if you've got time to spare, is worth a visit for the dramatic views. A large, unusually shaped rock stands near the village, the source of a spring of warm, thermal waters. All around lush vegetation flourishes. This is a popular area for hikers, many of whom take the opportunity to climb the **Calvario** Hill. At the summit there is a tiny **convent** which is built on the site where local folklore says a holy image was once seen. Many rare and colourful varieties of vegetation flourish on the slopes of all the surrounding hills.

Further south, the inland area is made up of a mountainous region which includes some of the highest peaks in eastern Spain. A starting point is OLLA DE ALTEA, about a mile and a half from the main coastal highway leading down to Benidorm and Alicante. Passing through Altea la Vieja and CALLOSA DE ENSARRIÁ, another small town built on steep slopes, the main road inland winds through some of the steepest and most beautiful countryside in the region.

The actual highest point on the Costa Blanca is **Mount Aitana** which stands over 1,500 metres high as part of the same mountain range which forms the Bernia range running alongside the coast. The nearest town to the peak is CONFRIDES, a very attractive mountain town which has managed to retain much of its rural charm, despite huge numbers of tourists passing through it each summer.

Nearby PENÁGUILA is another high town, some way off the main highway, which should be on the itinerary of any nature-loving inland visitor. One of the most dramatic sights is the ruins of **el Portalet**, the old Moorish castle. Several old seignorial mansions can also be seen, and the **Garden of Santos** is one of the major landmarks of the inland region. The large **safari park** near Penáguila is a popular excursion from Benidorm, and it is open from 10am–5pm during the winter months; 10am–6.30pm in the summer.

Ten miles away is **ALCOY**, one of the largest inland towns in the Costa Blanca. This sprawling industrial town tends to give a rather more gloomy impression than it deserves. The jagged skyline is dominated by little red roofs and a couple of huge domes which stand over two of the largest churches in the town. Many of the larger houses were built by the wealthy bourgeoisie towards the end of the last century when the Industrial Revolution finally hit this part of Europe in a big way. Even today, a large textile factory in Alcoy is one of the oldest in the Iberian peninsula. Alcoy is much better known today, however, as the home of *peladillas*, one of the finest sweets manufactured in Spain. Don't leave here without trying them!

Among the points of interest in Alcoy are the **Church of Santa Maria**, the **Castle of St George** and the imposing **town hall** building. If you take a few minutes to stroll round the Plaza de España you will see some very fine modernist façades, but you will really see local culture at its very best if you have the chance to visit the town around 22–24 April. This is when the annual *Moros y Cristianos* is celebrated, a colourful fiesta which also takes place in many other parts of the Costa Blanca to commemorate the Reconquest, but it is undoubtedly seen at its very best in Alcoy. A cardboard model of a huge stone castle is erected in the main square, and a series of parades and displays culminate in the appearance of

Saint George. The noise, the smell of the firecrackers and the colourful costumes blend into the background of wild, live music and the sight of hundreds of people generally enjoying themselves. The fiesta is known to date back at least until the eighteenth century and some of the finest costumes have been worn by generation after generation of Alcoy locals. Many of the older ones can be seen in a small museum of local treasures inside the town's castle.

Although one of the most popular inland destinations for day trippers, Alcoy is not a resort. There are relatively few places to stay in the town, which is a little surprising for a town the size of Alcoy, but a couple of suggestions for the independent traveller are the three-star **Reconquista** (Tel: 330 900), on Puente San Jorge, which has 77 well-appointed rooms open throughout the year, and the larger, one-star, **San Jorge** (Tel: 543 277) along San Jorge de Ribera. This hotel/*residencial* is also open all year round, and has 86 bedrooms, all with showers and private toilet facilities. Book well in advance, especially if you're keen to stay here during the fiesta period.

PRIVATE. Keep Out   Eight miles from Alcoy you can visit the sanctuary of FONT ROJA, a peaceful spot which couldn't be further removed from the bustling coastal resorts further east. Most visitors, however, prefer to head back towards Altea. This particular road is one of the highest above sea level in eastern Spain, and one which is frequently blocked by snow during the winter months when the temperature falls significantly below the 61°F (16°C) winter average for most of the Costa Blanca region.

The area directly inland from Alicante is known as the Route of the Castles. Between this great sea port and Villena, this district of the Costa Blanca is densely populated, although none of the towns or villages merits a particular visit unless you arc keen to see one of the many magnificent old castles which give this part of the region its name. One of the first you should aim for is the **Castle of La Mola**, clearly signposted about a couple of miles off the main road close to Novelda. The castle is a large Arab fortress which was constantly besieged and set on fire throughout the troubled Middle Ages. Its most striking feature is the main tower, a dramatic triangular shape which is known to date from the early Christian period. Another well-known castle is the Gothic-style **Sanctuary of La Magdalena** nearby which embraces many features typical of the Catalonian modernist architects.

Another ten miles away, at PETREL, there is another fine castle which dates from the Middle Ages, standing as an interesting reminder of the type of link which, out of necessity, grew up between a town and its castle. The settlement crowded itself inside the impenetrable walls, but in more peaceful centuries has spread outwards into the surrounding farmland. Seven miles away, the **Castle of La Atalaya** has to be seen as it represents one of the finest examples of medieval military architecture anywhere in Spain.

The fascinating inland town of **ELCHE** lies fifteen miles west of Alicante, and would merit a visit if only to see its hundreds and hundreds of palm trees. The vast majority began life as early saplings planted by the Carthaginians in the third and fourth century BC, although, naturally, they have been carefully looked after and propagated since then. The Moors described them as having 'their feet in water, heads in the fire of heaven'.

All the palm trees are grown in dense groves around three sides of the town, no mean achievement for a town with a population of over 100,000! There is a serious point to all these trees, of course, as they provide the town with its main industry, producing succulent dates. It is a testament to the methods of Abderraman III, a tenth-century invader, that the irrigation system he devised is still the one which keeps the palm trees watered today. As one might reasonably imagine, a town with so many palm trees has a spectacular celebration on Palm Sunday, although advance hotel booking is essential if you wish to share in this marvellous spectacle.

Both the **Hort del Chocolater** and the **Hort de Baix** are worth visiting if you are at all botanically minded. Either will give you a greater understanding of one of Europe's most 'concentrated' horticultural towns. It's worth reflecting that, for every resident in Elche, there are over ten acres of greenery in the immediate area. The **municipal park** is less formal; another sight in Elche worth seeing is the **ayuntamiento** (town hall).

Try not to leave the town before you have managed to visit the magnificent **Alcázar de la Señoría**, a fantastic old Moorish palace, with large, solid towers. In earlier centuries, many great nobles and monarchs came here. Both James the Conqueror, and Ferdinand and Isabella are known to have stayed here during the Middle Ages. The palace grounds alone are well worth an afternoon visit.

The town has a good museum which will give you a much better insight into the history of this often-neglected part of inland Costa Blanca. The **Municipal Archaeological Museum** is situated in the municipal park, and is open workdays and public holidays from 11am–1pm and again from 4–7pm. The **Museum of La Alcudia**, at the nearby archaeological site of the same name, is open on a much more informal basis all day every day except Mondays and one or two public holidays.

Elche is not a resort, but a couple of suggestions for accommodation include the very appealing four-star hotel, the **Huerto del Cura** (Tel: 458 040), one of Spain's famous paradors. This luxurious building has 59 well-appointed rooms and a host of additional facilities such as a swimming pool, tennis court and occasionally organized evening entertainments. More modestly, the two-star **Candilejas** (Tel: 466 512) with 24 bedrooms, or the very basic one-star **Maria** (Tel: 460 283) are open throughout the year.

Costa Calida

The Costa Calida is probably the least-known of the Spanish costas, often being regarded as part of the Costa Blanca. It is essentially the coast of the province of Murcia, and, although there are a few resorts, is very limited in scope.

The developing resorts of LA MANCHA DE MAR MENOR, Los Alcázares and Santiago de la Ribera have an up-market air that is slightly spoilt by the high-rise concrete blocks that have been built here. However, there are excellent beaches and water-sports and year-round bathing in the great sea-water lagoon, safely enclosed behind the spit of La Mancha.

The large port and naval base of Cartagena, just to the south, have little to offer the holiday-maker, with the possible exception of a rather heavy nightscene, and the southernmost resort on this costa, Aguilas, is recommended principally for the sandy coves to be found just outside the town.

The climate in the area is similar in most respects to that of the Costa Blanca, with temperatures ranging from about 11°C (the low fifties Fahrenheit) in winter to about 23°C (the mid-seventies Fahrenheit) in summer. Inland, it can become unbearably hot in summer when the *calina* settles over the land and temperatures can reach an absolute maximum of 44°C (113°F).

The first of the resort areas on the Costa Calida is to be found at **Mar Menor**, a salt-water lagoon shielded from the sea by a long 'spit' formation that forms a large bay area off the coast. The lagoon has become a popular spot with tourists, due in large measure to the miles of wide and sandy beaches which are found on both sides of the spit, known as LA MANGA DE MAR MENOR. There are excellent **water-sports** facilities around the lagoon, and a couple of smallish resorts – LOS ALCÁZARES, and SANTIAGO DE LA RIBERA – are to be found on its mainland edge.

The up-market resorts are still undergoing some development and, sadly, are architecturally unattractive. The major recommendations of this destination are the sports facilities, and beaches, which are good for swimming. Of the available hotels, a better choice would be the middle-range **Cavanna**, which offers around 400 clean, comfortable rooms plus a pool, garden and tennis facilities.

On the southern edge of the Mar Menor Lagoon is LA UNION, which some guides describe as a resort. In fact, it is a dreary and run-of-the-mill mining town, and is certainly not to be recommended for even the shortest of holiday visits.

A few miles on along the coast road is the ancient town of CARTAGENA founded, as you may have guessed, by the Carthaginians in 220 BC. Cartagena has always been important and powerful, and today it is Spain's leading commercial port and a major naval base. Although it is of some historical significance, it is not an especially attractive place for the average tourist, though it does have quite a lot of nightlife. If you do find yourself passing through, the major sights include the **Museo Arqueológico** (to the North) which has some interesting Roman relics, and the beautiful **gardens** around the remains of the **Castillo de la Concepcíon**.

To the south of Cartagena is PUERTO DE MAZARRÓN, a quiet and unremarkable little resort in the early stages of its development. There is a good, sheltered sandy **beach** which can get quite busy. Nearby, there are a number of small sandy coves which may be attractive to the Sun Worshipper and – if you can find a quiet enough spot – the naturist. For accommodation here try the 100-room **Hotel Dos Playas** which has a pool and tennis facilities (Tel: 594 100).

The last of the resorts on this rather limited costa is AGUILAS, originally a small port. The **beach** in the town itself is polluted, but about four miles to the south-west there is a long, wide stretch of very fine, white sand where the sea is much cleaner.

Inland from the Costa Calida, the provincial capital of MURCIA may be a worthwhile day excursion. Lying in fertile lands in the Valley of Segura it is an ancient and pleasing place, a mixture of brash new buildings and faded old ones, clustered along narrow medieval streets.

The outstanding attraction of the place is the **cathedral**, begun in the fourteenth century but not completed until the eighteenth. The design is basically Gothic with a Plateresque façade and a tower in Renaissance style. Inside, many of the chapels reflect the design of the façade, and the **Capilla de los Vélez** is especially beautiful. There is a **museum** featuring some primitive sculptures in the cloister. You should also take the opportunity to climb the tower from which there are some excellent **views** across the city to the *huerta* (fields).

Other sights in Murcia include a **museum** commemorating the local artist **Salzillo** and containing some of his renowned processional figures; the **Museo Arqueológico**; and the **Museo de Bellas Artes** on Calle Obispo Frutos with works by Velázquez.

Costa del Sol and Costa de Almería

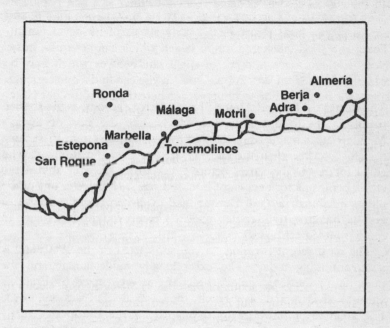

INTRODUCTION

The section of Spain's long southern coast, from the tiny British colony of Gibraltar in the West right the way across to the developing resort of Vera in the East, is one of the best-known regions in Spain. Geographically, more than half the region is made up of the Costa de Almería, an interesting stretch of coast and easily the least-developed of all Spain's Mediterranean seaboards with fewer than half a dozen British tour operators offering holidays to no more than four or five destinations. The remaining stretch is the Costa del Sol, the most heavily developed part of the Spanish coastline, which is relatively short but dominated by three of Europe's largest resorts: Marbella, Torremolinos and Málaga, and it is to them that we shall devote most attention in this chapter.

Beginning at Vera on the eastern edge of the Costa de Almería, our tour of the region will run from east to west looking, in turn, at all the coastal resorts in detail relative to their size and popularity with British tour operators. Once again, we conclude with a look at one or two suggested inland excursions.

HISTORY

The Costas del Sol and Almería have a history as long as the Iberian peninsula itself, and it is one which, like the rest of Spain's Mediterranean seaboard, is marked by constant invasion. First came the Phoenicians, then the ancient Greeks, then the Romans, who ruled for several centuries before the Moors took over almost the entire peninsula for over eight hundred years. Granada is one of the oldest inhabited parts of Europe, and its close proximity to Africa and the lucrative trade routes made it a keenly fought-over region in more troubled centuries.

The most recent invasion, of course, started in the 1960s and is still continuing today. The exceptionally mild climate and the potential of the long, golden beaches was recognized by Franco's cultural advisers and, as a result, the Costa del Sol was one of the first areas to become heavily developed for the European (chiefly British) package-holiday market. You won't be surprised to learn that there are as many tourists in the costa thirty years later as there ever have been.

GETTING THERE

Almost all visitors to the Costas del Sol and Almería arrive on a charter flight at the large international airport close to Málaga. There are regular scheduled and chartered flights to and from most European capitals and also New York and North Africa. The two main sea-ports in the region are at Málaga and Algeciras, and there are regular shipping connections with Marseilles, Morocco, Sydney and Cape Town. Train and bus services to the rest of Spain, further west as far as Ayamonte and the Portuguese border, and north into the European mainland proper, are excellent. The train service to Madrid from Málaga, for example, operates four or five times daily and takes about eight hours.

CLIMATE

The region receives over 320 days of sunshine each year: of the remainder you can expect four foggy days a year and just one to be thundery. The warmest months are July and August when the daily average is around 29°C (84°F) – with virtually no rain ever recorded at this time of year. The temperature remains mild throughout the year, and the coolest months are February and November when the average is a 'chilly' 23°C (74°F).

CULINARY SPECIALITIES

Among the rich variety of specialities in this region, a favourite is *pescaito frito* (deep-fried fish), bathed in olive oil and tangy herbs. During the summer months, *gazpacho* is a popular type of soup which is made from bread, olive oil, garlic, water and tomato. Fresh peppers and local cucumber are often added. A traditional dish from the inland area is *las habas a la granadina*, which includes Trévelez ham, bay leaf, mint and parsley. Among the ten recognized varieties of local wine, *Oloroso* is dark and golden with a high alcohol content of around 18–20% as compared with the 9–11% average of French or German wine sold in the UK.

WHERE TO GO FOR WHAT

If you head away from the well-known resorts right on the coast you will find that the Costas del Sol and Almería can provide surprising contrasts. The Sun Worshipper and the Socialite will feel content in any of the big resorts: Málaga (especially), Torremolinos and Fuengirola, although Benalmadena is gaining in popularity and its gently sloping beaches make it a favourite for Family Holidays. The Sightseer will love Málaga: despite extensive tourist development, its medieval heart remains intact with plenty to see. The inland towns of Antequera and Ronda also have plenty to see. The Nature-Lover will enjoy the Nerja Caves and the hills and lakes of most of the inland region.

The most easterly resort in the region is VERA, the administrative and judicial capital of the surrounding district. This is an area of traditional agricultural importance, and a short drive inland will lead you through some of the best parts of Spain for growing oranges, cereals and the famous olives which go to make up some of the vast quantities of olive oil consumed on the Iberian peninsula. There is little in Vera to recommend a specific trip, but it really comes alive between 7 and 10 June each year as it celebrates the reconquest of the town by the Catholics in 1488.

Practically next door, **MOJÁCAR** is one of only three resorts of any size in the Costa de Almería. It is an excellent place to visit for a day, or even an afternoon, if you wish to escape the crowded beaches further east. Countless hidden coves are a Nature-Lover's paradise, and you might just be lucky to find one all to yourself to sunbathe in quietly. The town itself splits neatly into two parts: the old village high on the hill and the new town further down. The countryside all around is bleak and barren until you get a few miles inland, and Clint Eastwood fans might recognize the surrounding area as the setting for a number of his classic spaghetti westerns.

In the old town, the maze-like old back streets and their quaint little shops and houses make up the principal attraction of the resort apart from the beach. Jewellery and crafts shops are among the most popular shops in Mojácar, but if you have come here looking for a good beach then you won't be disappointed.

The coastline is suitable for bathing for several miles around here, although the texture of the beach varies from fine golden sand to coarse shingle at the farthermost end. The main beach stretches for well over a mile, although the best stretch is near the Hotel Indalo where the slope is gentle and the sand clean and safe for children. Water-sports facilities are reasonable, but more suited to the amateur pedalo enthusiast than the devoted sportsperson.

Non-self-catering accommodation in Mojácar is limited to a handful of three-star hotels. The best-known is the **Indalo** (Tel: 478 001) which sits at the far end of the main beach and, for those who want to visit the resort centre, a packed courtesy bus runs regularly from just outside the hotel. It looks out onto a wide, shingle beach, but a golden, sandy stretch is only a short stroll away. The hotel has 308 bedrooms, all with private facilities, balcony and a seaview. Many were refurbished shortly before the 1988 summer season. Organized entertainment is excellent, with a disco nightly and live music three or four evenings per week.

One other hotel of note is the **El Moresco** (Tel: 478 025) which is superb for those looking for an 'away-from-it-all' break in this part of southern Spain. It sits in an area of outstanding natural beauty, with fine views over the surrounding mountains, rolling plains and down to the sea. The beach is over two miles away, although a courtesy bus is provided. All 145 bedrooms are simply but comfortably furnished and most have wide vistas across to the distant Mediterranean.

From Mojácar, the coast continues south as far as the CABO DE GATA, one of the most southerly points on the Iberian peninsula. The village of Cabo de Gata itself is unremarkable apart from the spectacular views from the sea-front. It is not a resort, but it is a popular spot for day trippers and you can still see evidence of the local fishing industry flourishing long after the impact of tourism made it economically unviable further west. The water round this part of the coast is among the clearest and least polluted in the Mediterranean.

Further west, **ALMERÍA** is the regional capital of the Costa de Almería, and a fascinating town whose long history should make it a 'must' on the itinerary of any visitor to the region. Early settlements dating as far back as the third millennium BC have been found in the area around Almería, and it is reckoned that, as prehistoric settlements go, this was a relatively sophisticated part of the European continent. In later centuries, lead, silver and copper ore were found in abundance near here; indeed, this was one of the few places in the world where pure silver could be mined.

The town of Almería reached its peak of commercial importance in the eleventh century when it was one of the world's major silk suppliers. Believe it or not, Almería was briefly the second most wealthy city in Europe, after Constantinople, during the period of Moorish occupation, but the main industry swiftly turned from silk to smuggling after the Moors left in the late fifteenth century.

Easily the most impressive sight is the magnificent **Alcazaba**, the remains of an enormous fortress which was built by Abderraman III in the tenth century on the site of much earlier fortifications. Successive rulers of the province built onto and extended the great walls, and at its peak the fortress housed a palace, mosque, gardens, hot baths and even a small reservoir to help look after the needs of the 20,000 inhabitants of the fortified buildings. The Christian forces of Ferdinand and Isabella eventually captured the fortress in 1489 and it gradually fell into disrepair in the generations which followed.

Severe earthquake damage helped the Alcazaba's deterioration, and it is only in the decades since the end of the Second World War that steps have actively been taken to restore it. Many of the original walls and interior buildings have gone, but you can still walk round most of what remains and appreciate the scale of the Alcazaba. During the summer it is open from 10am–1.30pm and again from 4–7.30pm; in winter the opening hours are slightly longer, from 9am–1pm and again from 3–7pm.

Among the other points of interest in the town are the **cathedral**, another deliberately enormous building which also owes its origins to the Moorish invaders. It is unusual in that it was designed to be as much a fortress as an ecclesiastical building: tall, windowless walls are topped by rows of high battlements that have seen their fair share of action. Much of the present building was a reconstruction of an earlier church which had been destroyed by the fifteenth century. The interior is much more fascinating then the stark exterior, and one of the largest of several more recent stained-glass windows depicts the city's patron saint, San Indalecio. The cathedral is open daily from 8am–12 noon, and again from 5–8pm.

The Old Town will give you an insight into the history and background of Almería. There are a large number of churches, mostly open to the public only for services or by prior arrangement, but the nineteenth-century **Plaza Vieja**, now better known as the Plaza de la Constitución, and the much older **Calle de las Tiendas** were the principal centres of activity in the Old Town in earlier times.

If you are keen to see some of the best examples of the many thousands of archaeological finds from the Almería area, the **Archaeological Museum** is the place to head. It contains many fine objects from the Bronze Age right through to late medieval times and the end of the Moorish era. Its opening hours are short: 10am–2pm Tuesday to Saturday, so bear these times in mind and visit early.

Nightlife is non-existent apart from a few bars and cafés around the harbour area and, of course, during fiestas when the whole town comes alive. Almería's other main attraction, apart from the places of historical interest, is its shops. Some of the best bargains to be found in the whole region can be had at Almería's weekly market, but no matter what day you visit the town you can be sure of finding a good selection of locally made pottery, ceramics and thick blankets. Embossed leather goods are an interesting choice of souvenir, and quality guitars are made in the town – although if you set your heart on a Spanish guitar you might reasonably expect a few problems transporting it home if you travel by air.

Accommodation for all budgets in Almería is limited: the best hotel is the large **Costasol** (Tel: 234 011), a good three-star hotel which has a certain style, even if its public rooms look and feel rather dated. It is located on the town's main street, within easy reach of all the main sights and amenities. One budget suggestion for the independent traveller is the **Casa La Francesca** (Tel: 237 554) along the Calle Narvaez. This simple, clean house is one of the most popular places to stay for visitors on a limited budget, so advance booking is strongly recommended.

If you are staying in Almería, one of the best places to visit if you want to enjoy the facilities of a good beach is **AGUADULCE**, about six or seven miles west of the town. The main beach here is long and sandy, although, overall, this area is undeveloped by the standards of resorts further west. One or two basic water-sports are available, and there is the usual collection of beach bars and cafés, but if you want anything more sophisticated then this isn't your destination.

A couple of suggestions from the limited range of accommodation options in Aguadulce include the large, four-star, **Hotel Playa Dulce** (Tel: 341 274) which has been renovated to a very high standard over the last few years and now occupies the prime position overlooking the beach. All rooms have private facilities and most have fine seaviews as well. The **Satélites Park** (Tel: 340 600) lies about 300 yards from the beach and is a good alternative. It offers either self-catering apartments or the same apartments with full hotel service. It is well located for the short drive into Almería proper.

A little way round the Bay of Almería is **ROQUETAS DE MAR**, an expanding resort which is already the largest of a handful of holiday destinations on the Costa Almería. Roquetas is a man-made resort chosen primarily because of its picturesque location rather than the stretch of beach it overlooks. The beach is long and narrow, and mainly shingle except for one strip of golden sand near the eastern end. Water-sports facilities are available, although this is not one of the best beaches for sports enthusiasts, and Sun Worshippers are not recommended to go any further than the harbour as the coast deteriorates into rocky sea-front beyond there.

In the evening you shouldn't be stuck for somewhere to go. Many of the bars, cafés and restaurants have some sort of live show during the summer months, and the large hotels almost always have at least a disco or some other form of organized entertainment. Look out for the open-air flamenco dancing which quite often takes place at **El Pirata**, about halfway along the beach. For somewhere to dine out, **Restaurante Chino Fong Shau** is a very popular Oriental place, specializing in Chinese and Indonesian food which you might find a welcome contrast to the international fare served in most of the hotels.

The majority of hotels in Roquetas de Mar are comfortable, modern three-star hotels catering for a high turnover of international package holiday-makers. One of the newest is the magnificent **Golf Trinidad** (Tel: 324 211) which was only opened in 1987. This large, futuristic hotel has nearly 400 bedrooms, all with a fridge and colour television (with satellite pictures too!). It lies close to a large part of the shingle beach and has an excellent programme of entertainment for all the family. A superb hotel all round except, perhaps, for young singles.

The **Sabinal** (Tel: 320 600) is an enormous, clean hotel with over 400 bedrooms and very attractive public areas. It overlooks the shingle (not sand) beach and is ten minutes' walk from the resort centre: one of the resort's better hotels but not one of the region's best. The **Playamar** (Tel: 320 250) is a better choice for families as baby-minding and cots are readily available in its 291 bedrooms and there is plenty for Mums and Dads to do in the evening. Live music is organized most evenings, and residents can also use the facilities of the Playamar's sister hotel, the three-star **Zoraida Park** (Tel: 320 750) at the opposite end of the resort. The Zoraida Park, incidentally, is a reasonably quiet hotel, but the facilities and quality of service leave quite a bit to be desired so we don't recommend it highly.

ADRA lies a little way up the coast, and has a long, narrow beach made up of coarse sand with no facilities to speak of. This is a popular spot for independent travellers with caravans or tents, as there are no fewer than four camp sites nearby. The next resort is **MOTRIL**, a well-known town with a population of over 40,000 and, considering its size, surprisingly little to offer the visitor. There are no sights to speak of, and the best beach is a large strip of coarse sand some way to the west of the town which definitely isn't worth a special visit.

A suggestion for somewhere to eat in Motril is **La Caramba** (Tel: 602 578) along the Avenida de Salobreña. This unassuming little place offers some really good, traditional Spanish dishes, and if you've yet to try a definitive *paella* then look no further. The independent traveller might consider the two-star **Tropical** (Tel: 600 450) along Avenida Rodriguez Acosta for somewhere simple and relatively inexpensive to stay. The Tropical also has an excellent restaurant. You'll find them both at the east end of the town close to a filling station.

The last town on the Costa de Almería is **ALMUÑÉ-CAR**, a thriving settlement with a population of over 16,000 and a long history. Dominating the town from above is the old **Castillo de San Miguel**, a fascinating old ruin which the Romans originally built on Greek foundations, only to have it considerably altered by the Moors. During the War of Spanish Independence, British warships blasted great chunks of it to oblivion, but most of it has survived and you can walk round a considerable area which has now been excavated.

Another of the town's most striking sights is the **Roman aqueduct** which is believed to have been built in 1 BC. Not all the structure has survived, but the best sections lie near the old Granada road. Many relics of the town's history are preserved in the **archaeological museum** in the Cueva de Siete Palacios – signposted within the walls of the *castillo*. Easily the most remarkable item is an inscribed Egyptian vase which has been positively dated to the seventeenth century BC; interestingly, it was found in a seventh-century BC Phoenician tomb and is reckoned to be the oldest inscribed object ever found on the Iberian peninsula. The museum is open from 6–8pm Tuesday to Friday, and 12 noon–2pm at weekends; it is closed on Mondays.

There are long beaches to the front and to the east of the town: both are a combination of sand and shingle but neither has much in the way of water-sports available. For those, you'll need to head a few miles further west to **La Herradura** where you will find one or two very picturesque little coves lying near **Salobreña**. The closer you get to Nerja, the first town on the Costa del Sol, the more difficult access becomes to the isolated (non-developed) beaches. Further information about beaches, what there is to see and do, and information about where to stay in Almuñécar can be obtained from the **Tourist Information Office** (Tel: 631 125).

Beyond Almuñécar you cross into the Costa del Sol proper, one of the few Spanish regions where there seems to be little dispute about precisely where the boundaries start and finish. The first town you will reach is **NERJA**, a prosperous place with a population of nearly 12,000. Archaeologists have discovered traces of Palaeolithic man having lived in the surrounding hills nearly 20,000 years ago, but the district had an unremarkable history until the arrival of the Moors during the Dark Ages. It was at that time that a predominantly agricultural economy was converted to a silk-manufacturing economy and, as a result, helped make Spain's southern coast, with its convenient location close to major trade routes, one of the most prosperous corners of medieval Europe.

Easily the most popular tourist attraction at Nerja is the famous **Caves of Nerja** which were discovered more than forty years ago by some schoolboys hunting for bats! They are among the most significant archaeological finds of the century, and although many of the more interesting ones are not yet open to the public, the ones which you can see are fascinating. Safe, well-lit walkways guide you through the former homes of Palaeolithic Man, and one of the most impressive galleries contains the world's largest known stalactite which measures nearly 200 feet. You can't miss it! The caves lie a few miles out of town, and are open from 9.30am–9pm from May until mid September, and 10am–1.30pm, and again between 4 and 7pm, for the rest of the year.

In the town itself, the most striking man-made feature is the enormous **aqueduct** which dates from the last century. Another feature which you should try to see is the picturesque tree-lined main avenue which is known as the **Balcón de Europa**. King Alfonso XII was passing through the town at the end of the last century, and was so struck by the beauty of this avenue that he said it was the 'Balcony of Europe'. Needless to say, the king's flattering description stuck. For further information about what there is to see and do in Nerja, there is a **Tourist Information Office** (Tel: 521 531) along the Puerta del Mar.

Many of the bars in town have some sort of organized entertainment during the week: live flamenco shows are the most popular. Two ideas for somewhere to eat are **Pepé Rico's** (Tel: 520 247) along the Calle Almirante Ferrándiz which specializes in sizzling steaks; and **Udo Heimar** (Tel: 520 032) on Pueblo Andaluz. Udo is an enthusiastic German who offers a wide range of German and other international dishes in a bright, modern restaurant. One of the best-value restaurants away from the large resorts further west.

The choice of accommodation in town is limited, but one of the best hotels is the three-star **Balcón de Europa** (Tel: 520 800) on the famous avenue of the same name. This old hotel has a subtle Spanish character which will appeal more to independent travellers not trying to save too much on accommodation, and who might be looking for somewhere a bit more impressive than the average, modern, tower-block hotel favoured by most tour operators.

Another three-star hotel worth considering is the **Nerja Beach Club** (Tel: 520 100), a small hotel with just 50 well-appointed rooms. Despite its name, the beach is a good fifteen minutes' walk away but that shouldn't detract you as it is one of the finest stretches of sand in the immediate area. The hotel has a reasonable range of facilities suitable for most types of holiday-maker except young singles and families. Entertainment is limited to the occasional disco and 'Alberto', a real character who plays 'live' music each and every evening. He is guaranteed to become one of your most vivid memories of this resort!

For something really upmarket, one of Spain's great paradors sits right above the beach at **Playa de Burriana**. This four-star luxury hotel is perfect for enjoying this part of Spain at its very best – but you can reasonably expect to pay for the privilege as, in 1988, the average rate was £30–£40 per person.

A short drive from Nerja is FRIGILIANA, a delightful little rural village often visited by holiday-makers on the Costa del Sol who tire of the sea and the sand for a day. There is nothing much to see here, other than some of the finest, uninterrupted views of the surrounding area from the top of the village. A wander along a few of the quiet back streets will give you a vivid reminder of what ALL the major Spanish resorts were like just a few decades ago!

Further west, you gradually notice the coastal countryside becoming more built up with whitewashed apartment complexes and large hotels. The area between Nerja and Málaga is reckoned to be one of the most unattractive stretches of coastline in the whole of southern Spain; certainly there is plenty of evidence to suggest hasty development some years back when the demand for places to stay in Spain's sunny costas far exceeded the number of available beds.

Roughly half-way between Málaga and Nerja is TORRE DEL MAR, one of the least attractive patches of development on the coast which is much more popular with Spanish holiday-makers than British visitors. There is nothing to see or do here apart from 'enjoy' the long strip of coarse, dusty beach which really can't be recommended. Nearby TORROX COSTA isn't much better although the sand is a little finer, and there are one or two reasonable restaurants, including the **Don Sancho** (Tel: 530 311), which cater mainly for the enormous numbers of German visitors who flock here annually.

A few miles further west and you reach **MÁLAGA**, the provincial capital of the Costa del Sol and easily one of Europe's most popular package-holiday destinations. Unlike many of Europe's mega-resorts (for example, Benidorm), the tourist side of Málaga developed long after a flourishing city had been in existence. Many visitors are surprised when they discover that Málaga is a city the size of somewhere like Edinburgh, with a comparable population of well over half a million and a history to rival many of the larger inland towns and cities.

In ancient times, Málaga grew up around its large port and became an important fish-salting location; indeed, the name Málaga comes from *malac* which means, literally, 'to salt'. The Romans made the town one of their principal ports on the Iberian peninsula and were one of the first to exploit the rich silver deposits in the surrounding hills. Málaga's mild climate made it a popular 'resort' for visitors even two thousand years ago!

Today, Málaga has a number of fascinating points of interest for the Sightseer to enjoy. At the top of the city is the **Alcazaba**, the magnificent remains of an eleventh-century Moorish fortress which was, for several centuries, the residence of the Arab Kings of Málaga. A long walled double-rampart approach connects the fortress to Gibralfaro Hill. Sadly the magnificent building fell into disuse after the eighteenth century, and it is only since the 1930s that work has been undertaken to restore it.

The heart of the Alcazaba was a Moorish **palace**, and this is where the bulk of the energy to restore the building has been concentrated. A small **archaeological museum** contains many fine ceramics and some of the best artefacts which have been found during excavation work in and around the Alcazaba. Look out for the remains of a small **Roman theatre** which, sadly, was partly obscured by early restoration work on the walls of the fortress before its historical importance was realized. The Alcazaba is open from 10am–1pm, and again from 4–7pm during the winter months, and 11am–1pm and 5pm–10pm during the summer. Your admission ticket allows you to see all the features of the Alcazaba including the Roman theatre and the museum.

On top of the Gibralfaro Hill you can enjoy some of the finest views of the city, and also explore (free of charge) another Moorish **castle** which was built by the great Arab leader Yusuf I as a direct copy of an earlier Phoenician fortress. One of the most obvious landmarks is the city's **cathedral**, a rather disappointing sixteenth-century ecclesiastical building which was the work of Diego Siloée. The second tower, as you will see, was started in the mid-eighteenth century and never actually completed. It is commonly believed that church funds were diverted to the American War of Independence, but its most bloody period was earlier this century, during the Civil War period, when Republican forces occupied it for more than seven months. A number of priests were killed and the cathedral's treasures looted.

Two other churches of note in Málaga are the **Iglesia del Sagrario**, with its magnificent sixteenth-century high altar and ornate Gothic façade. The church is a designated national monument, and is open from 10.30am–1pm and 3.30–7pm daily. The **Iglesia de Santiago**, on the other hand, is a much less ornate building which was constructed on the site of a much older Moorish mosque around the middle of the sixteenth century. The imposing tower is all that remains of the original Arab structure, and the church is open daily from 7–11am, and again from 5–8pm.

Málaga has a good range of museums and galleries, the traditional haven for visitors on rainy days, but the region's fine weather, particularly during the hot summer months, means that you will need to find another excuse if they wouldn't normally be one of the attractions of a new city for you to visit whilst on holiday. The **archaeological museum** is inside the Alcazaba and contains an important collection of exhibits dating from prehistoric times right through the Greek and Roman era to the end of the Arab occupation. Admission is included in your ticket for the Alcazaba. The **Bellas Artes Museum**, on San Agustín, is inside the palace of the Condes de Buenavista and contains a fine range of exhibits ranging from a Moorish stone cross to Roman mosaics. In addition to a small library dedicated to the artist Pablo Picasso, who was born in the city in 1881, there are works of arts on display by Picasso and many other great artists including El Greco, Murillo and Ribera. The museum is open 10am–1.30pm, and again from 5–8pm except Mondays. The actual house that Picasso was born in is about a hundred yards away in the Plaza de la Merced, although it is not open to the public.

The **Museo de Semana Santa** belongs to the religious fraternity of Santisimo Cristo de la Expiracion and contains a very impressive collection of statues and other religious relics devoted entirely to the celebration of Easter. It is open from 10am–1pm and 3.30–7.30pm. The **Museo de Artes Populares,** on Pasillo de Santa Isabel, is a remarkable permanent display of domestic art and is open 10am–1pm, and again from 5–8pm.

Sports facilities in Málaga are excellent, although water-sports are non-existent because beach facilities, in common with most cities and large towns, are appalling. There is a nine-holf golf course a few miles east, operated by the **El Candado Club de Golf.** Karting is possible at the **Karting Villa Rosa,** near the airport, and the best place to play tennis is at the **Club de Tenis de Málaga** at Pinares de San Antón. For more information about what there is to do or see in Málaga, consult the **Tourist Information Office** (Tel: 213 445) on Marqués de Larios, or else at the airport (Tel: 312 044) if you have time after you arrive.

Nightlife in Málaga really swings, and never more so than during one of the many colourful fiestas which take place throughout the year in the city. Most occur during the summer months, when the sun shines longer and the still night air is warm and pleasant. On 6 June, for instance, the Feast of Corpus Christi culminates in a long procession and traditional bullfight together with a large fireworks display. On 16 July, the sea procession of the Virgen del Carmen takes place and you will be able to see the image of the Virgin being retrieved from the seabed and then ceremoniously returned to the deep. Around the same time, the national Spanish arts festival reaches the sunny south coast.

A succession of festivals takes place between 4 and 12 August, and this is also the peak of the bullfight season in this part of Spain. One of the most popular fiestas is the Grand Festival of 'Verdiales', Folk Music of the Province, which takes place between 26 and 28

December. This bright celebration includes the participation of the traditional 'pandas' of the Montes de Málaga in Venta del Túnel.

A couple of suggestions for nightlife in Málaga are **Café Teatra** near the cathedral. A favourite meeting place for artists and performers for decades, you can always be sure of some form of impromptu live music and/or theatre near here. **Miguel Angel**, on Calle Cánovas de Castillo, is a popular 'piano pub' which surprisingly few foreigners seem to stumble across. Good fun if you are prepared to join in the entertainment.

Málaga has a wealth of places to eat out, although it is interesting to note just how few restaurants offer international menus. In the expensive bracket, two of the best restaurants are **Café de Paris** (Tel: 225 043) which is one of the exceptions, with a good range of continental dishes and a relaxed setting; **Antonio Martín** (Tel: 222 113) is one of the city's oldest restaurants, having been founded over a century ago and flourished ever since. It is almost a tourist attraction in its own right and, quite apart from the superb food (seafood is a speciality), it offers one of the most atmospheric places to eat out in the entire region. Book in advance if possible, otherwise you might be disappointed.

For somewhere less upmarket, **Pámpano**, on the Avenida de Pries, has exceptionally long opening hours so is ideal for that late night meal or early morning breakfast if you're planning a long journey. **El Tormes**, just off the Calle Granada, is a bustling favourite with the locals, and a rival to the nearby **La Tarantella** as Málaga's best-value eating place.

The bulk of the hotels in Málaga is in the town centre, ideally situated for the excellent sights and shopping facilities but liable to be noisy. Easily the most striking hotel is the **Parador Nacional de Gibralfaro** (Tel: 221 902), another of Spain's magnificent paradors which occupies a fantastic position high above the city and close to the Alcazaba. Centuries ago, an ancient inn is said to have stood on the site of the parador but modern-day visitors can expect a much higher standard of comfort and service. It more than deserves the three stars awarded by the Spanish Tourist Authorities and is an extremely popular hotel with locals for a meal or even a quiet drink in comfortable surroundings at weekends.

Even if it doesn't command the best location, Málaga's best hotel is the attractive five-star **Málaga Palacio** (Tel: 215 185), a magnificent hotel right in the heart of the city, along Cortina del Muelle, which retains a lot of authentic Spanish character. It is a good three miles to the nearest beach from here, but hotel facilities include a swimming pool, hairdresser, and television in every bedroom.

Casa Curo (Tel: 227 200) is an attractive three-star hotel on Calle Sancha de Lara, ideal for those looking for a traditional quality hotel within easy reach of the city centre. There is a reasonable selection of simple, good value hostels and pensions for the independent traveller or visitor who may be travelling on a tight budget. Two suggestions are the **Hostal Residencial Chinitas** (Tel: 214 683) along the Pasaje Chinitas, and **Pensión Ramos** (Tel: 227 268) near the Alameda Principal. The Ramos is one of the cheapest options in Málaga, but the standard of accommodation is extremely basic and the place is likely to be very busy during the peak summer months.

Eight miles west from Málaga lies **TORREMOLINOS**, one of the most developed Spanish resorts which receives well over half a million visitors every year, more than half of which are British. About three dozen British tour operators offer literally hundreds of thousands of holidays to Torremolinos each summer in a variety of self-catering and hotel accommodation, and with prices to suit virtually all pockets.

Four decades ago Torremolinos was a tiny fishing village with a single inn to welcome the occasional stray visitor who might happen to be wandering down the one wide street. The town had an undistinguished past, having had little more than a modest flour-producing industry to its name until the 1930s when that went into decline. There are no ancient ruins or sights in what is now a prosperous coastal town with over 25,000 inhabitants, many of whom have helped build the town's reputation almost entirely on the tourist market.

In the 1960s, when Spain's ageing dictator Franco decided to put his country firmly on the European tourist map, Torremolinos' long beach, superb year-round weather, and the proximity of an international airport four miles away made it an obvious choice for rapid development and promotion as a 'super, sunny, fun-filled' holiday destination – and that was precisely what happened. The resort's popularity since then has grown and grown and, provided you are prepared to accept that the town is severely over-developed to cater for the package market, Torremolinos may well be the place for you.

The resort is built on a rocky slope at the bottom of the rolling foothills of the Sierra de Mijas. One natural attraction worth looking out for is the ancient **Manantiales**, the famous pure water springs known to the Romans and, even today, as the source of all the water supply for both the cities of Torremolinos and Málaga. The highest peaks around the town are the Sierra Nevada, which stands over 3,700 metres (11,000 feet) high, and the Sierra Tejada which overlook the beautiful bay that made Torremolinos such an attractive site for developers in the first place.

What remains of the old village, as it was before the tourist era, is focused around the well-known San Miguel Street, although a host of popular boutiques and fashionable chain stores has sprung up where once small independent traders flourished as they looked after the needs of a much smaller community. Torremolinos today is a popular conference centre as well as a holiday destination, and the huge **Congress and Exhibition Centre** regularly plays host to some of Spain's most prestigious gatherings.

Sports facilities in the town are superb – a much wider range than in most coastal resorts is on offer. In addition to the usual water-sports, golf, horse riding, and underwater fishing can be arranged; for hunting enthusiasts, hare, rabbit and partridge can be found in abundance but, obviously, you MUST consult the appropriate authorities first before you go charging off into the hills to hunt the local wildlife! Contact the **Tourist Information Office** (Tel: 381 578) at Calle Guetaria.

Apart from the obvious water-sports concentrated around the beach areas, there is an eighteen-hole golf course run by the **Club de Campo Torremolinos** virtually next door to the resort's imposing parador. The course was opened in 1925 and lies about two and a half miles from the centre of town. Horse riding can be arranged with **El Ranchito** (Tel: 383 063) at La Colina, Camino del Pilar, and, for the tennis enthusiast, the best courts are run by the **Club Tenis Torremolinos** about three miles out of town.

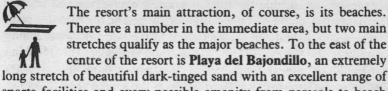 The resort's main attraction, of course, is its beaches. There are a number in the immediate area, but two main stretches qualify as the major beaches. To the east of the centre of the resort is **Playa del Bajondillo**, an extremely long stretch of beautiful dark-tinged sand with an excellent range of sports facilities and every possible amenity from parasols to beach bars to make your trip to the beach as enjoyable as possible. Children will love the little boating lake near the Hotel Don Pablo.

The second beach is **Playa de la Carihuela** to the west of the town centre. It is the less attractive of the two as it narrows considerably in parts and has large patches of shingle which is never very comfortable for children (or adults, for that matter) to run along or sunbathe on. Like Del Bajondillo, this beach has plenty of beach bars, cafés and basic shops selling everything from suntan oil to British newspapers. Whichever beach you decide to visit, rest assured that it will be packed!

Torremolinos has no shortage of nightlife: quite apart from the discos and programmes of entertainment organized by virtually all the main hotels, the resort centre positively reverberates with bars, clubs and discos throughout the hectic summer season. A great many of these nightspots are extremely poor imitations of the best discos and clubs in the cities, and you may well be disappointed to find some of them with little more than out-of-date taped music after you've paid several hundred pesetas to get in.

Many of the best nightspots are the ones which retain some hint of an authentic Spanish flavour; after all, it is a shame that so many holiday-makers return from a fortnight's package holiday on one of the costas and reflect that they may have seen little or nothing of what the country really has to offer. A couple of suggestions are **Molino de la Bóveda** (Tel: 381 185) along the Calle del Tajo which has live music nightly and is one of the resort's best clubs if you want to see authentic flamenco dancing. It has been transformed from an old mill, one of several made redundant after the town's flour-producing industry started to decline in the 1930s. **El Jaleo,** in a small square close to the Calle San Miguel, is another option for sampling some traditional nightlife.

One of the delights about a large, cosmopolitan resort like Torremolinos is the huge selection of cafés and restaurants. Most styles of continental cuisine are represented in the town, and one or two of the best restaurants include **El Caballo Vasco** (Tel: 382 336), a magnificent rooftop place offering traditional Basque country cuisine in very attractive surroundings, and **Cucho's** (Tel: 383 112), which is an informal, homely restaurant specializing in thick steaks, heavily influenced by traditional Spanish sauces. Try their *solomillo à la pimienta* for a real treat.

One of the resort's most expensive restaurants is **La Yuca** (Tel: 384 200), at 17, Avenida las Palmeras. This place is bright and formal, and the superb international menu is dominated by the talents of the English head chef. If you cannot live without the best British-style cooking you are likely to find in Torremolinos, then make sure not to miss La Yuca. It opens each evening until midnight and closes only on Wednesdays during the summer season.

The severe over-development in and around Torremolinos means that there is an enormous collection of hotels from which you can choose one best suited for your individual or your family needs. As we cannot, obviously, feature all the hotels in the resort, we have carefully selected a representative sample of nine which we recommend as being among the best in Torremolinos.

Arguably the resort's best hotel is the five-star **Castillo de Santa Clara** (Tel: 383 155), which has 224 extremely well-appointed bedrooms, plus a further 150 apartments, all featuring large balconies and with the added advantage of a fridge and television on request. The Castillo commands a superb position on a headland overlooking both the town centre and La Carihuela village. The sandy beach is a short lift-ride away and among the features of the hotel is one of the resort's best nightclubs: the bar prices are steep but a visit is highly recommended!

Among several good four-star hotels, the **Cervantes** (Tel: 384 033) stands out as one of quality. Its distinctive L-shape stands out from some distance, and it is located close to the resort centre, within a few minutes' walk of the beach. Facilities for all the family are excellent, and the informal, welcoming attitude of the hotel staff is a distinct plus. A good value, all-round, family hotel which comes highly recommended.

The **Don Pablo** (Tel: 383 888) is an enormous hotel with 400 bedrooms over ten floors. It is busy, and not the best choice if you value your peace and quiet. There are 16 mini-suites and, together with the remaining bedrooms, all have private bathroom facilities, air conditioning and a balcony. The full entertainment programme is likely to appeal more to young singles and older couples who still feel 'young at heart' than families or retiring holiday-makers.

Another good four-star hotel is the **Al Andalus** (Tel: 381 200) which lies in the Montemar part of the town about fifteen minutes from the resort centre. The beach is ten minutes' walk away, but the main attraction of this 170-room hotel is its overall relaxing atmosphere which is likely to appeal to older holiday-makers. Evening entertainment, including a disco, is organized most days, but this is never obtrusive.

The **Guadalmar** (Tel: 319 000) is a most impressive four-star hotel about four miles from the centre of the resort. Formerly a Holiday Inn hotel, the Guadalmar overlooks its own stretch of (man-made) private beach and has 200 large bedrooms over eight floors. The public areas, both inside and outside the hotel, are clean and tidy, and perfectly safe for children although the relative isolation of the hotel does not make it an obvious choice for families with active youngsters who might get easily bored with 'just' the large pool.

Among the three-star hotels, both the **Azor** (Tel: 381 123) and the **Barracuda** (Tel: 385 400) can be highly recommended. The Azor is the smaller of the two, with 163 bedrooms over seven floors compared with the Barracuda's 245 bedrooms on ten floors. The Azor is ideal for couples looking for a relatively quiet holiday as facilities for young singles and children are very limited. It lies in a residential part of the town close to both a railway underpass and, more noticeably, the main flight path for aircraft approaching Málaga Airport. The Barracuda, on the other hand, is perfect for noisy family holidays and it is located near La Carihuela village.

Two final suggestions, from among the three-star hotels, are the **Flamingo** (Tel: 383 855) and the **Principe Sol** (Tel: 384 100). The Principe Sol is yet another first-class Sol hotel offering a very high standard of comfort and accommodation. It is a massive hotel, with nearly 600 air-conditioned bedrooms, but it has an excellent position close to the main beach. The Flamingo offers good-value, if a little basic, accommodation in 239 rooms over ten floors. The steep hike down to the beach doesn't make it ideal for older visitors or very young children.

The coast west of Torremolinos is one of the most densely built-up areas of hotel and apartment development in Spain. Immediately after Torremolinos, the next resort you will come across is **BENAL-MADENA**, which is closely followed by the enormous Fuengirola, although it is becoming increasingly difficult to make out where the break is between the three adjoining resorts.

Benalmadena is a spread-out resort which dominates the best stretches of several miles of good beach. It lies fourteen miles from Málaga and has little discernible identity from either of its large neighbours, although it has a small **archaeological museum** which contains a reasonable selection of mainly local artefacts proving that the town was flourishing even in pre-Roman times. Look out for the pieces of pre-Columbian art which were brought across from South America, and also the marble entrance floor which came from the wreck of an eighteenth century cargo ship, sunk off the coast two centuries ago. Cynics have long suggested that it might have had a better chance of survival if it hadn't had to carry the marble floor!

Half a mile from the beach, the old suburb of ARROYO DE LA MIEL makes an interesting afternoon's visit. Originally this was a small village inhabited by farmers and fishermen and their families, but the arrival of package tourists in large numbers has brought with it the more lucrative tourist industry and transformed the economy not only of this suburb but of much of Spain's Mediterranean coast. The greatest amount of apartment and villa development around Benalmadena has taken place near Arroyo.

Apart from strolling round the old back streets of Benalmadena and admiring the fine views from the top of the oldest part, the only other sight is the **Castillo de Bil-Bil**, a cultural centre built in Moorish style which plays host to many major exhibitions, conferences and musical concerts each year. The main **Tourist Information Office** (Tel: 443 395) is also located here.

Benalmadena is a reasonable shopping centre and, even if you can't find what you are looking for here, there is an extremely efficient local bus service connecting the main resorts with Málaga and with each other. It takes just ten minutes, for instance, to travel from Benalmadena into the centre of Torremolinos.

One of the main attractions of Benalmadena is its beaches: they are good, but by no means the best on the Costa del Sol. The better ones stretch out for several miles west of the town although they vary in width and quality quite considerably. A number of horseshoe breakwaters provide shelter from the very infrequent breezes, and all the main beaches have the usual beach bar and basic sports facilities. There are a number of very small, man-made beaches near the marina but, like the larger natural beaches, these get extremely busy in summer.

An evening alternative to the beaches, for all the family to enjoy, is the **Tivoli World Fun Park** just outside the town. This marvellous fun-park complex is open between April and October, from 5pm each evening until late, and it includes a wide range of amusements, fun rides, restaurants and side-shows. Don't be put off by the rather hefty admission price as this includes nearly three dozen rides and side-shows.

For adults, the resort's most glamorous nightspot is the **Casino** at Torrequebrada, which is open daily between 8pm and 4am. You need to be over twenty-one to be allowed in (and have your passport to prove it), and smart dress is essential. This sophisticated gambling place has all the usual games, including French and American roulette, chemin de fer, baccarat and blackjack. It is well worth spending a few hundred pesetas (slowly, unless you are extremely lucky or extremely rich!) just to savour the atmosphere and watch the big-time gamblers in action.

Next door to the casino is the **Fortuna Nightclub** (Tel: 383 140), one of the Costa del Sol's principal nightspots, which has two completely different shows every evening. In addition, it has a superb restaurant, and a busy café if you feel like eating less formally. Advance reservations for the shows are strongly recommended to avoid disappointment.

Disco nightlife is available through most of the larger hotels in the resort, but the most popular 'in' place since 1986 has been the **Borsalino Palace** disco in the heart of the bustling new town. This is very much a young persons' nightspot, with inflated drink prices and the best European disco dance music to match. If you happen to be in the resort around 14 August then the whole town comes alive. This is when a great fiesta – one of the region's most colourful – takes place in honour of Nuestra Señora de la Cruz.

There are few really good restaurants in Benalmadena, which is surprising for a large resort, but a couple of the better ones are **Chef Alonso** (Tel: 443 435) and **Senang** (Tel: 444 831). The former is one of the resort's most popular eating places with foreign visitors, not least because of its superb range of Spanish speciality dishes, and you can be sure of an informal atmosphere and good service. It is open throughout the year (except Tuesdays) but serves lunches only during the low season, from October to April. Senang, on the other hand, is a more sophisticated place which offers a remarkable range of Eastern dishes: Indian, Chinese and Indonesian. The choice is outstanding and the quality more than matches the diversity of sauces and finely cut meats. Live music is an added bonus during the summer months.

Benalmadena has a very good selection of hotels, the majority of which are three- or four-star, as graded by the Spanish Tourist Authorities. One obvious exception is the fine five-star **Triton** (Tel: 443 240) which, as part of the Inter Group, offers 200 bedrooms, including ten suites, in a select beach location. Facilities include two swimming pools, spacious sun terraces, a sauna and massage parlour and one of the finest hotel dining rooms in the region: up to six courses are offered nightly.

The **Aloha Puerto Sol** (Tel: 387 066) is probably the best four-star hotel in the resort and is extremely popular with British visitors. Another Sol hotel, it has 420 suites which come complete with balcony, adjacent lounge area, mini-bar, and balcony with seaview. The sandy beach is directly opposite, and a nightly programme of evening entertainment is well thought out to appeal to all age groups and all types of holiday-maker.

The **Alay** (Tel: 441 440) is another large four-star hotel, this time with 265 bedrooms, which comes highly recommended. It also overlooks the beach and is about five minutes' walk away from a reasonable group of shops. The interior is smart and tidy, and all the bedrooms have a good seaview. This hotel is an excellent base for young singles, although the in-house entertainment is likely to appeal to a slightly older age group.

A third four-star hotel worth considering is the **Costa Azul Fiesta** (Tel: 442 840), a 312-bedroom hotel which is part of the Fiesta Group. It sits close to a very good sandy beach; additional features include a kidney-shaped swimming pool and live music and/or a disco most evenings. The one obvious drawback is its rather isolated position a little way out of the resort centre, on the main coast road which links Benalmadena and Fuengirola.

Among the three-star hotels, the **Palmasol** (Tel: 443 547) is very popular and enjoys a quiet location overlooking the harbour and sea-front. It has 244 rooms, all with private facilities and a balcony, but the location and limited entertainment make this a more sensible choice for older holiday-makers. The **San Fermin** (Tel: 442 040) is a first-class two-star hotel which is perfect for young singles and families. It is ten minutes from the beach and resort centre, but its 316 bedrooms are well appointed for a hotel in this class, and the large swimming pool (plus separate children's pool) are often more popular than the short (uphill) trek to reach the beach.

A couple of miles west of Benalmadena is **FUENGIROLA**, another former fishing village which, like Torremolinos, exploded in size and popularity twenty years ago with the arrival of the mass package-holiday market. Fuengirola today is a first-class resort which can be recommended highly to all age groups, and the range of hotels is likely to include something to suit most holiday-makers.

The town has a population in excess of 30,000, a nucleus of which is descended from Spaniards who settled in Fuengirola centuries ago. The most obvious relic of the resort's history, and, indeed, the only site of note, is the remains of the tenth-century **Castillo de Sohail** which was one of several such castles along Spain's southerly coast built by the Moorish king Abderraman III. The Christian Reconquest of the region at the end of the fifteenth century saw the partial destruction of the old castle, but it was rebuilt three centuries later and flourished for a while as a base for the local authorities to supervise and stamp out smuggling. It is easily Fuengirola's most distinctive landmark, and its crumbling walls are the perfect vantage point to overlook the entire resort.

A Roman **façade** was discovered some years ago, and partially reconstructed, in the Castilla Square in Los Boliches. Four large columns of white marble were built in the nearby Las Salinas Quarry and later abandoned before they ever reached the site they were originally intended for. The street Los Boliches, incidentally, was so named after the street traders from Genoa, who were called Bolicheros, and who settled here during the fifteenth century.

One other attraction which the kids will love is the town **zoo**. It has a small, but carefully selected choice of the most popular zoo animals, and you can visit it any day throughout the year on the Calle Camilo Cela. Opening hours are from 10am–2pm, and again from 5–9pm during the summer (including Sundays and fiestas), and 9am–1pm, and 3–7pm during the winter months.

Shopping offers many possibilities in Fuengirola – among the best buys are gold jewellery and precious stones. The days of finding a ridiculously cheap bargain are long gone (look VERY carefully if you think you've found one) but you might be lucky to pick up a ring or bracelet at a significantly lower price than you would pay back home. Don't buy too much, though, or else you'll find yourself paying considerable duty at customs on your return.

Fuengirola has a number of good beaches, although the most common feature about them all is the fact that they are invariably very crowded. In total, they stretch for over four miles from the castle across to Carvajal, in the East. All the beaches are wide and clean, and the two most popular – **Santa Amalia** in front of the town and **Los Boliches** – shelve gently, so are perfectly safe for children. The water-sports enthusiast should be content with the range of activities which are available, although the water is likely to be quite crowded!

Sports facilities in general are good in Fuengirola. In addition to the obvious water-sports, golf can be enjoyed at the **Mijas Golf Club** (Tel: 472 912) which lies about two and a half miles outside the resort. Access is gained from the main town bypass, just off the N340, and there are two eighteen-hole courses which visitors can enjoy. Horse riding is possible at **Rancho el Cañaón**, near the Mijas Golf Club, and for the courageous (or foolhardy!) there is a superb roller-skating rink on the Avenida Jesús Santos Rein.

The range of hotels in Fuengirola is surprisingly limited for such a well-known resort. Among the better hotels is the four-star **Las Piramides** (Tel: 470 600) which has 320 very comfortable rooms, including 40 'standard' suites and a sumptuous Royal Suite. Most have seaviews, and all have private facilities and a balcony as standard. The hotel is split into two large blocks, each standing eleven floors high, but both are located close to the main beach and resort centre.

A superb three-star hotel is the **Angela** (Tel: 463 445) which sits opposite the beach and quite close to local shops. It is extremely popular with British holiday-makers and has 261 bedrooms across eleven floors. It is a modern hotel, but has a quiet informality more commonly associated with more established, older places. There is a reasonable selection of nightlife, but this is aimed more towards young families or older couples rather than energetic singles.

Another good three-star hotel is the **Florida** (Tel: 476 100), an older building with over a hundred comfortable rooms overlooking either the seafront or hills to the rear. It lies close to the resort centre and is definitely an obvious choice for older visitors keen to escape from noisy singles and young families. It is surrounded by extremely picturesque gardens, and the interesting programme of organized entertainments includes flamenco and cabaret evenings.

Inland a little from Fuengirola is **MIJAS**, a prosperous little town which sits over 400 metres above sea level. From here you can enjoy some of the finest views across the rolling mountains and verdant countryside which distinguish much of inland Costa del Sol. For many centuries before the arrival of the mass tourist industry the town had a flourishing economy based on the almonds, figs and olives which add life to the scenery round about this part of the region.

In ancient times, Mijas was little more than an unimportant farming village until the Romans arrived and realized the full industrial potential of the food growing in the nearby forests and fields. The Romans built huge ramparts, which the Visigoths later strengthened, but the conquering Moors destroyed them in the eighth century. One of the most colourful tales from the town's long history happened during the Reconquest, in the fifteenth century: the Catholic forces recaptured the town relatively bloodlessly, but the eight hundred Arab inhabitants they found were stripped of their belongings and either forced into slavery or exchanged for Christian prisoners in North Africa. After a brief interlude, when the town struggled against pirates to re-establish itself, it quickly regained its early prosperity and has retained it ever since.

Mijas is not a large resort: only a few British operators offer holidays here each summer, and most of them are limited to self-catering/apartment accommodation. Nevertheless, Mijas is one of the fastest developing parts of the Costa del Sol, and its sun-drenched back streets and good shops make an interesting excursion. Two sights of note are the eighty-year-old **bullring** and the magnificent old **church** which was originally built as a mosque in the ninth century. Much of the present building was converted into a Christian place of worship by the Catholics in the early fifteenth century, and it was around that time that the Mozarab Tower, which you can still see, was added.

The town offers virtually nothing in the way of evening entertainment, and even the range of cafés and restaurants is limited. One suggestion is **La Alegría de Mijas** (Tel: 485 720) on the Pasaje del Compás which offers a wide range of traditional Spanish fish and meat specialities. Similarly, there are very few hotels or *hostals* for the independent traveller to consider but, of the ones there are, the best hotel is the four-star **Hotel Mijas** (Tel: 485 800). This charming old hotel lies on Urb Tamisa and offers a level of intimate sophistication which you cannot find in any coastal hotel.

The Mijas district borders about eight miles of the Mediterranean coastline, stretching west from the castle in Fuengirola towards Urb Calahonda, which is known as MIJAS COSTA. Although you might be lucky to find one or two isolated coves, there are very few recommended or even safe beaches on this strip of coastline. Water-sports are out of the question along most of the eight miles, and the few obvious beach areas are tiny and made up of coarse sand. None are suitable for children because of hidden rocks just below the waterline at a number of the coves. Stick to the known resort beaches; they may be crowded but at least they're safe.

The last giant resort on the Costa del Sol is **MARBELLA**, a noisy, over-developed town whose reputation has been redeemed by the construction of some very fine four- and five-star hotels in recent years. This is an area of high financial investment: everyone from millionaire pop stars to notorious bank robbers flock to this once subdued little town which has already become one of the most rapidly growing population centres in Spain.

The first settlers were Neolithic cavemen, whose primitive paintings have fascinated archaeologists ever since their discovery earlier this century. The Romans founded the first known town a century before the birth of Christ, and the impressive remains of a fine **Roman villa** can still be seen today at the mouth of the Rio Verde. Little remains of the large castle built by the Moors in the tenth century, and the Reconquest street-plan for the busy agrarian community remains, essentially, the heart of Marbella today.

There is practically nothing to see in the way of sights or obvious attractions, although the **Old Town** is still very attractive and contains some marvellous little shops tucked away in the more obscure back streets. There is a Renaissance **fountain** in the Plaza de los Naranjos, and a small selection of the best local artefacts can be gazed at in the **archaeological museum** which is open most mornings and late afternoons throughout the summer. Close to the Rio Verde lie the remains of a **Roman villa**, but these are still in the process of being excavated. For more information about what there is to see and do in Marbella, contact the **Tourist Information Office** (Tel: 771 442) which you'll find on the Avenida Muguel Cano, 1.

It has been claimed more than once that Marbella has something for everyone: for the young single, the family, the sports enthusiast, the sunlover, and the older holiday-maker. Certainly Marbella gives the impression of being all things to all people, although it is only fair to say it is much more a young person's resort than an older holiday-maker's.

Like all the towns on Spain's south coast, Marbella has its fair share of fairs and festivals. Major parades take place throughout Easter week, and during the second week in June a great procession commemorates the Fiesta de San Barnabé, the town's patron saint, as the Catholic recapture of the town in 1485 is remembered. On 16

July each year, an unusual ceremony takes place as the townspeople hope and pray for a good fishing catch in the coming year.

One of the most popular attractions of Marbella is the magnificent range of sports activities on offer. All the main watersports are available on the beaches, and these include windsurfing and waterskiing. Six miles west of the town, there is an excellent golf course, designed by Robert Trent Jones and opened in 1977. Slightly nearer to hand, **Golf Las Brisas** (Tel: 785 544) is a very attractive eighteen-hole championship course, opened in 1968, with a handy practice course as well for the beginner or rusty amateur.

Horse riding is another popular activity which can be organized through the **Club Hipico de Marbella** (Tel: 770 539) which is based at Hacienda Cortes. Many of the major hotels have their own tennis courts but, for those which do not, there are six public courts along the Urb Aloha run by the **Club de Tenis Aloha**. For the more adventurous, you can enjoy roller skating at **Top Roller**, on Calle Magallanes; it is open daily from 6pm–12 midnight.

Marbella has a number of good restaurants, most of which are clustered around the town centre. A couple of the best ones are **Gran Marisquería Santiago** (Tel: 770 078) on Duque de Ahumada, and **El Mesón del Pasaje** (Tel: 771 261) at Pasaje, 5. Gran Marisquería is easily one of the town's most popular restaurants for the locals – and you can be sure that is always a good recommendation for visitors to follow! Fresh seafood and fish dishes are the specialities of the house. El Mesón, on the other hand, is built out of an old town house near the picturesque Plaza de los Naranjos. It has a very traditional interior, and is open throughout the year except Thursdays and the damp month of November.

Accommodation in Marbella presents the visitor with a wide choice: the first hotel built in the resort was the Hotel Commercial, which appeared in 1918, although it was another half century before a collection of small chalets started the tidal wave of modern hotel building. Today Marbella has some of the Costa del Sol's best hotels, from which we have selected a few, and some of the worst as well – which we have naturally ignored.

If you are prepared to spend quite a bit of money on really good accommodation, then Marbella is just the place for you: there are at least half a dozen five-star hotels alone, two of the best of which are the **Don Carlos** (Tel: 831 140) and **Los Monteres** (Tel: 791 700). The Don Carlos has over 200 superb rooms, all with air-conditioning, private facilities, wide balconies (with good sea or mountain views), and the option of studio apartments, executive suites, or even one of two Presidential Suites if you are prepared to really invest a small fortune in your holiday. Large landscaped gardens lead down to a fine stretch of sandy beach and, in the evening, there is a good programme of organized entertainment.

Los Monteres has a more isolated location, about four miles from the resort centre, but it has 171 air-conditioned bedrooms and an excellent range of facilities including a huge swimming pool set in tropical-style gardens, live music occasionally and a very good restaurant which is popular with residents and non-residents alike.

One more five-star hotel worth looking out for in tour operators' brochures is the **Puente Romano** (Tel: 770 100). It lies about five minutes away from a reasonable patch of shingle/sandy beach, and is one of the region's most expensive hotels. The Puente Romano has 242 luxury apartments, each with private facilities, air-conditioning, lounge area, colour television and a mini-bar. This is considered to be one of Marbella's most exclusive hotels, and it easily falls into the category of 'if you have to ask the price, you can't afford it'; as a clue, though, the Royal Suite, for one night, will cost you well over the price of a reasonable week-long package holiday in a two- or three-star hotel further along the Costa . . .

The **Golf Guadalmina** (Tel: 781 400) is a popular four-star hotel: with just 65 rooms it is small enough to remain relatively intimate. Its isolated location eight miles from the town centre will suit committed 'away-from-it-all' holiday-makers or golf fanatics, because there are two eighteen-hole courses either in or adjoining the hotel grounds.

ESTEPONA is the last resort proper in the region. This unassuming town of nearly 25,000 inhabitants has a curiously uncertain history. The consensus amongst historians is that the Romans founded it around the first century BC, but archaeological evidence does not support this. It is known, however, that, by the Middle Ages, the flourishing Islamic community of Estebbuna was in existence on the site of the present town, but exactly who preceded the Moors is unclear.

There are no sights of note in the town, but one attraction for the Nature-Lover is the magnificent **Sierra Bermeja**. From the summit of Los Reales you can see as far as Marbella, Gibraltar, and even the coastline of North Africa on a clear day. The road from Estepona is clearly signposted and the surface good.

One suggestion for accommodation in the resort is the four-star **El Paraiso** (Tel: 783 000), an isolated 200-room hotel about seven miles from the resort centre. It overlooks an eighteen-hole championship golf course, partly designed by Gary Player, and facilities for guests include free courtesy transport to Marbella and two swimming pools. Another possibility is the **Seghers Club Sol** (Tel: 800 100), a three-star complex made up of 81 apartments, which looks onto the resort's reasonable beach.

One final 'resort', which is not quite on the Costa del Sol but nevertheless is worth considering for a day trip, is ALGECIRAS. The beaches on either side of the town are filthy and invariably polluted. The town's most obvious attraction is its reputation as the gateway to Morocco. Ferry services operate several times daily to Tangier and Ceuta, and it is perfectly possible to take a day trip across to another continent IF you are prepared to endure the crowded ferry and occasionally over-zealous Moroccan customs. For the social experience it is well worth it, but if you've got children with you, or are a woman travelling alone, forget it.

INLAND

The inland part of the Costa del Sol and Almería offers a wide range of possibilities for the visitor, not least because the scenery provides a total contrast to the crowded coastal resorts and long, sandy beaches. The Nature-Lover will enjoy just driving through mile after mile of rolling hills, lakes and forests, from the mountain ranges of Ronda, Mijas and Almijara to the countless villages and towns full of history and life further west.

As none of the inland towns or villages are major resorts, we have not attempted to give you as detailed a description as we have with most of the better-known coastal towns. Nevertheless, we have highlighted the main points of interest in a number of inland destinations and, taken on their own or two or three at a time, they should give you a few ideas about where to go for a day or even an afternoon excursion.

FRIGILIANA, near Nerja at the eastern end of the Costa del Sol, sits more than a thousand feet above sea level, and its whitewashed houses make it a typical example of an Andalusian village. Nearby CANILLAS DE ACEITUNO lies at the foot of the 770-metre-high Sierra Tejeda, and this is one of the best vantage points to admire the highest peak in the region: the 2,500-metre-high Pico de la Maroma.

MACHARAVIYA, about thirty miles from Málaga, used to be known as 'Little Madrid' as it was once an important market town for the surrounding district. Today, though, it has fewer than 4,000 inhabitants and is dominated by a huge church that was built in 1785 by Don José Gálvez, Marquis of Sonora. José served for a while as Minister of the Spanish Indies, and his family made their fortune through Spain's colonial exploits in the seventeenth and eighteenth centuries.

Thirty-one miles from Málaga, ARCHIDONA has a long history dating back to before Phoenician times. Among the sights in this busy inland town are **Ochavada Square**, the churches of **Las Monjas Mínimas** and **Santa Ana**, and the only **Moorish mosque** which still exists in the entire region. Lavish and colourful celebrations take place in Archidona during Easter week.

ANTEQUERA is the largest inland town, with over 40,000 inhabitants and excellent communication links with the rest of the region. It lies on the edge of a wide fertile plain, and takes its name from the Roman town of Antakira which grew up on the site of the present town. Prince Fernando of Antequera conquered the town from Moors in 1410, and it was renamed in his honour. The town lies on steep slopes, dominated by the **Real Colegiata de Santa María la Mayor**, a magnificent sixteenth-century Basilica built in an Italian Renaissance style. Another building dating from the same period is the **Colegiata de San Sebastián** with an ornate façade designed by Diego de Vergara, and a huge Baroque-style Mudejat Tower which was added between 1700 and 1706. The **municipal museum** is located in a large eighteenth-century building, striking because of its tall watch-tower and cloistered courtyard, and it contains many artefacts found in the town and surrounding area. A number of **prehistoric dolmens**, huge Neolithic stone monuments, can be seen around the outskirts of the town, and more information can be obtained about them at the **Tourist Information Office** (Tel: 842 180) in the Plaza de Coso Viejo.

The town of CHURRIANA lies six miles from Málaga, and is best known as the former home of writer Ernest Hemingway. Nearby, ALHAURIN DE LA TORRE is another beauty spot, built on the remains of a Roman town, which preserves a picturesque Andalusian atmosphere. It lies at the foot of the Sierra de Jabalcuzar and in the Valley of the Guadalhorce.

Alhaurin de la Torre shouldn't be confused with ALHAURIN EL GRANDE, a larger town which lies in a beautiful valley, between two rivers, about five miles from Coin. Pine forests on the surrounding hillsides house a nature reserve for rare birds and, in the town itself, you can still see the remains of the **Roman aqueduct** and many other reminders of the town's earliest known settlers. There is a large **Renaissance-style church** built over the ruins of an ancient castle.

COIN is a busy market town set in the Valley of the Guadalhorce. Among the sights here are the remains of a fifteenth-century **castle** and a number of sixteenth-century public buildings which include the **Church of San Andrés**, a restored **Moorish palace**, and **Mozarab Tower**. Look out for the quaint Arab quarters in the neighbourhood of Plaza de San Andrés and Santa María. A final suggestion for an inland excursion is the vast natural wonder of the **Gorge of Los Gaitanes**, near the small town of Ardales.

Costa de la Luz

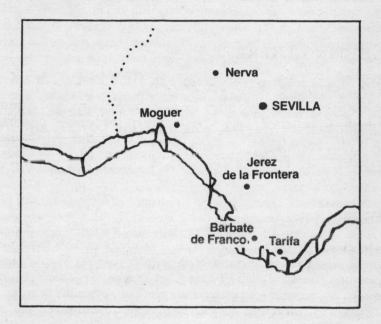

INTRODUCTION

Stretching from Algeciras and Tarifa at the very southernmost tip of
Europe around the Spanish coast to Isla Cristina on the Gulf of
Cádiz, Spain's Costa de la Luz (Coast of Light), offers some of the
country's best beaches, and some excellent resorts.

The Atlantic beaches are of fine, golden sand fringed by dunes,
and although the sea is naturally colder than the Mediterranean, for
most of the year the costa presents a real alternative to its better-
known, busier rivals.

Only now being developed at all for mass tourism, many of the
destinations here are quieter and less flashy than other Spanish
resorts and are ideal for peaceful, family vacations.

In Cádiz, the visitor will find a charming and atmospheric city with some notable sights; and the Coto Doñana National Park in the flat marshlands around the Guadalquivir River teems with wildlife to attract the Nature-Lover.

GETTING THERE

The costa is relatively well served with communications. It has a major road linking up the whole coast either side of Cádiz. There are also good connections to the rest of the country. Rail connections are also good, and buses link up the resorts too. The major airport is at Seville, where scheduled flights can be had in addition to holiday charters.

CLIMATE

The climate of the Costa de la Luz is relatively equable, with the travel season taking in most of the winter months. Winter temperatures (average 12°C/55°F) are lower than on the Mediterranean costas, but summer temperatures are more or less similar at around 23°C (73°F). Inland, in Seville, summer temperatures can rise as high as 48°C (118°F).

Rainfall is low in summer, with July and August unlikely to see more than 1mm (1/32") of rain, but is high in winter. The November figure may be as high as 120mm (4¾").

Wind may cause most problems on this costa as the southernmost areas, especially Tarifa, are *very* windy. A constant average of up to 20 mph in this area all year round would be predicted.

CULINARY SPECIALITIES

The Costa de la Luz and the Andalusian region in which it lies have few really notable specialities. However, the coast is noted for its **seafood**, especially fried fish (try it at Chipiona or Puerto de Santa

Maria), and **gazpacho**, the cold, tomato-based soup, is a regional dish.

Jerez is, of course, the centre of the sherry trade, and many varieties can be sampled at El Puerto de Santa Maria. The pale, golden, dry variety called **Manzanilla** originates in Sanlucar de Barrameda.

WHERE TO GO FOR WHAT

The costa's principal attraction must be its numerous **beaches** of fine, golden sand, and for this reason the Sun Worshippers should find that most of the resorts provide the facilities they need to enjoy the sun.

A number of the resorts are relaxed and quiet and provide good destinations for Family Holidays; notable here are Conil, Rota, and Mazagón. These might also find favour with the Recluse, though for a really quiet place with just one hotel Zahara de los Atunes might be preferred.

The Nature-Lover will be enthralled by the bird and animal life of the Coto Doñana National Park.

For the Sightseer, Tarifa, Europe's most southerly point, may be of interest. Vejer de la Frontera is also worth seeing: for a flavour of old Spain this distinctive hill town with its Moorish atmosphere is a winner. Cádiz too, although not one of the world's 'great cities' may be attractive to the Sightseer.

ALGECIRAS, the first of the resorts on the Costa de la Luz, stands across the bay from Gibraltar, and despite the excellent views of the famous Rock, has little else to recommend it. Indeed, it scarcely deserves to be called a resort, being an unattractive and down-at-heel sort of place.

It is notable for being full of Moroccans en route home – just across the Mediterranean – and this at least gives the place some atmosphere, but it really can't be recommended.

From Algeciras south towards Tarifa – mainland Europe's most southerly point – you will travel through some marvellous scenery. As you pass through the hills towards the tip of the continent there are some excellent **views** down to Gibraltar and across the narrow straits to the Moroccan coast. You can see, on a clear day, the distant Rif Mountains rising on the African continent.

TARIFA is an attractive town with a Moorish feel, full of atmosphere. The older parts of the town are particularly pleasant, with parts of the **old walls** very well preserved, and a maze of narrow lanes to investigate.

The principal site is the **Castillo de Guzmán el Bueno**. A Moorish creation, the castle is named after a former commander, Guzmán, whose son was taken hostage during a siege. The price the enemy attached to his son's life was total surrender, and Guzmán chose 'honour without a son'.

Also notable is the most southerly point of mainland Europe, not far from the town, at **PUNTA DE TARIFA**.

For accommodation in Tarifa, try the **Balcón de España** hotel (Tel: 956 684 326), a small place, if a touch expensive. (Pool.)

To the north of Tarifa, one finds an excellent **beach**. Five miles long and a quarter of a mile wide in places, it is dune fringed and relatively undeveloped. Being on the Atlantic coast of Spain it may, of course, be rather windy, but there are sheltered, quieter spots as one moves north. Like many of the beaches on this costa it has benefited from the lack of commercialization that resulted from the whole of the coast from Algeciras to Cádiz being declared a military zone.

| PRIVATE. Keep Out | A little further along the coast from Tarifa, ZAHARA DE LOS ATUNES has another excellent beach. The place itself |

is remarkably quiet, with few tourists and only one small hotel.

Travelling northwards, we reach **BARBATE**, another moderately unattractive place. It is redeemed by excellent beaches of fine, golden sand, both in town and at **Playa de los Caños de Meca**. The town stands above Cape Trafalgar where Nelson triumphed over the Spanish and French in 1805, and lost his life doing so.

Slightly inland from Barbate is **VEJER DE LA FRON-TERA**. Although it is not a resort, it is worth visiting if you are at all interested in getting a real flavour of this part of Spain.

Set between surrounding hills, it has a distinctive Moorish aspect and is redolent with old world charm. Its remarkable jumble of whitewashed houses clustered around a Moorish castle and its dramatic setting make it a memorable place to see. Don't miss it.

There are few places to stay, though a more expensive, new hotel is being constructed in a former convent. Meantime, there are a number of private rooms and a reasonable pension at Callejón de Amano, 5.

Returning to the coast, and a little off the main road, we come to CONIL, a small, simple resort which is growing in popularity, though it is still far from being fully commercialized. Here you can enjoy eight miles of quiet, sandy **beach**, fringed by dunes. The busier parts offer beach bars. Otherwise, there are no real 'sights' in Conil. Nevertheless, a quieter resort and perhaps a good family destination. The tourist accommodation available is of a reasonable, if unremarkable type.

The last town of importance before we come to Cádiz is CHICLANA DE LA FRONTERA. Standing on the fringe of an area of salt marshes, it lies slightly inland. The **beach** is therefore a few miles away, and is again very pleasant, offering two to three miles of fine sands fringed by pine trees.

Marvellously situated at the end of a long promontory, the ancient port of **CÁDIZ** is, as you approach, a striking expanse of white against the backdrop of the sea.

Cádiz has a long, diverse history, having been founded by the Phoenicians, and later ruled by Romans and Moors before becoming one of the Spanish nation's chief ports. Although little of its pre-eighteenth-century history remains today much of the town retains an historic atmosphere and a relaxed charm.

Cádiz's sights include the new and old cathedrals which stand adjacent to each other just to the south of the lively **Playa de San Juan de Dios** with its cafés and restaurants.

The **old cathedral** dates from the thirteenth century, but was destroyed and rebuilt in the seventeenth century in a Renaissance form. More interesting, however, is the **new cathedral**, built in eighteenth-century Baroque style. It can be easily identified by its striking yellow dome, and features paintings by Murillo, the tomb of the composer Manuel de Falla, and, from the east tower, excellent **views** across the city. There is an associated **museum** open daily (excluding Sundays) 10am–1pm, 4–6pm.

North of the cathedrals, you will find yourself in the older parts of town, with their narrow streets and pleasant squares. Here, on Calle del Sacramento, you will find the **Torre del Vigia**, standing over one hundred feet high. Nearby, is the **Municipal History Museum** on C. Sagasta. It houses a number of interesting exhibits including an unusual ivory and mahogany eighteenth-century model of Cádiz. (Open: Monday–Saturday, 9.30am–1.30pm, 5–9pm; Sunday, 10am–2pm.)

Not far away, on C. Rosario, is the oval-shaped **Chapel of Santa Cueva** with three works by Goya to be seen. The chapel can be entered by ringing the bell at C. San Francisco, 11.

Other religious sights of note include the **Chapel of Hospital de Mujeres** to the south of the old town, which features a marvellous El Greco – his *St Francis in Ecstasy*; and the **Church of Santa Catalina** on Avenida Primo de Rivera. This latter houses Murillo's last work, the *Mystic Marriage of St Catherine*, on its high altar. The artist fell to his death in 1682 whilst painting it.

More fine paintings can be seen in Cádiz's **Museu de Bellas Artes y Arqueológico**, on Playa de la Mino to the north of the town. It has works by Murillo, Rubens, and Zurbarán, together with archaeological relics from the Phoenician cemetery, among them a unique sarcophagus. (Open: Tuesday–Sunday, 9am–2pm, 5–8pm. Small admission charge.)

At the north-west edge of the promontory you can take some sea air and enjoy an excellent **view** as you wander through the **Parque de Genoves**. The park features an attractive palm garden and the **Teatro de Verano** theatre.

Much of the pleasure of Cádiz lies simply in walking around the older parts, savouring its atmosphere and architecture amongst the winding streets. A useful map of the town can be had from the **Tourist Office** on C. Calderon de la Barca to the north (Tel: 211 313). (Open: Monday–Saturday, 9am–2pm, 5.30–7.30pm. Closed Sundays. Shorter hours in winter.)

For accommodation, the **Francia y París** hotel on Playa Calvo

Solelo (Tel: 212 318) is good but tends towards the expensive. A cheaper alternative is the **San Remo** at Paseo Maritimo, 3 (Tel: 232 202) with a beach view.

For a meal, there is a number of good, inexpensive restaurants on the Playa San Juan de Dios, which has the advantage of lively atmosphere. More expensive, but offering good cuisine, is **Español** at Duque Victoria, 6 (Tel: 211 893).

If you have the time, you should not miss the opportunity to make the trip inland to sample the splendour of Spain's fourth city – **SEVILLE**. Cádiz and Seville are connected by a major road – the A4. By bus – there are eight each day – the journey takes about two hours. Travelling by train is not much faster, but however you go you are likely to find it a journey worth making.

Seville, capital of the region of Andalusia, is a graceful and charming city with a unique personality, which has gained a deserved reputation amongst city-lovers. Spreading out along the fertile banks of the Rio Guadalquivir, it offers the visitor the chance to take in some magnificent sights. Those you shouldn't miss – the cathedral, the Giralda Minaret and the Alcázar – are all conveniently situated adjacent to each other in the central area of the old town.

The **cathedral** is Seville's crowning glory. Dating from the fifteenth century, it is one of Christianity's greatest creations and the largest Gothic building ever created – 124,000 square feet!

Built on the site of a former mosque, its well-proportioned interior represents grandeur on a vast scale. Among the highlights to be seen inside are altar pieces by Murillo to the right of the main entrance. The **Capilla Mayor** chapel is decorated with a beautifully carved **retablo** (altarpiece) depicting scenes from the Bible. In the **Sacristia Mayor** are paintings by Murillo, and Ribera, and elsewhere in the building you can see works by Zurbarán and Goya, amongst others. Also to be seen is the **Monument to Columbus**, with four huge black and gold coffin bearers carrying Columbus' remains aloft. The **Patio de los Naranjos** (Court of Orange Trees) are pleasant gardens in which to pause and marvel at the splendour of it all.

At the north-east corner of the cathedral is the **Giralda**. Built by the Moors in the twelfth century, this tower – rising to around 110 metres – was once the minaret of the old mosque. There are fine **views** across Seville from the gallery.

To the south-east of the cathedral is Seville's third unmissable sight – the **Alcázar** – the palace of Moorish and Christian monarchs, which is still used today by King Juan Carlos. Dating from the fourteenth century when it was constructed for Pedro the Cruel, the entrance leads through a courtyard to the main façade of the building – an excellent example of Mudéjar architecture. Inside are a number of very fine apartments – one of the most impressive is the **Ambassador's Hall**.

Among Seville's other attractions are the Mudéjar-style **Casa de Pilatos** and the **Museo de Bellas Artes**, with an important collection of Spanish art. The **Torre del Oro** is also worth seeing – originally a defensive tower, it now houses a maritime museum and an aquarium of some quality. For sheer atmosphere, take a stroll through what was once the Jewish Quarter of Seville, the **Barrio de Santa Cruz**. This area is a maze of twisting alleyways knotted together with such unplanned complexity that it is virtually impossible to map. Risk getting lost, and wander amongst the streets and courtyards bedecked with flowers and ivy.

More information about the city, and a useful map, can be found at the **Tourist Office** on Avda de la Constitución, near the cathedral (Tel: 221 404). Open: Monday–Saturday, 9am–7pm, Sunday (summer only), 9.30am–1.30pm.

If you plan to stay in Seville there is a reasonable number of good, moderately priced hotels. A good bet in the one-star range is the **Hotel Simón** at García de Vinuesa, 19 (Tel: 226 660) housed in a modernized mansion. It has a traditional feel, and is clean and comfortable, with singles at around 2,600 pesetas and doubles from around the same price in a room without private bath. (With bath, around 3,700 pesetas.)

Returning to the coast, EL PUERTO DE SANTA MARIA, across the Bay of Cádiz, is a rich commercial town with a refined air about it. At one time it was the port for all sherry consignments for the nearby centre of the sherry trade, Jerez. Today, a number of important sherry firms still have *bodegas* here, and many visitors come to town just to take advantage of the **free tastings** they offer. Among the firms are Terry, Osborne, de Cuesta, and Caballero, and most offer tastings in the mornings only.

Among the other sights and attractions of El Puerto, which is also now a developing tourist destination, are the Moorish **Castillo de San Marcos** and a number of good beaches, including **Playa Puntilla**, **Playa Andalucia**, and **Playa Fuentebravia**.

There are a number of good hotels, principally on the western side of town.

A little further around the bay is ROTA, an outstandingly pleasant beach resort of growing popularity. As with most of the Costa de la Luz, the **beach** is sandy, clean and offers good bathing.

A US airbase in the town means that good English is spoken by the locals, although there have been some tensions with the Americans. There is also a large gypsy population and you should beware of pickpockets and other petty theft while here.

For accommodation here, the **Playa de la Luz** hotel is priced in the mid-range, with good facilities on offer.

Northwards along the coast you pass CHIPIONA, a small, quiet resort in winter which becomes very busy in summer, despite the fact that some of the water here is not of the cleanest, and reach SANLUCAR DE BARRAMEDA.

Sanlucar is a rather basic place as far as facilities for visitors go – it's certainly far from being a full-scale resort. There are a few sights, although nothing really outstanding. Among these are the 'palaces' of **Montpensier and Medina Sidmia** and the **Castillo Santiago**, perched high on Cuesta de Belen and offering marvellous views.

The **beach**, on the Rio Guadalquivir River is some way out but is pleasant enough.

Nature-Lovers will be particularly interested in the **Coto Doñana National Park** across the bay. The marshy landscape is scarcely enthralling, but the fauna rather than the landscape is the attraction here, with a wide variety of wildfowl to be spotted, not to mention mongooses, eagles, buzzards, and lynx. **Tours** of the park are available – free short tours are given after taking a cheap boat trip across the bay, and more expensive, four-hour guided excursions by Land Rover are organized by the Cooperativa Marismas del Rocio (Tel: 430 432). The park opens from Tuesday to Sunday.

This marshy reserve has an important effect on the surrounding area which should be mentioned: mosquitoes. These breed readily in the conditions of the park so that Sanlucar, and further north, Torre Le Higuera, are affected by these pests more than other Costa de la Luz resorts.

TORRE LE HIGUERA, which is also known as PLAYA MATALASCA-NAS, is a large, modern, fast-growing and rather impersonal resort. Nevertheless, the excellent beach is long and sandy, with a range of water-sports on offer.

As a larger resort, Torre le Higuera also has a slightly livelier nightscene than is found in some of the previously mentioned places.

The resort of MAZAGÓN, a little further north on the same stretch of coast, is an attractive, quiet place with an excellent beach of fine sand. An ideal family destination.

Edging further around the Gulf of Cádiz, one comes to PUNTA UMBRIA, not far from the unpleasant industrial town of Huelva. Standing at the end of a promontory, Punta Umbria is a popular resort with a little nightlife and another good beach. There are no real sights to see, however, and it is principally a sun and surf destination.

The last of the costa's main beaches at LA ANTILLA and ISLA CRISTINA are, again, both worthwhile. Isla Cristina offers reasonable accommodation.

Wrested from the Spanish in 1704, **GIBRALTAR** is an extreme parody of modern-day Britain – more British than the Brits, some would say. Sterling is the official currency, blue-suited policemen pound the beat and fish 'n' chip shops abound. Proximity to Spain is not without its effects, however, and the inhabitants of the 'Rock' are likely to speak Spanish just as fluently as English.

The colourful and turbulent history of the promontory begins in ancient times when, as one of the legendary Pillars of Hercules, it was regarded as the edge of the world. A succession of Phoenicians,

Carthaginians, Romans and Visigoths settled on the Rock until the eighth century, when the Moors seized it as part of their conquest of the Iberian peninsula. They named it Jbel-al-Tarik, which has become modified over the years to 'Gibraltar'. During the Christian Reconquest, Spain retrieved the Rock, but lost it again three centuries later during the Spanish Wars of Succession to the British forces.

British sovereignty of Gibraltar continues to be a contentious issue. Spain views the British rule as a perpetual affront, while Britain, and more importantly, the inhabitants of the Rock, refuse to cede to Spanish rule. However, with the death of Franco and more recently Spain's entry into the EEC, hardline attitudes have softened somewhat and traffic between Gibraltar and the Spanish mainland now goes unimpeded (the borders were re-opened in 1982).

Getting to Gibraltar couldn't be easier. Apart from the numerous coach tours, there are local buses departing every half hour from La Linea, the nearest Spanish town to the Gibraltarian frontier. Driving is not advisable as the Rock has chronic traffic problems, and traffic jams are frequent and frustrating. Also remember to take your passport or you will not be allowed through customs.

Once there, pick up a map of the island at the information stand and catch a bus or walk into the town. The town centre is basically one long main street, full of British chain stores and off-licences. As a tax-free zone, Gibraltar is the cheapest place to shop in Europe (cheaper than the duty-free at airports too), so take plenty of sterling with you. Some of the smaller shops will accept pesetas, but if you are changing money at banks, remember to ask for sterling, otherwise you will be given Gibraltarian money which is not valid anywhere apart from the Rock. Customs allowances for alcohol and cigarettes follow EEC regulations (*see* 'Customs' on page 30), and additional goods worth up to £30 are also permitted.

For sightseeing, the Rock and its famous apes are the most obvious priority. The cable-car at the end of the street or an inexpensive taxi ride will take you to the summit. Once at the top, after the obligatory viewing of the apes, guides will point out the fresh-rainwater reservoirs which supplement the island's sparse natural supplies and will also lead you through the tunnel blasted out from one side of the Rock to the other.

Halfway up the Rock, there are tours of St Michael's Cave. A huge natural cavern, complete with stalactites and underground lakes, it was used as a hospital during the war and now functions occasionally as a subterranean concert hall. Descending further, the road goes past the Upper Galleries: vast tunnels hewn out of the rock in the eighteenth century for military purposes.

Back in the town itself, the **Gibraltar Museum**, Bomb House Lane (open Monday–Friday, 10am–1pm, 3–6pm, Saturday, 10am–1pm) tells the story of the Rock from prehistoric times to the present day. Otherwise, there is the **Trafalgar Cemetery**, where the graves of those who died in battle can be seen. **Tourist Offices** may be found at Cathedral Square (Tel: 76400) or the Piazza, Main Street.

From Main Street, taxis operate round-the-island trips, lasting approximately two hours and costing around £6. Alternatively, take a taxi to the small village at CATALAN BAY or head for one of the beaches. Visitors also have the opportunity to take a full day trip to Tangier in Morocco, only a couple of hours away by boat. The boat fare to Morocco is expensive (approximately £30 a head) but if you can afford it, well worth the money for a flavour of this fascinating and exotic country.

As far as eating out goes, there is a wide variety of restaurants and cuisines available, ranging from American-style fast-food joints to places specializing in Chinese, Spanish or Italian food. For some authentic British fare (well, almost!) try the **English Eating House**, 13 Market Lane (Tel: 77313) or the restaurant at the **Rock Hotel**, 3 Europa Road (Tel: 70500). Seafood and fish restaurants are also a good bet – **El Patio**, 54 Irish Town (Tel: 70822) has a particularly good and moderately priced seafood menu while the **Village Inn** in Catalan Bay (Tel: 75158) specializes in lobster and swordfish dishes. Probably Gibraltar's most prestigious – and certainly one of the most expensive – eating places is the restaurant attached to the **Casino Royal**, Europa Road (Tel: 76666). The sumptuous surroundings are impressive – the food even more so – although if you don't fancy spending over £12 a head for their mouth-watering fare, you'd be best to look elsewhere!

Gibraltar is surprisingly lively at nights. Open-air restaurants and terraced cafés in Main Street positively hum with life and it is here that most of the activity is to be found. For a more bohemian atmosphere, head for the **New Marina** area, where you can sip drinks and watch the sun set over the sea. There are one or two discos and nightclubs on offer, but these generally start very late (around 11.30pm–12.00 midnight) and even though Gibraltar is a duty-free zone, drinks in the nightclubs are still twice the price of those on sale in bars. Away from the main town, the only other disco available is at **Hotel Caleta Palace** (Tel: 76501), overlooking Catalan Bay. This is open most nights and can be reached by a short taxi ride from the town centre. For a more luxurious night out, where you can take your chance on anything from a fruit-machine to a roulette wheel, the **Casino Royal**, Europa Road (Tel: 76666) is the place to head.

If you're thinking about staying on the Rock, then you may end up disappointed if you haven't pre-booked. A number of tour companies operate packages to Gibraltar now and tend to use up a substantial amount of the few moderately priced hotels available. At the top end of the scale there is the **Holiday Inn**, Governor's Parade (Tel: 70500) which is pricey but maintains the standards expected of this international hotel chain. A more atmospheric alternative is **The Rock**, 3 Europa Road (Tel: 70500) which is being restored to recreate the ambience and elegance of a grand European hotel. On the other side of the peninsula at Catalan Bay, **Hotel Caleta Palace**, Catalan Bay Road (Tel: 76051) is a well-equipped, comfortable hotel overlooking a fine sandy beach and the little fishing village of Catalan Bay. For those of more modest means, the **Bristo**, 10 Cathedral Road (Tel: 76800) or **Queen's**, Boyd's St (Tel: 74000) are adequately equipped and reasonably priced.

The Canary Islands

LA PALMA
Santa Cruz
de la Palma
TENERIFE
Laguna
LANZAROTE
Arrecife
GOMERA
Galdar
Puerto del Rosario
Grandilla
Las Palmas
Telde
HIERRO
Hierro
FUERTEVENTURA
GRAND CANARIA

INTRODUCTION

Less than one hundred miles off the coast of West Africa, just north of the Tropic of Cancer, the Canary Islands are only five hours from Britain by air and are one of the top holiday destinations in Spain. A group of seven islands, they offer a climate that is warm and sunny throughout the year, but thanks to the refreshing Atlantic winds is never excessively hot.

From the large resort developments of Tenerife and Gran Canaria, to the tranquillity and seclusion of Gomera and Hierro, these islands offer something for everyone. Whether you are looking for sandy beaches, sun, and extensive water-sports facilities, or peace and quiet in a beautiful setting, the Canaries have a destination for you, and offer a tremendous variety of scenery and holiday atmospheres from which to choose.

GETTING THERE

In general, most tourists arrive in the Canary Islands by plane, though it is possible to book a passage on a number of cruise ships without taking the full cruise. All the islands except tiny Gomera have their own airport, and Tenerife has two.

There are also good air links between the different islands with several flights each day, although most visitors choose to stay on just one. Certainly island-hopping can add considerable variety to your stay, and there is such diversity in the scenery and attractions of the different islands that this can be a very worthwhile thing to do.

Alternatively you can island hop by sea, making use of one of the regular car ferries. Naturally, this is a cheaper way to travel but it is also much slower – the longer connections can take as much as eight hours to reach their destination. A faster alternative for those travelling between Tenerife and Gran Canaria is the one-and-a-half-hour jetfoil trip. There are four connections each day and the cost is about the same as the air fare – and, of course, you get to experience a new way of travelling.

Transport on the islands themselves is generally quite good. All seven islands have good taxi services which are relatively inexpensive – fares are metered for short trips and you can strike a bargain for longer journeys. Taxis are often a good way of sightseeing too, but mainly if you are in a group of three or four and can split the cost – it becomes much less economical for one or two people.

Most of the islands also have good bus services, with reasonable fares, and on Gran Canaria and Tenerife you can also make use of the co-operatively owned mini-buses known as *waa-waas*. The service on the smaller islands is less useful for the visitor and is often very limited indeed.

Car hire is readily available on all the islands and is often very worthwhile for a few days, to take in the sights of your island. Hertz and Avis cars can be hired at all the Canarian airports. In general, the roads on the Canary Islands are fairly good, but bear in mind that the more remote areas and the smaller islands are naturally less developed in this respect, though even Hierro's main roads are now completely tarmacked.

CLIMATE

The climate of all the Canary Islands is warm and sunny throughout the year with an average temperature of around 21°C (70°F) in the winter months of December and January and 29°C (84°F) in the summer, when the hottest months are July and August – although the tourist season peaks in March and April.

The sun is usually stronger than in the Mediterranean resorts and it can be sunny for as much as seventy to eighty per cent of possible hours in each year. However, it should be remembered that the more mountainous islands can attract cloud.

There is quite a lot of variation in the amounts of rainfall experienced on the different islands at different times of the year and even in different parts of the same island. Most rain falls in the winter with December usually being the wettest month with anything from 25 to 55mm (1–2¼"), depending on the island. The driest island is Lanzarote, which lies closest to the African coast and to some extent mimics the dry climatic conditions of North Africa. Lanzarote can also be rather windy in comparison with the other Canaries. The wettest of the islands are La Palma, Gomera and Hierro to the West.

When choosing an island and a resort in the Canaries for your holiday you should also remember that the North of the mountainous islands – principally Tenerife and Gran Canaria – is wetter and more cloudy than the southern areas. Thus resorts like Los Cristianos on Tenerife may be preferred to, say, Playa de San Marcos, as far as the dedicated Sun Worshipper is concerned. This is not to say, though, that the northern resorts are perpetually shrouded in cloud.

CULINARY SPECIALITIES

As in much of Spain, a particular favourite on the Canary Islands is the saffron-flavoured rice dish *paella*, served with seafood or meat. That other typical Spanish dish, *gazpacho* – a cold soup made with a tomato base – is also popular here.

Not surprisingly, fish is a particular speciality on the islands, and is usually served grilled, often accompanied with *mojo picón*, a light sauce of olive oil, vinegar and spices which enhances and complements the fish beautifully. Fish varieties peculiar to the Canaries include *Sama*, and *Burro*.

Other Canarian specialities include a vegetable and meat stew called *puchero* and *papas arrugadas*, potatoes boiled in their skins and served in a special sauce. *Sancocho* is a delicious fish stew with potatoes. On Lanzarote, where many of the local people keep goats, *queso blanco* is a white goat's cheese with a mild, light flavour.

There are some local wines, which, if not world famous vintages, are certainly palatable. Lanzarote produces a strong, medium sweet white wine called *Malvasía*, whilst the village of Monte on Gran Canaria is the source of a mellow red.

WHERE TO GO FOR WHAT

The Canaries have something for every type of holiday-maker from the Socialite to the Recluse. As you will have seen from the climate information above, all the larger islands should suit the Sun Worshipper, though some are better than others in this respect.

The best destinations of all for sun-soaked holidays are Lanzarote and Fuerteventura, with the latter just ahead by virtue of its excellent beaches: vast tracts of soft white sand stretching for miles. They allow visitors a fair amount of privacy, and this, together with the extensive areas of dunes, has made parts of Fuerteventura popular with naturists. Nude bathing is also popular amongst the dunes of Playa de Inglés on Gran Canaria.

The beaches on Lanzarote are also of a good standard but are less extensive. On Gran Canaria, there are good sandy beaches at Las Canteras, in the capital of Las Palmas, and in the resorts of Playa del Inglés and Playa de Maspalomas. Sun Worshippers on Tenerife will have to be content with lying by the hotel pool, or on one of the small black-pebble beaches that are found in most of the resorts. The best of the Tenerife beaches is probably the one in Los Cristianos which is soft and brown rather than black and gritty. It should also be remembered that the North of both Tenerife and Gran Canaria lie in the shadow of the islands' central mountain ranges and can cloud over at times. The smaller islands to the West are wetter and less sunny, and there are few really good beaches of any size. They are not really good destinations for the Sun Worshipper.

By far the best islands for the Socialite type are Tenerife and Gran Canaria, which are the most highly developed tourist centres. On Gran Canaria, Las Palmas and Playa del Inglés have a large number of bars and discos – in the latter, many are housed in large, multi-storey 'commercial centres'. Nightlife in Maspalomas and Puerto Rico is more limited. On Tenerife, the top spots for nightlife are to be found in the resort of Puerto de la Cruz but all the larger resorts should be reasonably lively.

For the Nature-Lover and the Sightseer there is no shortage of interesting spots in the Canaries, though the islands are not among the best destinations for those with this type of interest: the emphasis is on scenery pure and simple rather than fabulously rich galleries and great museums of history and culture.

Probably the scenic highlight of the archipelago is Lanzarote with its unique, lunar-like landscape of volcanic badlands which are strangely beautiful and are designated as a Spanish National Park. Tenerife's Teide Mountain, and the generally lush vegetation of that island's interior are also attractive. On Gran Canaria, you can enjoy the spectacle of the undeveloped interior with its plunging ravines and rugged mountain areas. The central volcanic basin of Cruz de Tejeda is an outstanding attraction. La Palma, Gomera and Hierro to the West all offer the possibility of excursions through lush, undeveloped interiors. The Valle Gran Rey on Gomera is especially wonderful.

For the Recluse, it is the western islands which must be the first choice – if you don't find it quiet enough here you may as well give up, such is the lack of tourist development. In particular, the smallest islands of Gomera and Hierro are amazingly tranquil, with only a few hotels each. There are also quieter resorts on most of the other islands which would suit those who want peace and quiet rather than total seclusion. Puerto de Santiago on Tenerife is a good example of this type of destination.

The Sportsperson in search of a healthy holiday will find that there are a number of possibilities in the Canaries, especially for water-sports. Fuerteventura is one of the world's top windsurfing desti-nations, and this is also popular on Gran Canaria and Lanzarote. These two islands are probably the most promising all-round sports destinations. For golfers, there are courses on Gran Canaria, Tenerife and Lanzarote. Water-sports, including water-skiing, scuba diving and sailing, are available on Gran Canaria, Tenerife, Fuerteventura and Lanzarote. And, of course, there are tennis and squash facilities in many of the islands' better hotels.

For Family Holidays, many of the resorts on the main resort islands are ideal, with large, well-equipped hotels and safe beaches. Among the better choices for families are Playa Blanca on Lanzarote, and Puerto de la Cruz on Tenerife. But really, any of the major resorts should be acceptable for most families.

TENERIFE

The Coast

Tenerife is the largest of the Canary Islands and the capital of the provincial group which takes its name from the island's main town – Santa Cruz de Tenerife. It has a considerable variety of scenery, ranging from the lush greenery of the northern coast, with its banana plantations and palms, through the stark central plateau of volcanic rock, to the dry and more sunny southern coast.

The island is dominated by the highest mountain in the Canaries, and indeed in all Spanish territory, Mount Teide, which stretches upwards to a height of 3,700 metres (12,200 feet).

There are a number of popular resorts on the island, which has a lot to offer, although it does have the disadvantage that the beaches – where they exist – are composed of black sand and pebble.

The capital, SANTA CRUZ DE TENERIFE, lies towards the south-east tip of the island, and is a fairly large town with a population of around 200,000. It's a major seaport and is not unattractive, having some pleasant gardens such as the García Sanabría Park in which to enjoy a stroll, but it doesn't really have any significant sights to offer.

If you are taking a look around the town, you might like to visit the **Church of San Francisco**, notable for its finely carved altar of gilded wood and impressive ceiling paintings. The **Museo Municipal**, to the West of the church on C. José Murphy, offers a collection of paintings by Spanish and Canarian artists. Also of some possible interest is the **Castillo de Paso Alto** at one end of Avenida de Anaga, which houses a small military museum.

To soak up some sun here there is an excellent man-made bathing **beach** of, unusually for Tenerife, white sand at Las Teresitas, just outside town.

For **golfers**, there is an eighteen-hole course eight and a half miles outside town at El Penon. Clubs can be hired for a small charge; green fees can be up to 1,200 pesetas.

For more advice and information about the island and its facilities, the main **Tourist Office** is located on Palaçio Insular (Tel: 242 227).

Although visitors do come to Santa Cruz, it is not one of the island's principal tourist resorts. The first of these – LAS CALETILLAS – lies fourteen miles eastwards along the south coast. It is not, however, to be recommended. A down-at-heel, dull sort of place, it is chiefly noted for its power-station – an irritatingly excellent view of which can be had from the stony **beach**. This is a resort to be avoided, which shouldn't be too difficult since it was recently dropped by UK package firms.

EL MÉDANO, the next resort along this coast, is scarcely more promising. Situated close to the airport – which causes noise problems – it too is rather dull and isolated, and a bit run-down. It is partially redeemed by the smallish beach, on which the main hotel stands, which is more soft and sandy than some of the others and is possibly the best on the island. Accommodation is principally in the **Hotel Médano**, a reasonable three-star place jutting out into the sea.

The COSTA DEL SILENCIO (also known as Las Galletas) not far along the coast from El Médano is more a colony of apartment complexes than a resort. The coast here is somewhat unappealing and the **beaches** are of pebble rather than sand. Nevertheless, most of the apartment complexes offer pools, bathing areas and other reasonable facilities. If you do come here, try to choose a well-equipped complex – the **Ten Bell** is one of the largest and best and provides accommodation particularly suitable for families.

 On the western coast of the island, the resort of LOS CRISTIANOS is of much more interest than those on the southern coast. Centred around a small fishing town with a little character, this resort has a fairly good **beach** – by Tenerife standards – of soft, brownish sand which has a tendency to get crowded. Unfortunately, its location next to the port has also brought some pollution, although the problem is not serious and the resort should still be of interest to the sun-seeker.

The pleasant, palm-fringed promenade offers a number of inviting open-air cafés, and some restaurants – try the **Restaurante Casa del Mar** on the third floor of a building near the harbour. There are good views across the harbour to the sea, and the prices are reasonable – a decent meal should cost around 1,300 pesetas. Menus in English are available.

Accommodation in Los Cristianos tends towards the down-market. Among the better hotels is the **Oasis Moreque**, a three-star place on six floors ten minutes from the beach. There are good facilities, including an average-sized, attractive pool fringed by palms; the food is reasonable too. For a livelier time the **Princesa Dacil** offers a nightly disco, tennis court and nearby facilities for water-sports. Again, it is a generally clean and comfortable three-star hotel.

Next door to Los Cristianos is **PLAYA DE LAS AMERICAS**. This is a commercialized resort in its purest form, entirely purpose-built for tourism. Although it suffers from the plague of concrete blocks common to most purpose-built resorts, many of the hotels offer good-quality accommodation and facilities. There is a reasonable, sunny **beach** of black-brown sand, although this tends to get crowded, a problem made worse by the excessive and growing amount of accommodation.

Water-sports are available, and the resort may well be ideal for the sun-seeker who can find space on the beach.

There is some **nightlife** outside the hotels, with a fair number of bars and discos noisily competing for your custom.

From the wide selection of hotels, some of the better accommodation can be found at the **Hotel Flamingo**, a small 60-room establishment with three stars ten minutes from the beach. It offers a good pool and relaxed atmosphere with excellent facilities for tennis – something of a speciality here. The dining room serves reasonable food from an international menu, and there is a nightly disco. A more expensive, four-star alternative might be found in the **Park Troya**, a large hotel of 314 rooms suitable for most types of holiday-maker. Close to the beach, it has good facilities including a large pool, sauna and tennis court. There is regular live music, and you can select your meals from an international menu – with the option of dining à la carte.

PRIVATE. Keep Out | Further along the western coast of Tenerife, and nestling under the vast cliffs known as Los Gigantes, **PUERTO DE SANTIAGO** is a quieter, smaller-scale resort with just two hotels and a number of apartment complexes. The reclusive sort of holiday-maker may feel comfortable here. The cliffs are picturesque and there is a 200-metre **beach** of black sand – with another larger beach not far away. Among the attractions of this resort is an inviting 'Beach Club' which offers a pool, restaurant, bar and other facilities.

The **Hotel Los Gigantes Sol** merits four stars, and is friendly and comfortable. A nightclub – open each evening – provides a large part of the nightlife in the resort. The other facilities include tennis, squash and a gymnasium. The **Hotel Santiago** is a recently built place of a similar sort to the Los Gigantes Sol, if somewhat larger and a little more lively.

If you are in the mood to eat outside your hotel, a good choice would be the **Bamboo Restaurant** which offers a varied menu of European food – anything from Chateaubriand to Spanish lamb – cooked to a high standard. The restaurant is smart and welcoming, and a meal would cost you around 1,700 pesetas per person.

Situated on the less sunny, wetter northern coast of the island, PLAYA DE SAN MARCOS is scarcely a resort at all, offering only apartments. There is a very small beach of black sand. The nearby town of GARACHICO may be of passing interest to the sightseer with its **Castillo San Miguel** – a survivor from an important town that was destroyed by a volcanic eruption in the early eighteenth century. From the roof of the castle, there are excellent views of the town and out to sea. The local **Church of Santa Ana** may also be worth seeing.

Much more significant for most tourists is Tenerife's main resort, further along the northern coast – **PUERTO DE LA CRUZ**. The resort lies at the end of the verdant Orotava Valley, below Mount Teide – a picturesque setting that adds much to the attraction of the place. The town, which was not exclusively created for tourism, retains at its heart some original features from the time when it was a simple fishing port, and is the better for this. It is not, of course, without high-rise concrete developments; there are many. But although commercialized, Puerto de la Cruz is slightly less brash than some of its Canarian competitors.

One drawback here is the beach – a wholly inadequate 300 metres of black, gritty sand. Swimming here can be dangerous, as the beach is only partly sheltered from the heavy Atlantic swell. To cope with this problem a well thought-out, attractive **lido** has been built, with several seawater pools, changing rooms, bars, restaurants and sun terraces. There is an admission charge, but your ticket allows you to go in and out throughout the day. For the serious sun-seeker, a word of warning: although Puerto de la Cruz gets a *reasonable* amount of sunshine, this can be limited by the cloud build-up caused by the mountains.

In the evenings, there is plenty of **nightlife**, with a wide choice of bars and discos, and a small **casino** on Parque Taoro which offers blackjack, roulette, baccarat and slot machines.

There are few sights but the **Jardín Botanico** (Botanic Garden) on the road to the town of Orotava, which features exotic flora from all over the globe, is of some interest. The gardens are open from 9am to 7pm with a small admission charge. Of minor note is the **Church of Nuestra Señora de la Peña** on the Plaza de la Iglesia which has an exquisite altarpiece of gilded wood in the Baroque style.

Also worth seeing is the **Casa Iriarte**, at Calle San Juan, 21. This eighteenth-century mansion house is now a **craft centre** for the island and also houses a **maritime museum**. The visitor can watch local craftsmen working with leather, wood, gold, silver and embroidery and can purchase the high-quality results at reasonable prices. The maritime museum includes maps and scale models and historical exhibits. There is a small admission charge.

The **Loro Park**, just outside town, houses a large collection of parrots as well as flamingos and chimpanzees, in a pleasant garden setting. Children will enjoy watching the brightly coloured parrots playing with miniature bicycles and skates, and performing tricks. The park opens from 8.30am–6pm, and there is an entrance fee which includes the bus trip to and from the town.

The choice of accommodation available is vast. From amongst the hotels available, a good all-round winning combination is the three-star **Hotel Dania Park/Magec/Magec Park complex**. These three hotels, popular with British visitors, and offered by several tour operators, together offer over 500 rooms. The excellent facilities include rooftop pools, with pleasant views, tennis court, table-tennis, and a games room. There is a regular disco and a cabaret in the hotel, which is also situated conveniently close to the main attractions in the centre of the town.

A smaller, and quieter alternative is the four-star, 166-room **Hotel La Paz**, which overlooks the town from its hillside position twenty minutes' walk away. (There is also a five-days-a-week hourly courtesy bus.) There are panoramic views over the ocean and the Orotava Valley, and the hotel is set in small but attractive gardens. The facilities include a large pool and tennis court, and there is a nightly disco. The La Paz should suit most types of holiday-maker, though older people may be uncomfortable with the walk into town.

For a meal, try the **Restaurant Viking** on Avenida General Franco. Good food – some of it Scandinavian – comes cheap here. A set meal is likely to cost around 650 pesetas, an à la carte selection around 1,000 pesetas. Portions are generous, and the atmosphere quiet and welcoming. Also worth sampling is the Spanish cuisine served at **La Papaya** at Calle de Lomo, 14 (Tel: 382 811). The owner greets his customers at the door of the restaurant with a glass of sherry, and you'll be shown your table in any one of a number of rooms in this converted house. The menu includes *paella*, fish dishes, beef, pork and rabbit, cooked in a range of Spanish styles. A meal here will cost you between 1,400 and 2,000 pesetas per person.

Just inland from Puerto is **LA OROTAVA** which features some impressive old Canarian **mansion houses**, one of which is now a **craft shop and museum**. There is a magnificent **view** of the lush Orotava Valley from the nearby **Mirador Humboldt**. You can also visit the **banana plantation** of Banañera el Guanche where you can learn about the cultivation of this fruit and enjoy a glass of banana liqueur. The plantation also has a small souvenir shop. (It is open 8am–7pm. There is an admission charge.)

North of Puerto de la Cruz, **MESA DEL MAR** scarcely rates a mention. It is too small a place really to merit the title resort, and is notable chiefly for its obscurity. The beach of black sand is completely unsheltered from the Atlantic waves which pound it relentlessly. There is a number of villas here, and one rather upmarket apartment complex – but that is all.

Northwards again, towards the north-eastern tip of the island, is BAJAMAR. A somewhat isolated resort with just four hotels, it is attractively set on the coast below the Anaga Mountains. There is no beach, and a lido is amongst the few available facilities. UK package companies abandoned the resort in 1984, but it may suit the reclusive types – if they can find a way to get there!

Inland

The interior of Tenerife provides a number of opportunities to escape the resort life, and sample some fascinating scenery. One of the most popular excursions is to the Mountain of TEIDE. Any of four roads from the coast will take you up to the crater of LAS CAÑADAS which forms a vast, barren plateau at the centre of the island, an expanse of hard volcanic rock relieved only by patches of scrub, above which rises the mountain peak.

You can take a cable car to a point just below the summit, and from there a rough path leads on upwards to the very top. Throughout the climb you will be able to enjoy excellent views, and when you have reached the summit you will be rewarded with a magnificent panorama across the crater and the rest of the island to the sea. The air at these altitudes is thin, however, and the less fit and older visitor may find the final walk from the cable-car station to the peak too strenuous – the views from the station itself are, however, well worth seeing in themselves.

For those in search of unusual accommodation, the **Parador Nacional Cañadas del Teide** stands of the plateau formed by the crater. Rooms in the luxurious chalet-style hotel cost as much as 6,000 pesetas for a double. The facilities include a dining room serving Spanish cuisine, and a pool.

The island's former capital of LA LAGUNA, about five and a half miles inland from Santa Cruz, is a delightful place which is worth visiting. The narrow streets are full of traditional Canarian architecture – aristocratic buildings with sculpted façades of lava, carved doorways and balconies. Among the sights of La Laguna is the nineteenth-century **cathedral** with some interesting paintings and carvings, and the **Church and Monastery of Santo Domingo**.

To the north-west of La Laguna, towards the northern edge of the island, is the rugged, hilly area of the MONTAÑAS DE ANAGA and the MONTE DE LAS MERCEDES. The slopes are covered in Canarian pinewoods and this area is particular good for those with a taste for **hiking**. The tourist office in Santa Cruz provides a very useful series of maps of the Tenerife *senderos turisticos* or tourist walks, which also give useful practical information – picnic places, bus stops and so on.

GRAN CANARIA

Gran Canaria, the third largest of the Canary Islands, is the capital of the Las Palmas province, which also includes Fuerteventura and Lanzarote. The almost circular island is a top tourist destination and offers vast, sandy beaches of good quality. It is probably also the most scenic of the popular Canary Islands, and indeed, such is the variety of its scenery and vegetation that it is often described as a continent in miniature.

The North of Gran Canaria is verdant and fertile, swathed in woodland and banana plantations; the almost desert-like South, where many of the resorts are located, is principally an area of sandy beaches and concrete tourist developments. In striking contrast to both is the spectacle of the beautiful, undeveloped interior, with its plunging ravines and rugged mountain slopes.

Gran Canaria's capital is **LAS PALMAS**, situated on an isthmus to the north-east which widens out into the Atlantic. Las Palmas has managed to pull off a surprising double act, for not only is it a major seaport – the busiest in Spain – and the commercial hub of the whole Canary Islands group, but it is also an important resort.

Fortunately, the isthmus on which it stands has provided a natural break between the city's commercial and tourist activities, with the harbour area being situated on one side, and the main resort area on the other. Thus, the excellent **Las Canteras Beach**, fringed by modern hotels, has escaped the threat of pollution.

The resort area of Las Palmas is a busy, energetic sort of place with a lively nightscene and a lot of atmosphere. It might tend, however, to be rather noisy for some and much of the town can hardly be described as architecturally attractive, having succumbed to the problems of sprawling concrete developments (there is still some building work going on). But if it's nightlife you are after, this may be the place. Otherwise, some of the island's other resorts have more to offer.

Bearing these reservations in mind, Las Palmas does have some attractions besides nightlife and the beach. Not least of these is its status as a duty-free port – there are a number of shops offering duty-free goods, and it may well be worthwhile haggling to get an even better price!

There are also a number of attractions for the sightseer. The **Parque Doramus**, for example, is a large and picturesque park which houses a zoo as well as a swimming pool, tennis courts and the renowned **Hotel Santa Catalina** – an attractive example of eighteenth-century architecture.

To the South, the old quarter known as the **Vegueta** is centred around the Plaza de Santa Ana. Standing on the square is the great Gothic **cathedral** of Santa Ana, with its impressive neo-classical façade. Inside, you can admire the Baroque high altar, and from the towers take in fine **views** across the city. Outside, facing the cathedral, are two bronze statues of dogs from which the islands take their name, the Latin for dog being *canis*.

Not far away is the **Museo Canario**, standing on the corner of Calles Dr Chil and Dr Verneau. It features an important collection of remains from the period before the islands' conquest by the Spanish, as well as geographical exhibits. (Open: Monday–Friday, 10am–1pm, 3–6pm; Saturday, 10am–noon. Admission charge.) The **Casa de Colón** nearby was the home of Columbus before he sailed for the New World, and is now a museum to both its former occupant and to the conquest of the islands. The Casa is notable for its magnificent doorway, and for the grace and beauty of the interior. It also houses a small art collection. (Open: Monday–Saturday, 9am–1pm. Small admission charge.)

To the North of the Vegueta is the **Ciudad Jardin** or Garden City, close to the Playa de las Alcaravaneras, which features the **Canary Village**, an exhibition of island architecture and folklore, and the **Museo Nestor**, which preserves works by the artist from which it takes its name.

The choice of accommodation in Las Palmas is reasonable, with a fair selection of hotels available in most price ranges. Among the better hotels popular with tourists is the four-star **Hotel Imperial Playa**, situated centrally, with easy access to the nearby beach and also to nightclubs, bars and restaurants. A medium-sized place, it offers more character than some of the standard 'concrete blocks' to be found in this resort, and the English-speaking staff are attentive and helpful. The atmosphere is relaxed, and possibly the only disadvantage of the Imperial Playa is the absence of a pool.

For a meal outside your hotel there is a number of good quality restaurants, most of which are situated in the resort area. One worthwhile place to try is **Kim's Steak House** at Alfredo L. Jones, 19 in the Puerto de la Laz area. Run by an English couple, the Steak House is popular with visitors and locals alike – a reasonable meal should set you back about 1,500 pesetas. From the à la carte menu, don't miss the chance to sample their excellent New York cut steak. After your meal, relax with one of the Steak House's speciality coffees – anything from Jamaican to Spanish blends is offered. Alternatively, seek out the simple Spanish charms of the **Mesón Vasco Kal-Aide**, where a meal will cost you around 1,000 pesetas. Traditional Spanish cuisine is served here in the cool interior of an old, stone-walled building with metal-grilled windows. The Mesón is at Dr Grau Bassas, 35.

From the capital, it is around an hour and fifteen minutes' journey by road to the island's southern coast and the trio of popular resorts that occupies the five to six miles of rolling dunes around Maspalomas. San Agustín, Playa del Inglés and Playa Maspalomas are the busiest of Gran Canaria's resorts and are set amidst acres of sand and dunes, rolling breakers, palm trees, and the inevitable concrete monuments to commercialization. These are the places to come for sun. Indeed, the resorts revolve around their beaches – and that is how most tourists here spend their time.

The first of these three resorts, **SAN AGUSTÍN**, is smaller and quieter than its neighbour. It is generally well laid out if unremarkable and lacking in local colour to add atmosphere to your stay. The beaches – of which there are several – are not as good as those in the adjacent resorts, with some rocky and stony patches.

In general the built-up areas of this resort are modern and reasonably smart – though there are some scruffy exceptions – and the hotels, though fewer in number than in Maspalomas and Playa del Inglés, are of a good standard. There is enough nightlife to keep the average visitor occupied in the evenings – including Gran Canaria's only casino, adjacent to the Tamarindos Sol Hotel – don't forget your passport if you pay a visit here. Altogether, a highly acceptable destination for the Sun Worshipper.

Among the hotels of San Agustín, the upmarket, four-star **Costa Canaria** is thoroughly recommended. A clean, comfortable and modern hotel of 154 rooms – all with private facilities and a seaview – it is located right on a good, sandy beach within walking distance of the resort centre. The good-sized pool is set in pleasant gardens to the front, and there is also a children's pool and playground. A regular programme of sports and entertainments is arranged, and an added bonus is that all guests are allocated their own sunbed on arrival – putting an end to disappointments and arguments liable to spoil your holiday.

A good three-star alternative for those with shallower pockets, is the **IFA Beach Hotel**, which shares a building and facilities with the Hotel Hapimag. The IFA Beach overlooks a sandy beach and has 202 rooms which, though on the small side, are extremely comfortable. There are two large pools as well as a children's pool, and ample numbers of sun loungers. Live entertainments are organized weekly, and there is a nightclub in the adjacent hotel too. This is a good, generally recommended hotel, although those with a taste for a very quiet life should bear in mind its size and fairly central location.

PLAYA DEL INGLÉS, the largest and busiest of the three resorts in this part of the island, adjoins the western side of San Agustín. It is a large, sprawling and untidy sort of resort, with no real heart – or soul. Bars, nightclubs, shops and restaurants have been housed in multi-storey 'commercial centres' which can make the hotels close by unbearably noisy. A number of the hotels are situated at uncomfortably long distances from the beach – implying a long, and sometimes uphill walk there and back. Older travellers and those for whom easy beach access is important should therefore choose carefully.

The saving grace of Playa del Inglés as a tourist destination, and undoubtedly the principal reason for its popularity, is the **beach**: acres of golden white sand on which to soak up the ultra-violet make this the Sun Worshipper's dream. And for those who like to get an all-over tan, the miles of rolling dunes offer the possibility of **nude bathing** in privacy.

Playa del Inglés is, then, highly recommended for the Sun Worshipper and for the younger Socialite type who doesn't mind the noise of the commercialized centre – there is certainly no shortage of nightlife.

From amongst the enormous choice of hotels in this resort, a number stand out as offering particularly good value. From amongst the four stars, the **Hotel Dunamar** is a medium-sized, cool and comfortable place, just five minutes from the beach. The hotel, which recently won a gold award from Thomson's, the tour operator, offers the usual facilities, including a good-sized, clean swimming pool, and a free sauna and gymnasium. The attractive dining room is situated on the sixth floor and offers an à la carte service in addition to the tourist menu. Live entertainments are organized most evenings.

Also worthy of mention is the **Hotel Neptuno**, a recently opened four-star hotel located in the centre of the resort. It maintains consistently high standards and is friendly and welcoming. The principal disadvantage of the Neptuno is the twenty-minute walk to the beach.

In the three-star category, the **Hotel Continental** is a good choice. Just five minutes from the beach it's another modern building on eight floors, well decorated and comfortable. The well-cared-for facilities include a large pool, children's pool, bar and pizzeria. There is a nightly disco and live entertainments are a regular event. All 383 rooms are equipped with private facilities and a balcony, some with seaviews.

The third in this chain of three resorts is **PLAYA DE MAS-PALOMAS**, separated from Playa del Inglés, four miles away, by sand dunes and by one of Gran Canaria's two eighteen-hole golf courses – the other being inland at Caldera Bandama. The beach is essentially just a continuation of the Inglés Beach, and is of the same high quality. The resort itself is quieter and considerably more attractive than its neighbour, having escaped from the worst excesses of aggressive commercialization. Development in Maspalomas has been largely confined to a single shopping street and to a limited number of hotels.

This is undoubtedly a more relaxing place than Playa del Inglés, with only a limited amount of nightlife, mainly confined to the hotels. For the Sun Worshipper, the resort retains all the attractions of its neighbour, and may even be preferred.

Those with a taste for the sporting life may also find this an interesting destination – in addition to the golf course, horse-riding, water-sports and sub-aqua activities are available, and there are tennis, table-tennis and archery facilities in the hotels.

There are only three hotels in Maspalomas – two four stars and a five star. It may not be worth paying five-star prices for this particular resort, so from amongst the available options it is probably best to go for either of the four-star hotels – the **Faro** and the **Palm Beach**. The latter is almost twice as large, with 358 rooms, and is therefore likely to be both livelier and somewhat noisier. Otherwise there is little to choose between them, with both offering high-quality facilities and nightly entertainments.

Although there are few sights in any of the resorts in the Maspalomas-Playa del Inglés-San Agustín group, visitors to the area might be interested in the gardens and aviary at **Palmitos Park**, just inland.

PUERTO RICO is the fifth and last of Gran Canaria's resorts, situated about 35 miles from the airport, on the southern coast. A relatively new development, Puerto Rico is undeniably a purpose-built, commercial resort, spreading down from steep hillsides to a large, crescent-shaped, sandy beach which does tend to get pretty crowded during the season. For all that, it's not uninviting for a basic sun and surf holiday, having managed to retain a more civilized and relaxed atmosphere than the brash and uncompromising Maspalomas.

A popular family destination, there is a good choice of bars and restaurants, as well as two discos to add to the entertainments offered by the resort's single hotel – most accommodation being in the multitude of apartment complexes and villas which carpet the hillsides. The resort is still developing with some building work going on, and seems likely to become an increasingly popular destination.

The above-mentioned one hotel is the **Rio Sol**, located a mile and a half from the centre of the resort and the beach – a courtesy bus is provided for guests. The facilities include two pools and a separate children's pool as well as good sun terraces, well equipped with loungers. This is an aparthotel and consequently, the 210 rooms are all equipped with a small kitchenette, complete with hob. There is also a small dining room which offers a rather bland, international menu, and bar snacks. There is a nightly disco and regular entertainments are organized. Although comfortable and friendly, this accommodation may be more suited to younger travellers and to the active, sport-orientated type.

Sights of Gran Canaria

For the Sightseer and Nature-Lover, both the coast and the interior of Gran Canaria offer a great deal – possibly more than any other island in the Canaries.

The northern coast is fecund and green, rarely visited by tourists. THE AGAETE VALLEY is one of the lushest areas of all, with fine views – especially of the Pinar de Tamadaba **pine forest**, situated inland. The small fishing port of PUERTO DE LAS NIEVES, on the coast here, is famous for its fish restaurants. CENOBLO DE VALERÓN, to the west of Las Palmas, offers some interesting caves once occupied by the Guanches – the original inhabitants of the island. However, the main attraction of the western and northern coast lies not in specific sights, but in the general scenery. A drive along the spectacular, twisting coast road can make a refreshing change from resort life.

On the eastern side of the island, south of Las Palmas, is Gran Canaria's second town, TELDE. It is not especially picturesque, but if you find yourself here the fifteenth-century **Church of San Juan Baptista** is worth visiting to see its beautiful Flemish altarpiece – probably the most valuable art treasure on Gran Canaria. Other sights of passing interest here include the **Basilica of Santo Cristo**. In the nearby CUETRO PUERTAS are further remains of the Guanches – here, there is the so-called Sacred Hill of the Guanches, including a large chamber which may have been used for council meetings of their leaders.

Undoubtedly, the best of Gran Canaria's sights are to be found in the interior. Most spectacular of all is CRUZ DE TEJEDA, right in the centre of the island. Here, there are marvellous views from a look-out point over the central volcanic basin. On a good day you can see as far as Mount Teide, on Tenerife. The village of Tejeda lies, amid orchards, in the basin itself, and there is also a parador here, offering high-quality accommodation. Six miles along the ridge, from POZO DE LAS NIEVES, the island's highest point at 2,450 metres, there are all-encompassing panoramas across the whole of Gran Canaria.

The village of TEROR, just to the North of Tejeda, has some excellent examples of old Canarian houses and the eighteenth-century **Church of Nuestra Señora del Pino**, dedicated to the island's patron saint.

Other inland sights include FATAGA, to the south-east of Tejeda, with some pleasant palm woods and SANTA LUCÍA which is set in some very attractive scenery and has a small archaeological museum.

LANZAROTE

The Canary Island lying closest to the African coast, Lanzarote is also the most striking of the group, with scenery unique not only amongst these islands but almost to the entire world. Like the other Canary Islands, the North is greener and more fertile, whilst the southern coast is dry and sandy, but what sets the place apart is the barren, almost lunar aspect of the *malpais* or badlands that cover two thirds of its area – more than 200 square miles.

These badlands are great tracts of fine volcanic ash, black and browny-red in colour created by massive volcanic eruptions in the Timanfaya area during the seventeenth and eighteenth centuries. Today, they give much of Lanzarote an eerie, alien look, and render a large part of the land infertile – little vegetation has yet managed to survive to soften this stark, uncompromising landscape. All over the island one comes upon the craters and remains of extinct volcanoes.

In a few areas, careful management and irrigation has created oases of fertility, and the local farmers manage to grow a few melons, potatoes, grapes and tomatoes. Dry stone walls are used to shield the fields from the wind – which, since Lanzarote is comparatively flat, blows unchecked straight from Africa.

The towns, villages and resorts of this island are smarter and better laid out than on any of the other islands, thanks to strict local development laws and the influence of a locally famous designer and architect César Manriqué, who has advised the local administrators for much of his life. Hotels over five storeys high and villas over two storeys are not permitted, nor are billboards. All new buildings are constructed from natural, local materials in either green or white, and there are strict regulations on where new development can take place. All this has helped to create a distinctive, almost chic look for the island and its resorts.

Perhaps surprisingly for a place famous for its black ash landscape, Lanzarote offers the added bonus of beaches of soft, golden sand. Altogether it is a unique and particularly appealing destination.

Lanzarote's capital is **ARRECIFE**, located on the east coast about three miles from the airport. It is a busy commercial city, more notable as a fishing port than as a holiday destination, and there are few reasons to stay here. Although there is a pleasant promenade, the town beach is not terribly clean and there is little nightlife of any note, although the **Snipe Disco** may be a passable place to spend an evening out. The disco is on Avenida Mancommunidad and tourists get in free if they bring their passports along.

There are only a few sights in the capital. These include the **Castillo de San Gabriel** which houses a museum of archeology and the **Castillo de San José**, above the harbour, with a collection of contemporary art that is worth a short visit.

Hotel accommodation in the capital is limited, and most hotels are situated in the centre of the town. The four-star **Arrecife Gran** is the island's only skyscraper with 150 rooms on fourteen floors overlooking the harbour, mostly with good seaviews. It is not among the best of the Canaries' four-star hotels but is generally comfortable and quiet with good public areas and reasonable standards in the dining room. The alternative is the **Miramar**, a three-star *residencia* on Calle Coll (Tel: 810 438) which is a safe bet for a clean, comfortable, if basic, room and a friendly welcome. There is a small restaurant with waiter service and an international menu.

The resorts of Lanzarote have far more to offer the holiday-maker than its capital, and the first of these, **PLAYA DE LOS POCILLOS** and **PUERTO DEL CARMEN**, lie adjacent to each other a few miles down the coast and about four miles from the airport.

This is Lanzarote's largest and most developed resort area, and is set against an attractive backcloth of hills. The long, wide **beach** is large enough not to become overcrowded even in high season, and is composed of dark coloured sand. For those who want a lot of space, or peace and quiet, the Playa de los Pocillos area is the less busy. There are adequate numbers of bars, restaurants and supermarkets, and these resorts are generally pleasant if rather characterless.

In the evenings, the better discos and nightclubs – and there is a large choice – include the **Vilson Disco** on Calle Reina Sofia which is large and very popular with clientele spanning the generations. Entry is free until midnight, though some of the drinks can be expensive.

In common with the rest of the island, much of the accommodation in these resorts is in apartment complexes, often with their own pool and sun terraces, but there are a few hotels too. Amongst the best of these is the **Hotel San Antonio**, which stands right on the beach at Playa de los Pocillos. It's a four-star place ten minutes from the resort centre. Facilities include a Discotheque Beach Club open each evening, floodlit tennis courts, and a solarium and gymnasium. All 331 rooms have seaviews and private facilities. The pool is medium-sized and very clean, and there are plenty of sunbeds both around it, and under the surrounding trees and canopies.

Alternatively, the **Hotel Los Fariones** in Puerto del Carmen provides modern accommodation to a four-star standard. Built on four floors, this recently refurbished hotel stands in a pleasant, sandy cove. All the usual four-star facilities are available and all 200-plus rooms have seaviews.

From amongst the numerous apartment complexes, a good choice available from British tour operators would be the **Playaclub Apartments**. A fairly recent development, these are situated conveniently near the resort centre and close to the beach. The attractive white apartments are enhanced by the amenities available which include a pool, sun terraces, gardens and bar.

If you are dining out in this resort the **Las Vistas Bar** is a good place to try. Here, you can enjoy your choice from a well-chosen international menu in the attractive courtyard or inside, under a vaulted ceiling. Both set menus and à la carte meals are available, with prices ranging upwards from 900–1,000 pesetas. Among the best choices from the menus are seafood soup, prawns, and grilled sole, which they cook to perfection. You can find this delightful restaurant at Calle Guardilama, 20 (Tel: 825 010). It is closed on Mondays.

Lanzarote's third resort is **PLAYA BLANCA** on the scenically rugged southern tip of the island, forty minutes from the airport. It is a relatively small resort, with a small, sandy beach and a smart promenade area. It has grown up around a pleasant little fishing village, yet has not lost its character through development –

which is still continuing. The amenities come down to a few shops and restaurants and a number of bars. There is no disco or nightclub, and what nightlife there is is confined to the hotels and apartment complexes which climb the slopes behind the village. This is, then, a resort for those in search of a quieter kind of holiday. Ideal for families and possibly for the more reclusive type of holiday-maker, not so ideal for the Socialite type.

For a meal out in Playa Blanca, the restaurant which bears the name of the resort is a good bet. The **Playa Blanca** is housed in an attractive white building on the sea-front with excellent views. You can eat outside in the sea air if you wish, as the tables are pleasantly sheltered from the wind. The culinary standards are high, and some of the seafood dishes are heartily recommended. Count on spending around 1,600 pesetas on a good meal.

There is only one hotel in Playa Blanca, the **Lanzarote Princess** (Tel: 830 000) and that was only opened in 1987. The hotel now provides excellent four-star accommodation on four floors laid out in a semi-circular design. Situated about ten minutes' walk outside the resort itself, and a few minutes' walk from the beach, the facilities are well up to the standards expected in this class of hotel and include a nightly disco – the only one in Playa Blanca – mini-golf, tennis and squash courts. For children there is a special pool and a playground area as well as a baby-patrolling service. Well-recommended.

The last of Lanzarote's main resort areas is the **COSTA TEGUISE** close to Arrecife. The backdrop of surrounding hills is attractive, though some of the surrounding countryside is rather desolate. The resort doesn't really have a centre, having developed in an *ad hoc* way around the five-star **Los Salinas Sol Hotel**. The beach is small and rocky in parts but many of the visitors to this area seem to prefer the poolside facilities of the hotel or their apartment complex.

There are a number of modern villa developments such as the **Los Molinas Complex** and a new aparthotel has recently opened, the **Los Zocas**. Nightlife and other facilities are principally *within the accommodation* – although the **golf course** is nearby.

In terms of accommodation, if you have the money, the Los Salinas Sol (previously the Los Salinas Sheraton) is obviously *the* place to stay on the Costa Teguise. Many of the 310 luxury rooms are grouped around a large, very attractive central water garden; others are arranged on six floors in a stepped design. All rooms have the usual five-star facilities and a private terrace area. The choice of sports available to guests includes table tennis and tennis, sailing, subaqua, windsurfing, water-skiing and deep-sea fishing. The hotel also has a well-equipped gymnasium and easy access to the nine-hole golf course. The beautifully designed pool is large and sectioned, and there are plenty of sunbeds in the pool area and elsewhere. And naturally, the cuisine available is also of an outstanding quality – breakfast and lunch can be taken from a buffet by the pool, and in the evenings dinner is a culinary delight, with three or four choices available on the table d'hôte menu. Prices for all this luxury are naturally high!

In a lower price range, the **Los Zocas** complex is awarded three stars by the powers that be and, as mentioned above, is a recent development. Although it is somewhat isolated, the surrounding area is developing fast – though not so fast as to become a problem. There are 244 rooms on three floors, all with private facilities and a kitchenette area which provides a self-catering alternative to the three small dining rooms serving an international menu with three choices. À la carte is available. Live entertainments are organized each evening and there are adequate sports facilities. On the whole, it is a typical aparthotel with quite high standards.

In addition to the various resorts, there are a number of excellent beaches which the serious Sun Worshipper will find worth checking out. Amongst the best is **Playa de Papagayo**, situated at the southern tip of the island. Here the sand is soft and golden, the water outstandingly clean. It is also a particularly quiet beach, and at times may be almost deserted. Perhaps for this reason Papagayo has become popular with nude bathers in the know.

Sights of Lanzarote

Lanzarote is one of the more scenic of the Canary Islands, and has a great deal to offer the Sightseer. Probably the most outstanding attractions are the **Montañas del Fuego**, which lay at the very epicentre of the eruptions of the eighteenth century. The area around these mountains – now called the **Parcque Nacional de Timanfaya**, is an eerie wilderness of black lava, ash and craters, tinged with red and brown. There is still some subterranean activity going on, and the tremendous energies locked up under your feet are aptly demonstrated by pouring some cold water into a hole or small crater. Fractions of a second later a miniature geyser of white-hot steam shoots up into the air!

This energy has been put to productive use in the restaurant at ISLOTE DEL HILARIO, the ultimate destination of most tours. The restaurant and bar here have been built onto what was once the hut of the hermit Hilario. It is claimed to be he who planted the fig tree that grows up through the centre of the restaurant, a lonely specimen of plantlife in this volcanic desert. From the viewpoint at Islote del Hilario there are superb views across the whole National Park area.

For the more adventurous visitors, camel rides are available to the crater of the largest of the 'mountains of fire' – TIMANFAYA. Leaving from a station near the entrance to the park, they make their way up the slopes of lava – a peculiar but very popular journey which is not excessively expensive. These excursions are only available in the mornings as the camels are put to work in the fields outside the park after lunch.

For those keen on coastal scenery, the south-west coast is the most spectacular, with the Atlantic waves pounding the black volcanic shoreline – **Los Hervideros** is especially beautiful. Another beautiful spot is **El Golfo**, a crater right on the coast which has formed a lagoon of bright green water, unknown in depth. The salt water lake here is good for swimming. Nearby, are the saltpans of JANUBIO, where you can view the processes involved in extracting the salt from seawater – essential to Lanzarote, which has no natural source of fresh water.

At the northern tip of the island the MIRADOR DEL RÍO is a viewpoint blasted out of the cliffside and offers a marvellous vista of

Lanzarote's western coast and the offshore islet of LA GRACIOSA – thanks to the island's ubiquitous designer Manriqué who was responsible for its construction. (Open: 11am–7pm; admission charge.) You can enjoy a drink and a meal here, at the **Bar Restaurante Los Roques**. Eat outside if you can, weather permitting.

Around the tip of the island, on the eastern coast are the volcanic **Cuevas de los Verdes** caves, with galleries which run for over three miles. Once used by the islanders to hide from pirates, the caves are now a deservedly popular tourist attraction, and a guided tour is available for a small charge. Parents of young children and the elderly should bear in mind that some of the paths can be quite steep and the lighting is not always bright enough to ensure absolute safety from slips and falls. (Open: 11am–6pm.)

The **Grotto Jameos del Agua** nearby is another cave, but in this case it has been converted into a subterranean **restaurant** and **nightclub**. At the centre is a lake full of blind, white crabs, and birds fly over your head as you dine. There is a small entrance fee in the daytime, which rises when the nightclub opens later on. This unusual attraction was designed by – you guessed it – César Manriqué.

The island's original capital, now its second city, is TEGUISE, situated inland, towards the northern part of Lanzarote. It is relatively untouristed and retains a pleasant air of antiquity. The **Castillo de Guanapay** castle, dating from the sixteenth century, stands on the top of a nearby volcano, on the edge of the crater, and offers marvellous views, in all directions, across the island's interior to the coast.

FUERTEVENTURA

Lying just one hundred miles off the African coast, Fuerteventura is hot and dry. Much of the landscape of low-lying hills is covered by infertile, dry scrub, providing a sparse covering for the scorched earth below. It is not a landscape that can easily be described as scenic or picturesque, but in the light of dawn or dusk it can take on a kind of stark, uncompromising beauty that may appeal to some.

Many of the people are poor, living a life of subsistence on the plains and in the wide central valley of the island and, despite being the second largest of the Canary Islands, Fuerteventura's population is relatively tiny.

All of this may seem to hold out little promise of being the ideal destination for the average holiday-maker, but Fuerteventura has one outstanding feature that draws in hundreds of visitors each year – its beaches. This is a desert island in the truest sense, with vast tracts of soft white sand along most of the coast offering the chance for even the most escapist of visitors to find their own tranquil spot. Indeed, the wide open spaces have found growing popularity with naturists.

The island offers a quieter, more relaxed type of holiday, centred mainly around the beaches, and with far less in the way of sophisticated nightlife than is found on other Canary Islands such as Tenerife. Definitely an away-from-it-all destination.

Fuerteventura's lack of commercial development has also saved the surrounding sea from the problems of pollution, and the almost transparent water provides excellent opportunities for water-sports, in particular scuba-diving and windsurfing – for which Fuerteventura has become the world's fifth most popular destination.

The island's capital is **PUERTO DEL ROSARIO**, an uninspiring, run-down and drab little place with little to recommend it. It is not really geared up as a tourist resort though it could potentially serve as a base for exploring the very limited sights in the interior of the island. The airport is situated close to the town.

Of considerably more interest to the holiday visitor is
CORRALEJO, the island's principal resort, which has grown up
around a small fishing village. Although quite small, compared with
some resorts, Corralejo is increasingly popular and still expanding.
The village offers a number of bars, restaurants and disco, but is more
or less a simple and unsophisticated place so that much of the nightlife
– such as there is – is centred on the hotels. If the disco does appeal, it's
called **Freddy's** and can be found at Calle la Iglesia, 29; it is very
popular with the windsurfing set. (Entrance charge for men includes
first drink; women get in free.)

The **beach**, around which life in Corralejo revolves, is vast, its
only disadvantage being the lack of shelter from the wind –
hence the popularity with windsurfers. For those interested in trying
out this sport, boards can easily be hired by the hour or day for
anything from 900 pesetas upwards.

Accommodation in this resort is in one of a small number of hotels
or in the attractive and comfortable Hopalco Apartment Complex on
the outskirts of the village. Of the hotels, one good option is the
four-star, 356-room **Tres Islas**, set just by the beach. It offers a wide
variety of excellent facilities, including tennis courts, a very large pool
with island bar, and windsurfing facilities. There are two restaurants
and an à la carte grill room, and the management organizes a weekly
gala dinner. It should be noted, however, that the Tres Islas is not
cheap, but may be worth a splurge.

A less expensive option is the **Hotel Oliva Beach**, set amongst
dunes close to the sea. Facilities include a pool and solarium and
regular discos are organized in the evenings.

Fuerteventura's second resort is MORRE DEL JABLE, a relatively new
development at the southern end of the island. It is not especially
attractive from the architectural point of view but has an excellent
beach. It is centred around another small, simple village with limited
facilities for visitors. Accommodation is available in a limited range of
hotels and apartments, including a large, comfortable Robinson Club
hotel with a wide range of facilities.

There are a number of other small resorts around Fuerteventura,
essentially consisting of a few hotels and apartments and the beach.

JANDÍA has a particularly good beach, stretching along the coast for more than twenty miles, and has found popularity with naturists. The resort also offers an unusual **aqua-park**. Accommodation is limited, but what there is is of a good standard. Other simple hotel-beach combinations can be found at PÁJARA and TARALEJO. Taralejo's beach is, however, one of the island's less appealing, consisting of dark brown lava sand rather than the soft, golden white variety found in the other resorts.

A final holiday option is the isolated **Hotel Los Gorriones Sol** situated on a wide expanse of **beach** and surrounded by sandy hills. The hotel is largely self-contained with a wide range of facilities, and entertainments are organized day and night. Tennis, mini-golf, volleyball and windsurfing are available. The hotel, with 321 rooms, is a comfortable and friendly three star, and is offered by a number of British tour operators, including the British Airways company, Enterprise.

If you want to dine out on the island, one popular and friendly place to try is the **Restaurante Bar Oscar** in Corralejo on Calle la Iglesia. A large, traditional-style place with red-checked tablecloths, it serves a range of typical Spanish dishes such as *paella* as well as excellent T-bone steaks and the speciality of the house – bananas flambé, which are irresistible for dessert.

Sights of Fuerteventura

The prospects for the Sightseer on Fuerteventura are very limited indeed. The capital of Puerto del Rosario – as mentioned above – is virtually worthless in this respect, and in most others!

BETANCURIA situated inland, in the middle of the island, has more to offer, having been the first capital of Fuerteventura after the Spanish colonization in the fifteenth century. This green oasis in a landscape of arid scrubland remains the island's second most important town and a visit to the eighteenth-century cathedral and the small but interesting archaeological museum may make for a break from sun, surf and sand. For those who find the desert-like landscape appealing, a drive around the island may be another sightseeing option, but the scenery is far from spectacular. Cars are easily hired.

The other large town (bear in mind that the population of the capital is only a few thousand) is GRAN TARAJAL on the south-eastern coast. However, it has nothing to recommend it to even the most easily pleased of sightseers!

LA PALMA

PRIVATE.
Keep Out

La Palma, the most westerly of the Canaries, is also one of the most unspoilt, having only recently seen a little development as a tourist destination. It is probably the world's steepest island, for within its 45-kilometre length and 30-kilometre width it reaches heights of 2,400 metres (8,000 feet).

It is amongst the most verdant and beautiful of the Canaries, with flourishing plantations of tobacco and banana on the lower slopes and dense woods of almond and Canarian pine higher up providing shelter to a wide variety of animals and birds. At the heart of the island lies the vast crater of the volcano which gave birth to it, now a National Park offering some breathtaking views.

There are a few beaches of dark, low-quality sand and rock and the island is principally attractive as an away-from-it-all destination for the Recluse and Nature-Lover, for whom it should have considerable charms.

The capital of La Palma is **SANTA CRUZ DE LA PALMA** in the centre of the eastern coastline. It is set against a backdrop of hills, with a small harbour and narrow, steep streets graced with picturesque local buildings and some stately old mansions with ornate balconies. Once an important port, it retains an air of relaxed dignity and faded grandeur, and possesses considerable charm.

Among the sights of Santa Cruz are the sixteenth-century **ayuntamiento** (town hall) and the **Iglesia de San Salvador** (Church of San Salvador), both on the Plaza de España, off the attractive main street, Calle Real. The church dates from 1503 and is notable for its distinctive Moorish roof and for the painting by Esquivel, *Transfiguration*, which adorns the high altar. Also on the square is **La Cosmologica**, a worthwhile museum of history.

The **Castillo de Santa Catalina** defended the island against pirates during the sixteenth and seventeenth centuries. Amongst the marauders was Peg-Leg, a Frenchman who ransacked the capital in 1553. Thirty-two years later a cannon-ball fired from the castle managed to sink Francis Drake's flagship as it approached the island. Seafaring exploits are also recalled by the full-size replica of Columbus' flagship *Santa Maria* which houses a small **naval museum**.

Also worth visiting in Santa Cruz is the **Santuario de la Virgen de las Nieves**, a sanctuary dating from the sixteenth century. Chief amongst its possessions is a treasured Gothic sculpture in terracotta which depicts the island's patron saint, Señora de la Nieves. The saint's feast day – 5 August each year – sees tremendous celebrations across the island.

The choice of accommodation in Santa Cruz, and indeed on the whole island, is confined to a handful of hotels and a parador. The **Parador Nacional de Santa Cruz** is on the Avenida Maritima. The rooms and service are up to the usual high standards of all paradors, and the building itself is a typical Spanish mansion. Previous guests include King Juan Carlos. Expect to pay around 6,000 pesetas for a double room.

The largest of the two hotels, the two-star **San Miguel** on Avenida de José Antonio (Tel: 411 243), provides comfortable accommodation to a reasonable if unexceptional standard. There are 242 rooms on ten floors and prices for doubles start at around 3,800 pesetas for a room with private bath. There is no dining room, but a snack bar will provide simple meals and breakfast. Alternatively the 68-room, three-star **Hotel Mayantigo** is friendly and comfortable with access to a poor-quality beach. None of the staff – in common with most of the native people of La Palma – speaks English. The Mayantigo is on C. Alvarez de Abreu (Tel: 411 740).

For a meal try the **Restaurante Canarias**, close to the parador. This is a popular and welcoming place serving typical Spanish cuisine – the *paella* is excellent and the prices for most dishes economical.

Sights of La Palma

If you come to La Palma at all, you come for the scenery and the seclusion – and this island has both in large measure. Any reasonable tour of the island will imply hiring a car as there are no coach tours.

To the North of Santa Cruz you travel through a region of luxuriant vegetation through the rather unremarkable town of PUNTALLANA and on to SAN ANDRÉS where you can swim in a natural seawater pool. Further north, the principal attraction is scenery pure and simple, as the twisting road, full of potholes, leads on through the laurels of the Los Tilos Forest and banana plantations. At FUENTE DE LA ZARZA there is a cave dwelling of the island's original Guanche inhabitants.

On to the north-western edge of La Palma, and you come to CUEVA BONITA, a beautiful seawater grotto which can be visited by boat. Further south, off the side-road for La Cumbrecita there is an excellent **viewpoint** over the CALDERA DE TABURIENTE crater which lies at the very centre of the island. Also on the western coast is TAZACORTE, another heavily cultivated area, where there are some reasonable **beaches**.

In the centre of the island is the NATIONAL PARK, where you can travel through forests of chestnut and Canarian pine trees to the volcanic core of the island, with its craters and rocky landscape centred on Mount Caldera. Make it up to the end of the road and you will be able to take in some spectacular panoramic views. Not far away is the OBSERVATORY at Los Muchachos, which houses the Isaac Newton refracting telescope and the giant William Herschel reflector. The place is certainly worth seeing but is only open to visitors on the fifteenth of each month.

In the South of La Palma, FUENCALIENTE offers the chance to see another couple of volcanic craters and at SAN ANTONIO there is a pleasant walk marked out. This is the area of the most recent volcanic activity: the volcano of Teneguía erupted in 1971.

GOMERA

Gomera is the second smallest and least-visited of the Canary Islands. Almost perfectly circular in shape, it is covered by lush vegetation and scored by deep valleys. It has no airport, no resorts and almost no hotels that merit the name. Its attractions lie in its unspoilt beauty and tranquillity which will undoubtedly find favour with the Nature-Lover and Recluse alike.

The trip from Tenerife by ferry takes an hour and a half, and you will arrive at the island's capital, **SAN SEBASTIAN**, a quiet little place of 7,000 people where Columbus once docked to take on supplics for his trip to the New World. There are few sights, but you may want to see the tiny **museum** housed in the **Torre del Conde** (Count's Tower), a sixteenth-century fortress. The house where Columbus stayed is known as the **Casa de Colón**, and there is also a scattering of colonial houses of some architectural interest.

Accommodation on Gomera is *very* limited. Indeed, your choice comes down to the more expensive but very comfortable **Parador Nacional**, which has three stars and 39 rooms, or the more simple facilities offered at the **Hostal Canarias**, a three-star pension with 44 rooms. There are also apartments at Calera and Vueltas.

Sights of Gomera

Taxis and cars can be hired in San Sebastian for scenic tours around the island – don't come here for anything else; there is nothing else to do! Most of the main roads are now made up to a reasonable standard, so this shouldn't pose many problems.

The most attractive areas to head for lie in the North and West, where the vegetation is at its most lush. The valleys of VALLEHERMOSA and HERMIGUA are extremely pleasant but the most scenic is the VALLE GRAN REY, one of the most heavily cultivated parts of the island. The valley is extremely steep, marked by crags and hairpin bends in the twisting road. Some of the **views** are quite wonderful.

As to settlements, there are no real towns of any size, just small, picturesque villages like AGULO and CALERA where there is a reasonable beach with probably the cleanest water to be found off any Canary Island. CHIPUDE, inland, is home to a cottage industry of pottery which may provide you with an unusual souvenir.

HIERRO

 Hierro is the smallest and most westerly of the Canaries, once thought to be the very edge of the world. It is almost completely undeveloped for tourism and for the visitors it does receive it offers a startling contrast in landscapes. Parts of the island are desolate areas of volcanic wilderness, covered in black rocks, and cones of ash – of which there are more than 1,500 on Hierro. Elsewhere there are forests of Canarian pine, cultivated fields and rolling hills, and meadows filled with flowers. There are no resorts and few sandy beaches, but it is undoubtedly a beautiful island and provides probably the ultimate destination for the reclusive holiday-maker.

The capital, **VALVERDE**, lies on a small plain in the North of the island and has a population of just 5,000. It is an attractive little place, with ornamental gardens and orchards. There are no real sights in the capital.

There are, however, sights worth visiting on this remote island outside the capital. These include the fertile valley of EL GOLFO in the West, with its scattering of small villages. The valley is, in fact, part of the rim of a vast crater that is mostly submerged beneath the waves of the Atlantic. There are a number of **viewpoints** around the area offering very attractive vistas.

SABINOSA is one of the villages in the West of the island with a small spa but no accommodation. LA RESTINGA at the southern tip of the island is a tiny port with a poor beach of black pebble. Other beaches are to be found at the main port, PUERTO DE LA ESTACA, where there is sand but also the threat of pollution, and at TAMADUSTE, which is good for swimming.

Accommodation is very limited indeed. There is one three-star hotel in the capital, as well as a couple of *hostales*. The best place to stay is probably the **Parador** at El Puerto de la Estaca. As might be expected, nightlife is non-existent.

Vocabulary

In the main resorts and large towns, there is generally no problem making yourself understood as English is widely spoken in hotels, tourist offices and restaurants, although obviously the further you stray away from the major tourist areas, the more likely you are to run into difficulties. This is when a good English/Spanish phrasebook proves to be invaluable and if your pronunciation isn't too impressive, you can always take the easy way out and just point at the appropriate phrase.

Spanish is an easy language to learn, especially if you have a smattering of Italian or Portuguese, as Southern European languages are very similar to each other. The basic rule to remember when speaking Spanish is that every letter is pronounced, thus both 'r' and 'e' in *tarde* are pronounced. Letters whose pronunciation is not obvious are: 'c' before 'e' or 'i' and 'z' which are pronounced 'th' as in *thin*; 'g' before 'e' or 'i' and 'j' which are pronounced 'ch' as in *loch*.

English	*Spanish*
Yes	Sí
No	No
Please	Por favor
Thank you	Gracias
Good morning	Buenas días
Good afternoon	Buenas tardes
Good night	Buenas tardes

Goodbye	Adiós
Goodbye (literally 'until tomorrow')	Hasta mañana
Excuse me	Perdóneme
Where is/are?	Dónde está/están?
When?	Cuándo?
What?	Qué?
How?	Cómo?
Who?	Quién?
Why?	Por qué?
I understand	Entiendo
I don't understand	No entiendo
Do you speak English?	Habla usted inglés?
Can I have?	Puedo tomar?
I would like	Quiero
A single room	Una habitación sencilla
A double room	Una habitación doble
A room with a bath	Una habitación con baño
A room with a shower	Una habitación con ducha

What is the price per night?	Cuánto cuesta por noche?
What is the price per week?	Cuánto cuesta por semana?
It is	Es
It isn't	No es
Is there/are there?	Hay?
There is/there are	Hay
Good/bad	Bueno/malo
Cheap/expensive	Barato/caro
Big/small	Grande/pequeño
Where can I get a taxi?	Dónde puedo coger un taxi?
Take me to this address, please	Lléveme a esta dirección por favor
Where's the nearest bank, please?	Dónde está el banco más cercano, por favor?
Where can I cash some traveller's cheques?	Dónde está el banco más cercano, por favor?
Can you show me on the map where I am?	Puede enseñarme en el mapa donde estoy?
May I have my bill, please?	Puede darme la cuenta, por favor?
Where's the ladies' toilet?	Dónde está el lavabo de señoras?

Where's the gents' toilet?	Dónde esta el lavabo de caballeros?
Call a doctor	Llame a un médico
Call an ambulance	Llame a una ambulancia
Call the police	Llame a la policía
One	Uno
Two	Dos
Three	Tres
Four	Cuatro
Five	Cinco
Six	Seis
Seven	Siete
Eight	Ocho
Nine	Nueve
Ten	Diez
Sunday	Domingo
Monday	Lunes
Tuesday	Martes
Wednesday	Miércoles
Thursday	Jueves

Friday	Viernes
Saturday	Sábado
Today	Hoy
Tomorrow	Mañana
Yesterday	Ayer

Katie Wood and George McDonald

Fontana Holiday Guides

No one can afford to take a chance with their holiday – yet people often do. Whether you want to sightsee or sunbathe, birdwatch all day or dance all night, the Fontana Holiday Guides tell you all you need to know to plan the best possible holiday for *you*: which resort, which tour operator, where to stay, how to travel, what to see and do.

Easy to read, objective, well researched and up to date, they are indispensable guides to getting fun – and value for money – out of your holiday.

Titles available:

Holiday Greece
Holiday Portugal
Holiday Turkey
Holiday Yugoslavia

Katie Wood and George McDonald

Europe by Train

Every year cheap European rail travel entices hundreds of thousands of people to sample for themselves the diversity and pleasures of the Continent.

Designed specifically for students and those on a tight budget, this is the only guide which looks at 26 countries from the Eurorailer's viewpoint. It is full of essential, practical information on:

* Train networks and station facilities
* The best routes
* Maximizing the benefits of rail passes
* What to see
* Where to sleep and eat
* Where the nightlife is

No traveller wanting to see Europe inexpensively can afford to leave home without this guide.

Ken Walsh

Hitch-Hiker's Guide to Europe

An invaluable guide for anyone wanting to travel cheaply in Europe, including the British Isles, Western Europe, Scandinavia, Iceland, the Eastern Bloc, North Africa, Turkey and the Middle East.

Packed with useful information on:

* What to take	* Routes
* How to travel	* Useful phrases
* Where to sleep	* Emergencies
* What to eat	* Local transport
* Best buys	* Working abroad
* Roughing it	* Currency hints

'Practically researched . . . colossal fun to read'
Observer

Katie Wood and George McDonald

The Round the World Air Guide

The long haul travel market is dramatically expanding and for little more than the price of a return flight to Australia you can now circumnavigate the globe. *The Round the World Air Guide* has been written specifically for the new breed of serious traveller and whether you are on a round the world ticket or using conventional long haul options, it will guide you to the best places and the best prices. It is the only book which covers all you need to know to plan and book your trip *and* acts as a practical guide to the world's fifty major destinations.

Full of essential information on:

* How to cut costs and get the most out of your ticket
* Stop off possibilities and side trips
* Airport facilities around the world
* Where to go and what to see
* Where to sleep and what to eat
* Dining out and nightlife

No frequent traveller can afford to take off without it!

Fontana Paperbacks
Non-fiction

Fontana is a leading paperback publisher of non-fiction.
Below are some recent titles.

The Round the World Air Guide *Katie Wood & George McDonald* £9.95
Europe by Train *Katie Wood & George McDonald* £4.95
Hitch-Hiker's Guide to Europe *Ken Walsh* £3.95
Eating Paris *Carl Gardner & Julie Sheppard* £2.95
Staying Vegetarian *Lynne Alexander* £3.95
Holiday Turkey *Katie Wood & George McDonald* £3.95
Holiday Yugoslavia *Katie Wood & George McDonald* £3.95
Holiday Portugal *Katie Wood & George McDonald* £3.95
Holiday Greece *Katie Wood & George McDonald* £5.95
Waugh on Wine *Auberon Waugh* £3.95
Arlott on Wine *John Arlott* £3.95
March or Die *Tony Geraghty* £3.95
Going For It *Victor Kiam* £2.95
Say It One Time For The Broken Hearted *Barney Hoskins* £4.95
Nice Guys Sleep Alone *Bruce Feirstein* £2.95
Impressions of My Life *Mike Yarwood* £2.95

You can buy Fontana paperbacks at your local bookshop or newsagent.
Or you can order them from Fontana Paperbacks, Cash Sales Department, Box 29, Douglas, Isle of Man. Please send a cheque, postal or
money order (not currency) worth the purchase price plus 22p per book
for postage (maximum postage required is £3).

NAME (Block letters) _____

ADDRESS _____

_____

_____